Korea Between Empires, 1895–1919

The East Asian Institute is Columbia University's center for research, publication, and teaching on modern East Asia. The Studies of the East Asian Institute were inaugurated in 1962 to bring to a wider public the results of significant new research on modern and contemporary East Asia.

STUDIES OF THE EAST ASIAN INSTITUTE

Korea Between Empires, 1895–1919

Andre Schmid

COLUMBIA UNIVERSITY PRESS   NEW YORK

COLUMBIA UNIVERSITY PRESS
Publishers Since 1893
New York   Chichester, West Sussex
Copyright © 2002 Columbia University Press
All rights reserved

Library of Congress Cataloging-in-Publication Data

Schmid, Andre.
    Korea between empires, 1895–1919 / Andre Schmid
      p. cm. — (Studies of the East Asian Institute)
    Includes bibliographical references and index.
    ISBN 0–231–12538–0 (cloth : alk. paper) — ISBN 0–231–12539–9
    (pbk. : alk. paper)
    I. Nationalism — Korea — History. 2. Korea — History — 1864–1910. I. Title.
II. Series.
DS915.25 .S36 2002
951.9′02 — dc21   2001058377

∞
Columbia University Press books are
printed on permanent and durable acid-free paper.
Printed in the United States of America

c 10 9 8 7 6 5 4 3 2 1
p 10 9 8 7 6 5 4 3 2

For Sonia

Contents

Acknowledgments

Acknowledgments are about origins.

The problem is that as a historian, I am a member of a profession that is notoriously unable to determine starting points. Self-reflections on my own work are no more definite. I might say that this study began as a dissertation project, pressured into a concrete proposal in a mad shuffle to meet a funding agency's deadline. But now that I have proposed one starting point, my historian's instincts to trace any phenomenon further back in time lead me to suggest that this study can also be said to have begun earlier, when some of the questions that I pose in this book first came to my attention during a solo-bicycle trip to the historical sites scattered around the city of Kyongju. Yet this might just be a contemporary history. This study could also be said to have a prehistory, one in certain long-term, diffuse interests in nationalism and in East Asian history that somehow, somewhere, had a rendezvous. That the precise origins are less than clear is my personal lesson in the problems of historical memory.

Acknowledgments are also about influences.

Thankfully, influences are somewhat easier to recognize. Over the indeterminate course of this project, I have benefited from the insights, comments, and cajoling of many generous friends, colleagues, and teachers with a startlingly array of scholarly and political preferences. I have often wondered what would happen if they all gathered in the same room. They haven't, but the pages of this book reflects some of the conversations and disagreements they might have had. The diversity in the following pages —

some might say schizophrenia — is certainly a debt to their various influences and good cheer, for which I will always be highly grateful. They have made the process of completing this work possible and enjoyable. Of course, I ultimately bear the responsibility for its final form.

Over wine and Mozart, Huynh Kim Khánh first gave me the courage to head in this direction. At Columbia University a triumvirate of Carol Gluck, Gari Ledyard, and Madeleine Zelin oversaw and guided this project through the dissertation stage. Michael Tsin asked the type of, at first, seemingly off-the-wall questions that slowly percolated until they flavored this work. In Korea, I was fortunate to learn much about Korean history from Professor Han Young-woo of Seoul National University who, in his lectures and discussions, opened the world of Korean intellectual history to me. Professor Choi Chang-jip of Koryo University, together with many of his graduate students, taught me much about Korean history and politics, both inside and outside the classroom.

Two fellow dissertation writers, Kim Brandt and Margherita Zanasi, have patiently followed this work through its many stages, dealing with various ups and downs yet always responsible for improvements along the way. Alexis Dudden has shared many of the interests and frustrations that shape these pages, her enthusiasm always revealing an upside. Hwang Jongyŏn, in New York City parks and Seoul cafés, has inspired me with his keen mind and questions to explore new areas of inquiry. Henry Em, a rare fellow aficionado for Korean historiography, has, through discussions, e-mails, and criticisms, helped me think more deeply about Korean historical works. Timothy Brook, Eric Cazdyn, Prof. Chŏng Okcha, Martina Deuchler, Prasenjit Duara, Carter Eckert, Kyung Moon Hwang, Merose Hwang, Y. G. Kim, Kathy Moon, Tetsuo Najita, Laura Nelson, Koichi Okamoto, James Palais, V. Ravindiran, and Michael Robinson all, in different ways, have made comments on this work that convinced, shamed, and seduced me into changing words, paragraphs, and even entire chapters — always for the better. The good times with Nicky may have delayed this work, but play always focuses one's mind. I am especially fortunate to have had a father who supported me in numerous ways for what now seems far too many years. Margaret B. Yamashita helped make my prose more scrutable. The many questions posed by the (sometimes unknown to me) participants at various seminars — at the University of Chicago, University of Toronto, Princeton University, University of California at Los Angeles, University of Washington, and Harvard University — have also been a benefit.

I am grateful to the publishers of my earlier published articles for allowing me to weave portions of them into this book, including "Rediscovering Manchuria: Sin Ch'aeho and the Politics of Territorial History in Korea," *Journal of Asian Studies* 56, no. 1 (February 1997): 26–47; "Censorship and the *Hwangsŏng sinmun*," in Chang Yun-shik et al., *Korea Between Tradition and Modernity: Selected Papers from the Fourth Pacific and Asian Conference on Korean Studies* (Vancouver: Institute of Asian Research, 2000), 158–71; "Decentering the 'Middle Kingdom': The Problem of China in Korean Nationalist Thought," in *Nation Work*, ed. Timothy Brook and Andre Schmid (Ann Arbor: University of Michigan Press, 2000); and "Looking North Toward Manchuria," *South Atlantic Quarterly* 99, no. 1 (Winter 2000): 199–221.

Those mad shuffles to produce proposals for funding deadlines led to a generous response from a number of agencies whose support made this study possible. I have benefited from a Fulbright fellowship, Korea Research Foundation dissertation research fellowship, Social Science and Humanities Research Council of Canada postdoctoral fellowship, and a traveling grant from the Faculty of Arts and Science, University of Toronto. My research has also benefited immensely from the generous support the Korean Foundation has annually contributed to the Cheng Yutung library of the University of Toronto.

Finally, my deepest debt is to Sonia, without whom, nothing. To her, this book is dedicated.

Introduction: A Monumental Story

In October 1905, a Korean newspaper announced an ar-
chaelogical discovery. A magnificent stele had been found. A hulking 6.5
meters of stone, it recorded the deeds of a famous king from the Koguryŏ
dynasty, Kwanggaet'o (375–415). Originally erected by his son to commemorate the king's accomplishments, the stele had been lost over the centuries
to the shifting soils of southern Manchuria, buried without any trace or
memory of its existence. As readers of the announcement learned, despite
Kwanggaet'o's reknown for victorious battles against China and the expansion of his realm to the farthest reaches of Manchuria, few specifics about
his deeds had been recorded in traditional histories. Now, as the newspaper
gleefully reported, this would change, for the stele was engraved with a
detailed inscription, stretching around the four sides of the stele and num-
bering more than 1,750 characters.[1]

Nevertheless the report registered a certain degree of despondency. The
stele had actually been discovered more than twenty years before the announcement to Korean readers in 1905. In 1882, hearing that a buried
monument had become partially exposed, a Chinese official hired laborers
to unearth what was to turn out to be the Kwanggaet'o stele.[2] Two years later
a Japanese military officer traveling in China made a rubbing of the stele.
This copy was now on display in Tokyo at the Ueno Park Museum, the
editorial pointed out, unbeknownst to any Koreans.[3] Only when a Korean
student in Tokyo obtained a copy of the rubbing and sent it to the offices of

the newspaper did the editors learn of the monument. To share the inscription with others, they reprinted the full text in the next six issues, allocating
it to the prominent space usually reserved for editorials. By reading the
stele's text, they wrote, other committed patriots would now be able to "know
the level of civilization and degree of national strength" in the days of
Kwanggaet'o.

To "know" these things, however, was not so straightforward, especially
when the stele's inscription was written in an archaic style incomprehensible
to all but the most highly trained classicists. Even the reprinted text in the
newspaper included footnotes to explain key terms and obscure phrasings,
marking the first Korean attempt in what was to be a long and still continuing
struggle over the interpretation of this impressive hunk of stone.[4] Other pundits quickly emerged, each emphasizing the significance of the stele as a
historical source that would provide direct access to a forgotten part of the
national past. "Only one or two records out of thousands" concerning
Kwanggaet'o were passed down, complained one.[5] Another commentator
described the monument as "truly the most powerful historical material in
ten thousand Korean generations."[6] It could serve, according to still another,
to rectify "the shortcomings of thousands of years of historical records."[7] That
the monument could be seen as revealing a glorious past was especially
welcome in an era when heroes were sought.[8] It was Kwanggaet'o's military
success and, more specifically, the resulting territorial aggrandizement that
appealed to these early interpreters. To one writer, the very size of the stone
was just one more reason to be in awe of the stele itself, as well as the man
for whom it was erected. It had withstood the fires of war, and foreigners,
despite their "love" for ancient relics, had been unable to move it.[9]

Yet because the stele had been buried for one thousand years, complained
one writer, it had not undergone the "rubbing and handling of scholars."[10]
This "rubbing and handling" — essential to what the newspaper's editors had
identified as the need "to know the level of civilization and degrees of national strength" — was an early step in transforming a monument originally
hewn from stone, engraved, and erected as an act of filial piety into a key
element of a newly emerging national story. The meanings that were to be
instilled in the Kwanggaet'o stele reflected many of the currents in nationalist thought during this era. Its metamorphosis — from discovery to publicity
to the creation of its national significance — was part of a process central to
all nationalist movements and the focus of this study: the production of
knowledge about the nation. Broadly defined, the production of national

knowledge involved the many, often competing and contradictory, ways that Koreans defined and represented their national community to one another. More narrowly, it was in debates and discussions about specific issues, events, and objects — be it the Kwanggaet'o stele, ruminations over the concept of citizenship, debates about personal hygiene, questions of local governance, or the appropriate dress for officials — that writers metaphorically or literally, unconsciously or not, articulated various ways of thinking about the nation. Pursuing these questions — How did they see themselves as a single unit? How did they articulate their vision of the nation's particular character? — is a line of inquiry whose main concern is not testing the accuracy of defining statements. Rather than measure such claims empirically — Did a peasant in Chŏlla Province *really* live in the same style of house, eat the same type of food, and wear the same cut of clothes as pearl divers on Cheju Island, ginseng merchants in Kaesŏng, or a student of Confucianism in Andong? — this study asks how representations, narratives, and rhetorical strategies shaped the parameters and content of nationalist thought. It is this realm of self-knowledge, mainly as expressed in the most powerful public medium of the time, newspapers and journals, as well as some textbooks and monographs, published in the years between the conclusion of the Sino-Japanese War in 1895 and the early years of the colonial period that constitutes the focus of this study.

In these years, as the power of the Qing Empire in China ebbed and the reach of Japanese imperialism extended to the peninsula — an era when Korea was situated both temporally and physically between two empires — a disparate group of intellectuals, reformers, and publicists made the nation the premier subject of intellectual exchange for the first time in the peninsula's history. In their newspapers, journals, and textbooks, they pursued the possibilities offered by such specific objects as the Kwanggaet'o stele, their interpretations both shaped by and further developing a veritable outburst of thinking and writing about the nation. Often grouped together by historians as a single movement — what in Korean is referred to as the Aeguk kyemong undong (the Patriotic Enlightenment Movement) — these individuals were observers of and participants in a loosely aligned nationalist movement designed after the termination of the Sino-Japanese War in 1895 to protect their newly won independence and, then, once this sovereignty was forfeited to Japan in 1905, to recover their lost national rights. One of the major contentions of this book is that the knowledge produced by these individuals and groups established the basis of modern Korean nationalist discourse. Armed with their presses and dominating the school movement, these nationalist writers produced many of the key texts and generated some of the most powerful social memories of the nation at an opportune time *before* the annexation of the peninsula into the Japanese empire — a situation quite different from the settings of most other colonized nations. Thereafter, the bounds of these debates in Korea were severely constricted by the colonial authorities, who were keen to subsume discussions of the nation into their goal of making Koreans loyal imperial subjects.[11] Whether the national knowledge these writers produced helped resist Japanese goals or whether it ultimately became complicit with Japanese colonial ideology was a dilemma they all had to face.

What interests me in this study is less the well-documented political struggle for nationhood than the cultural strategies of these groups in identifying just what denoted their particular nation as *Korean* during an era when the regional environment changed radically and they began committing themselves to the capitalist modernity that underpinned the global system. My approach distances itself somewhat from histories of nationalist movements which, because of their focus on the political fight for independence, have tended to draw stark divisions between external imperialist powers and indigenous forces of liberation, with the clash between the two offering the main narrative for national history and an important criterion for definitions of modernity.[12] Such histories have had the felicitous consequence of highlighting resistance against the abuses of power, yet in so doing they have tended to obscure an equally important story, the interplay between those internal and external forces that themselves constituted the nation. In recent years, much postcolonial research has sought to draw out this dynamic.[13] Eschewing a mode of analysis that sees nationalism as solely reactive to the impingements of foreign imperialism, these studies have traced the various ways by which both the colonized and the colonizer developed within these interactions. Most significantly, this approach problematizes the assumption that the nation was created independently of any cultural exchange with international forces or that self-understanding by various groups somehow arose from a deep well of knowledge that had lain untapped for generations. Strangely, we are often quick to acknowledge the socioeconomic impact of global participation, yet when it comes to questions of national identity, we hesitate to regard self-knowledge as anything other than the product of an autonomous imagination. I argue that the production of knowledge about modern Korea was a process deeply entwined with the international environment of that particular historical moment, that it was as much a part of the process of writers coming to terms with their new global position as it was one of rethinking their own nation, and that nationalism was the first consciously globalizing discourse. In the fifteen years between 1895 and annexation, nationalizing and globalizing forces intermingled, often to the extent that it is difficult to disentangle one from the other or to distinguish clearly the internal from the external. The two were neither as exclusive nor as oppositional as many pundits of globalization today assert.

This is not to deny the nationalist politics and goals of the era but, rather, to show that the urge to identify, express, and disseminate what many writers called the "character" of the nation was stimulated by the peninsula's integration into the global order at the end of the nineteenth century. As a number of recent studies by Arjun Appadurai, Etienne Balibar and Immanuel Wallerstein, and Prasenjit Duara have shown, the condition of globalization not only has influenced the political ideology of nations, ensuring that they define themselves as sovereign, but also has informed and structured the ways in which culture has been used, promoted, and forged in the name of the nation.[14] One of the ironies of a world order populated by nations is that claims to particularity are themselves universalized. The very act of possessing uniqueness is universalized: every nation is to have a unique character as part of its claim to nationhood.[15] It was this "national order of things," as Liisa Maalki has put it, that conditioned the desire of Korean writers at the turn of the century to think of the nation as a part of — though, to be sure, a singular part of — a larger ecumene, producing the types of knowledge necessary to identify what made this particular nation Korean in a world of many nations.[16] As is often postulated in studies of Korean nationalism, the outburst of writing about the Korean nation during these years certainly reflected a resistance to external political pressures, in particular to Japan after 1905. But this outburst also marked the greater participation of Korean elites in the global ideologies of capitalist modernity, ideologies that in themselves stimulated this rethinking of the nation and, as Harry Harootunian has observed, were the very signs of capitalist modernity rather than resistance to it.[17] The Kwanggaet'o stele was only one of a plethora of items through which this distinctive character was articulated.[18]

It is significant that the announcement of the stele and the claims about its nature were first made in the pages of that most modern of institutions, the newspaper. Many studies of nationalism have explored the relationship between this medium and the nation. Most famously, Benedict Anderson has argued that the nation's very origins can be traced to the rise of print capitalism and the appearance of mass vernacular newspapers.[19] There has been much debate about the applicability of Anderson's schema to East Asia,[20] but what interests me in this study is not as much locating a certain moment in the past when the Korean nation can be said to have originated as understanding the ways in which newspapers at the end of the nineteenth century tried to express particular visions and definitions of the nation. The content of nationalist ideology is not of interest to Anderson, yet I contend that it is precisely the formation of particular ways of understanding and ordering the nation that determines the direction of nationalist movements, the activities of its members, and the participation of the nation-state in the broader global arena. In this sense, newspapers must be seen not just as circulating commodities that can alter consciousness but also as producers and disseminators of specific modes of knowledge that enable and encourage certain types of activities. In noting how Anderson and other students of nationalism downplay the content of nationalist thought, Partha Chatterjee has written, "It is the content of nationalist ideology, its claims about what is possible and what is legitimate, which gives specific shape to its politics. The latter cannot be understood without examining the former."[21] At a time when Korea stood between two empires, newspapers gave voice to a variety of national visions that shaped, directed, and reflected that period's growing nationalist movement.

As a medium for producing national knowledge, newspapers were unrivaled. Segmented into discrete stories in each edition; divided into separate issues unfolding over days and years; and featuring pieces as diverse as advertisements, letters to the editor, poetry, editorials, and the like, newspapers offered a powerful medium for bringing together in a single space the disparate topics and objects that writers explored, hailed, and used for making claims for the nation. The segmented nature of the newspaper at once enabled diverse issues to be investigated, issues that, though seemingly unrelated, were connected explicitly or implicitly by the efforts of editors to elucidate their significance in terms of the nation. Constitutions *could* be related to sewers, and railways *did* have a connection to how one blew one's nose. Such topics belonged on the same pages of the same newspapers, were written about with the same conceptual vocabulary, and as readers were told, all bore varying degrees of relation to the health and wealth of the nation. The classification of the myriad facets of social, economic, political, and cultural life at the turn of the nineteenth century into national categories reflects the power of nationalism to offer an interpretative framework for everyday lives, as well as the ability of writers, in turn, to give voice to the nation through the quotidian.

This inclusivity, in which national significance could be instilled into all matters, did not translate into a uniformity, however. Despite all the editorial enjoinments to "solidarity" and "harmony," the segmented nature of newspapers enabled divergent visions of the nation to be expressed, often on the very same page of a paper. The cacophony of a daily newspaper — with its reports on happenings at court, complaints from irate readers, advertisements peddling fashionable hats, and editorials wishing more people would read the paper — captured the many voices claiming to speak on behalf of the nation and the diverse ways in which the nation could be invoked by these writers. It was the capacity to organize a wide range of issues, objects, and dissenting opinions and to relate them all to the nation that made the newspaper the organ par excellence for producing a wide and disparate body of national knowledge.

What is striking about the media of the era is the rather paradoxical juxtaposition of the sheer volume of national knowledge offered to readers at the same time as editors bemoaned the lack of information about the nation. This frustration may have been a necessary motivation for anyone wanting to write about the nation for an audience, but it also points to the continual urge to locate the nation in the constantly shifting political context of the period. The fifteen years between 1895 and 1910 were variously described as a time of change, an era of reform, a period of transition, and, most of all, a time of crisis. Korean newspapers detailed tremendous changes at a number of levels, whether on a world level as the peninsula was further integrated into the global system, on a regional level as Korea was annexed into the Japanese empire, or on national and local levels as shifts in the political balance of power on the peninsula buffeted the reform agenda of the various streams of the nationalist movement. The national knowledge produced in these years in many ways reflected a concatenation of these shifting local, national, regional, and global forces. Depending on the period and the particular issue at hand, the locus of the nation could be identified as residing in very different realms, creating various hierarchies of visions that might be simultaneously expressed in the same newspaper.

Most obviously, the nation was located in temporal and spatial terms. But as always, this worked at several levels. Seen as part of a new global ecumene, the nation needed to be brought into narratives of world history that plotted the trajectory of all nations along the same lines, ultimately leading to the modern. As part of a region identified as the East (Tongyang), the nation was linked with its two neighbors, Japan and China, with their shared attributes presented as a product of a common past that could be folded into narratives of world history yet still show the unique historical accomplishments and future potential of the region. At the level of the nation, the newspapers offered histories that established the country's autonomous subjectivity, proof, it was argued, of Korea's rightful claim to sovereignty in a world populated by nations. In the years immediately after the Sino-Japanese War, these various spatiotemporal approaches to the Korean nation appeared seamlessly interwoven, serving the purpose of disengaging Korea from the types of knowledge that had long structured understanding of the peninsula within an East Asian regional order centering on China.

The tensions among these different levels were revealed as Japan colonized the peninsula. Endorsing, as did their Korean rivals, capitalist modernity but deploying it for opposite ends, Japanese colonialists wielded their accounts of regional and world history to undermine Korean claims to autonomy and to usurp Korean sovereignty. For Korean nationalists, this presented a number of problems. The forms of national knowledge that had served their purpose of disengaging from an earlier regional order now threatened to segue into Japanese colonial ideology. They had indeed located the nation away from China, but the very self-critiques that had enabled this reorientation were now being co-opted by imperial Japan, rendering the knowledge produced in these newspapers less amenable to nationalist usage, if not complicit with colonialism. This conundrum again led some writers to search for a new location for the nation, outside the reach of colonial authorities, where again the nation's autonomy could be resurrected and different strategies of resistance could be formulated. This search moved in various directions — some pointing to the spiritual character of the nation, others seeking refuge in ethnic definitions of the nation, and still others finding a locus for the nation outside its borders.

In concentrating on the production of national knowledge at the expense of a history of nationalism as a political movement, this study nevertheless returns to the question of the political import of national knowledge. Indeed, as I point out, the decisions made and visions articulated for the nation by these writers informed and guided the actions and strategies of the nationalist movement, ultimately influencing the fate of the nation. Questions of representation, narrative, and definition in themselves had political consequences for individual writers, newspapers, and the nation as a whole. While the process of knowledge production was not in itself autonomous, the resulting knowledge was relevant to the political autonomy of the peninsula. It is in this sense that this book is a study of politics, except that the location of political struggle is not in anticolonial demonstrations, underground societies, or fund-raising drives but in the aesthetics of representation, the use of language, and the writing of history. Only by understanding the genealogies of these forms of national knowledge can the function of nationalist thought on a peninsula caught between two empires be understood. How this terrain was navigated by the editorial staffs of different newspapers and journals is the main topic of this book.

Civilization and the East

Korean editorial writers working at the beginning of the twentieth century would not have been surprised by recent scholarly trends emphasizing that self-knowledge was relational, part of a process in which cross-cultural representations function to distinguish the national self and to articulate difference or uniqueness.[22] On more than one occasion, writers acknowledged that the development of a sense of Koreanness had been enabled by comparative exchanges with the many peoples of the world — or as one writer observed, "Knowing others, one knows oneself [*chip'ijia*]."[23] I hasten to add, however, that in the case of Korea, this comparative endeavor was not marked solely by a duality between the East and West, a binary that has been the target of much criticism while still underlying many critiques.[24] To be sure, the West loomed large over the intellectual landscape of Korean writers at the beginning of the twentieth century. As discussed in chapter 1, nationalist intellectuals defined themselves as the bearers of "civilization and enlightenment," accepting both Western definitions and claims to the universality of these notions. It was in these notions of civilization, with their vision of historical progress, that Korean writers framed the nation as a member of a larger global ecumene. The nation was the product of these progressive forces of history, and it was through the nation, by means of commitment and willingness to reform, that the populace was to be civilized. In this way, civilization was positioned as an authority with the full backing of world history that could be invoked when calling for the transformation of the nation. The nation and civilization were seen as intertwined, inseparable parts of the same reform enterprise, in which the seemingly benign nature of civilized knowledge was to assist in preserving the nation.

Located as they were between two empires, one in decline and the other ascendant, Korean nationalists cast their gaze not just at the faraway West but at their two neighbors as well.[25] As I show in the following pages, shifting understandings of China and Japan were integral to Korean self-knowledge, largely overshadowing the East-West dynamic and giving Koreans several others against which to compare their nation's particularity. The tumultuous regional events in these years — the Sino-Japanese War, the Boxer Uprising, the Russo-Japanese War, and, finally, the 1910 annexation of the peninsula into the Japanese empire — resulted in historic changes in regional power formations that had important consequences for the ways that Koreans viewed not only their two East Asian neighbors but also, because of the deep linkages, the ways that they understood their own nation. In the years immediately after the Sino-Japanese War, the widely discussed situation of China became one of the primary ways of articulating notions of civilization and their relationship to newly emerging visions of Korea. One commentator on the Kwanggaet'o stele hinted at these changes when he detailed Kwanggaet'o's victories over the northern kingdom of Yan with its capital in Beijing, describing how Kwanggaet'o was "always able to take revenge against enemy countries, erasing the shame of previous kings and raising high the respect of the country within all the seas."[26] That historical victories in China were being remembered more than a millennium and a half after their occurrence was less a belated celebration than an indication of a deliberate cultural renewal that sought to recast the peninsula's historical relationship with its continental neighbor. Rethinking Korea meant reevaluating China.

In 1895, as part of the treaty that ended the Sino-Japanese War, the Qing Empire recognized Korea's independence, ending all the ritual ceremonies that symbolized Korean subordinance to the "Middle Kingdom." Although in the view of foreign powers, this treaty resolved the ambiguity of the peninsula's position vis-à-vis China, there still remained the far more complex cultural legacy of practices and knowledge shared with China resulting from centuries of exchange. The function of China as the "Middle Kingdom" in a transnational Confucian cultural realm had already begun to disintegrate by the time commentators on the Kwanggaet'o stele could hail his historical military victories as evidence that "our nation was originally strong and brave and did not have a weak and inferior character."[27] As I argue in chapter 2, this shift in China's function was an integral part of a process of reconfiguring the nation according to the new knowledge and notions of civilization that had been introduced and enthusiastically adopted by Korean nationalist writers. The "Middle Kingdom" was no longer seen as occupying the center but was decidedly on the periphery, both globally and regionally. And as peripheral, China was anything but civilized. This reorientation called into question the full range of practices, texts, and customs that for centuries had been shared by Koreans as part of their participation in the transnational Confucian realm. Formerly accepted as universal, these were increasingly deemed Chinese and thus alien to Korea. Somewhat paradoxically, during an age when China's power, both political and cultural, was ebbing, Korean writers devoted much energy to discussing China.

A movement for cultural retrieval ensued as nationalist intellectuals unearthed purely indigenous practices and beliefs from the accretions of Chinese culture — what I call the decentering of the "Middle Kingdom." As much of the literature on cultural retrieval has shown, efforts to regain a purely authentic national culture generally result in the development of hybrid cultures.[28] But in turn-of-the-century Korea, the culture targeted for expurgation was not that of the immediate colonizing power, as is so often the case with colonies of the West, but that of its neighbor, China. Hybridization did not originate with the arrival of imperialism but was conceived as having been under way for centuries in East Asia. For Korean nationalists, the task of recovery was one of disentangling this hybrid into what they viewed as its component national parts, disavowing one and cherishing the other. If the Treaty of Shimonoseki marked a formal end to tributary ties, these efforts sought to expunge Chinese culture, viewing its seepage into Korea as a major cause for national weakness and inimical to their desires for an independent nation. While such cases as the celebration of Kwanggaet'o's victories over a Chinese kingdom reflected these desires, implementing the changes was not always so straightforward. Practices and symbols that for centuries had been shared as universal were not so easily segregated into two distinct national categories — and not everyone, due to divergent political or ideological goals, agreed.

These legacies could also be used to advantage. One newspaper, the *Hwangsŏng sinmun (Capital Gazette)*, despite its many calls for decentering the "Middle Kingdom," built on this common history to write about the East, or *Tongyang*, as a counter to the West. For a newspaper committed to a reform Confucianism, the East offered a means of not only expressing a vision of the region as a cultural entity united by its shared Confucian past but also showing how this past could be integrated into the new understanding of "civilization and enlightenment." As Stefan Tanaka has shown for certain intellectuals in Japan, the editors of the *Hwangsŏng sinmun* similarly used notions of the East to establish an equivalence with the West that laid claim to an equally worthy, if not superior, past, as defined by the criteria of civilization — a move that, in turn, enabled them to affirm the claims of civilization to universality.[29] Enlightenment could be presented as being as much Eastern as it was Western. Accordingly, reform of the nation was not so much "Westernization" as abiding by this single principle of human history — the "Way," in the parlance of the editors — that had been mastered in the distant Eastern past and could once again make the nation strong. As a result, the histories of East Asia and Korea were recast in the framework of enlightenment history, creating a style of Orientalist history in which the accomplishments of the sages and Korean reform thinkers came to be valued only insofar as they contributed to the ineluctable march of progress in global history.

Although in the years immediately after the Sino-Japanese War, the commonality of region was defined in the eyes of the editors of the *Hwangsŏng sinmun* as a legacy of an earlier shared Confucianism, this definition began to change as Japan became ascendant. Reflecting these geopolitical shifts, regional identity increasingly began to place Japan at the center of the East. As I trace in chapter 2, by the early years of the twentieth century, the cultural definitions of the East blossomed into a style of racial Pan-Asianism as the editors began to participate in an espousal of social Darwinian doctrine across East Asia. The yellow peoples (*hwangsaek injong*) against the white peoples (*paeksaek injong*) — this was the true historical struggle. As the *Hwangsŏng sinmun* argued, only by uniting the three nations of the East could the individual nations survive the onslaught of the white peoples. Their commitment to Pan-Asianism led the editors to welcome Japanese cooperation with Korean attempts at reform. The political naïveté of this position was revealed when Japan, as a direct result of its victories, was able to impose a protectorate on Korea in 1905, giving credence to oppositional views that the greatest threat to Korea came not from the white West but from a fellow yellow country. Although the *Hwangsŏng sinmun*'s editor in chief was thrown in jail and the paper was suspended for its attack on the Protectorate Treaty, the paper did not stop espousing its Pan-Asian doctrine. Instead, this Pan-Asianism developed as part of an editorial platform that staked out a middle ground in the Korean political spectrum, between the pro-Japanese collaborators and what the editors viewed as the anti-Japanese nationalists who unrealistically sought the immediate removal of Japan from the peninsula. Working under Japanese censorship from this politically exposed middle position, the paper struggled to hold onto its earlier notions of the East as one way of offering a critique, however muted, of Japanese colonial policies for violating the ideals of regional solidarity and Japanese responsibilities of leadership. What had at first seemed to be a shared enterprise was now turned by the editors against Japan, as Pan-Asianism could be wielded against the very nation that deployed it as part of its colonial ideology.

Colonialism and History

The aggression of Japan that led to the sundering of Pan-Asian ideals was hardly the only function of that country in Korean nationalist thought in these years. As the exhibition of the rubbing of the Kwanggaet'o stele in downtown Tokyo shows, Japan had already emerged as a powerful producer of knowledge about Korea. That a rubbing made in distant Manchuria, brought back for study, and displayed in Tokyo was discovered by a Korean student in Japan enabled the sequence of events and interpretations that enshrined the stele as a potent nationalist symbol. One of my arguments is that Korean self-knowledge in this period cannot be separated from the Japanese production of knowledge about Korea. That is, the expression of national identity in its many forms was not just a product of a reaction against the Japanese takeover of the peninsula but was also deeply engaged — whether to struggle against, to absorb, or, as was more often the case, some combination of these two — with Japanese writings about Korean culture and history. With the most powerful publishing industry in East Asia and media in which Korea frequented the headline news, more was published about Korea in Japan than anywhere in the world, perhaps even on the peninsula itself during the first few years after the Sino-Japanese War. This knowledge, like any other set of ideas, could be exported to Korea, and after 1905, the colonial authorities did their utmost to disseminate particular forms of representations about Korea that served to extend and maintain their rule.

This process was not just a question of colonial imposition. As I contend in chapter 3, regardless of their antagonistic political goals, nationalism and colonialism with their mutual endorsement of capitalist modernity shared much in their historical understanding and approaches to national culture. Most Japanese knowledge of Korea was framed in the very same vocabulary of civilization employed by Korean intellectuals in their own rethinking of the nation. During the ten years of nominal independence before the imposition of the Protectorate in 1905, the knowledge produced in Japan could be used to good effect by Korean writers, more often than not to borrow the authority of a Japanese expert to reinforce an argument made by the author. Such exchanges were not seen as complicit with Japanese interests but as complementing the shared and parallel commitment to "enlightenment and civilization," which in the case of Korea was seen as affirming sovereignty. But as soon became evident, this knowledge was not so benign.

As Japanese intrusions into peninsular affairs quickened, culminating in the 1905 Protectorate Treaty, the tension existing in the nationalist project became apparent. The seamless interweaving of nation and civilization, as had been regularly touted for ten years by the nationalist press, began to unravel. Was the nation paramount? Or did the global task of civilization take precedence? "Civilization and enlightenment" were now being wielded by the very country to which these Koreans had granted a special authority in this realm; only now it served to legitimize the colonization of their own nation. What they had appealed to as a higher authority to strengthen the nation was now cited by Japanese colonial authorities as a higher authority to extinguish the nation. Satirize as they did Japanese colonial discourse and decry the contradictions between rhetoric and action, these writers were caught in the double bind of "civilization and enlightenment." The dilemma they faced, I suggest in chapter 3, was how to extricate themselves from these ideologies that were undermining their goals for independence but on which they rested their own leadership of the nationalist movement and in which they had framed their very definition of the nation.

This conundrum extended to questions of cultural representation as well. Both nationalism and colonialism shared an impulse to appraise cultural practices (if not national culture as a whole) in terms of their compatibility with the ideals of the civilized nation and capitalist modernity. This shared dynamic, together with the interchanges between Korean and Japanese writers, led to a remarkably high degree of commonality in the ways that Korean culture was represented by nationalist and colonial writers, despite their opposing political goals. The Chosŏn-dynasty (1392–1910) elite, known as *yangban*, served as one of the most convenient metaphorical devices to critique traditional Korean culture in both nationalist and colonial writing, with their focus on factionalism, laziness, corruption, and the like displaying thematic similarities. Where they differed, of course, was the goal for which these images were invoked: in one case it was to urge the population to reform away from particular types of behavior, and in the other it was used to show that such practices made internal reform unthinkable. The danger for nationalists was that their own critique of past cultural practices, due to its representational overlap with colonial critiques, could be harnessed to the very colonial enterprise they were now resisting. This was the ultimate power of Japanese colonialism — the co-option of areas of nationalist thought developed autonomously before the 1905 Protectorate so that they not only could no longer be resorted to in defense of the nation but also segued into colonial ideologies. To be sure, such co-option was resisted. Korean nationalists even tried to convert colonial concepts to their own purpose. But with annexation and the closure of their presses in 1910, there was little time for these strategies to be fully developed.

Given this situation, both colonial authorities and nationalists paid great attention to how Korea and its culture were represented. Neither Japanese colonial authorities nor Korean nationalists needed to await the rise of postcolonial theory to understand that cultural representations were related to power, with consequences for the peninsula's political disposition. The contest between nationalists and colonialists extended into the realm of representation and the definition of terms. For nationalists, one strategy for escaping the dilemmas presented by the double nature of civilization was to create a separate realm in which definitions of the nation were not so deeply embedded in enlightenment-style notions of progress. Especially after Japan gained control of those state institutions that were central to the earlier visions of self-strengthening, resistance through reform appeared futile to many, since it meant working directly or indirectly with the colonial authorities. Consequently, as I show in chapter 4, some writers began moving away from state-centered definitions of the nation to contemplate an alternative location, one variously called the national soul (*kukhon*) or the national essence (*kuksu*). Like so much of the new conceptual vocabulary of the nation, this was a language shared by nationalists throughout East Asia. But in Korea, its political importance and usage were tied up with the politics of the Protectorate, in particular the search for a national locus outside the purview of the colonial state. This spiritually defined nation offered a form of resistance rooted not in civilizing reform but in the cultivation of language, religion, and especially history. Partha Chatterjee has shown how Indian nationalists developed similar notions of a spiritual realm under British rule, but unlike the situation in India, in Korea there was great concern that even this national soul could be violated by colonial power.[30] The spirit of the nation, as they regularly pointed out, might be located in history, but as became clear after 1905, it still was not clear who would control interpretations of that past.

Indeed, from the middle of the Meiji period (1868–1912), Japanese scholars had exhibited much interest in early Korean-Japanese relations. Myths from the first recorded Japanese histories offered intriguing accounts of Japanese relations with its closest neighbors on the peninsula. As part of their first modern national histories, scholars used these early relations to extol the accomplishments of the Japanese imperial house. These histories were quickly taken up by the Japanese media and used by colonial authorities, as certain aspects of these myths — particularly the claim that Empress Jingū had conquered the peninsula and set up an administration over its southern portion — were woven into colonial ideology. These novel Japanese theories appeared on the peninsula at precisely the time aspiring Korean historians were exploring the possibilities of writing their own national histories. Consequently, as I show in chapter 4, even before annexation, Japanese historical theories about Korea had begun to appear in Korean school textbooks and geographical studies. Other authors were more leery, treating these theories with skepticism. Nevertheless, all historians in this period engaged in some way with Japanese versions of the Korean past, whether this was to accept them outright, adapt them to their own purposes, or set them up as a foil to develop oppositional histories. It is in this broader context that the development of modern Korean historiography must be situated.

Because of the power of Japanese versions of the Korean past, it remained for Korean historians to develop a locus for the nation that could escape the conundrum presented by "civilization and enlightenment." It is in this sense that the work of Sin Ch'aeho, an editorial writer working for the *TaeHan maeil sinbo* (*Korea Daily News*), is so important. As I explain in chapter 5, Sin offered in 1908 a new interpretation of the past that capitalized on a number of the era's intellectual tendencies to offer some solutions to these problems. In keeping with the trend away from state-centered definitions of the nation, Sin adopted an ethnic definition of the nation, what was known as the *minjok*. He also highlighted an old foundation myth about Tan'gun (a mythic figure himself) to create a history that descended through time in a manner reminiscent of the patrilineal family records used in the Chosŏn dynasty. The result was a genealogy for the Korean people that, when combined with the type of martial historical figures promoted as national heroes, offered a masculine conception of the nation. Adopting a social Darwinian vision that left little room for an enlightenment-style history, Sin made the bloodline of the ethnic nation his subject, with its survival amid constant threats of extinction serving as his main narrative dynamic. In placing the ethnic nation at the core of his history, Sin deliberately distanced himself from earlier Confucian narratives focusing on the court. By so doing, he created an autonomous subject for the nation that had no external referent or measure other than its own action, a move that made China irrelevant to the story of the Korean *minjok*, constituting the final step in decentering the "Middle Kingdom." His history also offered an objective definition of the nation, a nation that existed through historical time, regardless of whether the Korean people were aware of its existence. But in the special circumstances of a colonized nation — when state and territory, in the parlance of the time, had been "stolen" — the continued existence of the ethnic nation depended on mass awareness, and Sin's history promised to forge and sustain that collective memory. Sin's historiographical maneuveurs served many purposes at this time, but most important, they created an autonomy for a nation squeezed by two empires, simultaneously decentering Korea away from China in the past and offering a version of the nation that enabled a particular form of resistance to Japan in the present. These maneuveurs were quickly taken up by other historians, who proposed a wide range of alternatives within the parameters set out by Sin. The repercussions of Sin's history spilled over into many other issues, one of which was the question of national space.

The Boundaries of the Nation

Discovered on the northern side of the Sino-Korean border, the location of the Kwanggaet'o stele raised a number of questions about territorial limits. What were the spatial bounds of the nation in the past, and where should they be in the present? For a unit that was seen as a territorial entity, this was a question touching the fundamental definition of the nation. Nationalism tolerates no amibiguity in the disposition of lands; sovereignty over territory must be clearly delineated. But at the end of the nineteenth century, the exact location of the Sino-Korean border to the east of Mount Paektu in the upper reaches of the Tumen River was anything but certain. This was not a novel issue, but in the last quarter of the nineteenth century when both Korea and China began to explore the new conceptual vocabulary of territorial sovereignty for ordering their own territorial realms, this remote section of border became hotly contested as each side sought a different location for the limits of their nation.

Much of the work on the modern nation emphasizes the disruptive effects of nationalism. This has often been presented as a "clash" between premodern and modern forms of collective organization. Or to use more recent terminology, it represents "epistemic violence," in which the indigenous and the Euro-American are equated with the premodern and modern, respectively, the latter riding roughshod over the former as capitalism extends from the West to the rest of the world. Whichever set of terms (together with their divergent assumptions) is used, one tendency in these studies has been to point to the paradoxical force of appeals to tradition at the time when the nation itself is being "invented," "constructed," or "imagined."[31] These approaches have opened new ways of analyzing the nation and shape much of the work in this book as well. Yet by describing the origins of the nation as a move from and to the essentialist categories of modern and tradition, respectively, these approaches have tended to neglect the interactions between nationalist and prenationalist discourses, thereby oversimplifying the genealogy of the modern nation.

Research on the spatial character of nations has often taken this general approach, stressing the modern nature of territoriality, in particular its linkage with Western forms of cartographic knowledge. This approach contrasts the modern with the premodern and Western with indigenous to offer a vision of the nation as an externally generated transition from a nonterritorial entity to a territorially delimited nation.[32] In chapter 6, I show how the transition toward defining the peninsula as a sovereign, delimited unit of space was more complicated that the mere replacement of indigenous geographic discourses with their Western counterparts. By the time the Western powers arrived, the centralized state bureaucracy of the Chosŏn dynasty had administered a relatively stable realm for well over four centuries. Out of administrative practices and geographical studies, both sponsored by the state and individually written, a sense of territory had already developed well before concepts of sovereignty arrived. Works on territory and history written since at least the seventeenth century, if not earlier, had created a sense of space that transcended any single dynasty. This was not a nationalist conception of the territory, in which notions of citizenship were extended to the entire population within the borders of the nation as a locus of political sovereignty. Nor was there a movement that actively sought to produce and disseminate spatial knowledge. But that such a spatial understanding existed was crucial in the late nineteenth century, since it meant that early nationalist writers did not need to imagine from scratch the nation as a spatial entity. The Chosŏn dynasty was not a blank sheet waiting to have Western definitions of space written on it. Instead, the texts from and social memories of the late Chosŏn dynasty needed to be reconfigured, even retrofitted, in line with the new knowledge of the West while at the same time these understandings mediated the reception of Western discourses on space.

This long-standing sense of space was central to the Korean position on its border dispute with China at the end of the nineteenth century. The basic position of the Korean government in this territorial dispute followed arguments that had a long history in the late Chosŏn period. Although differences over the positioning of the border were contested in a new international vocabulary based on the notion of territorial sovereignty, these new concepts came to be interwoven with themes and issues dating back to the mid-Chosŏn dynasty. In many cases, Koreans used new notions of space to affirm and rearticulate received understanding about the border, and in turn, this rearticulation resulted in certain shifts in the way that space was claimed for the nation.

The dispute over the northern border ensured that the peninsula would emerge as the dominant spatial metaphor for the nation. Yet the location of the Kwanggaet'o stele on the other side of the border — outside the peninsula, so to speak — led many writers to ponder the relationship between the peninsula and the vast lands of Manchuria. As I show in chapter 7, this tendency developed into a romantic vision as writers cast their historical gaze back to an earlier age when the nation extended beyond the peninsula into the lands of Manchuria. During the Chosŏn dynasty, some Koreans had felt nostalgic about the north. But now with a new national subject, the *minjok*, linked to its mythical progenitor, Tan'gun, a novel way of claiming Manchuria as central to the nation arose. As most extensively explored in the work of Sin Ch'aeho, the rightful realm of the *minjok* was defined as the lands initially settled by Tan'gun and his early descendants, in other words, the peninsula *and* Manchuria. The vicissitudes of the *minjok*'s presence in Manchuria emerged as a measure for narrating national success and failure — a poignant assessment of the Korea of the day. Such a history, though most boldly envisioned by Sin, found its way into rival newspaper editorials, essays by other prominent writers, and textbooks produced by religious groups, leading to a widespread sense of the centrality of Manchuria in Korea's national history. In this vision that rested on historical interpretation and vacated the language of territorial sovereignty, the nation's spatial dimensions were defined as much by what had been lost as by what had been retained. For some, the solution to the nation's crisis rested beyond the peninsula in an irredentist hope that a history with Manchuria at its center would enable Manchuria to be reclaimed in the present. This was a history of loss, in which regaining the north was the only route to redemption.

Contemplation of Manchuria's role for the past and future of the peninsula was not the only way the locus of the nation could be shifted beyond the peninsula. It had, after all, been a Korean outside the country who had first stumbled across the rubbing of the Kwanggaet'o stele and reported its existence to those back home. This migration abroad, not only to Tokyo, but also to Hawai'i, Mexico, Russia, Manchuria, and the United States, became the subject of much editorial scrutiny in the domestic press. That Koreans were crossing their borders to distant lands at the very time that the nation was regarded as a population congregated in a discrete territorial space raised troubling questions about the dominant definitions of the nation. These individuals had left behind the national territory that supposedly defined them. Reports back from diasporic communities, especially San Francisco, forced domestic writers to conceptualize the relationship of these deterritorialized immigrants to the peninsula. What is clear from the domestic press of this era is that the diaspora was integral to general debates about the nature of the nation — a centrality that I believe must be reincorporated into our understanding of the nationalist movement and not relegated to an external history of "Koreans over there." I argue in chapter 7 that the dichotomy of inside/outside developed in these reports on the diaspora enabled new strategies for exploring questions of national character and, ultimately, enabled the dominant spatial logic of national discourse to be turned inside out. This logic — namely, that national territory and culture are isomorphic — was challenged by both domestic and overseas writers as the colonial presence of Japan deepened while the patriotic activities of Koreans in San Francisco increased. As diasporic newspapers crossing the Pacific Ocean disclosed to the chagrin of peninsula-based editors, the future of the nation might best lie with those beyond the peninsula who were uninhibited by colonial power. Koreans in San Francisco eagerly accepted this responsibility, claiming that they alone could preserve a nation whose physical boundaries had been tainted by Japan's presence. With the homeland stolen, the assumptions that allowed some domestic writers to scold Koreans abroad for not preserving their culture were reversed: deterritorialization now became a prerequisite for true nationalism, and in the eyes of some, it was better to live outside than inside the peninsula.

In these many ways, the Kwanggaet'o stele, like so many other objects, debates, and events, became a specific issue through which writers explored various ways of locating the nation in relation to shifting national, regional, and global environments. This exploration did not stop with annexation in 1910 but continued throughout much of the colonial period, though always constricted by the vacillating press restrictions of the colonial government. With liberation in 1945 and the reemergence of a powerful indigenous publishing industry, writing on the nation freed itself from some of the most obvious constraints of colonial rule, allowing an unabashed nationalism to be explored on the peninsula for the first time in almost four decades — although now constrained by the politics of the cold war. On the peninsula, this nationalism was manifested in the entrenchment of two rival regimes, who after their internecine war (1950–53) invested many resources in competing interpretations of the past in support of their claims to sole legitimacy. As I maintain in the epilogue, the official histories of both the Democratic People's Republic of Korea (DPRK) and the Republic of Korea (ROK) have treated the legacies of turn-of-the-century newspaper writers quite differently, the former dismissing them as ineffective in the face of Japanese colonialism and the latter embracing them as part of a nationalist movement that eventually resulted in the formation of the southern state. Regardless of these divergent appraisals, I believe that one of the legacies of these early newspaper writers was to solidify many of the parameters and conceptual frameworks that continued to shape nationalist discourse throughout the colonial period and into postliberation Korea.

The crisis that at the end of the nineteenth century shook the institutional and ideological foundations of the nearly five-hundred-year-old Chosŏn dynasty created the opportunity to rethink modes of collective life in the capitalist modernity of the global system, a system that, despite tremendous changes since the outset of the twentieth century, remains with us today and continues to structure our national lives. Issues first raised in early Korean newspapers still are part of contemporary debates about the Korean nation in areas as diverse as language, history writing, and spatial limits, demonstrating the power of the national knowledge produced by these writers and the ability of their conceptual frameworks to adapt to changes in the do-

mestic and international environments. The stir caused by the announcement of the Kwanggaet'o stele at the beginning of the twentieth century has
certainly subsided. But just as the stele is featured in the official narratives
of both the DPRK and ROK and models of the stele are prominently displayed
in both Seoul and Pyongyang museums, the lines of inquiry first established
in early Korean newspapers and journals continue to shape debates about
the nation in both Koreas today.

1   The Universalizing Winds of Civilization

Who will breathe in the winds of this new civilization that are
night and day crossing over to this side of the Pacific Ocean, accompanying the
ships and telegraphs? Who will light a torch in the deep and long night?
— *Sŏbuk hakhoe wŏlbo,* February 1909

Nationalism thrives on crisis. And in the closing years of the
nineteenth and the opening years of the twentieth century, perhaps the only
area of agreement across the full spectrum of Korean society—from conservative Confucians residing in the countryside, to leading reform officials
in the capital, to resident foreign observers—was that the peninsula was in
quite a predicament. Editors did not shy away from colorful metaphors to
portray the crisis. A single article could describe the nation as a "flimsy ship
crossing a raging river," "an old house threatening to collapse," and "a sick
body."[1] The people were referred to as "fish in a boiling cauldron," "sparrows
on a burning column,"[2] and "crows in a basket,"[3] while the imperialist powers were likened to tigers and wolves surrounding the nation,[4] a group of
thieves encircling a house,[5] and a typhoon advancing from all four directions.[6] It was as if Korea were being "shot on four sides by arrows."[7] Others
avoided such dramatic language, suggesting only that the national situation
was so dire that "it was unspeakable."[8]

In such a precarious situation, the people should be "preparing the house
for a huge storm"—and a growing number tried to do just that.[9] These were
nationalist writers and publicists who tried to escape the crisis by producing
and disseminating particular types of knowledge about the nation in support
of a reform agenda. In the newspapers, journals, and textbooks that they
created, these writers for the first time made the nation the unrivaled subject
of public discourse, linking all matters however seemingly trivial or however
seemingly grand—from the style of haircuts to constitutions, from popular

rights to the use of umbrellas — to the nation's health and wealth in a global order. The diversity of information about the nation was largely united by an underlying commitment to the ideologies of capitalist modernity as captured in the period's most popular phrase, "civilization and enlightenment" (*munmyŏng kaehwa*). Touted as universal, *munmyŏng kaehwa* spurred a reform package that sought to strengthen and enrich the nation by disciplining the population into certain modes of behavior and bringing both individuals and the nation in line with international standards. In this way, *munmyŏng kaehwa* offered a new spatial and temporal unit that linked all three levels: the behavior of individuals shaped the fate of the nation that performed within the historical laws that, in turn, were seen as having produced the contemporary global ecumene. Nationalism in these years resorted to a form of globalization as a way of salvaging the nation, a project informed by the temporal and spatial vision of *munmyŏng kaehwa*.

With their segmented format and long runs, newspapers were ideally suited to investigate and disseminate the many new ways of articulating national visions in this changing ideological environment. In an era when no other media could rival the power of newspapers and journals, the writers who controlled them dominated public discourse about the nation and world, enabling them to offer visions of Korea that positioned themselves as enlightened leaders while shunting aside alternatives that might contest the assumptions of their nationalist reform project.

Internal Disorder, External Calamities

Events both on and surrounding the Korean peninsula in the last few years of the nineteenth century neatly fit the classical Confucian definition of crisis as captured in the phrase *naeu oehwan*, "internal disorder, external calamities." At this time, few writers committed to new notions of progress were keen to employ such a mode of analysis with its connotations of cyclical dynastic decline. Nevertheless, most contemporary analysts, as well as historians today, agreed with the basic premise of *naeu oehwan*: that the crisis of the waning years of the Chosŏn dynasty resulted from the confluence of internal and external trends. Externally, the conspicuous arrival of the West's new technologies, capital, and knowledge had helped spur a reconfiguration of state-society relations while internally, less conspicuous but equally significant long-term socioeconomic trends had undermined the state's ability to rule. Parochial matters that in an earlier age had been the concern of only village heads and magistrates were now interlinked with globalizing processes, and what had been seen as local matters came to be interpreted anew in world historical terms. No other period in the previous few centuries had witnessed such profound shifts in the ideological makeup of Korean society.

The sense of crisis took a specific form in 1894 when a peasant uprising almost overthrew the 502-year-old dynasty. Led by Chŏn Pongjun, the peasants in a southwestern county rose up against their corrupt local magistrate, who, after coercing them into building a water reservoir, had the temerity to charge them for using that water. By the end of May, slightly more than one month after the outbreak of hostilities, the peasant armies captured the capital of Chŏlla Province. Historians have tended to contextualize the events of these days as long-term trends marking the decline of the Chosŏn dynastic order. The magistrate who initiated the uprising with his demands, Cho Pyŏnggap, has come to personify the corruption that made state institutions in the last century of the dynasty unable to adapt to a changing socioeconomic order, thereby exacerbating the pressures on the rural economy through their personal exactions from the peasantry. The ability of the uprising's leaders to mobilize peasants rapidly in areas far removed from the site of the original crisis are seen as a reaction to the widespread difficulties in the countryside resulting from long-term changes in the agricultural economy and intensifying commercialization.[10] These shifts brought with them various types of dislocation between status and economic power while arguably impoverishing large numbers of participants who had been unable to take advantage of the changes.[11]

Other historians have paid close attention to the affiliation of many of the peasant leaders with a new religion that since the 1860s had expanded throughout the country. Called Tonghak, or Eastern learning, this syncretic religion provided some of the organizational infrastructure for the peasants, and as some scholars have contended, its advocacy of social equality and calls for social change posed an indigenous ideological challenge to the state's Confucian orthodoxy.[12] Despite these differences over the precise origins and nature of the peasant uprising, historians generally agree that the successes of the peasant army and the ineffectiveness of the state were rooted in a growing imbalance in the institutions and ideology that had served the dynasty for more than half a millennium.

Never was this clearer than in June 1894 when government troops failed in their attempts to retake the capital of Chŏlla Province from the peasant armies. With their troops routed by the "Green Bean General," as the leader of the peasants had come to be affectionately known, the court telegraphed Beijing for assistance in suppressing what had developed into a virtual civil war that threatened the very existence of the dynasty. When Qing officials responded affirmatively, Japan, which had been carefully monitoring the events, seized the opportunity to send its own troops to the peninsula, setting up the conditions for the outbreak of the Sino-Japanese War. What had begun as a dispute over a reservoir in a remote county escalated into a war that fundamentally changed the geopolitical landscape of the region.

From the earliest years of the Meiji period, Korea had been an important foreign policy issue for Japanese leaders. Since the "Conquest of Korea" debates (Seikanron) of 1872–73, the question of how best to protect and maintain an ever shifting array of Japanese political, security, and economic interests dominated discussions of Korea.[13] Outside the government, various groups pursued their own, often highly imaginative efforts while the government sought to do so by mastering the conventions of international law, even though brute force was always a ready option.[14] In a demonstration of how quickly Japan had learned the style of gunboat diplomacy, which only a short time before had been used against it, a ship was sent off the shores of Korea to provoke an incident. The following year, beating the Western powers at their own game, Japan signed the Treaty of Kanghwa with the Korean government, opening the peninsula to an ever widening array of international commercial activities. One of the treaty's objectives had been to weaken Korea's ties with China, but in fact, because of various political shifts within Korea, combined with a newly aggressive Chinese stance on the peninsula, the treaty did not translate into an attenuation of Sino-Korean ties. State and private support for reformers inside the country dominated Japanese efforts to shift the political balance for the next two decades, but by the early 1890s, despite a burgeoning trade, Japan had been unable either to persuade or to force a reconfiguration of Korea's relations with the Qing.[15]

When in 1894 the Chosŏn government requested assistance from Qing officials to suppress the Tonghak peasant armies, Japan used the opportunity to end Chinese influence on the peninsula. That the government and peasant armies had agreed to cease hostilities before the Japanese troops arrived was a minor inconvenience. Japan rejected proposals to withdraw. In July 1894, Japanese troops captured the Korean palace and sequestered the king, actions that triggered the outbreak of the Sino-Japanese War. In control of the government, the Japanese established a reform-oriented cabinet that launched a sweeping reform movement, known as the Kabo reforms. In the countryside, however, news of Japan's actions led the Tonghak armies to reorganize, this time directing their attacks against the foreign invaders. Hopelessly outarmed, they were defeated by Japanese troops, and Chŏn Pongjun, together with other key leaders, were captured. By the next spring, Japan's success in the Korean countryside was followed by an even more resounding victory when its army and navy completely routed the Qing forces. In the Treaty of Shimonoseki, the document signed to conclude the war, the first clause forced China to recognize the objective pursued by Japan for many years, an end to tributary ties with Korea.

Within a week of each other, Chŏn Pongjun was executed and the Treaty of Shimonoseki was signed.[16] While these two events may have been satisfying to many Japanese, they did little to assuage the sense of crisis that prevailed in Korea. The independence acquired from the Treaty of Shimonoseki, while certainly welcomed by many Koreans who had long been working to end the tributary relationship, was seen as a hollow sovereignty. Granted rather than earned, it was sovereignty in name only, according to one style of critique. Independence proffered by outside forces, it suggested, could never lead to a completely sovereign nation.[17] Internally, although the defeat of the Tonghak peasant forces dispelled the immediate military threat to the dynasty, sporadic local uprisings, sometimes involving Tonghak members, continued for many more years. Indeed, the central government's reform program, with its top-down and heavy-handed approach, often aggravated the situation in the countryside. These years were also the high tide of concession diplomacy in East Asia. Whether it was Americans seeking railway construction or gold mining rights, Russians demanding forest concessions, or Japanese obtaining fishing rights, the Korean government was regularly pressured and cajoled into handing over concessions to foreign commercial interests.

The history of the next fifteen years until annexation is often recounted along three narrative lines, all tracing various dimensions of the crisis. The most prominent narrative, focusing on the royal house, offers a high-level political history in which the king and his family serve as a metaphor for the nation. A legacy of lingering court-centered Confucian historiographical practice, this narrative line renders the drama surrounding King Kojong into a style of national history that follows the steady decline from nominal independence to colonialism. It was not a happy slide. In one of the most telling moments in the history of the royal house, on October 8, 1895, a group of Japanese ruffians organized by Miura Gōrō, the newly appointed Japanese consul to Korea, broke into the royal palace. The queen was targeted for removal, having been vilified in the Japanese media as a conservative obstacle to reform and the expansion of Japanese interests. She was slain that night by Japanese swords. In a vain attempt to hide evidence of the deed, her body was burned at the back of the palace, an action that earned international opprobrium for the newly "civilized" Japan, but not enough for Miura to be convicted by the Japanese courts.[18] Fearing for his own safety, King Kojong shortly afterward hid in his consort's palanquin leaving his residence for the Russian legation, where he remained ensconced for a contentious eleven months. Upon his return to the palace, he and his officials launched a series of reforms — a restoration (chunghŭng), in the classical parlance in which the changes were framed — that tried both to salvage the throne's tarnished reputation and to strengthen the court's hold over the state bureaucracy and society.[19]

Despite these efforts at reform, the state was unable to resist Japan's sustained encroachments. During the Russo-Japanese War, the court declared the peninsula to be neutral, but Japan took advantage of the wartime emergency to wrest control of many government functions. Two months after Japan's victory, Itō Hirobumi, accompanied by a group of soldiers, marched into the palace to force the official imperial seal to be placed on a treaty making Korea a protectorate. In a letter published on February 1, 1906, in a national newspaper, Kojong announced he had never consented to the treaty, and the following year, he dispatched a secret mission to the International Peace Conference in the Hague, only to have his delegates refused admission to the proceedings. These acts of recalcitrance were enough for his Japanese handlers to force Kojong to cede the throne to his reputedly more feckless son, Sunjong. The military was disbanded, and in 1907, a new treaty effectively handed control of internal administrative matters to a coterie of high-level Japanese advisers. Three years later on August 22, Emperor Sunjong proclaimed the annexation of Korea, relinquished his throne, and was soon, in a move symbolic of Japanese claims to reuniting a long separated family, accepted as a "prince" in the Japanese imperial line.

A second narrative thread through the years after the Sino-Japanese War traces the ultimately doomed efforts at state-generated reform. Attempts by various groups to initiate change in the 1880s gained new impetus in the postwar environment. With Japan now pressuring the court to pursue a re-

form program, many officials and even exiled reformers had an opportunity
to pursue the style of government and social changes that they had long
advocated but had never had the political power to implement.[20] Between
July 1894 and February 1896, wide-sweeping reform decrees announced
what amounted to a thorough overhaul of Korean institutions and social
legislation. Socially, the status system of the Chosŏn dynasty was officially
abandoned. The hereditary elite, or *yangban*, at one end of the social spectrum was deprived of state support for many of their traditional privileges
while, at the opposite end, the remaining slaves were freed. One of the
defining features of the patrilineal system — the prohibition of widows' re-
marrying — was outlawed, although the patrilineal ordering of families was
not challenged. The king's authority was limited: the imperial purse was
separated from the state budget, and his control over the bureaucracy
was restricted. The traditional examination system was abandoned as a
means of recruiting officials, while schools with a new curriculum were
opened and students were sent to Japan at government expense. Over this
year and a half, more than 660 reform documents were announced.[21] Certainly for the local official receiving this onslaught of unprecedented orders
from the capital, it was a tumultuous time indeed.

After King Kojong finally left the Russian legation in February 1897 to
return to his palace, a new set of reforms was initiated. Frequently referred
to by the new reign date, Kwangmu, these reforms were more restrained
than the Kabo reforms, in some cases even resurrecting pre-Kabo administrative practices. Reform was now equated with the strengthening of royal
powers, and the king was elevated to imperial status.[22] Financial reform was
pursued, in part so as to alleviate the pressures on the royal household. In
addition to the imposition of new taxes on various services and ginseng, a
land survey was launched. Although a lack of capital hampered the efforts
to measure landholdings and to issue ownership certificates, eventually
about two-thirds of the nation's land was recorded.[23] Efforts were made to
strengthen the military. Investments, often underwritten with foreign loans
or concessions, were made in the nation's economic infrastructure, in telegraph lines, road improvements, or the construction of major railways.

By 1907, when King Kojong was forced to abdicate, it was clear that in
the last ten years of his reign, immense changes in both the apparatus and
ideology of governance had taken place. That the designs for reform were
often bolder than their implementation was a common critique. How effectively these changes were carried out by a state that could not confidently

impose its will on the localities remains a question of much debate. The difficulty of extending reforms outside the capital is one reason that questions of local governance were discussed so widely in these years. Whatever the answer, it is clear that even in the more conservative Kwangmu reforms, the assumptions about governance had shifted as dramatically as the old balance of forces that had maintained the stability of the dynasty for more than half a millennium had been undermined.

A third story line for these years, one interwoven with the account of reform outside the state, is the growth of a nationalist movement. Besides the now scattered forces of the Tonghak peasant armies, two nationalist streams arose. One was the "righteous armies" (*ŭibyŏng*), who traced their intellectual pedigree back to the earlier "Protect the Orthodox, Repel the Heterodox" (Wijŏng ch'ŏksa) advocates who in 1876 had vociferously opposed opening the country to Japan. Now, in addition to the inflammatory memorials submitted to the king, they added to their repertoire armed resistance to the Japanese presence on the peninsula.[24] Until 1911, when the few survivors were squeezed out of the peninsula into Manchuria, skirmishes of various sizes with the Japanese military dotted the countryside.

The second stream of the nationalist movement, often called the Patriotic Enlightenment Movement — the focus of this study — similarly traced its origins to before the war.[25] In the short term, this included the Enlightenment Party of Kim Okkyun, Pak Yŏnghyo, Sŏ Kwangbŏm, and others who, out of frustration at their inability to reform the government from within, switched tactics. In December 1884, at a dinner celebrating the opening of a new postal system, they captured King Kojong in a coup d'état. For three brief days they ruled, proclaiming radical reform proposals in the name of the king. But Chinese troops, led by Yuan Shikai, attacked the new government, killing those who did not manage to escape to Japan. Several later returned to take prominent positions in the cabinet during the Kabo reforms. In the longer term, many of these intellectuals saw themselves as the heirs of reform thinkers of the late Chosŏn dynasty, such Pak Chiwŏn, Yi Ik, and Chŏng Yagyong.[26] Some intellectuals could even trace their teacher affiliations back to these thinkers. Kim Okkyun and many of his co-conspirators in the 1884 coup d'état had studied in the home of Pak Kyusu, the grandson of Pak Chiwŏn, renowned for advocating an open door policy before the Treaty of Kanghwa.[27] The advent in the late nineteenth century of a style of reform thought that engaged with the West cannot be separated from the long history of reform thought in Korea during the seventeenth through

nineteenth centuries. Other leaders of this movement, as much of the English-language literature has pointed out, were deeply influenced by their
conversion to Christianity.[28]

The year 1905 occupies an important position in all three of these story
lines. On November 17, the Japanese imposed a protectorate on Korea,
assuming control of its foreign affairs. It is all too easy to draw a direct line
following Japan's gradual accumulation of power starting with the end of the
Sino-Japanese War until the Meiji government was able to annex the peninsula in 1910. As a number of studies on decision-making processes at the
upper levels of the Japanese government have shown, however, Japanese
leaders were divided over how best to pursue their economic and security
interests in the peninsula.[29] It is less easy to recapture Korean reactions to
this tumultuous series of events without imposing our historical hindsight
on the figures of these years. What is striking is that until the outbreak of
the Russo-Japanese War, very few Koreans predicted the train of events that
eventually culminated in the loss of sovereignty at the hands of Japan. To
be sure, there was a general sense of crisis to which Japan was seen as
contributing with its special concerns and specific challenges to Korean
sovereignty. But until Japan's actions during the war revealed its less than
benevolent intent toward the peninsula, there was no generally shared understanding in the public media that Japan presented a greater threat than
Russia or that the imposition of a protectorate was imminent. Until this time,
newspapers were just as likely to recall with a degree of gratitude Japan's
function in forcing the Qing government to recognize Korean independence as to condemn Japan for its peninsular activities. One overseas student
in the United States recalled this situation in 1908 in a letter to a Korean
newspaper. He described coming across a copy of an old American magazine
from 1905 that had an editorial cartoon depicting Japan, Russia, and the
United States struggling over two dishes, one called Korea, the other Manchuria. It went on to illustrate how Japan would get the right to eat the
dishes with no American interference. Such prescience in an editorial cartoon confounded the student, who expressed wonderment and disillusionment that at a time when foreigners clearly understood that Japan was seeking to acquire the peninsula, many Koreans placed their trust in Japanese
claims of charitable intentions.[30] If the Protectorate Treaty of 1905 caught
Koreans off guard, many responded over the next few years by forming nationalist associations and building schools for the promotion of a nationalist
curriculum.

To writers in the newly arisen press — people who were participants in these events as well as their recorders[31] — what proved most frustrating was the ineffectual response of officials and the general population. In what emerged as one of the most common metaphors of Korean nationalists — indeed, of nationalist intellectuals around the world who were dissatisfied with the results of their attempts to mobilize their compatriots — the nation was said to be still "asleep," undisturbed by recent events.[32] Such a description, of course, assumed that the observer, unlike his compatriots, was not only awake but also knew how to shake the nation out of its slumber. In the years immediately after the Sino-Japanese War, the number of groups willing to appoint themselves this task grew dramatically. To sound the reveille, they outfitted themselves with newspapers in which they propounded a new message.

Globalizing the National and Nationalizing the Global

That new message was *munmyŏng kaehwa* — "civilization and enlightenment." Although most exuberantly promoted by the newly emerging newspaper presses, by 1895 the message had become familiar. It had insinuated itself into speeches by the king, and even regulations listing changes in the curriculum of that venerable Confucian academy, the Sŏnggyungwan, appealed to *munmyŏng kaehwa*.[33] At the extreme opposite, advertisers, always quick to capitalize on the latest trends, flogged their products — whether medicine or milk — as suited for a "civilized age" and fitting the discriminating taste of "civilized" consumers.[34] Able to sell both reform and products, *munmyŏng kaehwa* emerged as the vocabulary of the era.

The power and seductiveness of *munmyŏng kaehwa* lay in its ability to link seamlessly the individual, nation, and globe into a historical and spatial unity. As a modern discourse par excellence, *munmyŏng kaehwa* offered a conceptual framework in which various groups could come to terms with their recent integration into the global capitalist system. At the same time, its underlying drive for change served to deepen that participation. Today, although nationalism and globalization are often juxtaposed as oppositional or exclusive processes, in Korea at the end of the nineteenth and early twentieth centuries, the two were mutually constitutive: nationalism was the vehicle for accelerating the peninsula's inclusion in the global capitalist order, and these globalizing forces — in particular what was called the "new knowledge" (*sinhak*) — stimulated a radical rethinking of the nation and its identity. One editorial captured this relationship: "In this era the joint advancement of globalism [*segyejŏkchuŭi*] and nationalism [*kukkajuŭi*] constitutes the path toward civilization."[35] The appropriation and dissemination of *munmyŏng kaehwa* resulted in a historical shift in the spatiotemporal definition of the peninsula. Now the nation was seen by nature as just another member of a community of nations that stretched around the world, sharing a historical trajectory.

While *munmyŏng kaehwa* claimed a temporal and spatial universality — applicable to all nations at all times — its usage was conditioned by its long history in the West. As Norbert Elias has shown, the idea of *civilité* had originally been a means for medieval European, especially French, aristocrats to separate themselves from the lower classes. By the eighteenth century, this idea had been diffused across the social spectrum to become a widespread social precept, spawning its nominal form, "civilization."[36] As Europeans traveled beyond their borders, they carried this notion of civilization with them, moving it from the domestic social sphere onto the international stage, as it offered a useful rationale for both protecting their citizens in faraway lands and using force to extend their political and economic interests.[37] By the time Korea established relations with outside powers in the latter half of the nineteenth century, civilization had become the foundation of international law and, with its claims to universality, had become the central tenet of an international modern discourse.

It was within this discourse that Korean intellectuals tried to position their nation, and in so doing they accepted this Western-derived concept and promoted its claim to universality. As evident in the early efforts to provide didactic introductions to this concept, Korean writers focused not on its particular history but on its universal validity. Yu Kilchun, one of *munmyŏng kaehwa*'s greatest advocates, wrote that enlightenment was what leads "the thousand affairs and ten thousand matters of humanity to reach the stage of greatest good and greatest beauty." There were various types of enlightenment, he explained, ranging from the enlightenment of government to that of machines; only when these various types were combined could one begin to constitute a "complete enlightenment."[38] A prominent newspaper described enlightenment as a means "to open wide one's state of absolute ignorance and strive to undertake myriad tasks while taking into account actual circumstances and natural laws."[39] On a later occasion the editors explained this meant that the fundamental way of progressing toward enlightenment consisted of correcting mistakes, learning new knowledge, and pursuing superior ways of doing things.[40] Such nebulous definitions suggested that anyone, anywhere, and at any time could, with the appropriate effort, become "enlightened."

These definitions also reveal the activist impulse at the heart of *munmyŏng kaehwa:* something needed to be *done* to the nation. Precisely what reform was needed was the question around which much of the political jockeying of the era revolved. It was over the issue of reform that observers of the political scene at the time, and historians today, divided activists into various political stripes: conservative, moderate, or radical. Editors vied, officials clashed, and speakers debated over whether the cutting of hair was a necessary step for enlightenment, how much Confucian teaching could be inserted in an enlightening curriculum, how the currency should be reformed, and what system should be used to hire and promote officials in the localities. Underlying these specific, contentious issues were a number of assumptions about reform and its relation to the nation that reflected the power of *munmyŏng kaehwa* to link individual efforts to the nation and, more broadly, the world.

The very structure of reform writing revealed these relationships. A typical piece began with a laudatory description of some feature of the civilized world before shifting — usually after an exclamatory cry of despair, *aigu!* (alas) — to what was presented as the benighted or ignorant status of that same phenomenon in Korea. Comments about what a shame this was, leading Korea to be derided in the world, were followed by reform proposals of varying specificity on how to bridge the gap. As illustrated in one newspaper's celebration of the founding in 1904 of the TaeHan Women's Association (TaeHan puinhoe), by concentrating on a specific reform issue, such pieces served to group Korea into the same global community and historical narrative as the countries of the West.[41] One of the most written-about subjects of the time, gender issues — the status of women, women's education, early betrothal, the sale of girls, or the remarriage of widows — were commonly used as markers of national backwardness. Women were metaphorically equated with the past, a past that needed to be overcome by altering their status and behavior.

In this editorial, the universality of *munmyŏng kaehwa* was established from the outset by a description of the earliest periods of humanity, when all people, wherever they lived, were in the same benighted state. "In the countries of both the East and West, during the age when society was ex-

tremely ignorant, the status of women was such that they were considered
nothing more than a piece of property or a plaything of their men." Then
the editors followed a narrative of progress, recounting how in the history of
the West the position of women continually improved. Continuing until the
French Revolution, the editors observed that the freedoms and rights of
women continued to expand so that at least in terms of their ability to serve
in national politics, they enjoyed the same status as men. Especially impressed by the fact that in a number of countries women had acquired the
right to vote, they asserted that "it is no exaggeration to say that today in
America and the countries of Europe, when the position and rights of
women are compared with those of men, there are no large differences."
This initial passage established progress as the narrative and the West as the
measure, setting up a contrast to the situation in Korea:

> As described earlier for the prehistoric period of ignorance, [in Korea
> today] women are in the situation in which they do not have the tiniest
> of freedoms and are only fettered and oppressed by their husbands.
> Even if they are women with intelligence and skills, they have no way
> of making use of their natural abilities. They are simply one of the
> abandoned goods of human society.

In these Korean representations of the West, the (in)accuracy of statements — "there are no large differences"! — was less the issue than the way
the exaggerated successes of Western women and the overly pessimistic view
of the achievements of Korean women were woven together. Western and
Korean women, ancient and contemporary, were brought into the same
story of *munmyŏng kaehwa*. The "beautiful deed" of founding the TaeHan
Women's Association was not solely a Korean matter but was also Korea's
contribution to the furthering of this global process. "This is important not
only to the glory of the single country of Korea, for it also expresses sincere
sympathy for the human way [*indo*] of today's civilized world." In this way,
Korea was being written metaphorically through specific reform issues —
here the status of women but also in such diverse areas as habits of hygiene,
government systems, and education — into a universal vision of time and
space.[42]

According to the temporal logic of *munmyŏng kaehwa*, the contrast between the superiority of specific Western practices was not an essential difference, but one of time. Such comparisons underscored the potential for

catching up to the West but always presented Korea as lacking or backward. "Looking back at the history of Western countries, two or three centuries ago their repressive and barbarous customs as well as their corrupt and chaotic governments resembled those of Korea today."[43] One editorial compared a generic "Western farmer" — whatever this may have been — with a Korean farmer, depicting the latter as five hundred years behind his Western counterpart, with the gap explained as the consequence of "enlightenment."[44] Even chicken-raising techniques could be structured in this fashion. As one enterprising company advertised, better techniques in the West had created magnificent fortunes, while in Korea, chicken-raising techniques were still "immature and childish."[45] The ad offered a book for only thirty-five *chŏn* that would allow one to master these techniques, in effect insinuating that Koreans could become enlightened by the "mature" raising of chickens. Whether in a grandiose scheme of reform or something as pedestrian as chicken raising, the very method of urging reform illustrates how the concept of *munmyŏng kaehwa* was predicated on a division between the East and West, serving to reinforce Eurocentric definitions of a historically inferior East. Used sweepingly, representations of the West had less to do with the social reality on the other side of the world and more to do with a writer's desire to contrast a targeted feature of his nation with that of a superior Other in order to muster a rationale for reform.

The blandest invocation of this sort could carry great power. Readers could be shown the way something was done in "ten thousand countries" (*man'guk*) and "every country" (*gakkuk*) in order to learn that Korea, too, could match these supposedly universal practices. As was always the case, these universal ways were conflated with an idealized and reductive vision of "Western ways." When readers learned that "every nation" had an arboretum day, the implication was clear: Korean schoolchildren should devote a day every year to planting trees.[46] When an editorial asked, "Where in the world are there countries that do not have insurance companies?" the expected answer was "Korea," confirming that the peninsular nation did not conform to the "civilized" ways of the world.[47] When a horse galloping on the streets of Seoul injured a mother and child, a report could castigate the government for not passing the type of "regulations of ten thousand countries" prohibiting such careless activity.[48] It was this representation of Korea, according to the logic of *munmyŏng kaehwa*, as "lacking" or "behind" that supported the nationalist intellectuals' chorus for reform.

Determining how far a nation lagged behind this ideal was the key task in the common practice of ranking nations into hierarchies of civilization. At its simplest level, the differences between nations were twofold: those in the dark and those in the light.[49] More commonly, however, a three-tiered typology was offered. Yu Kilchun divided the world into the civilized, the semicivilized, and the barbarian. Countries in the middle rung, as he defined them, were content with small accomplishments, had no long-range plans, and did not commit themselves to the various forms of enlightenment. Below them, at the foot of the hierarchy, were "the most pitiable under Heaven," countries where one cannot even "distinguish what they can and cannot do."[50] For most writers busy creating such taxonomies, Korea fell firmly into the middle rank. But semicivilized, viewed from the opposite perspective, could be read as semibarbaric, and more often than not writers focused on these less than enlightened features, venting their rage and sighing in despair at these uncivilized characteristics to the point that they seemingly forgot their claim about Korea's middling rank. As one writer demanded to know, "How has it come about that in all the world, Korea is the weakest, Korea is the poorest, Korea is the basest, and Korea receives the least respect from others?"[51] The answers to the question were many, and they all positioned the nation as an object in need of reform.

Munmyŏng kaehwa was always linked with another complex set of ideas derived from the West, social Darwinism. Like *munmyŏng kaehwa*, social Darwinism was considered spatially and temporally universal, but if *munmyŏng kaehwa* was the result of the progressive lessons of history, then social Darwinism represented the inviolate laws of human society. It, too, had hierarchies of nations, hierarchies that neatly overlapped with those of civilization. The civilized countries, after all, were usually the strongest countries. The same types of knowledge distinguished nations for these two hierarchies. Although *munmyŏng kaehwa* implicitly offered an idealistic, perhaps even naïve, vision of a common enterprise uplifting all of humanity and viewed the ideologies of capitalist modernity as a benign force, social Darwinism saw this same knowledge in more utilitarian terms, enabling the "strong to make the weak their fodder," as the expression went. In this sense, social Darwinism had a much bleaker vision of the world, one of struggle, in which to act other than self-defensively was to threaten the future of the nation. In its emphasis on carnal metaphors — eat or be eaten — social Darwinism regarded the nation less as a collection of individuals seeking to acquire knowledge for the betterment of the collective unit and more as a biological entity seeking to ensure its survival. On the question of law — an

issue central to *munmyŏngng kaehwa* as a rational regulator of human society — social Darwinism stressed its use as a tool of the powerful. As one
paper had a person in an editorial declare about international law, "These
so-called public laws, righteous principles, alliances and treaties, and morality all are nothing more than words on a piece of paper." Put more bluntly,
"In the world we live in today, if one wants to treat people with benevolence
and righteousness, then one must be a very stupid person in a deep sleep."[52]

While these two strands of thought coexisted in the same newspapers and
journals, after the Protectorate was established in 1905, the naïve confidence
that many writers held for *munmyŏng kaehwa* began to waver. To be sure,
they had always been aware of its double standards, since they had closely
observed how the powers invoked civilization as a self-serving platform for
their own political and economic interests. But with the creation of the
Japanese Residency General in 1905, they could now witness firsthand how
munmyŏng kaehwa was used to undermine their national sovereignty and
even push them out of the civilizing process. As the double nature of *munmyŏng kaehwa* became more apparent, many writers began to steer away
from its most obvious uses toward its counterpart, social Darwinism, which
now seemed to offer a more realistic accounting of Korea's slide into colonialism. Although they pointed out the underside of *munmyŏng kaehwa* and
stressed social Darwinism, no writers went the extra step to question or challenge the concept of "civilization and enlightenment" itself. Their vision of
the nation in a new global order was so dependent on the historical and
spatial underpinnings of *munmyŏng kaehwa* that it was difficult to speak of
national reform at the same time as they tried to extricate the nation from
its logic. Moreover, their self-definition of leaders of the nationalist movement rested on this conceptual framework. As a result, writers switched between *munmyŏng kaehwa* and social Darwinism according to their whim or
purpose. In some cases, fully cognizant of the double standard, they urged
a rise to the top of the heap where the benefits would work in their favor.
More often, however, civilization continued uneasily to underlay their writings about the nation as they tried to preserve nationalist uses of the concept,
resisting its complete co-option by Japanese colonial authorities.[53]

The Pundits of the Nation

This vision of the nation as an entity to be reformed was fundamental to
the self-definition of newspaper writers as progressive individuals in line with

the forces of world history. More than any common social or geographic ties, it was the shared commitment to these goals that linked their efforts, even though they did not hesitate to rail at one another over specific issues. As professed in their charters and manifestos, the newspaper writers' commitment to *munmyŏng kaehwa* implied that their organizations were open to any person willing to adopt their goals. This was an age, after all, when active citizenship (*kungmin*) was offered as a panacea for the nation: all the people, being equal, would work in solidarity to reform the nation. For a country that had been structured primarily around status affiliation and family lineage for several centuries, this openness itself was quite radical. The often-acclaimed power of nationalism to level social differences received one of its earliest boosts in Korea in the ideological realm.[54] Although equality was hailed as a social goal in its own right, it was harnessed to the purpose of self-strengthening. The people *were* the basis of national power. Any obstacles to the participation of any social group in national life was seen as inhibiting the potential of the nation, even though in practice these calls were easier to make than to realize.

This supposed openness was frequently used vis-à-vis class and gender, two divisions criticized for having weakened Korea in the past. The celebrated example of Pak Sŏngch'un served in the eyes of many reform leaders as positive proof of this openness. As part of the demonstrations sponsored by the Independence Club on the downtown streets of Seoul, this member of the *paekchŏng*,[55] one of the most despised social groups of the Chosŏn dynasty, gave a speech that exhorted those who in an earlier era would have been seen as his "betters." Pak opened his speech with a nod toward the traditional linkage of social status and knowledge, admitting that because of his status, he was largely ignorant. He then proceeded to debunk this very notion in a series of remarks that would have been fitting from the mouth of any senior leader of the club. "The idea of loyalty to the sovereign and patriotism is the way to benefit the country and the people," he declared, "but this is only possible once the people and the officials have united their hearts."[56] The publicity surrounding this speech presented Pak as the new citizen, formerly discriminated against because of his status and now elevated to an ostensibly equal level by his commitment to self-improvement and national reform. That even a lowly *paekchŏng* could join the cause of the nation was the message underlying his public display as well as reports of his speech.

Just as common as claims about the movement's openness to class were assertions that the nation could transcend gender. Accordingly, the period

witnessed the beginning of a redefinition of gender roles to suit the needs
of a civilizing nation.[57] In this tumultuous period, when reformers hoped to
abandon unenlightened past practices to move toward a more civilized age,
women were a common measure of progress — if only because women
served as the prevailing metaphors for backwardness. Family was juxtaposed
with nation, the former being the source of superstition and the latter associated with "civilization and enlightenment."[58] Any woman able to reform
and leave "the women's chambers where they had been locked up for two
thousand years"[59] was considered a boon to the nation and its reputation, a
development to be hailed by reprinting the charters of women's groups and
schools. Consequently, women's education emerged as the most commonly
featured gender issue in the media. Espoused as a means of overcoming the
backwardness of the past, women's education was also deemed a source of
national power.[60] Since women constituted half the population, the reasoning went, the nation would be only half as strong if women were not educated.[61] In an age of competition, according to the charter of the Academy
for the Education of Women, "the need for women's education is one of
the means for national survival."[62] As another commentator bluntly warned,
countries without women's education are destroyed.[63]

The function of women's education was still largely conditioned by their
gender, primarily as mothers to ensure that the next generation was not
raised in a household full of superstition and as wives to support husbands
in their missions to reform the nation. This point was encapsulated in one
editorial:

> When boys grow up , they become officials, scholars, merchants, and
> peasants. When girls grow up, they become the wives of these people.
> If these women have the same learning and knowledge as their hus-
> bands, then household affairs will turn out well. Moreover, when they
> bear children, these wives will know how to raise the children and
> educate them. . . . As a result, we should not value the role of women
> less than [that of] men. All the responsibilities of nurturing future
> generations of the nation rest with the women.[64]

Educate women, many editorials overtly urged, even though the implicit
assumption in these enjoinments was that they would be educated *as* mothers, *as* wives, and *as* the reproductive bearers of the nation. Given this approach, it is not surprising that few, if any, women were active in the era's
press. Even publications specifically targeting a female audience were op-

erated and largely written by men.[65] As an issue for publicly exploring issues of national modernity, women's education remained mainly the domain of the male leaders of the nationalist movement. To be sure, women were to be brought into the national fold, only this was a nation to be led by men, whose publicly acclaimed heroes were male and whose history was largely masculine in orientation.[66] New women's associations could be congratulated, the opening of women's schools hailed, and the occasional letter by a female reader published, yet such entries in the period's newspapers invariably affirmed the civilizing assumptions of the reform project.[67] By profiling the achievements of women, they purported to offer an inclusive image of the nationalist movement, one that claimed to be just as open to gender as it was to class.

Claims of inclusivity were tempered by the reformers' self-appointed status as leaders, however. In Yu Kilchun's exposition on enlightenment, he equated his own role and that of his fellow reformers with those of the civilized leaders in the West, noting how in every country, whatever the national level of development, enlightened individuals existed. The crux of the matter, he explained, was the ratio of these individuals to the bulk of the population.[68] This formula immediately separated Yu and the other self-appointed custodians of enlightenment from the people, granting themselves status as part of an international cosmopolitan elite while saddling the people with the primary responsibility for the nation's woes. People like Pak Sŏngch'un and the students of the Academy for the Education of Women were the exceptions in the eyes of the leaders, the ones who verified the validity of the enlightenment project and could be offered proudly in the presses as indications of successful leadership. And as hortative exceptions, they confirmed the view of the population, in the parlance of the time, as little more than "ignorant people" (umin). Harsher depictions — "like children who cannot understand"[69] or "stupid and illiterate people no different from dolls of earth"[70] — were just as common.

The cover of Yu Kilchun's textbook (Nodong yahak tokpon) for laborers attending night school captures these nationalist reformers' ambivalence toward the population (see the cover of this book).[71] Standing on the right of the frame, the author has symbolically doffed his hat in the presence of a worker, who in turn is not only engaged in a Western-style handshake with Yu but is also, in a departure from Chosŏn-dynastic practices, looking Yu in the face rather than casting his gaze to the ground. The dialogue has Yu urging the worker to labor and learn for the nation. The speech levels are somewhat ambiguous, again not indicative of what in the Chosŏn dynasty would have been clearly delineated speech levels separating a scholar from a worker. Yu speaks in a formal level of speech, indicating respect for his interlocutor, while the worker registers his affirmative response in a somewhat more colloquial level of speech while still using a form of respectful address. These speech forms suggest that the worker, as a nameless representative of the people who, at least in theory, were the basis of the nation, deserved the respect of the teacher. These signifiers of social equality were novel for the era, an indication of the efforts to level traditional social categories. Nonetheless, the worker's significance is somewhat moderated by the artistic flourishes that privilege the author. Identified by name, as opposed to the generic depiction of the worker, Yu is shown with the emblems of civility — frock coat, top hat, and full moustache — marking him as a man of this internationalized age. It is Yu, it appears, who has taken the initiative to strike up the conversation and extend his hand, as if symbolically inviting the worker to join him. Yu's erect posture, frontal perspective, and highlighted coloring, in contrast to the worker's slight slouch, rear perspective, and lighter coloring, makes Yu the center of attention, even though this is a book for laborers. The two might join hands in the same struggle, but in the author's eyes, it was clear who actually spoke for the nation.

This ambivalence is partly explained by the fact that while the much-lauded goal of the movement was the protection of national sovereignty, the immediate task was teaching the population to adopt certain behaviors. This was where nationalism intersected with the various ideologies of capitalist modernity on issues as seemingly dissimilar as the body and economy. Countless articles and editorials deployed a style of chain logic, beginning with the individual or, more precisely, the behavior of an individual and then explained how through education this improper behavior could be modified into a more desirable form. If everyone pursued this path, the nation would inevitably become stronger and richer. Such chains of logic could focus on virtually any practice or belief and by promoting education, that all-important disciplining action, offer a strategy for becoming a more "civilized" nation. In the blunt language of one editorial writer, "If Koreans want to become like the people of other countries, they must correct the way they think."[72] Consequently, at a time when the specific concept of capitalism had yet to be introduced, much of the writing in the economic realm did not focus on structural questions but on how the behavior of the population could be modified and regulated so as to encourage commerce (*sangŏp*).[73] Nurturing an entrepreneurial spirit, encouraging self-help, respecting merchants, making good use of talent, knowing market prices, valuing time, and standardizing weights and measurements — all these became areas for modifying individual behavior as the immediate way of revamping the country's economic orientation and aligning it with the capitalism of the world system. This globalizing function helps account for the appeal and power of nationalism during this period in Korea.

Resorting to chain logic, however, was not the only tactic available to writers. Just as common, and perhaps more powerful, were the efforts to inculcate shame and anger into the readers. This could be at the general level of the nation — shame or anger, for example, at Korea's lowly place on the ladder of civilization and the resulting humiliating treatment, in the words of more than one editorialist, received by the world's powers.[74] Shame and anger also could be deployed on a more personal level to alter individual conduct. Modern discourses on the body used embarrassment as a way of spurring change, as seen in the flood of writings on hygiene, exercise, and comportment. As Norbert Elias showed for what he called the civilizing process in Europe, shame was a powerful motivating force for individuals to change their behavior. According to Elias, if Europeans had to be taught that farting at the dinner table was shameful conduct, then many Korean writers similarly tried to embarrass those, who "without any sense of shame, urinate and defecate in the streets."[75] It was embarrassing and, moreover, unhygienic.

In one of those metonyms that found its way into nationalist reform movements around the world, the health of the nation ultimately rested with the health of the individual.[76] In these ways, the urge to discipline the population linked questions of hygiene and the body through the same self-strengthening logic to issues such as the proper utilization of resources and the construction of railways. For these writers and speechmakers, leadership was not just a benign didactic exercise but one that used all the tools of rhetoric to cajole, hector, and badger as well as sway, convince, and persuade their audience to adopt behaviors deemed beneficial for both the nation and *munmyŏng kaehwa*. In this self-contained logic, all who resisted these enticements were easily dismissed as benighted. Their position on the outside of the project affirmed the leadership of the writers and the urgency of the project.

Not everyone, of course, was prepared to act like the idealized worker on the cover of Yu's book, nodding agreement and thanking intellectuals for their hectoring prose and efforts to control popular behavior. Who speaks for the nation is a question just as much concerned with local power, the relation among different segments of the national movement, and the political consequences of defining the nation in certain ways. Nationalist intellectuals were fully aware of this political competition. With their newspapers, their close associations with the burgeoning school movement, and their speaking tours in the countryside, these nationalist intellectuals attempted to be the sole voice for the nation, even if it meant shunting aside rival groups. Any individual or group that stepped outside the bounds of its project risked becoming the object of the intellectuals' invective, which the "righteous armies," or *ŭibyŏng*, who were fighting the Japanese in the countryside, knew all too well.

At the time of Queen Min's assassination in 1895, these various militia groups formed to offer armed resistance to the Japanese presence in the peninsula. With the establishment of the Protectorate in 1905, the *ŭibyŏng* received a new injection of energy as more men joined their forces. Prominent scholars in the countryside used their authority to encourage uprisings and organize militia, even if as in the case of one famous seventy-three-year-old Confucian, Ch'oe Ikhyon, his aged legs did not allow him to take to the hills with the forces he called to arms. In a daring maneuver in December 1907, Yi Inyŏng led more than ten thousand *ŭibyŏng* in a coordinated attack that reached the northern outskirts of Seoul before being repelled by the superior-armed Japanese military. The Japanese response to this escalation in fighting was ferocious. More troops were deployed to hunt down the scattered remnants of the *ŭibyŏng*, and the consequences for any villages supporting them, according to a number of foreign observers, included being burned to the ground.[77] Between 1907 and 1911, Japanese police reports estimate that more than 17,600 people were killed.[78] Despite Japanese claims to the contrary, annexation was anything but a peaceful process.

Newspapers kept a careful eye on these battles in the countryside, offering many reports to their readers.[79] Although editors displayed a certain degree of sympathy toward the patriotism of the *ŭibyŏng* leaders, they were united in condemning their tactics, since the leaders' use of violence conflicted with the editors' own vision of civilizing reform and education as the primary means to rescue the nation.[80] The editors of one newspaper encapsulated this divergence in their use of the classical dualism *munmu*, the first syllable of which indicated the cultural or literary, as distinguished from the latter syllable, *mu*, the martial. "In this era, the way to recovery is not to resort to military means [*mu*] but to cultural methods [*mun*]," it stated.[81] This artful use of the phrase *mun*, the same character used as the first syllable of the word *munmyŏng*, established a link with the central purpose of the newspapers.[82] As the editors argued more explicitly, even if all the people devoted themselves to education, working for the country, and advancing civilization, it still would be difficult to recover the country's national rights — how much more so, they asked, when the eight provinces were aflame with uprisings?[83] The *ŭibyŏng* might be called ignorant people (*umin*), but unlike the general population, the *ŭibyŏng* were deliberately pursuing a line of action that undermined both the nation and the leadership of the intellectuals, ensuring that the censure leveled in their direction would be especially severe. They were "calamitous demons who are ruining the country and poisonous sores that are harming the people."[84] The paper repeatedly denied them the use of the term *ŭi* (righteous), arguing that this was an empty name that their actions did not merit.[85] An alternative offered was *t'obi hwalchŏk*, (bandits and thieves), a form of mudslinging that was taken up by others.[86]

A second newspaper was hardly any more supportive. It also criticized the *ŭibyŏng* as "bandits," frequently pointing out that despite the patriotism of its leaders — who, it admitted, in some cases might deserve the title "righteous" — many others in the armies took advantage of the turmoil caused by the fighting to extort food and money from the population.[87] The editors stressed the inevitability of the *ŭibyŏng*'s loss: "Even if the power of the entire nation was garnered to resist Japan, it would certainly be dispersed with a mere shake of Japan's hand and a kick of its foot."[88] Like other papers, it stressed patience, urging that a program of reform must be undertaken to nurture national strength and await the proper moment to move.[89] Their sympathy for the patriotism of the *ŭibyŏng* had its limits, however, for ultimately the best outcome, they contended, was for the *ŭibyong* to be suppressed by the government as soon as possible.[90]

This criticism did not relent even when the substance of the *ŭibyŏng*'s demands shifted. After many of the early *ŭibyŏng* leaders were captured or killed, a new leadership less attached to the classical learning that had shaped their predecessors' worldview began to command the rural forces. This was especially true after the Korean military was disbanded by the Japanese Resident General in the summer of 1907, when former officers and soldiers

who had received modern military training and were likely avid readers of
the press moved down into the countryside to join the anti-Japanese movements. Gradually the early movement's designs shifted: calls for the protection of King Kojong and his family remained, but the prior focus on the
need to preserve the teaching of the sages was replaced with demands resembling those being articulated in the nationalist press. Included in the
thirty demands sent by Hŏ Wi, a leading general, to the Japanese Resident
General in 1907, freedom of the press, education, and association were
combined with demands concerning Japanese concessions, control of Japanese immigrants, and circulation of Japanese currency.[91] These new demands indicate the power of the *munmyŏng kaehwa* message. Now even the
ŭibyŏng, despite tracing their intellectual line back to the isolationists who
had been committed to expelling heterodox thought, were reading newspapers and "breathing the airs of civilization." Regardless of this expanding
common ground, the newspaper editors did not relent in their criticism, and
no effective alliance was ever established between these two segments of the
nationalist movement.[92]

Accordingly, the many calls for the solidarity (*tanhap*) and unity (*kun*) of
the population, found in all publications in these years, amounted to little
more than an enjoinment to follow the leadership and program of the writer.
It was behind their own visions for the nation that nationalist reformers
expected the people to unite.[93] Although the newspapers offered a voice for
the nation, it was the cacophonous voice of intellectuals committed to *munmyŏng kaehwa*, who could just as easily use their papers to try to drown out
rival strategies or divergent visions. "Who speaks for the nation?" was a
politically fraught question, which, put differently, meant "Who could struggle up onto the national stage to make his voice heard?" Getting onto that
platform included nudging others out. Their control of newspapers meant
these groups had unrivaled power over the means of disseminating knowledge about the nation. The state had no equivalent way of reaching out to
the population. Other streams of the nationalist movement, whether the
remnants of the Tonghak forces or the *ŭibyŏng*, could not, with their handwritten manifestos posted on doors and lists of demands nailed to trees,
challenge the dominance of the Seoul-based intellectual elite. Although
these publications did not offer the only visions of the nation at this time,
given their dominance over knowledge production, anyone dealing
with national questions had to engage with the specific forms of national

knowledge disseminated by this most public of media that had risen so rapidly.

The Eyes and Ears of the Nation

In 1895 there was not one privately managed Korean-language newspaper on the peninsula.[94] A dozen years later, more than a handful of newspapers and a dozen educational magazines were circulating throughout the country and even overseas. Called "the eyes and ears of the nation," newspapers were the preeminent medium of the nation. Indeed, rather than just witnessing and hearing, as the metaphor suggested, they gave vision to and informed the nation in multiple ways.[95] At a time when universities and research institutions had not yet been established, these newspapers and journals served as the primary producers of knowledge about the nation. With their diverse reportage, poetry columns, foreign reports, editorials, advertisements, letters, reprinting of documents, and personal solicitations, newspapers offered a single space for the many voices that lay claim to the nation and explored its various facets. Newspapers rarely featured detailed treatises on the nation — the pace and finances of publication did not permit long essays — but within their often bewilderingly wide-ranging articles, newspapers reached across the spectrum of the day's social, economic, and political concerns, relating them all, whether explicitly or merely by their position on the page, to the national concerns of their editorial staff. With so many articles in a single issue and long publication runs, newspapers did not reflect a united voice with an unwaveringly consistent editorial policy. Rather, the papers' shifts and contradictions often reflected tensions in the nationalist movement or, just as frequently, ambivalence in the beliefs of the editorial staff that played themselves out in different issues.

The rise of the press shortly after the Sino-Japanese War began with the *Tongnip sinmun* (*The Independent*). Established in 1896 by Philip Jaisohn,[96] a returned Korean American, and Yun Ch'iho, a prominent Christian and essayist, it was the first vernacular newspaper in Korean. The most iconoclastic paper of the time, it combined its zealous calls for reform with a pro-Christian message, before being shut down together with its supporting institution, the Independence Club, in 1899 for what was seen by the court as its overly aggressive political tactics.[97] One year before its suspension, more moderate members of the Independence Club, who were less enthusiastic about its Christian message and more interested in advocating a hybrid mix of reform rooted in Confucian traditions, established the *Hwangsŏng sinmun* (*Capital Gazette*, 1898–1910). Lasting thirteen years until annexation, this paper, with its mixed vernacular–Chinese character script (*kukhan honyongch'e*) and classical allusions, targeted the Confucian-trained elite, urging them to participate in a renovation of government and society that both headed in new directions while remaining faithful to certain core practices of the past.[98] The *Cheguk sinmun* (*Imperial Post*, 1898–1910) chose its name in celebration of the emperor, but as its first editorial stated, the paper was for the people. Like the *Tongnip sinmun*, it published in the vernacular and was said to have the widest circulation among the uneducated and women.[99] The *TaeHan maeil sinbo* (*Korea Daily News*, 1904–10) covered Japanese actions on the peninsula in more detail than any other paper of that period. Owned by an Englishman, the *TaeHan maeil sinbo*'s protection under extraterritorial laws gave the paper and its Korean staff the political leeway that guaranteed its spot as the most popular paper of the day. By 1907 it was publishing three daily issues, one each in vernacular Korean, mixed script, and English.[100]

Editors and writers came from all over Korea to the capital city to work in the press. While some local Korean-language newspapers did exist, the tradition of Seoul as the heart of the peninsula's intellectual activity was only reinforced by the rise of the new media.[101] After 1905, with the widespread formation of groups to promote education, regional associations assumed a more vital function as the organizing principle for nationalist writers. Chŏlla, Kyonggi-Ch'unchŏng, the northwest, and southern Kyŏngsang, among others, had their own associations to raise funds for schools in their area and publish monthly journals. These monthlies advertised their efforts and offered a voice to regional perspectives and differences on the nation. A form of gentle one-upmanship — Who was the most enlightened? — can be found in these writings, presenting the people of their region and their group as contributing the most to the nationalist project. The Northwest Educational Association, for example, teased readers from other regions about how their own members were the most advanced, boasting about their region's special connection to the nation's founders.[102] Central dailies would comment on the level of reforms in certain regions, comparing them with their own past records or other areas of the peninsula, such that northern P'yŏng'an could be praised as the province that had sold the most books, bought the most newspapers, and built the most schools.[103]

Yi Songhŭi has examined the Northwest Educational Association, analyzing the social background of its membership. Between 1906 and 1908, the number of people willing to pay the one-time entry fee of one *wŏn* and monthly dues of twenty *chŏn* (later reduced to ten) expanded from the 108 founders of the organization to some 1,027 individuals. These included school principals, teachers, and students as well as county magistrates, prefecture heads, an assortment of minor officials at both the central and local levels, and individuals identifying themselves as lawyers, translators, and businessmen.[104] Significantly, for many people, membership was determined by the new category of career, as opposed to the status affiliations of the Chosŏn dynasty. This was a new professional elite combined with the old elite of officialdom. Biographies of leading writers and editors reveal that all were highly educated, usually in traditional Confucian schools, and that some had even passed the government examinations before they were abolished in 1895.[105] Most were of either *yangban* status or what Kyung Moon Hwang has called "secondary status groups," those groups between the *yangban* and the commoners, including the *chungin*, who filled technical positions in the bureaucracy, the *hyangni* or clerks, who ran day-to-day operations in local districts, and the *sŏŏl*, the illegitimate offspring of *yangban*.[106]

As the membership roles of the Northwest Educational Association suggest, there was a great deal of interaction among government officials, nationalist organizations, and newspapers. The Independence Club, sponsor of the *Tongnip sinmun*, was known in its early years for its debates on current affairs that brought together leading government officials with its nonofficial members. Only in its last year, when its reproach of the heads of ministries intensified and the court's support began to erode, did officials withdraw their membership.[107]

At a time when journalism had yet to emerge as a stable profession, career paths reflected this interaction as well, as many people involved with the press served stints in the bureaucracy. For those people who wanted to coax and berate the state into undertaking reforms, it always must have been tempting to move into positions of power where they could do what they themselves had urged. Yun Ch'iho, one of the prominent publishers of the *Tongnip sinmun*, served in various positions in the government after the paper was shut down. In 1903, he became the magistrate of Ch'onan County and later a cabinet minister. Sŏng Agyŏng, general manager of the *Hwang-sŏng sinmun*, left after nine years at the paper to become the magistrate of P'ŭngch'on County in 1907.[108] Less typical was the peripatetic career of Kim Kyohŏn, a major publicist and second patriarch for the Tan'gŭn-worshiping religion, Taejonggyo. Kim resigned from a string of official positions at the age of thirty-one to join the Independence Club, only to return to the employ of the government as an editor of its publications after the club was disbanded in 1899. In 1906, he accepted an official position in local government, transferring once again to the government-publishing bureau in 1909 before finally quitting in 1910 to devote himself full time to the Taejonggyo.[109] The desire of the members of some organizations like the TaeHan Hyŏphoe to enter the government was sufficient, according to Pak Ch'ansŭng, for them to refrain from any serious criticism of officials for fear of alienating potential future employers.[110]

Except for the most prolific and prominent writers, journalism was a less than reliable career path, in part because the newspaper and journal enterprises rested on shaky financial foundations. To be sure, newspapers were commercial enterprises, but for the most part they were undercapitalized, their ability to stay afloat indicating more their commitment to nationalist causes than an elusive profitability. The *Hwangsŏng sinmun* raised capital with an initial offering of five hundred shares at ten *yang* each, with the profits from advertising and sales to be distributed to the shareholders. Like so many of its competitors, however, the *Hwangsŏng sinmun* hardly rated as a successful enterprise: not all the shares were sold at first, and a subsequent offering made in 1905 to alleviate financial pressures also proved disappointing.[111] Those with the resources to invest were clearly wary of committing their capital to such a newfangled institution. Their apprehension was well founded. Few newspapers in this period attained financial stability. The *Cheguk sinmun* closed its offices on four occasions between 1899 and 1907 because of financial shortcomings, and readers of the *Hwangsŏng sinmun* were constantly greeted with front-page notices warning of the paper's imminent collapse.[112] Part of the problem stemmed from advertising revenues, which despite editorial enjoinments to businessmen explaining that ads "open the eyes and ears of all under heaven . . . and reap enormous benefits," were insufficient.[113]

Another difficulty encountered by the press, as every editor bemoaned at one time or another, was inadequate readership. Newspapers may have caused a stir in the heated political environment of these years, but their readership still constituted an exclusive club. The editors of the *Tongnip sinmun* complained that Koreans were not even interested in becoming enlightened, citing popular purchasing habits as proof: they will buy cigarettes but will not spare a single coin for a newspaper.[114] Many Koreans "don't even know what a newspaper is," lamented the *Hwangsŏng sinmun*. "This newspaper has already been published for eight or nine years, but still there are people who have not given it a glance."[115] Notices in the *Hwangsŏng sinmun* stated that circulation over its thirteen-year history hovered around three thousand copies. The *Cheguk sinmun* fluctuated more dramatically. Averaging between two thousand to three thousand copies, its circulation fell as low as one thousand and, for a number of months, even topped four thousand copies.[116] The *Tongnip sinmun* wavered between two thousand and three thousand copies.[117] Educational journals published after 1905 reached similar levels of circulation.[118] The *TaeHan maeil sinbo* captured the widest readership. At its inauguration, fewer than four thousand copies were printed, but by 1908, once it had set up separate Korean-language, mixed-script, and English-language editions, its total circulation reached more than thirteen thousand.[119]

Most distressing for the papers' financial backers was that these figures represented printed, not paid, copies. It was common practice to send off copies before payment. As many editorials complained, readers too frequently were tardy in remitting their subscription fees. This situation was exacerbated by the eagerness of some papers, like the *Cheguk sinmun*, to send multiple copies to local officials with the expectation that these would be made available to the people in their jurisdiction, only to be surprised that not all officials wished to support the press with timely payments for unrequested subscriptions.[120] According to one likely exaggerated accounting, the *Tongnip sinmun* was owed the staggering sum of more than U.S. $175,000 by delinquent officials.[121] Distribution difficulties abounded as all the papers depended on the newly founded and not always reliable postal system.[122] Late deliveries became worse after 1905 under the Japanese Protectorate. Readers' letters regularly complained that they did not receive the paper for days on end and that their copies often arrived in bunches.[123] A priest in Pongsan County listed each issue that he had failed to receive: a total of forty-one over a five-month period, which was still better than the predicament of another reader who complained that he had missed about half the issues.[124]

Because of the lack of capital and the difficulties in persuading readers to send in their subscription fees, most of the publications depended on the largesse of their readers. Only with subventions could they stay afloat. On a number of occasions, Emperor Kojong made significant donations, in 1903 contributing five hundred *wŏn* to the *Hwangsŏng sinmun*, in addition to two thousand *wŏn* and a new printing press to the *Cheguk sinmun*.[125] Even the popular *TaeHan maeil sinbo* is said to have depended on regular, secret contributions from the emperor to avoid bankruptcy.[126] The *Hwangsŏng sinmun* at one point launched a subscription and donation drive, in which the names of all contributors were regularly printed under the title "A List of the Civilized" (*Munmyŏngnok*).[127]

Circulation rates alone do not capture the full range of the newspapers' audience, however. Newspapers appear to have quickly become a part of the oral culture of the cities and villages. "Every time one passes through the streets or markets," described one observer of the *Cheguk sinmun*, "there is either a youth or a white-haired old man, holding a copy of a paper in his hands, reading aloud at the top of his voice."[128] Reform-minded county magistrates would have someone at public gatherings read from a paper such as the *Tongnip sinmun*, and at least one reader wrote letters to the paper, urging other officials to do the same.[129] Still others noted how frequently newspapers exchanged hands, one hearing of a case in the countryside in which a single copy of the *Tongnip sinmun* was read by no fewer than eighty-five people.[130] Another reader noted he received his copy of the *Hwangsŏng sinmun* from his scholarly friends.[131] Even a conservative scholar residing in the countryside noted that when the *Hwangsŏng sinmun* arrived in his locality, people in "all four directions" competed to be the first to buy and read it. A perhaps overly nostalgic former publisher of the *Tongnip sinmun* remembered that when a subscriber had "finished reading it [the paper], [he] turned it over to his neighbors, and in this way each copy was read by at least two hundred people."[132]

The small circulation of newspapers also belied their political influence during this period. Isabella Bird, the famous Victorian traveler, testified to their impact, commenting that the *Tongnip sinmun* was "becoming something of a terror to evil doers."[133] Indeed, the best indication of their power was that these so-called evil doers repeatedly tried to muzzle the press. Korean government officials, unaccustomed to the external scrutiny and criticism of their activities, mulled over the possibility of restricting the press on a number of occasions after the inception of the *Tongnip sinmun*. Foreign diplomats secretly encouraged controls, especially after the *Tongnip sinmun* published in 1898 some secret documents divulging Russian and Japanese attempts to exact concessions from the Korean government. An active nationalist press, it was feared, could interfere with their concession diplomacy by mobilizing public opinion against the granting of special privileges. By 1899, Emperor Kojong ordered that appropriate laws be prepared, but none was actually promulgated.[134]

It was not until the outbreak of the Russo-Japanese War that editors had to take censorship into account. On August 20, 1904, the editors of the *Hwangsŏng sinmun* and *Cheguk sinmun* were called into the offices of the Japanese military command and informed that reports on military movements would be prohibited.[135] All newspapers would be reviewed and censored before they were published, a process that over the next few years expanded to include impermissible topics well beyond military matters. Initially explained as a wartime measure and not formalized in any legal statutes, the power to censor was not about to be relinquished due to the inconveniences of peace.

Although the war ended, censorship did not. After 1905, censorship was under the control of the police, though still not legally codified. Writers, generally a more clever breed than censors, nevertheless found creative ways to get their message past the police.[136] Two years into his mandate, the leading Japanese official remained less than satisfied. As Itō Hirobumi told his audience in a 1907 Tokyo speech, one stroke of a Korean editorial pen had far more power to move Koreans than "one hundred words from my own mouth."[137] Coming from a man whose record in Japan showed that he brooked no dissent, such a public statement, while attesting to the influence of the Korean press, was an ominous signal. Sure enough, less than half a year later, the first set of formal censorship laws was announced, intended to rein in the press and make Itō's words more powerful than Korean editorial pens. Any overt challenge or criticism of Japanese rule was sure to be blocked out. Over the next three years, the editors of Korean publications had to work within these laws, leaving readers with the added titillation of trying to puzzle out just what words might lie under the censor's black stamp.

Only the *TaeHan maeil sinbo*, a paper owned by a former reporter for the London Daily Chronicle, the Englishman Ernest Bethell, escaped the scrutiny of the censor. Protected by Bethell's extraterritorial status, Korean writers worked unhindered by the censor, often writing scathing articles about Japanese policy on the peninsula and thus ensuring it the largest audience of any newspaper. Political pressure by Japan through its ally

Britain did succeed, however, in tempering the tone of the paper and even landed Bethell in jail.[138] But the paper maintained a critical editorial platform until it was effectively shut down upon annexation and turned into the official mouthpiece of the colonial authority, the *Maeil sinbo* (*Daily Newspaper*). From this point on, no other Korean-language newspaper operated on the peninsula. A few magazines stripped of any overt political content continued, but otherwise this was a period that historians of the Korean press have often termed the "dark period."[139]

Whether due to press restrictions, problems with distribution, or the disinclination of much of the population to take this new institution seriously, none of the papers that arose during the period grew to the level of mass-circulation dailies. The Korean nationalist movement grew rapidly between the 1890s and the March First Movement of 1919, when as Japanese-arrest reports show, participants in the pro-independence demonstrations numbered as many as 2 million people, ranging across all socioeconomic classes, both genders, and various geographic regions.[140] Newspapers and journals, though not the sole agents, were certainly handmaidens to this growth.

Print media were also just as important to mediating the incorporation of the peninsula into the larger global ecumene, explaining changes on and around the peninsula and making them part of their readers' daily lives. They were the most visible public organs engaged in redefining the Korean nation, both spatially and temporally. To use Benedict Anderson's terms, newspapers were the primary location for the reimagining of the nation away from the conceptual framework inherited from the late Chosŏn dynasty toward a nationalist vision rooted in global ideologies of capitalist modernity. It is in this sense, as producers and disseminators of knowledge about the nation, that newspapers were so important to the nationalist movement in Korea. From the initial printing of the *Tongnip sinmun*, when only four pages were offered three times a week, to the last years before annexation, when there were literally hundreds of pages available each month for every reader, the Korean nation emerged for the first time as the primary subject of public discourse. In these pages immense quantities of information about the nation as well as new conceptual treatments of the peninsula were produced to shape the social, political, and economic behavior of their readers. In the years immediately after the Sino-Japanese War, one of the top priorities in this process of reimagining was both to disengage from and to reconstitute the ways in which the nation had been understood in relation to China and the region.

2 Decentering the Middle Kingdom and Realigning the East

We hope we do not become like that.
— *Cheguk sinmun* on China, July 5, 1900

An 1895 school textbook, *An Elementary Reader for Citizens*, (*Kungmin sohak tokpon*), opened a chapter on China with a seemingly innocuous geographical statement. "China, like our nation," it stated, "is one country in the Asian continent."[1] At the time of its publication, though, such a statement resonated with meanings that extended beyond its geographical significance. In its first seven words, this single utterance captured the shift in China's position at the end of the nineteenth century: China was now little more than the equal of its former tributary nation, Korea. This brief phrase reflected what was to grow into a far-reaching endeavor, sponsored for the first time by dynastic institutions but carried out most widely in the period's media, to reexamine Korea's historical relationship with China — what can be called the decentering of the Middle Kingdom.

This decentering was more than a political readjustment. The impulse in nationalist thought to articulate a unique identity for the nation led to a reappraisal of centuries of Sino-Korean cultural interaction in ways that reflected Korea's growing participation in the modern ideologies of the capitalist world system. Integral to the production of national knowledge in these years, the process of decentering rested on a number of assumptions about the relationship between national culture and sovereignty. For Korea to protect its independence, many writers felt that a break with the transnational culturalism of the East Asian past was necessary, one that would be marked by a rejection of those previously shared symbols and practices as alien. Only the recovery and sustenance of a pure culture, they assumed, could rescue the nation. Yet as some were to discover, the legacies of an earlier East Asian regional order were not always so easily subsumed into the nationalist ideals of the new global order, since the political and ideological interests of select groups could run counter to this project of cultural renewal.

In addition to asserting Sino-Korean equality, the textbook statement drew attention to the position of Korea and China in Asia. Interest in the implications of Korea's continental location grew over the next few years as Asia became a unit of regional identity that tempered certain aspects of the decentering dynamic. Definitions of what was called the East (*Tongyang*) shifted dramatically after 1895, following changes in regional geopolitics. In the years after the Sino-Japanese War, one of the most adamant champions of this new regionalism, the newspaper *Hwangsŏng sinmun*, offered a cultural vision of the region, whose past accomplishments could be displayed to argue for the universality of *munmyŏng kaehwa*. In offering a history that stripped the West of any monopoly over "civilization and enlightenment," the editors delocalized the particularity of the Korean and Eastern past, incorporating the region into global narratives of progess. But as memories of a historical Chinese empire came to be superseded by the power of an ever intrusive Meiji empire, the paper shied away from this cultural vision toward one of the East as a racial unit, whose paramount concern was not with China but with Japan. Quickly developing into a kind of Pan-Asianism intended initially to protect the sovereignty of Korea against the West and support Japan in its conflict with Russia, the editors of the *Hwangsŏng sinmun* eventually used the East to establish a middle ground in the political spectrum. From this exposed position, they offered a vulnerable critique of Japanese policies in the peninsula after the 1905 Protectorate Treaty.

Demoting China

In the first clause of the Treaty of Shimonoseki, signed in 1895 by the Qing and Meiji empires to conclude their recent war, the Qing dynasty recognized the absolute sovereignty of Korea for the first time. For many years leading up to this treaty, a number of Koreans — most notably the leaders of the 1884 coup d'état — had called for an end to the tributary relationship, but it was only with this treaty that practices symbolic of Korean subordination and impinging on Korean sovereignty were once and for all abandoned.[2] So ended the centuries-long tributary relationship.

During the following decade and a half, the nationalist press explored the consequences for Korea of this political shift. Although many differences existed among the various papers of that era, they all agreed that China's military loss to Japan was symbolic of what they referred to as the "old knowledge" (*kuhak*) succumbing to the "new knowledge" (*sinhak*); namely, the Western learning on which Japan based the reform programs enabling its victory. This conclusion reflected the shift in the definition of civilization that underpinned the self-defined mission of these newspapers, a shift away from one hegemonic system with its geographical locus in China toward another, centered on the West. For the editor of the *Hwangsŏng sinmun*, this amounted to an outright reversal: "In the past, what one said was right today is felt to be wrong; and what in the past was felt to be wrong, today is understood to be right."[3] Accompanying this shift, the relationship between previous understandings of universals and particulars began to change. And as Koreans sought to assert their status as a sovereign nation, China was correspondingly demoted, stripped of its formerly privileged position.

A *Tongnip sinmun* editorial addressed the changes that followed the adoption of Western norms of civilization. Remarking that Koreans had lived in "one corner of the Eastern Sea" for thousands of years without knowing anything about the larger world, it continued,

> The only thing [Koreans] knew was to revere China as the central plain [*chungwŏn*], scorn Japan as the country of *wae*, and call all other countries barbarians [*orangk'ae*]. Now, for more than ten years, our doors have been open, and we have welcomed guests coming from all places. With our ears we can hear and with our eyes we can see the customs and laws of Western countries. We can now generally judge which countries are the civilized ones and which countries are the barbarous ones.[4]

If Korean writers could "now generally judge" the civilized from the barbarous, many busied themselves with drawing up taxonomies of the world's nations according to these standards. In such efforts, China became the most common example of a nation lacking civilization. Such representations unfolded over entire editorials as writers, wielding multiple examples and emotive exclamations, explored the reasons for China's condition.

Accounts of the hurly-burly of Chinese politics at the turn of the century were explained in terms of civilization — or, more strictly speaking, the lack thereof. In a year-end summary for 1897, one newspaper bluntly stated that all China did during the preceding twelve months was give up territory and rights to others, making no progress toward civilization.[5] A little more than a year later, in April 1899, newspapers reported that the Danish assembly had allocated funds to dispatch a warship to China. The *Hwangsŏng sinmun* noted that it was no longer just the powerful nations that were "dismembering China." Now Denmark, "a small country isolated on the North Sea coast," was joining the action. China would soon "be shamed by even Denmark."[6] By the beginning of the next year, the same paper listed China's foreign concessions, noting that a higher percentage of its population and territory fell under British rather than Chinese authority and that in those areas of Chinese authority, not a single railway had been built or mine opened.[7] The *Cheguk sinmun* blamed the chaos in China on its stubbornness in dealing with the West, claiming that "in all the world China was the least able to strengthen and enrich itself."[8]

Few events captured as much attention as the 1900 Boxer Uprising. Through a steady stream of reports and frequent editorial comments, the *Hwangsŏng sinmun* informed readers of the increasingly tense situation in northern China. By the time foreign troops were heading for Beijing, the editors had already sounded the alarm. Ever since the Wuxu reforms, they explained, the obstinacy and stubbornness of the court had further hardened while its attitude of barbarism (*ya*) and ignorance had heightened.[9] Xenophobia had become prevalent, they pointed out.[10] None of the officials was talented or knowledgeable; all were conservative, interested only in rehearsing the past and unwilling to pursue reforms. The editors even raised the licentious behavior of the empress dowager in her Xian refuge as further evidence of China's plight.[11] At the height of the uprising, the editors became so distraught at the possibility that the disturbances might spill over the Yalu River into Korea, they published a special editorial — on the front page rather than its usual position on the second page — calling for extraordinary border defense preparations.[12] China's turmoil, they feared, could even reach Korea.

More pervasive than such commentary, however, were the brief mentions of China — often no more than one line — on matters that ostensibly had no direct bearing on the country per se but that provided a minatory example of what became of nations if they did not engage in the civilizing process. The corrupt nature of Chinese law[13] and its inhumane penal institutions[14] were as common as its dirty streets and hospitals.[15] Nor did writers refrain from assailing the Chinese national character, charging the people with being lazy and claiming that "idleness had become a custom."[16]

Contrasts with the West were inherent in these representations of China. Decentered as barbarous, China functioned as a counterweight to Korean representations of the West as civilized. These comparisons, usually implicit, could also be made explicitly. In the year of the Boxer Uprising, one piece compared English and Chinese patriotism, noting that the British population donated money and supplies to the military and that soldiers unflinchingly entered battle. China, however, could not even protect its own land, it pointed out, because of its arrogance and loss of spirit over the last few centuries. The lesson of this comparison was that Koreans should avoid China's self-destructive ways.[17] More mundane matters were equally important. In an editorial linking sanitation and civilization, the *Tongnip sinmun* pointed out that civilized countries arranged for ready supplies of potable water for their populace. As proof of this, it offered statistics comparing the daily per capita consumption of water in several Western cities — Washington, New York, Paris, and London — with China's Guangdong. Guangdong's water usage was only a fraction of that of the Western cities. The implication was clear: just as the water consumption of Chinese residents was a fraction of their Western counterparts, so too was their degree of civilization.[18]

Reports of Chinatowns both abroad and at home reinforced such representations. This topic was a special favorite of the editorial staff of the *Tongnip sinmun*, whose chief editor, Philip Jaisohn, had studied in Philadelphia where he was undoubtedly exposed to American anti-Chinese writings. One early editorial berated the Chinese who had emigrated to the United States. Even though these immigrants now lived in a civilized nation, he complained, they were not able to reform their "savage" customs. On the issue of Chinese immigrants in Korea, the editor was no less restrained. The Chinese in Korea, the editor charged, make our already dirty streets even filthier and introduce our people to opium. "There are not even the slightest benefits that accrue in their coming to Korea," he continued, "only many harms." Comparing the Chinese merchants to leeches, the editor lambasted them for merely making profits for themselves without engaging in civilizing enterprises. "We don't want such people coming to Korea," he concluded.[19]

To be sure, writers did differ in their representations of China as barbarous. But in a press that, despite divergent political stances, uniformly defined its mandate as enlightening the people, these difference were mainly a matter of tone. The *Tongnip sinmun*, one of the most zealous advocates of civilization, treated China with scorn, calling it "the laughing stock of the world."[20] In contrast, the editors of the *Hwangsŏng sinmun* wrote with an empathy reflecting a consciousness of ancient bonds and possibly shared fates. "We are extremely worried for China," they frequently informed their readers.[21] A more ambivalent note was struck by the editors of a primary school reader who followed a statement that China is the object of the "world's ridicule and humiliation" with the simple conclusion "How pitiable. How laughable."[22] Whatever the tone, civilization and China during these years were linked in the pages of nationalist publications. Like its counterpart in Meiji Japan, civilization intruded on all matters Chinese, and China was regularly cited as an exemplar of barbarity.[23] If the Treaty of Shimonoseki had disengaged Korea from the ritual-political structures of tribute, representations of China as barbarous marked Korea's participation in the ideologies of the global system in which China played not a central but a peripheral role. Such a shift became integral to the rearticulation of Korean identity outside the bounds of the East Asian regional order.

Authentic Culture, Pure Identities

The decentering of the Middle Kingdom led also to a reconsideration of the long cultural interaction between the peninsula and its continental neighbor. As many studies have shown, nationalist movements frequently frame expressions of identity as projects of cultural recovery through which authentic national cultures are retrieved intact from the precolonial past.[24] In Korea, public calls for resurrecting a pure, lost culture first emerged in the nationalist press after 1895. Unlike in the colonial states of the West, in Korea the culture targeted for resistance, even expurgation, was not that of the immediate colonizing power, either the West or Japan, but that of Korea's neighbor, China.

For Korean nationalists, recovery was the task of removing the accretions of Chinese culture that had come to conceal the indigenous through their predecessors' long participation in the transnational realm of East Asia. Former representations of national particularity were reconstituted in relation to the new conception of universal civilization, while the former universals, rooted in a now largely discredited Confucian epistemology, came to be particularized, more often than not, as "Chinese." National meanings — Korean or Chinese — were imposed on common beliefs, symbols, and practices that previously had born few connections to the nation. As nationalist reformers sought to assert the purely Korean, practices that had earlier been shared without any privileging of geographical origins were sifted to determine just what could now be categorized as foreign so as to identify the Korean. Geographical origins came to be privileged so that the nationality of cultural forms was inscribable almost wholly by its spatial source. If a manufactured good could be identified by its "nation of origin," so too could a cultural practice. Consequently, a crucial component of the reconstruction of Korean national identity in these years was the attendant reinvention of the category Chinese. Just what it was that marked this particular nation as Korean was to be counterbalanced with just what it was that made their neighboring nation Chinese.

For these reasons, after the Sino-Japanese War when the most immediate threat to Korean sovereignty came from Japan and Russia, Korean writers devoted a surprising amount of attention to historical China. Independence in the contemporary world system came to be contrasted with what was increasingly decried as past Korean dependence on China, an opposition captured in the period's vocabulary, like *tongnip* for independence, using the characters for "stand alone," and *ŭiroe* for dependence, using the characters for "leaning on lazily."[25] This latter expression, together with its many derivatives — slavishness (*nobisŏng*) and, later on, toadyism (*sadaejŏk sasang*), for example — emerged as one of the most expansive concepts in the nationalist writers' arsenal. Found in all newspapers, journals, and textbooks, dependence was linked to a wide array of nationalist concerns, used variously to criticize individual behavior, government policy, social structure, and factionalism, as well as to call for new types of knowledge — all the while linked to the objective of sovereignty.

Past national dependence on China, according to many analysts, stemmed from the behavior of individuals. The *Tongnip sinmun* portrayed most Koreans as scheming to find someone — be it someone in the family, one's underlings, someone with greater ability, or someone in the capital — to rely on for clothes and food.

> Everyone across the country relies on someone else, without any notion of self-reliance and independence. This is why even though in the morning the nation became the vassal of the Qing and in the evening is subject to the interference of Russia or Japan, the people do not have the slightest sense of shame.[26]

The link between the individual and the nation was literally parallel: "If a person depends on another, he loses his freedom, his status plunges, and he

cannot avoid slavery. . . . If a nation relies on another, it threatens its independence, loses its national face, and also cannot avoid slavery."[27]

The articulation of this question in the vocabulary of slavishness resonated with one of the principal issues of social reform, the manumission of
slaves. As an institution, slavery had long been in decline when in 1894, as
part of the social agenda of the Kabo reforms, it was outlawed. But eliminating a social category and its attendant practices that had been widespread
for centuries was not an easy task for a state that had difficulty in these
tumultuous years developing governance structures that could penetrate local society. As late as 1910, newspapers still called for a more effective manumission, in one case describing the scale of the remaining practice at "many
tens of thousands" of slaves.[28] These calls, while deploring slavery's cruelty
and inhumanity, also framed manumission as a question of self-strengthening: equality and fairness were necessary for true citizenship, and national
power depended on the citizenry as a whole.[29] Slavery as a social institution
and an impediment to the full participation of the population was in this
way linked to notions of "slavish mentality" as a behavior that was hobbling
the nation. Both sovereignty and citizenship acquired their meaning in contrast to slavery.[30]

The majority of writing on dependence centered on issues of knowledge
and identity. Countless editorials berated their predecessors for a centuries-
long political dependence that had been enabled by and, in turn, helped
spur an obsession with Chinese learning. Even the *Hwangsŏng sinmun*, a
paper sympathetic to Confucianism and replete with allusions to Chinese
history, complained that all the past historical records were stored "in stone
rooms atop famous mountains." What did circulate were histories of their
neighbor, so that people "did not read their own history but studiously read
short and comprehensive histories of China, making most of the people
know about another country but not know about their own."[31] It was like
"not being able to recount the pedigree of one's own household yet being
able to understand the genealogy of someone else."[32] This juxtaposition between future and past, sovereignty and servility, independence and dependence exaggerated both the extent of subservience in the long, often contentious, history of tribute and the degree of freedom associated with
sovereignty in the new global order. But this dichotomy served writers well
insofar as it buttressed their calls for a cathartic elimination of Chinese
cultural forms from the peninsula. Only by reestablishing cultural purity, it
was argued, could true independence be attained.

The veneration of past Korean heroes became one of the primary avenues for inculcating greater knowledge about the nation. If not an age of heroes, it was an age of writing about heroes.[33] To this end, the historical figure Ŭlchi Mundŏk, "the single greatest person in four thousand years of Korean history," according to one scribe, was prominently resurrected.[34] More than a millennium earlier, in A.D. 612, Ŭlchi had led a smaller Koguryŏ (37 B.C.–A.D. 668) contingent against upward of 300,000 troops of Sui Yangdi's invading army. With a number of ingenious stratagems and some ferocious fighting, Ŭlchi did more than just emerge victorious. He handily routed the emperor's army, leaving only 2,100 bedraggled troops to scramble back to the haven of Sui territory. Despite this achievement, Ŭlchi's triumphs had been treated only scantily in prenationalist histories.[35] But writers at the turn of the twentieth-century, eager to find heroes to inspire younger generations, discovered in Ŭlchi a figure that at once reflected a lost tradition of military greatness while displaying a tenacious spirit of independence vis-à-vis China. No reader of newspapers, journals, or textbooks in these years could miss the extensive pieces detailing the life and accomplishments of this Koguryŏ general. Statues were raised in his honor in front of schools,[36] and his name appeared in patriotic poetry.[37]

In his introduction to one of the more lengthy biographies of Ŭlchi, the historian and editorialist Sin Ch'aeho recounted his epiphany-like reaction to learning about the Koguryŏ general. Sin described how before hearing about Ŭlchi's deeds, he had always assumed that the history of Korea's foreign relations was merely one of endless foreign invasions, in which a single word from China would be received by a cowering court—a situation that, Sin wrote, led him to believe that the natural character of the nation was "inferior and weak." When he read about Ŭlchi, however,

> my spirit surged and my boldness leaped. Raising my face to Heaven, I shouted, "This! This is the nature of our nation! It is thus! Nothing in either the past or the present rivals such a great figure and such great deeds. This is how strong and brave is the nature of our nation![38]

As one advertisement for the book announced, this was a work that would "heat up the blood of those with cold blood and give bones to the boneless."[39] The hope of the likes of Sin and others, of course, was that such historical biographies would, at a time when the peninsula was being besieged by external powers, provide examples of selfless patriots fighting against the odds to protect the nation. Learning about these battles, as another author pointed out, would "summon up a second Ŭlchi Mundŏk."[40]

Ŭlchi also represented for many writers a time when Koreans were truly Korean, unsullied by contact with a debilitating Chinese culture. As the author of the preface to Sin's biography noted,

> Ever since Chinese culture entered our country, all our people have burned with the fever of revering the foreign and have stubbornly clung to the sickness of degrading oneself. Consequently, even in their dreams they did not think of great heroes like Ŭlchi Mundŏk.[41]

This shift toward an infatuation with things Chinese had begun fifteen hundred years earlier, according to one analysis. Before this time, Koreans had a "heart of independence" and thereafter a "heart of dependence," all because "a custom of imitating and revering China and a tendency to depend on others had been passed down."[42] Ŭlchi's defiance of China, as both a warrior who had repelled Chinese attacks and someone who had avoided the Confucian training of later generations, symbolized a glorious instance in the national past. More than this, Ŭlchi's very surname served as evidence of that purely Korean past for which they were searching. Yu Kilchun lamented that ancient surnames like Ŭlchi had completely disappeared, replaced by Chinese-style names, because Koreans had become addicted to Chinese characters as though they were opiates.[43] Elevating the very name of Ŭlchi thus became at once a means of exalting a lost Koreanness and a call for purging Chinese influence, both political and cultural.

The Language of Nationalism

Such calls for the recovery of an unadulterated Koreanness rested on an assumption that there existed a simple, natural separation between the cultural forms originating in the continent and those rooted in the peninsula, despite centuries of exchange, appropriation, and interaction. Just as an archaeologist could dig up lost relics of the past, national character could be unearthed from the sands of time. As though culture was as objective as shards of pottery, it could be sought, retrieved, and restored — in short, returned to an untainted, original state. The myriad traditions, practices, and symbols inherited from their predecessors could be winnowed out; the cultural forms newly identified as Chinese separated and cast aside so as to reveal an obscured but ever present Korean essence.

More than any other issue, the reform of writing best fit these assumptions. The transition from the use of characters to a phonetic alphabet is a well-known story that took place over several centuries.[44] What is of concern here is the active promotion after 1895 of the phonetic alphabet as a *national* script (*kungmun*) in place of characters, a process that reflected the impulse toward a "pureness" of language and was informed by changing definitions of knowledge.[45] From the inception of the alphabet at the behest of King Sejong in 1443 until the late nineteenth century, this system to "Teach the People the Correct Sounds" (Hunmin chŏngŭm), as it was first called, had yet to gain as its main attribute a connection with the nation. In the king's own promulgation of the alphabet, he highlighted the efficiency of the alphabet, noting that the "ignorant . . . though they wish to express their sentiments in writing, have been unable to communicate." The alphabet would allow people to write "conveniently in their daily life"—a statement that, despite pointing out the difference in the Chinese and Korean spoken languages, did not appeal to an inherent nationness of either writing system.[46]

For the many scholars who opposed the introduction of the Hunmin chŏngŭm, efficiency was not so much the issue as was the character's unique relationship with the truths of the classics. On the basis of this relation, the educated elite rejected King Sejong's invention. Scholars such as Ch'oe Malli vociferously attacked the new alphabet, arguing that knowledge and characters were inextricably linked. Since the classics were written in characters and deemed to be the source of all truth, abandoning them would be tantamount to losing access to this knowledge. In a long memorial presented in 1444, Ch'oe contended that the new writing system would undermine learning and harm the order of the world. The people, he maintained,

> would not know the writings of the sages and worthies, "they won't study, their faces will be to the wall." They will be blind with respect to right and wrong in the Pattern of things. They will be futilely expert in the Vulgar Script. But what use can be made of that! The Culture of the Right, which our country has amassed and accumulated, will gradually come to being swept from the earth.[47]

For Ch'oe, there was little use for a new script. He asked, "Why should we change from a long-used, uncorrupted script and separately create mean, vulgar, profitless graphs?"[48] In Ch'oe's memorial, neither the character nor the new alphabet was identified primarily through an association with a particular nation, as is frequently assumed today. Instead, the nature of each writing system was determined by its link to knowledge, one offering access and the other precluding it. Thus, for Ch'oe and successive generations of Chosŏn-dynasty scholars, the character would literally be deemed *chinmun*, the "true script," as only it provided access to truth, whereas King Sejong's alphabet, which could make no special claim to knowledge, could be ignored, dismissed as nothing more than ŏnmun, the "vulgar script."

As the "new knowledge" intruded into Korea along with the guns and capital of the imperialist powers, the privileged relationship between knowledge and characters was increasingly challenged. Confucian truths and epistemology were less frequently invoked as they were gradually supplanted by new definitions of civilization. A new knowledge was promoted, one to which access was no longer monopolized by an understanding of characters but was attainable through any writing system, be it English, Japanese — or King Sejong's alphabet. The *Hwangsŏng sinmun* attacked the idea that characters had a special nature, containing exclusive meanings. It rejected as "the confused words of corrupt Confucians" the idea that "because Chinese writing was made by the sages of the Middle Land [*chungt'o*], it contains ineffable meanings [ŏnoe]."[49] While characters might grant special access to the knowledge of the classics, it was precisely this knowledge that was deigned ineffectual for the new tasks of the nation.[50] One overseas student expressed this concern:

> Alas! Why is it that for the last five hundred years, our country's people have solely discarded their unique script as though it was a useless object, revering only the Chinese characters imported from abroad and vainly spending their lives discriminating the four tones and learning the eight styles of writing [p'alch'e]?[51]

Echoing this sentiment, another writer lamented that there were many reasons why "our country's brilliant five-thousand-year history has sunk into the wretched black clouds of today, among which the influence of Chinese characters is the greatest."[52] The formerly venerated knowledge was symbolized by the image of the ineffective scholar, who could be depicted as little more than a "rice-eating dictionary."[53] Useless for their home or country, characters served only to harm the economy:

In all the towns and counties, many scholars and Confucians pursue knowledge, are good at reading aloud, and are good at discussing theories. But they do not know whether the price of rice at the small market just outside their door is high or low. They are able to understand the obscure meaning of the classics, histories, poetry, and belles lettres, but they do not know what is happening in today's world [*set'ae*]. They waste forty or fifty years of their efforts and are good at recounting a hundred volumes of anthologies but are not able to establish a single means of livelihood.[54]

The counterexample of the West served this argument, as Britain, the United States, France, and Germany could be cited by one critic as wealthy and strong countries that had attained these levels without resorting to Chinese.[55] Stripped of any claim to holding exclusive meaning and denied any privileged relation to the new systems of knowledge considered useful in the quest for independence, characters were demoted to the level of any other writing system. No longer special, they now were judged merely in terms of their merits as a communicative tool.

But even when characters were appraised for their communicative abilities, few Korean writers gave them high marks. Characters simply were inefficient. As the linguist Chu Sigyŏng pointed out, "Life does not come twice," and since one had to devote one's entire life to learning characters, what else could one learn? "What is it that they know after wasting more than ten years of their studies? Only the script."[56] Consequently, only a minority could learn to read: no more than a few out of a hundred, according to the *Hwangsŏng sinmun*,[57] one or two out of a hundred by the count of Yu Kilchun,[58] or, in the opinion of the most pessimistic, a single person out of a hundred.[59] Again, the argument was advanced contrastively:

In general, why is that the areas of the world that use ideographs are ignorant, while those that use a phonetic script are enlightened [*kyemyŏng*]? It is certainly because the ease or difficulty of a script determines whether a people's knowledge will be superior or inferior, and whether a people's knowledge is superior or inferior determines the strength or weakness of a nation.[60]

As a phonetic alphabet, King Sejong's invention was seen as a form of writing that enabled everyone to acquire the types of knowledge needed for the nation, precisely because it was so easy to learn. The alphabet was equally convenient for "men and women, old and young, the high and low, the poor and rich and the noble and vulgar." "If a stupid child studies for only a single day," wrote Chu Sigyŏng, "it is enough to know the writing [system]."[61] Others frequently noted the facility of women in the alphabet as further evidence that it was easy to learn — so easy, they asserted in a common expression of the era, that "even women could learn it."[62] Indeed, women who learned the alphabet and acquired new knowledge could be ranked above those men who understood only characters.[63]

better a way to know Thus the Korean script as an efficient medium offered a superior means of attaining knowledge. It became the basic building block of the enlight-enment project. As one of the earliest students of the alphabet explained, "The most essential thing for civilization is the national script."[64] Or as another proponent declared, the national script was "truly the foundation for ten thousand generations of civilization and the guide leading forward to independence."[65] In this way, writers contrasted the characters imported from China with King Sejong's invented alphabet. Set off against each other — one deemed inconvenient, the other efficient — the characters represented the past, a time of weakness and ignorance when Korea was less than fully independent, whereas King Sejong's alphabet looked to the future, to the promise of a strong and enlightened Korea able to defend its sovereignty.

This reconfiguration of the relationship between the written word and knowledge enabled the full nationalization of both scripts. Korean writers began to tout King Sejong's alphabet as the only *Korean* writing system. What for nearly five hundred years had been known as "vulgar writing" was transformed into the "national writing" (*kungmun*). In creating these national meanings, writers commonly naturalized the link between nation and writing. Chu Sigyŏng used this linkage to legitimize Korea's claim to independence as natural:

On this planet, land is naturally divided, and a group of people [*han-ttŏlgi injong*] living in these areas make and use a language appropriate to the local sounds prevalent in this clime. Moreover, they create a script that fits the sounds of their language. In this way, the existence of a special language and script in one nation is certainly a sign that this country is naturally a self-governing nation [*chajuguk*].[66]

So, too, could this link be universalized. As the editors of the *Hwangsŏng sinmun* asserted without any attention to exceptions, "In all the nations under Heaven, none does not have its own national language and national script."[67] Here, in a classic formulation of a deterministic criterion for defining a nation, language in both its oral and written forms laid claim to the right to nationhood.

By naturalizing the link between the written word and nation, writers simultaneously undermined the claim of characters to national transcendence. Formerly considered a truth script for all, characters now were identified as *Chinese* characters. For the first time since characters had been introduced centuries ago, writers highlighted their Chineseness. As one commentator felt compelled to note, "Chinese writing is the national language of the land of China."[68] Writers downgraded the status of the "true writing" to that of the national script of just another foreign country. As another explained, "The national writing is our nation's writing. Chinese writing is the writing of China."[69] This rejection of the character as Chinese and alien was most symbolically manifested in the numerous demands for the physical relocation of its place of teaching. As many reformers argued, characters should no longer be part of the national curriculum and thus should be taught side by side with English and Japanese in foreign-language schools.[70] Writers promoted the national script not only as something to be used but also as an object worthy of reverence. If not so venerated, one writer feared, it would be like someone who "did not respect his own parents and loved only other people."[71] Chu Sigyŏng beseeched his compatriots to love their language and writing system,[72] and Sin Ch'aeho challenged the nationality of any Korean who did not, asking, "Today, if there still are people who scorn the national script more than Chinese writing, can we still call them Korean?"[73]

Clearly for Sin, the answer was no. But in one of the few pieces published in these years that called for retaining characters, at least one writer refrained from making such a judgment. This person was a relatively unknown teacher, Yŏ Kyuhyang, who in his article in the conservative journal the *Taedong hakhoe wŏlbo* (*Monthly of the Great Eastern Educational Association*), adopted the same nationalizing logic of the advocates of writing reform.[74] For Yŏ, this logic could be wielded equally to defend characters. His defense rested on the dismissal of his opponents' assertion that characters had "invaded" from abroad and had then been adopted by Koreans. Instead,

he contended that characters had been in Korea all along: "For four thousand years, since Tan'gun and Kija first established the country, we Koreans
have been using characters." Yŏ did not revert to the old and tried claims
about the special relationship between characters and knowledge nor claim
any special transnational status for characters. Rather, he creatively asserted
that with their putative origins in Korea, characters were Korean, not foreign,
and as a Korean writing system, he insinuated, it deserved to be preserved,
not purged. Despite its very different agenda, Yŏ's piece shows how deeply
the logic of nationalizing culture had penetrated intellectual circles by the
early twentieth century. The argument leveled against King Sejong's alphabet nearly five hundred years earlier by Confucian scholars in defense of
characters had little support among conservative nationalists. Even the em-
battled defenders of characters sought to frame their arguments in terms of
nation and geographic origins. This style of counterargument, sharing as it
did the same assumptions about writing and nation and dependent on the
spurious notion that characters did not come from China, had little chance
of stemming the increasingly widespread and ideological use of the alphabet.
Out of a neglected linguistic invention, advocates of the formerly "vulgar
writing" succeeded in creating one of the leading icons of the nationalist
movement.

The calls by nationalists to rediscover the indigenous and discard the
Chinese were most successfully realized in the writing reform movement.
It was in this area that the assumptions toward national culture most closely
matched the objects of reform. Few challenged the iconic value of the alphabet — which, in turn, served to reinforce the wider calls for authenticity
and seemingly to substantiate the assumptions about the easy divisibility of
Korean from Chinese culture. But despite the high-profile calls for writing
reform, many newspapers and journals did not actually abide by their own
pronouncements. The *Hwangsŏng sinmun* constantly raised the issue of the
alphabet, early on giving histories of the vernacular while devoting editorial
space for an explanation of the system's principles.[75] It urged that the vernacular be used in schools,[76] recommended that the government make public notices available in the vernacular so the population could understand
them,[77] called for more research into the standardization of the vernacular,[78]
and even went so far as to suggest that if people did not read vernacular
newspapers, the national character (*kuksŏng*) could not be preserved.[79] The
problem, of course, was that the *Hwangsŏng sinmun*, like the majority of

newspapers, journals, and even textbooks in this period, was itself not written in the vernacular. Instead, it used a mixed script in which Chinese characters were combined with Sejong's alphabet. The first editorial defended the use of the mixed script as an excellent combination while admitting that even though the vernacular was superior, the literati simply would not use it.[80] Despite devoting considerable editorial attention to writing reform, during its thirteen years of publication the *Hwangsŏng sinmun* did not write a single editorial in the vernacular.[81]

The newspaper's combined use of characters and alphabet was criticized in its later years. The young Yi Kwangsu, later one of Korea's leading literary figures, pointed out in an article published in the *Hwangsŏng sinmun* that this so-called mixed script was in fact just old-style Chinese with a smattering of the alphabet. Even the selection of characters, he complained, seemed to come out of the *Kangxi Dictionary*, a reference to an eighteenth-century volume famous for including the most obscure Chinese characters.[82] The reasons for this contradiction by the papers' editors — recommending the widespread use of the alphabet but not using it in their own pages — are many. In his article, Yi Kwangsu argued that the continued use of what for most of the population was impenetrable prose had much to do with the reputation of the writers and their desire to impress others with their knowledge.[83] A more generous reading of the intentions of the editors of the *Hwangsŏng sinmun* is that they were specifically targeting the more conservative literati, trying to engage them in their nationalist project by writing in the language most familiar to them. A commercial argument might suggest that this was the paper's niche market at a time when intellectual discourse throughout the country was still dominated by those who had received a classical education. There also were problems concerning the standardization of the alphabet. As even many of the alphabet's defenders admitted, until further research enabled a degree of uniformity in its use, the mixed script would have to do.[84] But whatever the motivation, the fact that the paper's prose remained rooted in a classical style undercut its calls for promoting the national script, suggesting that despite its commitment to reform writing, other concerns could prevail over its professed desire to expunge these influences.

Indeed, not all reform efforts included a pair of cultural objects that could be so neatly inscribed with two, contrasting, national origins. In other areas of reform, divergent political, social, or ideological concerns could equally work at cross-purposes to the assumptions about culture that underlay the calls to decenter China. As the impulse to nationalize culture was carried into other areas, a number of ambiguities and difficulties appeared, for the rhetoric notwithstanding, not every cultural form could be smoothly instilled with clear-cut national meanings.

From King to Emperor

The months following the conclusion of the Sino-Japanese War proved to be the nadir in the political fortunes of the Korean royal house, when in quick succession Queen Min was assassinated by Japanese agents and King Kojong escaped to the safety of the Russian legation. With the prestige of the royal house seriously damaged, the court initiated a series of efforts to reverse the monarchy's fortunes and reestablish its dignity and power. It was to be a "restoration" (chunghŭng), an expression with a long history among beleaguered courts in East Asia. This restoration was similar in intent to what Benedict Anderson has termed "official nationalism," only here the court was following on the heels of the already burgeoning nationalist movement, hoping to harness the agitation for independence to its own purpose of reasserting the centrality of the throne.[85] For an institution that had been so deeply implicated in the politics and culture of tribute, the calls for cultural purity as a precondition for independence created a number of difficulties. Initially, its efforts focused on the vestiges of the tributary relationship. Even while King Kojong was residing in the Russian legation, changes got under way: adherence to the Qing's taboo characters was terminated; an independent year title, Kŏnyang, was adopted in 1896; and ancient monuments such as the "Welcoming Imperial Grace Gate" (Yŏngŭnmun), where Chinese imperial envoys to Seoul had been greeted for nearly five hundred years, were razed.[86]

Such monumental changes did not end with their demolition, however. If the razing of the old monument represented an ending, the construction of another symbolized a fresh beginning. On a clear sunny afternoon in November 1896, more than eight thousand residents of Seoul gathered on the same spot where a year earlier the "Welcoming Imperial Grace Gate" had been demolished. At about 2:30, after listening to the Pai Jae College Glee Club sing the patriotic song "Korea," the crowd watched the president of the Independence Club, An Kyŏngsu, lay the cornerstone of a new gate, to be called Independence Gate (Tongnimmun).[87] The English-language edition of the paper editorialized that the new arch was an appropriate successor to the Yŏngŭn Gate:

> And now an arch is to be raised on the same spot to stand forever as a negation of Manchu dominance, to show that Korea is once and for all cut off from the blighting influence of Chinese patronage; cut off, we hope, also from the system of corruption and trickery that today makes the most populous empire the laughingstock of the world.[88]

While the destruction of the monument signified a severance with the past relationship of reliance, the construction of the Independence Gate symbolized a hoped-for future: an independent Korea, free of the control of foreign powers.

The most powerful symbol of Korea's former subordinate status rested in the king himself. As long as King Kojong kept his royal title — a title that in the ritual language of tribute was beneath that of emperor — the suggestion of subordination lingered. Court officials thus moved to eliminate any such implication, through changes centering on Kojong's form of address, changes marked by exhaustive rituals based on classical precedents but now invested with new meanings. The first steps were taken as early as July 1894 when it was announced that the king's conventional form of address would be raised one level from "sovereign" (Kunju) to "great sovereign" (Taegunju). In subsequent years, he was elevated even higher, coming to be referred to as "Royal Highness" (Chusang chŏnha) and then in 1896 as "Great Imperial Highness" (Taegunju p'yeha), each change representing a significant rise in ritual language. When Kojong moved out of the Russian compound, the final stage in this process began. In October 1897, a memorial requesting a change in the royal status was submitted. A flurry of activity followed as officials and rural scholars rushed to present petitions beseeching the king to abandon the royal title. For three days in a row, Kojong's top officials knelt in the palace courtyard for four hours each day, according to protocol, submitting nine separate requests. Kojong declined all the supplications — except, of course, the last.[89]

Even before the king assented, construction had already begun on the Ring Hill Altar (Wŏn'gudan), suggesting the publicly humble Kojong was privately not so modest.[90] Quickly constructed for his coronation, Ring Hill Altar was designed along the lines of Beijing's Altar of Heaven, with three terraces separated from one another by nine steps. After the appropriate sacrifices to Heaven in the early morning of October 12, 1897, Kojong doffed the red robes of kings and donned the dragon yellow robes of emperors.[91] King Kojong became Emperor Kojong. Using ancient rituals to support modern concepts, the reinvention of the throne signified that the source of Korean sovereignty rested unambiguously on the peninsula. In his first edict as emperor, Kojong reversed a five-century-long tradition, announcing:

> The foundation of independence has been created and the rights of sovereignty exercised. The officials and people, soldiers and merchants, have called out in one voice, requesting in tens of petitions that We should assume the title of Emperor. We refused them numerous times, but there was no way to end their requests. Thus, on the seventeenth day of the ninth month of this year, We informed and sacrificed to Heaven and Earth on the south of White Hill and ascended the Imperial Throne. Establishing the name of the realm as Great Han [TaeHan], We called this year the first year of Kwangmu.[92]

Not only had the king become emperor, but the kingdom of Chosŏn had also become the Empire of the Great Han. In 1394, the two-year-old dynasty had chosen two possible names for the new dynasty: Chosŏn, the name of an early kingdom in northern Korea which in 108 B.C. had been defeated by the Han dynasty;[93] and Hwanyŏng, an old name for the Hamgyŏng area where the founder of the dynasty had been born. Presented to the Beijing court for approval, the Ming emperor picked the former. But by the late 1890s, the origins of the dynastic name — a name that had been unchallenged for five hundred years — came to be seen in terms of new concepts of sovereignty.[94] Now associated with disfavored politics of tribute, Chosŏn was abandoned in favor of Han, a term traceable to ancient kingdoms on the southern half of the peninsula, an area, most significantly, that had never been invaded by China. With its connotations of independence, the tradition of the ancient Han kingdoms was claimed for the new emperor and his empire.

Throughout this process of reinventing the Korean royal house, a wide-ranging arsenal of imperial symbols and rituals was invoked. Ostensibly employed in conventional fashion, this mixture of symbols in fact functioned in imaginative ways. Citations from the *Book of Rites*, the time-honored precedents of the Three Emperors and Five Kings, the constant appearance of the sacred number nine (nine requests, nine steps), the use of criminal amnesties, appeals to the benevolent care of Heaven — all these were venerable symbols embedded in the traditions of the East Asian regional order, symbols known by all educated Koreans and regularly used in court debates, leisurely writings, and official documents. In the last years of the dynasty, however, these traditions were wielded untraditionally. Reinvented to serve the new purpose of independence, they maintained their external form while embodying fresh meanings.

Central to this reinvention was a reformulation of the concept of emperor. One Heaven, one Emperor had been the accepted order until Kojong donned the imperial robes. Only one man, the Son of Heaven, could sacrifice directly to Heaven, yet by mounting Ring Hill Altar and undertaking the supplicative rituals, Kojong was rejecting the exclusivity of Sinocentric definitions. His coronation as emperor marked a rupture with traditional protocols, challenging the solitary legitimacy of Beijing's own claimant to imperial status. It was this deliberate violation that paradoxically brought fresh meaning to the hoary symbols. The reinvention of the royal house offered a new definition of an independent nation with an emperor as its symbolic center or, in the words of Kojong, as "the foundation of independence."

At one level, the reinvention of the royal throne functioned, as did writing reform, to decenter the Middle Kingdom. The rituals created a metonym for the nation: just as Kojong could now claim equal status to his Beijing counterpart, so too could the Great Han Empire claim equality with the Great Qing Empire. When in 1898 a Chinese plenipotentiary arrived in Seoul to seek a commercial treaty, he carried a letter that began, "The Great Emperor of Great Qing respectfully greets the Great Emperor of Great Korea," marking the first communication ever between the two sovereigns as equals.[95]

Yet there was also a very different dynamic in this reinvention. Unlike writing reform, in which two divergent writing systems could be juxtaposed — one as "ours" and the other as "theirs" — court officials did not attempt to highlight any inherent nationness in the individual rituals themselves. Instead, meaning was interpreted solely from their function. This meaning — independence as signified through the willful violation of received protocols — nevertheless was derived from the still resonant potency of traditional East Asian symbolic orders. The sacrificial altar, the color of the robes, and the supplicative actions of the officials — all were symbols that in other circumstances could have been inscribed with Chinese meanings and, according to the logic of nationalizing culture, rejected as other. But the court did not invoke such meanings. Instead, the court's own political needs and motivations took precedence. In seeking to reassert its own power and prestige, these symbols and rituals proved useful because they linked throne, nation, and independence, making each essential to the other. In a period when various social groups were participating in a contested process to reconstruct the national identity, the court used the imperial rituals and symbols to position the king at the center of newly emerging visions of an independent Korea.

As with many public rituals, however, the emperor and his officials could not monopolize the meaning of the throne's reinvention. Individuals outside the court had strong reservations, not so much about the crown's newfound enthusiasm for independence, but about the means by which the court pursued the goal. Upon hearing about the plans to elevate the king's status, Yun Ch'iho, one of the editors of the *Tongnip sinmun*, wrote in his diary, "I wonder which of the many asses in the government has put this piteous notion into the royal head?"[96] Later, in the public forum of a missionary-run publication, Yun showed a more diplomatic side. Employing the logic of decentering the Middle Kingdom, he ridiculed the conduct of various rituals and dismissed the memorials as reflecting the "ancient classic style of China, full of obscure allusions and bombastic phrases."[97] The *Tongnip sinmun*'s editorial on these changes, to which Yun may have contributed, was even more optimistic. It focused on the court officials who, it noted, had until very recently always looked to China. That even these men now worked for independence was a "sign that Chosŏn is gradually becoming an independent nation."[98] But such compliments were tempered by the editors' resentment of the tendency to reduce independence to titular matters. Whether a nation was "an empire or a kingdom," they insisted that it was the level of enlightenment that determined a nation's status. Willing to accept a symbolic end to royal subordination, the editors of the *Tongnip sinmun* were less eager to endorse the court's plan of making the throne the "foundation of independence."

The delicate task of at once promoting the king as a symbol of patriotic loyalty while deferring to embrace the court's own efforts at repackaging the royal institution was manifest in the *Hwangsŏng sinmun*'s response to a Chinese newspaper's account of these events. According to the Korean newspaper, its Chinese counterpart, the *Wanguo gongbao* (International Daily), described the ritual using the terminology "to claim the throne" (K. *ch'ingche*, Ch. *chengdi*), instead of "to ascend the throne" (K. *chŭkwi*, Ch.

jiwei). In conventional ritual language, the former term implied an illegitimate usurpation of the imperial mantle, while the latter signaled the legitimate assumption of the throne by the individual holding the Mandate of Heaven. By choosing to describe the ceremony as Kojong "claiming the throne," the Chinese paper in effect rejected the legitimacy of the action. The editors of the *Hwangsŏng sinmun* barely restrained their tone of ridicule: "We laugh" at the Chinese scribes for such "self-adulation and for still being mired in the corrupt theories of Song Confucians."[99] Yet these so-called corrupt theories were the very ones invoked by the court in the imperial rituals. What the Chinese editors interpreted as illegitimate was precisely the violation of established norms that the court deliberately manipulated to symbolize the independence of the nation through the throne. Although the interpretation of these rituals depended on the same assumptions, very different conclusions were reached. Hesitant to criticize an institution that they too wished to promote as a symbol of patriotism, the editors of the *Hwangsŏng sinmun* had no reason to restrain themselves from scoffing at the *Wanguo gongbao*. To mock its use of these theories was to indirectly criticize the court's methods of restoration. The *Hwangsŏng sinmun* editors tried to separate the choice of the imperial title from these theories. When they asked, "Don't they know that every sovereign nation has the right to establish its own titles as it so desires?"[100] The choice of title was thus reduced to little more than a perquisite of sovereignty.

The editorial exemplified the transitional nature of the period. Written in classical Chinese without the use of Korean (perhaps for the benefit of the writers at the *Wanguo gongbao*), the piece was based on a grasp of the intended implications of the Chinese newspaper's manipulation of these terms. The editorial's objection, unlike the court's rituals, worked from outside Confucian legitimacy theory, denying its relevance. For the editors of the *Hwangsŏng sinmun*, the court's reinvention of the throne stripped of its rituals and symbols could nevertheless mean independence, but independence defined according to international conventions of sovereignty.

The divergent interpretations of these rituals reflected conflicting views of the status of the sovereign in a reformed nation. Nationalist reformers, eager to present themselves as champions of enlightenment and national progress, were not as enthusiastic about the court's attempts to use what they perceived as outdated rituals and symbols to reassert monarchical power. Moreover, any reassertion of the throne had implications for the reformers' self-perceived role as the rightful leaders of an enlightened society. This conflict over who best represented and spoke for the nation eventually came to a head. In November 1898, these contending visions spilled into the streets of Seoul. Rumors — possibly planted by its detractors at court — suggesting that the Independence Club planned to establish a republic began to circulate around the capital. This gave top officials an opportunity to crack down on an organization that through its newspapers and street demonstrations had repeatedly — and, in the eyes of these officials, presumptuously — criticized government policy. In one of the better-known incidents of the period, these officials unleashed the hooligans of the Peddlers' Guild, who attacked club members participating in a large demonstration on the central street of Seoul. By December, the court had officially banned the club, and its newspaper was shut down.[101]

A National Flag

The ways in which the shared traditions of the East Asian regional order were variously employed can also be observed in the most prominent symbol of the nation at the turn of the century, the national flag. The dual function of the flag is best reflected in one of the recurrent images, both visual and rhetorical, from this period: the Korean flag fluttering in a line of the world's many national flags. Flying as one among equals, the flag represented the sovereignty of Korea in a world populated by nations, and at the same time, the arrangement of design and color exhibited a national uniqueness within a single standard format.[102]

The nationalist press deliberately cultivated the association of flag and nation. The editors of the *Tongnip sinmun* complained that "when they [the people] see the national flag, they do not have reverent and loving thoughts."[103] Writers urged their compatriots to "bring glory to the national flag,"[104] sing patriotic songs to it, and consider it more important than their own lives.[105] Schoolchildren were inculcated with romantic feelings for the flag, "as the light of the sun shines onto the national flag and the national flag flutters in the wind, the entire sky is filled with a feeling of fortune."[106] Through such efforts, the flag emerged as a constant feature in the social life of the nationalist movement, appearing on newspaper mastheads and school textbooks, hoisted nationwide on the occasion of the imperial birthday, and even included prominently on the packaging of "Key" brand cigarettes.[107]

What is interesting about the promotion and use of the Korean flag is the silence surrounding its origins, not of the flag design itself, but of its constituent parts. The design used in this period — and still used in the Republic of Korea today — was supposedly first proposed as a national flag by the official Pak Yŏnghyo in 1882. According to Pak's own account, he had decided on the basic design of the flag before his departure on a mission as envoy to Japan. After making a few alterations during his voyage to Tokyo, Pak later sent back a copy to Seoul. Before even receiving official approval for the design, Pak began flying it over his residence in Japan. The following year, 1883, King Kojong confirmed Pak's design, officially proclaiming it as the national Korean flag.[108] In this design, nationality was asserted through a blue and red symbol known as the *t'aegŭk* on a white background, flanked by four sets of trigrams, one in each corner. Such venerable symbols with their associations with classical texts laid claim to an ancient cultural past for the nation, muting the significance of the flag's recent invention. As such, the *t'aegŭk* flag combined both new and ancient, universal and Korean. Both the *t'aegŭk* and the trigrams had been used in Korea for centuries, for a variety of purposes. The *t'aegŭk* has been generally associated with Neo-Confucian debates ever since its use by the Song scholar Zhou Dunyi (1017–73) in his *Taiji tushuo* (*Illustrated Explanation of the Great Ultimate*). On the peninsula, the *t'aegŭk* had been employed as more than an illustrative device for Neo-Confucian metaphysical debates, as it was used at a folk level in tombs, temples, and even in medical texts. The trigrams, also associated with metaphysical debates and the *Book of Changes*, were, at a popular level, used for fortune telling.

The use of these symbols reflected the indeterminacy of the national categories on which the move to nationalize cultures rested. Texts like the *Book of Changes* and the forms of knowledge from which the *t'aegŭk* and trigrams were derived were precisely the types of texts and knowledge that newspapers such as the *Tongnip sinmun* castigated for stifling Korean creativity and leading the nation into its precarious political situation. Observing the situation in China, the editors noted that tens of thousands of scholars had mastered the Four Books and Three Classics, yet "this knowledge is not in the slightest helpful; on the contrary, because they have this knowledge, they are dying like a sick body." The editors urged their readers to heed this evidence as a warning: "What use does learning this knowledge have for protecting the country?"[109] More simply put, "forget the Four Books."[110] In the eyes of these editors, such books could be dismissed as nothing more

than "Chinese knowledge."[111] But these same editors overlooked the association of the *t'aegŭk* and the trigrams with the very forms of knowledge and
texts decried as both useless and Chinese. Instead, in this one particular
context — stitched together on a white background — the symbols took on
the most national of meanings. By placing the flag's image on its front page
and calling for its wider use, the *Tongnip sinmun* helped make the national
flag one of the single most prominent icons of the nationalist movement.

The design and use of the national flag reveal the more complicated
process of creating national meanings than suggested by calls for cultural
retrieval based on a dichotomy between Chinese and Korean. If the characters and texts that constituted these forms of knowledge could be given
Chinese meanings, so too could other derivatives of the same forms of knowledge, such as the *t'aegŭk* and trigrams, be used to establish purely Korean
meanings in the specific context of a national flag. Both outcomes were a
part of the same process, one that was less an epiphany of national consciousness in which an inherent Chineseness or Koreanness was recognized
than an effort to instill nationality into texts and symbols, which until very
recently had been considered universal.

A Lost Korean and Eastern Civilization

This tension between the calls for decentering China and the various
practices running counter to its assumptions also was manifested in the effort
to think of Korea as part of a newly conceived region, the East (*Tongyang*).
The logic of decentering may have emphasized national uniqueness, but
notions of regional unity required that at some level, national uniqueness
be subsumed into a transcendent identity, either racially or culturally defined, shared by neighbors. Cultural approaches to the East — much as
Stefan Tanaka has shown for Japan — were introduced into debates about
"civilization and enlightenment," in particular the desire to displace the
claim of the East's other, the West, as the sole locus of historical progress.[112]
In its first few years of operation, the *Hwangsŏng sinmun*'s editors used the
notion of the East as a strategy for promoting the universality of *munmyŏng
kaehwa* in the language of its classically trained readership. Although this
vision of the East later was changed into a style of Pan-Asianism, it first served
as a means of appropriating Western concepts of civilization while offering
different evidence for their historical validity. In so doing, the subordination

of the East that by these very enlightenment standards had become so evident to Korean writers was deemed temporary. In offering a way out of this dilemma, reform along the lines advocated by various nationalist organizations might appear alien to recent Korean experience, but as the editors strove to show through their novel interpretations of Korean and East Asian history, such reform in fact followed principles inherent in a global history to which Korea, as part of the East, belonged.

Not everyone was eager to redefine the East in positive terms. Although the editors of *Tongnip sinmun* stressed *munmyŏng kaehwa* more than did any other paper in the period, for them *munmyŏng kaehwa* remained a set of practices and concepts firmly entrenched in the West and only recently revealed to the East. The possibility that the Eastern past could be judged as enlightened by these standards received little attention in its pages. More commonly, the paper dismissed earlier forms of Eastern learning as a "disease," a type of learning that had produced nothing worthwhile[113] and one that it advised students to forget.[114] One "cannot dare compare" Eastern and Western learning, it insisted.[115] Although the *Tongnip sinmun* accepted the East-West divide as fundamental, in its pages the origins and development of civilization lay firmly in the West, with no attempt to claim an earlier, lost civilization on behalf of the East.

On this point, however, the *Tongnip sinmun* was a minority voice. Far more common were attempts to dispossess the West of any proprietary right on civilization by discovering in the Korean and East Asian pasts cases of enlightened practices. Yu Kilchun emphasized this feature of this "extraordinary and admirable principle," writing that it "is not something that did not exist in the past and only started recently but is the natural reason for all things that is no different today than in ancient times."[116] By far the most articulate champion of this view was the *Hwangsŏng sinmun*. From its earliest days, the *Hwangsŏng sinmun* included Confucian morality as part of its definition of *kaehwa*, and by its final years it was devoting much editorial attention to advocating a style of reform Confucianism.[117] While the paper called for a new Korean curriculum for schools, writing repeatedly of the danger of past habits of relying on China, it often did so in tones reflective of its sympathy for China's plight. This deep sense of a shared past, together with a writing style that continued to use classical terms and allusions, became the basis of the paper's articulation of a cultural vision of the East.

Most prominently, the *Hwangsŏng sinmun* remolded Confucian-style narratives to fit the framework of enlightenment-style history, enlisting illustrations from both the Korean and Chinese past as evidence of a non-Western enlightened age. That examples from the Chinese classical period would be deemed relevant to Korea in these early years revealed that the roots of the editorial staff were in Confucian learning as well as that premodern notions of a transcendant culturalism could be usefully harnessed as a basis for a more contemporary regional identity. Particularly in the early years of publication, the editors of the *Hwangsŏng sinmun* continued to hark back to the Confucian past in China, again showing the limits of decentering the "Middle Kingdom." Combined with illustrations from Korean history, these citations offered an alternative locus of civilization, though one temporally distant, the historical East.

A conversation-style editorial featuring two characters captured this function of the East. One figure stood for people with a naïve trust in Western claims, while the second, more seasoned, character represented the editorial position. The former began by noting that in recent times enlightenment had come to mean the imitation of the West and then asked the latter whether enlightenment had been present earlier in the East. The response was a brusque "How could there not have been?" before a list of cases was presented, detailing several of the classical myths of the sages — of Fuxi, Shennong, Yu, Yao, the Duke of Zhou, and Confucius — and presenting them all as examples of enlightenment.[118] The paper also cited the accomplishments of enlightened Koreans, frequently mentioning the invention of the vernacular script by King Sejong in the fifteenth century and the construction of Admiral Yi Sunsin's turtle boats, used to defeat a Japanese invasion at the end of the sixteenth century.[119] Also high on the list were the creation of movable-print typefaces and ceramics,[120] while at a more mundane level editorials stated as further evidence the continual improvement of agricultural techniques first taught by the ancient sage Kija as well as the establishment of school systems.[121] Even when criticizing conservatives for their stubborn adherence to the teaching of the classics at the expense of any new reforms, the editors agreed that these Confucian scholars had one thing right: in the Korean past there were wonderful institutions and excellent customs.[122]

Such examples offered various moments in a distant past when Korea and the East had been advanced, presenting a counter to the contemporary civilized West. According to the logic of decentering the "Middle Kingdom," what was Chinese, and thus rejected, was in this fashion subsumed into the category of the East, to which these Korean authors could still lay claim. Yet as they openly admitted, this was a lost enlightenment insofar as these vaunted accomplishments could be cherished only in memory, for succeeding generations had failed to build on them.[123] As they pointed out, when Koreans renewed intercourse with the outside world, we saw that "Europe which in terms of enlightenment had lagged behind us was now ahead of us."[124] The East was made "to witness things never seen before and to hear things never heard before."[125] The reasons for this reversal was one of the most vexing questions for this period, and few people hesitated to offer answers. Whatever the specific reason cited, this notion of regression and loss became a means of establishing enlightenment as a principle over which no one held a monopoly that extended across time and space. What had led to the advances of the contemporary West, it suggested, was no different from what in an earlier age had produced an enlightened East. It was the same principle, one that underlay global history. This was not a history of relentless progress, since loss or stagnancy were essential tropes to explain the crisis of this once enlightened East. But *munmyŏng kaehwa* nevertheless provided the unifying concept for all nations, past or present, offering a unilinear vision of history in which all nations, whatever their rate of progress, were headed toward the same ultimate goal.

Much effort was expended on supporting this historical vision that linked the ancient sages and the richness and strength of the West. Two strategies predominated, one establishing a conceptual continuity and the other substantiating an equivalence in content. While the division between East and West was fundamental to this vision, the common principle bridging the two could also be rendered equivalent by means of a venerable expression from the Confucian classics, the "investigation of things" (*kyŏngmul*).[126] *Kyŏngmul* was seen as temporally transcendent, existing in ancient times just as it did in the present. What bothered the editors was that their contemporaries derided their predecessors as ancient, forgetting that in the past they had accomplished many things through "investigation," including such skills as the mastery of fire. But while the West had daily investigated the principles of the myriad things in the universe (*manmul*), laying the foundation for inventions like steamships, telegraph wires, and the railways, Koreans had *temporarily* abandoned the investigation of things, the editorial grumbled, not taking advantage of all the resources in the country. This was not because Koreans were insufficiently wise, the editors both reassured and complained, but because they had become lazy.[127] In short, the ancestors of Koreans had done it in the past and therefore Koreans could do it again. In this fashion the editorial maneuvered to link ancient and new — fire and the railway — through their common mode of discovery, a practice shared by the West and Korea, *kyŏngmul*.

A second, more frequently used technique established the equivalence of specific enlightened accomplishments of the Eastern past and contemporary practices in the West. In one piece, the editor recounted the befuddled reaction of an old man who could not understand why the editor, known for his advocacy of reform, would be reading a traditional book. The editor responded, "It is because I truly admire the [ways of] governance of the Two Emperors and Three Kings that I also speak of the beauty of Western ways. Let me explain the reasons for you." He offered a comparison, describing the organization, availability, and linkage to public service of Western school systems. "For the most part," he concluded with an affirmation of the universal, "this is similar to the ways [*pŏmyu*] of the Three Dynasties."[128]

Such an approach can be found in the *Hwangsŏng sinmun* for many subjects. When writing in 1902 about the use of specialized knowledge for proper governance, the editors pointed out how the Great Sage Yu had devoted himself to specific tasks, in contrast to the current government in which ministers rotated their posts from day to day. Drawing a contrast with the countries of Europe and America where "it is very different from this," the editors observed that specialization of knowledge had led to good governance and many inventions. "The Westerner's art of governance is nothing more than a match to the meaning of Yao, Shun, and Guanzi. [What they have done] is broaden this meaning."[129] The central position of trust in the relationship between the government and the people provided another issue to make this point. What had been achieved by the sages in the past was now the root of Western governance.

> Alas! The Way of governing during the reigns of Yao and Shun and during the Three Dynasties was truly nothing more than trust. Today the fundamental technique of making governance by the powers also is nothing more than this trust. How could it be that there would be two Ways of governing the base?[130]

In short, in the eyes of the editors of the *Hwangsŏng sinmun*, there could not be two ways, only a single way, a universal existing in the past as well as the present and extending around the globe to include, equally, Korea and the West. By using the Korean and Eastern pasts to verify a conception of a universal that the editors believed was currently manifested most clearly in the countries of the West, the *Hwangsŏng sinmun* opened a means for proposing reforms modeled on the West through appeals to either contemporary Western practice or a return to earlier enlightened practices. Both types of reform, it was believed, were based on the same Way or principle — *munmyŏng kaehwa*. Such a strategy facilitated the appropriation of civilization by Korean reformers. As articulated by the Western powers, civilization had always been presented as a universal. But the concept's roots in Western social experience together with the continued existence of rival definitions of civilization had always belied its claim to universality. The appropriation and active promotion of this concept by non-Euro-Americans such as the editors of the *Hwangsŏng sinmun* supported these universalizing claims by expanding its use, moving it beyond its contemporary deployment by the Western powers in the extension of their power around the world to one that offered a reinterpretation of the origins of the East. By finding evidence of civilization in the national past, the editors of the *Hwangsŏng sinmun* sought to sever the concept from its Western source, with their assent to its universal claims making it just as much Korean and Eastern as Western.

One paradoxical consequence of this strategy, however, was that it necessitated a reinterpretation of the Korean and Eastern past. This was a usable past. It fulfilled the purpose of legitimizing civilization's universality only when the standards of civilization themselves were cast over that past to determine what in fact was usable. Received narratives of ancient Korea and China were remolded accordingly; achievements that could be lauded as enlightened were highlighted while formerly acclaimed accomplishments, unable to fit into the parameters of the concept, were relegated to an unusable past. There was little room in this narrative, to cite one example, for the accomplishments of Confucian metaphysics. This history, then, was a selective past, the process of selection infused with Korean derivatives of an originally European notion of civilization and one that largely abandoned traditional assumptions about the motive forces of history. This strategy of appropriation thus delocalized the particularity of the Korean experience, incorporating Korea as but one more case in the relentless progress of history.

In vindicating the past, however, this approach also condemned the present. The very universality of *munmyŏng kaehwa* held Korea and the East to its standards. However enlightened they may have been in the past, their current conditions could only be regarded as backward and in need of change. This was a historical vision that championed reform to spur Korea in the direction of capitalist modernity at the same time that it confirmed the leadership of reform advocates such as the editors of the paper. In its structure and logic, this strategy adopted many of the features of Orientalist writing that, as Edward Said has shown, have been fundamental to the power and authority of the West. In particular, the editors' dependence on an East-West dichotomy on which the universal of civilization was based rationalized Korean and Eastern subordinance to the West, confirming the West's superiority as the product of a history that was both natural and global.

According to the logic of *munmyŏng kaehwa* and for the purposes of reform, however, this rationalization enabled the paper's editors to reject any suggestion of an exclusively Western dominance of civilization. A Korean could be shown admonishing a Westerner for daring to suggest that Korea was incapable of becoming civilized. For what reason, the Korean asks the foreigner, do you think that only the West can become enlightened (*kye-myŏng*)? "I have heard that soon you will be returning home. Tell the people of the West on my behalf," he sternly instructed, "that Korea too . . . will soon be headed in a progressive direction."[131]

Peace and Unity in a Racially Defined East

These arguments about the East found a prominent place in the editorial pages of the *Hwangsŏng sinmun* in its early years. But as the editors began to heed their own calls to distance China and promote Korean cultural knowledge, the paper's use of classical precedents and allusions to the Confucian sages became increasingly untenable. Moreover, as the contemporary relevance of China to the East was superseded by the rising power of Japan, cultural definitions that rested on an understanding of an earlier transnational culturalism centering on China appeared less appealing. Without any overt indication, this particular style of writing about the East gradually receded from the pages of the *Hwangsŏng sinmun*, even though attention to the deeds of Korean historical figures continued to serve their purpose of claiming past moments of enlightenment for the nation.[132] This did not, however, signal the end of writing about the East, but only a shift toward a different style of regional vision — one that grappled with the changing geopolitics of the region, emphasized a racial definition of the East, and sought to position the *Hwangsŏng sinmun* in the middle of the Korean political spectrum.

By the turn of the twentieth century, race had become a prominent category for intellectuals around the globe to divide and classify the peoples of
the world. Concepts akin to race can be found in the Confucian canons
and ethnic categories had long been used in East Asia as a way of describing
foreign peoples.[133] But even though such ethnic thinking had a long history
in East Asia, as writers began to engage with Western forms of knowledge in
the late nineteenth century, they also began to appropriate the racial categories constructed in the West. Korean intellectuals were no exception to
this trend. In his *Sŏyu kyŏnmun*, Yu Kilchun treated this issue in a section
entitled the "Races [*injong*] of the World." Placed together with such essays
as "Seas of the World," "Rivers of the World," and "Products of the World,"
race was as natural for Yu as the geographic features of the globe.[134] Although
he admitted that experts disagreed on just how many races existed — by
some counts, three races, he wrote, by others, eleven; and still others, twenty-
two — Yu settled on five: yellow, white, black, brown, and red.[135] Befitting
nineteenth-century anthropology, all the groups differed according to their
physical characteristics. The yellow race, Yu maintained, had yellow skin,
straight black hair, large protruding ears, small slanting eyes, a narrow fore-
head, and high cheekbones. Such racial categories became standard in this
period, regularly appearing in newspapers and even taught to primary schoolchildren, accompanied by pictures of representative "specimens" of the
groups.[136]

Yet the bounds of the yellow race were nebulous. At times this category
was stretched to encompass all the peoples in the eastern and central Asian
continent. Korean writers could thus hail the military conquests of the Mongols, vicariously sharing in the glory of their bygone empire by presenting
the victories as those of their people, the yellow race.[137] The *Cheguk sinmun*
extended this definition even further, representing all of Asia as the continent
of the yellow peoples.[138] More typically, however, notions of yellowness were
conflated with the East as defined by Korea, China, and Japan. The inhab-
itants of these three nations, according to the *Tongnip sinmun*, "live on the
same continent and because their seed [*chongja*] is the same, their bodies
and hair similar, they use a common script, and even have many of the
same customs."[139]

Promoted as a natural grouping of people, yellowness became the basis
for several groups around East Asia to propose regional alliances as a means
of resisting Western white imperialism. In Japan, where Pan-Asianist activity
was the earliest and strongest, groups were formed to disseminate these views

among the peoples of East Asia. Visions of an Asian unity varied from the
cultural approach of Okakura Kakuzo[140] to the activist approach of Miyazaki
Toten, with many versions of the political forms that such unity should
take.[141] In China, too, leading intellectuals were drawn to the possibilities of
Pan-Asianism. Whereas Liang Qichao, who wrote extensively on race, flirted
only briefly with the notion of a political force uniting yellow people,[142] Sun
Yatsen developed close ties with leading Japanese Pan-Asiansts, promoting
Asian unity in many of his speeches.[143] Pan-Asianist ideas also found many
advocates in Korea.[144] Most notorious was the Ilchinhoe, a political society
established in 1904 by Yi Yonggu and Son Pyŏnghŭi, which made unity of
the yellow race a central tenet of its collaborationist activity. The Ilchinhoe
quickly became the bête noire of all nationalists, causing a hullabaloo when
in December 1909 it presented a memorial to the throne requesting Korea's
amalgamation into the Japanese Empire.[145]

But the Ilchinhoe did not represent the only Korean approach to Pan-
Asian ideals in these years. One of the most articulate champions was the
Hwangsŏng sinmun, which by 1905 began to use the East as a means of
exploring a middle ground, uneasily resting between the overtly pro-Japanese
groups and the unabashedly anti-Japanese nationalists, that exposed the paper to criticism from both sides. The paper's racial approach to the region
built on its earlier cultural vision of the East. In its earliest years, the two
were often joined, as seen in the *Hwangsŏng sinmun*'s use of an East Asian–
wide expression suggesting that the 400 million people of China, the 20
million people of Korea, and the 40 million people of Japan were of the
"same continent, same race and same culture [*tongju tongjong tongmun*]."[146]
The *Hwangsŏng sinmun* shared this idea, central to all Pan-Asian formulations, that in its historical struggle, the yellow race must avoid becoming the
fodder for the all-consuming advances of the white race. As one reader's
letter exclaimed, ever since the opening of the ports, the white race (*paegin
minjok*) has been flowing to Asia "as though it were the Yangtze River."
Considering the amount of territory conceded to the West, he bemoaned,
"Alas! The lands of the East have so quickly fallen under the control of the
white race."[147] It was a dire crisis of the race, the editors repeatedly warned,
a crisis that could lead to the enslavement of the yellow people or even result
in their outright destruction.[148]

Where the *Hwangsŏng sinmun* departed from the Pan-Asianism of the
Ilchinhoe was that it sought to intertwine region and nation in a way that

offered independence to the nation while guaranteeing security to the East. The two were deemed mutually dependent. For the East to resist the advances of the West, the paper wondered, "how can it rest with a single nation? [Any strategy] must unite the bravery and strength of the three countries."[149] One editorial explained the melancholy caused by gazing at a map of the East by recounting the long and contentious history of the three countries, a problem reflecting their inability to unite:

> The three countries of our yellow race are mutually dependent, like an axle and cart or lips and teeth. We should combine our strength and unite our hearts in striving to protect our land and race. How is it that we do not consider the principle of helping one another and plan only temporary expedients, chase after trifling benefits, and forget the great duty?[150]

Not just the safety but also the future prosperity of the entire region depended on cooperation. Uniting the East and preserving the peace, the editorial argued, would allow the millions of members of the yellow race to prosper, permitting both large and small countries to live securely.[151] Yet as much as the editors trumpeted the virtues of Eastern solidarity, they specified that it should be an alliance of three individually sovereign nations. As a category transcending that of the nation, yellowness was not seen as undermining national sovereignty. An alliance of the yellow people of the East offered the best means for Korean nationalist goals to be attained. Without such intraracial harmony, they insisted, Korea would have difficulty maintaining its independence. The yellow race, the alliance of the three Eastern nations, and Korean independence were deemed mutually dependent. For the editors of the *Hwangsŏng sinmun*, the national, regional, and racial crises could not be separated. Solidarity offered the only possible salvation for each.

Calls for unity were tempered somewhat by the realities of regional geopolitics. The current situation of China, now decentered and ranked as an equal member of the yellow race, presented difficulties for this editorial vision, since the very features that had led to China's representation as lacking civilization also made it the weakest partner in the alliance. Unable to guarantee its own integrity, China threatened the stability of the entire region. To those who thought that China was now irrelevant to the peninsula, the editors countered with a metaphor that became a refrain in their paper:

The East was like a three-household neighborhood. If a fire in one house started as a fierce Western wind raged, the flames would soon engulf the house to the east. The owners of that eastern house should not merely blame their neighbor for their imprudence without stepping forward to help, they warned; otherwise by the time the fire reached their own home, they would run around in a panic, futilely attempting to extinguish the flames.[152] "How could the misfortune of China not be the misfortune of all of the East?" Korea, as one nation in the East, they warned, faced no crisis more serious than the disintegration of China at the hands of the Western powers.[153] Stripped of its privileged position as the "Middle Kingdom," China was still understood as central in terms of regional security, only now it was a central threat to the survival of Korea and the yellow race, showing just how far China's position had slid in the estimation of these editors.

Confident of China's role, the editors were more hesitant about Japan, reflecting a certain tension in their uses of social Darwinism and *munmyŏng kaehwa*. In social Darwinian terms, Japan as a member of the yellow peoples was grouped with the East, but in terms of *munmyŏng kaehwa* it was seen as on a par with, and at times classified as a member of, the rich and powerful countries of the West. The same dilemma that had bedeviled Japanese intellectuals from the early years of the Meiji period —Did Japan belong with the East or the West? —arose in the regional visions of the *Hwangsŏng sinmun*, only in its pages the paramount concern was Japan's fidelity to the East. At the same time, the very civilization of Japan that led it to be grouped, however tentatively, with the the West, proved enticing to the editors, since Japanese wealth and strength were crucial to the region's protection. The editors fully understood that a defense against the West could not be prepared "in one day and a night" and that education and commerce were needed to make the entire region rich and strong. To this end, they hinted at Japan's potential leadership role, asking, "How would the situation of the three countries be saved without the guidance of a friendly nation with foresight?" Japan had this capacity. "Fortunately, Japan has taken the lead in opening the way to enlightenment [*kyohwa*]."

The danger, as they fully realized, was that Japan might not prove so "friendly." Returning to the metaphor of the burning house, they cautioned, "If Japan is arrogant about its small power and does not improve its relations with Korea and China . . . then when the spreading fire reaches [its] house, it will be extremely difficult for Japan to save itself on its own. Japan should think deeply about the expression 'When the lips are lost, the teeth get cold.'"[154] Pursuing this analogy further in another editorial, they satirized Japanese rhetoric, describing a person who when observing his neighbors' houses being robbed merely self-righteously scolded, "Because you didn't renovate your houses, the two of you couldn't prevent thieves from breaking in. Do those thieves dare break into my home?" Warning that Japan's turn would soon arrive, the editorial predicted that the Japanese would receive little sympathy from Koreans and Chinese. "What can be done when it is only after a home has been robbed that [the homeowner] regrets his past actions?"[155] In the eyes of the editors of the Hwangsŏng sinmun, a civilized Japan, an ambivalent partner of the West, was likewise an uncertain partner of the East.[156]

The prevalence of such admonishments reflected the tension in the editors' vision of a united East and the very real consequences of Japanese activities in both Korea and China. All the newspapers in these years reported the intensification of Japan's penetration of the peninsula and the mainland. From the first days of Tongnip sinmun's publication in 1896 until the outbreak of the Russo-Japanese War in 1904, Korean newspapers carried accounts of and objections to Japanese demands for special privileges and concessions, such as for the right to build railways, catch fish in Korean waters, or harvest Korean timber. Stories recounting infringements of Koreans' rights by individual Japanese residents were common, and the government was castigated for allowing Japanese to cross freely over to Korea.[157] But the editors of the Hwangsŏng sinmun consistently failed to link the accounts of Japan's abuses on the peninsula with their treatment of the prospective alliance of the yellow race. Discussions of racial historical struggles were spatially separated, on both the pages and between issues, from accounts of Japanese encroachments, thereby leaving the readers to weave the two strands together. In certain cases, the editors seem deliberately to have separated them. Describing the advances of the white race into the East after the Opium War, the paper produced a long list of aggressions: the Anglo-French expedition in 1860, France's special privileges in Yunnan in 1894, Russia's acquisition of coaling stations off the Korean coast in 1895 and the forestry concessions near the Tumen River in 1896, the occupation of Jiaozhou by Germany in 1897 and of Kowloon by the British two years later.[158] Missing from this tally, of course, was any mention of Japan's participation in this frenzy of acquisition in Korea and China — a seemingly glaring omission but one that did not slow the paper's calls for racial solidarity.

The Disintegration of Eastern Solidarity

With the outbreak of the Russo-Japanese War in 1904, however, there was less room for such ambivalence. In January 1904, realizing the imminence of hostilities, the Korean government declared its neutrality. The *Hwangsŏng sinmun*'s editorial position paid lip service to this position, beginning several of its commentaries with statements attesting to the nation's friendly relations with the two belligerents.[159] But in the first editorial after Japan launched its surprise attack on Russian ships in Inchon, the paper began a long line of strongly worded appeals to regional and racial unity — all of which supported Japan.[160]

As in much of the rest of the world, the editors perceived the war in racial terms, as a conflict pitting white Russia against yellow Japan, in what might determine the destruction or survival of the yellow peoples.[161] Any Koreans who opposed this position became the object of their editorial wrath. A few months after the outbreak of hostilities, some Koreans reportedly welcomed rumors of an impending Russian victory, only to be berated by the editors of the *Hwangsŏng sinmun*. These "rumormongers" misunderstood the significance of the war for Korea: "If Russia emerges victorious and Japan is defeated, then the East will be rent asunder and the yellow race will be finished."[162] Making the link among region, race, and its own national survival, the editors continued, "How can little Korea hope to protect its ancestral altars and defend its land? It will certainly be difficult for the spirit of Korea to avoid the tragedy of the Jews of Poland."[163]

The paper's earlier ambivalence toward Japan was overshadowed by an even greater distrust of Russian ambitions in the region. Upset at how the Russians had variously proposed that Korea be partitioned or exchanged for Manchuria, the editors complained that Korea had not been treated by Russia with the respect due an independent nation. Since Russia had regarded Korea as if it were "a grave with no one in it," how could it remain neutral when the nation had been so insulted? If Korea had the strength, they suggested, it should mobilize troops to wipe out this shame.[164] The threat, however, extended beyond Korea, for Russian political strategy, they warned, was to swallow Manchuria and occupy northern Korea and then incorporate all of the East into its empire.[165] Again, wishing for greater national strength, the editors wrote wistfully of joining forces with its two neighbors and bravely advancing northward to cut off the Siberian Railway, pushing the Russians beyond the Ural Mountains, in other words, out of Asia.[166]

Opposition to Russia made Japanese leadership in the East a prominent issue during the war. Japan was no longer compared with someone watching its neighbors' houses burn but presented as the defender of the East. The editors admitted that Japan had its own national interests at stake in the war but overlooked any contradictions those interests might have on the professed goal of protecting the integrity of Korean and Chinese territory. "To befriend those who support us and to distance those who invade us," they concluded, "is obviously a self-evident principle."[167]

In 1904 one man who fit the *Hwangsŏng sinmun*'s definition of "those who support us" was the architect of the 1905 Protectorate Treaty, who later became the leading scoundrel for Korean nationalists, Itō Hirobumi. When Itō came to Korea in March 1904, the paper extended a welcome.[168] Stating that during the Sino-Japanese War, Japan had made the support of Korean independence its main task, the editors dispensed with their earlier worries to write that Japanese power "until today has secured the basis of Korean independence"—a situation for which Koreans were "most grateful" to Itō and the Japanese court. This was even more the case today, they wrote, when the Japanese mobilized their nation's armies and resources to cross thousands of miles to do battle with Russia, again with the goal of solidifying Korean independence and protecting Korean territory. Korean officials, they urged, must take advantage of Itō's visit:

> Korea and Japan must from this day onward unite their hearts and combine their strength. Without losing self-rule, we must together follow the principle of crossing the river in the same boat . . . and vigorously pursue the task of renewal [*yusin*]. If we are able to do so, then this will be not only fortunate for Korea, but also truly fortunate for Japan.[169]

This quotation captures the delicate balance the editors hoped to achieve. While they appealed to a sense of racial and regional unity to muster support for cooperation with Japan and while they realized Japan was striving to become the principal regional power, a regional alliance was not seen as necessarily compromising nationalist goals. A loose alliance could be formed by independent nations "without losing self-rule." Still, there was some unease. Reliance on Japan left the peninsula vulnerable, since those same troops that could defeat Russia ostensibly in support of Korean independence, they realized, could, after the war, be turned against Korea.[170] For this reason, the editors' calls for cooperation with Japan were accompanied by continued enjoinments for a broad reform movement. Increased national strength was necessary for both a stronger East and possible self-defense against Japan.

During the war, as Japan increasingly interfered in Korean affairs, this unease turned into outright alarm. In a special four-part article, the editors examined the reasons for Koreans' growing anger at Japan, for the first time explicitly questioning the gap between editorial notions of Eastern unity and Japanese actions.[171] From this point on, the Korean-Japanese relationship became the sole focus of discussions of the East, with China and earlier conceptions of a culturally defined East fading into the background. Still clinging to the notion of Eastern unity, the editors argued that if Koreans' rancor continued to grow, it would harm Japanese-Korean relations, leading to a rupture among the countries of the East.[172] In what was to become a common criticism, the editors pointed out the contradictions between Japan's actions and its own public statements. Japan had promised to act as an adviser to the Korean government and to protect its territory and independence — a role appreciated by all Koreans, it noted. But the only activities Koreans could observe, they wrote, were Japan's acquisition of the right to fish off the southern Korean coast, Japan's unilateral initiation of construction on the Seoul-Ŭiju railway, and Japan's control of all of Korea's mountains, rivers, forests, and swamps. Turning Japanese rhetoric against them, they asked, "Does this come from loyal advice [ch'unggo] for good government? Is this what is called a way of protecting territory? Even if you asked a small child to examine this, he would certainly not say that this is the goal of loyal advice or a means of protection."[173] Returning to the theme of peace in the East, the editors completed their series of editorials with a rhetorical question: "Would the protection of peace not be the fortune of the two nations?"[174] Still favoring the notion of a regional unity, the editors had nonetheless begun to note — however reluctantly and subtly — how Japanese imperialism had begun to conflict with their own view of preserving national independence through regional affiliation.

The final expression of disillusionment can be found in the most famous editorial in the newspaper's nearly thirteen-year-life span, entitled "Today We Cry out in Lamentation."[175] Published after the Protectorate Treaty was signed in 1905, this issue was distributed free of charge and without the

approval of the Japanese censors, an act that cost Chang Chiyŏn, the editor
in chief and writer of the editorial, three months in jail. The piece was a
reiteration of the nationalist commitment of the paper, its dramatic denun-
ciation of the treaty lifting it into the canon of nationalist writing.[176] Less
prominent in the memory of this editorial, yet equally significant in terms
of the paper's evolving editorial policy, was its expression of betrayal. The
editorial staff's ideals of a potential Eastern solidarity had been shattered by
the establishment of the Protectorate. Now, in what amounted to a self-
confessional lament, the paper sought to make amends for what seemed an
overly naïve position. Itō, once welcomed, was now villified. In an opening
salvo, it charged Itō with deceiving the Korean people with his promotion
of peace for the East and his advice for solidifying the nation's independence.
"Everybody from the ports up to the capital, from the officials down to the
people could not help but welcome him." Switching to the current dilemma, the paper admitted that

> in the affairs of the world, there are many that are difficult to predict.
> Where do these five clauses [the 1905 Protectorate Treaty] come from?
> This treaty not only destroys [*mang*] our nation, but it also is truly a
> sign of the splitting asunder of the three nations of the East. Where
> are Viscount Itō's original ideas?

Only after expressing its dismay at the collapse — the "splitting asunder" —
of the paper's long-standing notion of Eastern unity, its consequences for
Korean sovereignty, and Itō's duplicitous role did it turn its invective toward
the Korean officials that had traitorously "given over to others our four-
thousand-year-old territory and five-hundred-year-old ancestral altars, forcing
the 20 million spirits [of our people] into becoming the slaves of another."
This piece marked the end of the *Hwangsŏng sinmun*'s active promotion of
a loose alliance in the East. The uncertainty about Japan's amenability to
support Korean independence had always raised questions about the possibility of its vision of an alliance. Now faced with Japan's steadily growing
encroachments on Korean territory, culminating in the five-clause treaty of
1905, these hopes were dashed.[177]

This did not mean, however, that notions of the East and the category of
yellow people disappeared from the pages of the paper. As fundamental
categories for thinking about the world, the East-West / yellow-white dichotomy continued to structure many editorials dealing with the interna-

tional order, whether globally or regionally.[178] For the editors, it remained
the "major competition" in an era marked by struggle, one that superseded
the "minor competition" among nations.[179] Several years after the Russo-
Japanese War and the imposition of the Protectorate, they could still write
that when Russia's ambitions had threatened the entire East, Japan alone
had risen up to block its southward expansion. Now the worry was whether
Russian ambitions might be revived or whether the United States might take
over Russia's role as the dominant white player in the East.[180] All of Korea's
difficulties with Japan could not shake their belief that the threat of the
white peoples remained preeminent. The dilemma for the editors was how
to reconcile this historic vision of an East-West struggle with the contemporary reality that it was a fellow Eastern nation that presented the most
immediate threat to their sovereignty. The solution was to transform their
vision for the region into the basis for one of the more unusual critiques of
Japanese policies in the period.

The critique was accompanied by a more direct attack on Japanese policies, an attack conducted under the watchful eyes of Japanese censors. Itō
bore the brunt of these sallies. In one case an entire two-part editorial on
the newly appointed resident general was censored.[181] Nevertheless, these
editorials often contained a deepened sense of the earlier unease about Japan, only now it expanded into a self-righteous reproof of Japan's infidelity
to the region. Because of this growingly critical stance, the *Hwangsŏng sinmun* was forced to defend itself against accusations, leveled by the resident
Japanese press, of harboring and inciting anti-Japanese sentiment.[182] But
what, in fact, underlay this criticism, the editors freely admitted, was an
admission — anathema to other nationalist groups — that Koreans could not
unilaterally safeguard their independence. Even if Korea could expel Japan,
they argued, it could not subsequently maintain its own sovereignty. Ultimately, this pessimistic self-evaluation led the editors to maintain their commitment to the East as a means for saving the nation. As they saw the state of
affairs, "It is the natural logic of the situation for both parties to solidify their
unity."[183] For this position, some nationalists labeled the paper as pro-
Japanese, another accusation the editors repeatedly denied, defending themselves in part by attacking others as pro-Japanese. Criticized by both the
supporters of Japanese colonial interests and the anti-Japanese nationalists,
the *Hwangsŏng sinmun* struggled to establish a middle ground.

The term the editors used for unity (*kyŏrhap*) deliberately differed from
the expression for outright annexation (*pyŏnghap*) used by certain segments

of the Japanese media and Korean collaborationist groups such as the Il-chinhoe.[184] The *Hwangsŏng sinmun* adamantly opposed any suggestion that Korea be amalgamated into the Japanese empire, devoting considerable space to excoriating and ridiculing the "followers and flatterers of Japan," a strategy no doubt also intended to assure readers of the distinctiveness of their political position.[185] They even challenged the very Koreanness of these "flatterers": "Their bodies, though Korean, carry the blood of another type in their chests. Their faces, though Korean, harbor the spirit of a foreign country in their countless bones."[186] These were the types who, if the Japanese told them, "Be a cow," then they would become cows and till Japanese fields; if they told them "Be a horse," then they would become horses and wear a Japanese yoke.[187] The Ilchinhoe was a common target of the editors' invective, and they consciously distanced themselves from its policies. When the Ilchinhoe issued its notorious letter in 1909 urging that Korea become part of the Japanese empire, the paper called for the suppression of the organization.[188] Instead, as distinguished from annexation, *kyŏrhap* offered a possibility for critique, since as the editors repeatedly insisted, misguided Japanese policies regularly undermined the the potential for solidarity necessary between the two countries at this critical historical juncture. In short, as articulated in the *Hwangsŏng sinmun*, Pan-Asianism was delicately turned against Japan.

This critique targeted both high officials as well as the immigrants that made up the bulk of the Japanese resident community. When in October 1908 Itō made a speech explaining that Korean trust was necessary for the successful implementation of his policies, the paper retorted that distrust stemmed from the double standards of Japanese policy. Despite all the Japanese statements about harmony and cooperative work, how was it that the leaders were "solely concerned with the livelihood of Japanese people and disproportionately assisted them, whereas the livelihood of the Korean people is completely overlooked and they happily watch as we wander about to our deaths?"[189] It was not as Itō assumed, the editors argued, that a preexisting animosity by Koreans toward Japan interfered with his designs but, rather, that the Japanese policies themselves were engendering doubts and suspicions. Only if Japan sincerely pursued its announced goals of protection, leadership, enrichment, and cultivation of Korea's strength did they believe that these suspicions would cease.

The paper also turned its sights on the behavior of the "low-level" (*had-ŭng*) Japanese migrants, as the paper referred to many members of the Japanese resident community. Reports of improper behavior — the Japanese man who robbed two travelers of more than thirty wŏn on the outskirts of Seoul, to cite just one instance — regularly appeared in the news section.[190] Such people, they argued, needed to be controlled by the authorities. The activities of this minority made Koreans resentful and "despise everything Japanese."[191] Given the censorship laws, it was more common for the *Hwangsŏng sinmun* to offer more oblique criticism. Juxtaposing selfish with common interests was a useful technique in which the common was equated with the East and the selfish was linked to current Japanese policies.[192] Any actions or policy that favored Japanese interests undermined the common-weal. "We Eastern people must abandon our selfish ambitions of the moment and direct our thoughts to a program of mutually protecting the people of the same stock."[193]

That such policies led to anti-Japanese sentiment among the Korean populace was a special concern to the editors — so much so that they took upon themselves the task of discrediting various types of misinformation about Japan. As early as November 1905, the paper was debunking rumors concerning the celebration of the Japanese emperor's birthday by soldiers stationed in Korea. To be sure, as part of the exuberant celebrations, "booze flowed like the ocean and meats were stacked like mountains." Rumors soon arose, however, claiming that drunken soldiers had burst into Korean homes, in some cases raping women. Reports were coming in that people were now hiding the women of their households. "We do not know where these rumors came from, but they show the ignorance and inferiority of our people." They speculated that these rumors had been deliberately spread to stir up trouble. "Don't believe them even a little bit."[194]

The middle position that the *Hwangsŏng sinmun* tried to establish subjected the paper to attacks not just from zealous pro-Japanese groups but also from other nationalists, who were quick to suggest that the paper was pro-Japanese. In a two-part editorial entitled "A Critique of Easternism," the *Hwangsŏng sinmun*'s major rival, the *TaeHan maeil sinbo*, offered the first major public reproach of Pan-Asianism. The article began with a description of three different types of groups which it collapsed into the single category of "Easternists": those who misunderstood the country, those who fawned on the foreign, and those who were confused and ignorant.[195] It characterized the first group as sharing the belief that the current era was a period of struggle between the East and West, yellow and white peoples, from which only one would emerge victorious — precisely the position of the *Hwangsŏng sinmun*, although it did not mention the paper by name. After briefly identifying the other two groups — characterizing the second as those individuals eager to gain official positions and riches by being obsequious to Japan, and the third as the political chamelions who now wore the colors of the Ilchin-hoe and pro-Japanese officials — most of the piece focused on the first group, an indication that the *TaeHan maeil sinbo* saw this brand of Pan-Asianism, articulated in nationalist terms, as a more serious threat to both the country and its own style of nationalism. The editorial did not challenge the fundamental categories of the East-West / yellow-white dichotomy on which the calls of the *Hwangsŏng sinmun* rested. As with all writing from the period, these were taken for granted. Instead, it was the relationship between nation and region that the *TaeHan maeil sinbo* questioned.

Admitting that some time in the future, the struggle might be between the East and West, the editors insisted that the nation's current struggle was more pressing. Satirizing Easternism as being like a person who contemplates the day when the whole planet will be united in the face of a threat from alien life-forms, they asked, "How can one foolishly dream of a matter that might occur in a thousand or ten thousand years and resist the state of affairs that is right in front of your eyes?"[196] The favorite metaphor of the *Hwangsŏng sinmun* was turned around: "Whether or not a neighborhood is united [*tan'gyŏl*] has little bearing on the rise and fall of my own home."[197] In the end, the condemnation of Easternism rested on its perceived acquiescence to Japanese authority over Korea. Notwithstanding its proclaimed nationalist credentials, the *Hwangsŏng sinmun*'s argument was heaped together with all other advocates of Easternism, including the Ilchinhoe. The *TaeHan maeil sinbo* also was not willing to entertain the suggestion that some might advocate Easternism not for the sake of the East itself but merely as a tool for saving the country. To this, it responded, "No Koreans utilize Easternism as a means of saving the country, but some foreigners employ Easternism as a way of stealing the national soul [*kukhon*]. We must beware, we must be careful."[198] This warning ultimately emerged as the most common criticism, one that blurred the distinctions among different types of Pan-Asian thought, lumping them altogether as supportive of Japanese preponderance. Ironically, this critique, as much as Japanese colonialist perspectives, skewed the political spectrum to its two extremes: either one acceded to Japanese power, or one opposed it. Those, like the staff of the *Hwangsŏng sinmun*, who tried to establish, however tentative, a middle ground between these two ends, were given little room to maneuver by either the colonial authorities or their nationalist contemporaries.

The Pan-Asianism of the *Hwangsŏng sinmun* was just one of the many ways that notions of the East were presented during these years. Even for its critics, the East remained an important unit of analysis, as almost everyone in these years in one way or another appealed to that most slippery of phrases, "the peace of the East" (*Tongyang chi hwap'yŏng*). What such expressions concealed, however, were the differences in interpreting the nation's relation to the region. For Japanese colonialists, "the peace of the East" could be used to undermine Korean sovereignty, with regional security interests as defined by Tokyo rationalizing annexation as the best course for regional stability. Yet this same phrase could also be used by the most ardent of Korean nationalists, as seen in the case of An Chunggŭn, who cited the "peace of the East" in explaining his reasons for gunning down Itō Hirobumi, one of the most frequent users of this very expression, for his role in establishing the Protectorate.[199] Positioned between these two poles, the Pan-Asianism of the *Hwangsŏng sinmun*, in which "peace of the East" was a means of advocating solidarity, became untenable.[200] In this way, although the East served a number of shifting purposes for the editors of the *Hwangsŏng sinmun* — universalizing *munmyŏng kaehwa* as well as redefining a cultural regionalism away from China to a Pan-Asianism centering on Japan — their attempt to stake out a middle ground was ultimately undermined by the polarizing effect of Japanese colonialism. Growing Japanese aggression in the peninsula skewed the Korean political spectrum, rendering not only political positions but also various forms of national self-definition less amenable to nationalist uses.

3 Engaging a Civilizing Japan

The new way of destroying countries is achieved through the shared principles of progress and change.
— *Hwangsŏng sinmun,* May 4, 1907

Korean writers at the turn of the century were often frustrated by the lack of information so central to nationalist movements: accurate statistical data. As the editors of the *Tongnip sinmun* complained, people could only guess at the total population of the country. Estimates varied wildly, they reported, from as few as 5 million to as many as 20 million people.[1] In 1908, the editors of *Sŏbuk hakhoe wŏlbo* carried this concern over to the question of the peninsula's natural resources. But besides bemoaning the dearth of records tallying the nation's wealth, they admitted that there was one solution, what they called "risking the shame of learning about one's own national affairs from foreigners." By turning to a book entitled *The Wealth of Korea,* produced by Takahashi Hidemitsu from surveys conducted by the Resident General Office and the Ministry of Agriculture, Commerce, and Industry, the editors were able to inform their readers that on an average per capita basis, Koreans held assets worth about 200 *wŏn.*[2]

As humiliating as it might be perceived by some, turning to Japanese books was quickly becoming routine in the last years of the Chosŏn dynasty. One observer noted that the number of Koreans going to Japanese bookstores in Seoul was increasing by the day, and many were even going directly to Tokyo and Osaka to buy books.[3] The Korean publishing industry could not keep up with the need for translated works.[4] Even old Korean histories, such as the *Tongguk t'onggam (The Comprehensive Mirror of the Eastern Kingdom),* were easier to buy in Tokyo than in the Korean capital.[5] While this rush for Japanese books, in the eyes of this observer, was somewhat of a boon for the level of Korean "civilization," it came with certain risks, and not just to the domestic publishing industry. Describing the period as one when Japanese power in the peninsula was expanding while the Korean spirit was flagging, he warned that reading only Japanese books hazarded developing a "slavish tendency for venerating Japan."[6]

The dilemma was more than just a question of accurate data. It reflected one of the difficulties confronting nationalist intellectuals in colonial settings around the world: how to deal with knowledge about their home country developed in the colonial metropole. The production of national knowledge may have been a central function of the nationalist movement, but so too was knowledge of that country integral to the colonial enterprise. Just like any other forms of knowledge, Japanese understandings of Korea could be conveyed to the peninsula for the consumption of Koreans.

To be sure, Korean nationalism and Japanese colonialism had diametrically opposed political goals, but some of their aesthetic strategies and economic reform efforts must be seen in world historical terms as driven by a complementary endorsement of capitalist modernity. Because of this common commitment and intellectual pedigree, underneath the call for independence and injunction for colonization, Korean nationalists and Japanese colonialists shared much in the way of conceptual vocabulary, themes in cultural representation, and narrative strategies. It was precisely their rootedness in the same range of modern discourses that led nationalists and colonialists to represent Korean culture in very similar ways, a congruency that eventually jeopardized the nationalist meanings of some of these shared representations.

For Korean nationalists, *munmyŏng kaehwa* seemed to offer a means of ensuring their participation in the global ecumene in the same conceptual terms and on equal footing with the powers — if only the reform project they sponsored could be carried out effectively. However, as quickly became apparent after 1905, Japanese uses of these same principles of development and modernity made it all the easier for colonial authorities to co-opt certain types of cultural representation that Koreans had been mobilizing for nationalist purposes before 1905. As can be seen in treatments of the *yangban* as well as the concept of *sadaejuŭi*, the power of Japanese colonialism in this realm of national definition and representation challenged the viability of nationalist self-critiques, even threatening to render them part of colonial ideology. *Munmyŏng kaehwa* threatened to destroy rather than save the nation, as it had earlier seemed to promise. But by the time Korean writers realized the double nature of *munmyŏng kaehwa*, they had so deeply embedded their knowledge of the nation and their own self-definition as leaders of the nationalist movement in its framework that, despite their alarm, they had difficulty extricating themselves from the civilizing logic.

The Authority of Japan

In the eyes of many Koreans, the Sino-Japanese War had validated both symbolically and, in its very real demonstration of Japanese power, the steps taken in Japan to reform its polity. The ideological foundation of this reform program, *bunmei kaika*— "civilization and enlightenment" — was the very same set of ideological principles that in their Korean rendition —*munmyŏng kaehwa*— was being actively promoted by nationalist intellectuals as a panacea for Korea. As a result, Japan's victory confirmed the ideological underpinnings of the Korean nationalist movement and granted to Japan a certain authority to speak on those issues of "civilization and enlightenment" that had become so central to Korean nationalists.

It had not always been this way. During the Chosŏn dynasty, the Confucian elite had largely disparaged Japan as a country of lesser learning. What is striking is how little attention was paid to Japan in the first half of the Chosŏn dynasty. The Imjin wars, when Japan twice invaded Korea in the last decade of the sixteenth century, heightened scholarly interest in Japan. Afterward, as Ha Ubong has shown, memories of the war lingered, giving impressions of Japan a distinctly militarist bent.[7] This was depicted in a handbook of morality, *Tongguk sinsok samgang haengsilto* (*Illustrated Manual on the Conduct of the Three Relations in the Eastern Kingdom*), commissioned in 1614 to promote various forms of proper conduct, in which the illustrations in the section on virtuous women featured Japanese marauders hacking resistant women into pieces.[8] Few works captured so powerfully the double image of Japan in the late Chosŏn dynasty as uncultured and violent.

From the time the newly established Meiji government dispatched a mission to the peninsula to announce the 1868 restoration of the emperor, Japan had in various ways been connected with the West in the eyes of Korean observers. At first, this association was hardly positive. Adamant isolationists such as the fiery Confucian Ch'oe Ikhyŏn castigated their opponents for contemplating a new relationship with Japan, contending that "the Japanese and the Westerners are one and the same."[9] The similarity in clothes and

hairstyles of early Japanese envoys to those of Westerners was sufficient for
the likes of Ch'oe to extend his opprobrium. But as the exchanges with Japan
deepened over the remainder of the nineteenth century, the relationship
between Japan and the West became a subject of much investigation for
those Koreans intrigued by the possibilities of the "new knowledge" (sinhak).
Would-be reformers turned Ch'oe's reductive formula on its head, seeing
the positive in those haircuts and smoking jackets and pondering their relevance to what, by the 1880s, was already an evidently stronger and richer
Japan. Some, such as Kim Okkyun, a reformer turned revolutionary who,
with Japanese backing, managed for three days in 1884 to overthrow his
government, looked across the Eastern Sea for inspiration. But Kim and his
co-conspirators were a minuscule portion of the intellectual elite, let alone
the overall population, and had no forum in which to advance their program.
Kim's premature gambit for power heightened the court's suspicion of Japan,
making reform from within its ranks all the more difficult. Although in the
economic realm, ties continued to deepen, looking to Japan as a source of
motivation for reform had become politically risky for individuals, a point
publicly made by the government in 1893, when one of its own officials
lured Kim Okkyun out of his Japanese exile to Shanghai, where he was
promptly assassinated.[10]

The political environment changed with the Tonghak peasant uprisings
and the subsequent defeat of China by Japan. By 1895, hostility to Japan at
the court had been temporarily sidelined, and organized opposition in the
countryside had been suppressed with defeat of the Tonghak peasant armies.
In the capital, the first in a succession of reform cabinets was established
with the backing of a now preponderant Japan. Including members such as
Kim Hongjip implicated in the 1884 coup d'état, the cabinet launched the
massive Kabo reform program, aimed at renovating the country's finances,
overturning the social order, and reforming governing institutions. It became
once again possible to raise Japan as a hortatory example. With the rise of a
new press in 1896, such efforts moved out of the privacy of the reformers'
homes into the much more visible site of newspaper editorials.

One consequence of histories that focus on tracing the confrontation
between the rising Japanese imperialism and the burgeoning Korean nationalism is that they overshadow the extensive intellectual interaction between Japanese and Koreans. The political contest over the future sovereignty of the peninsula has been seen as carried out by two discrete and
exclusive entities, the colonized and the colonizer, an approach that, in

highlighting the oppositional character of the contest, tends to conceal the substantial resonance between colonial and nationalist thought. There was, in fact, a great deal of interaction and overlap between the two, even before 1905 — exchanges made all the easier because both structured their respective political projects around "civilization and enlightenment." This exchange and overlap, in turn, affected the political contest, showing how the form and content of national knowledge were deeply rooted in the structures of power underlying Japanese colonialism. Indeed, the power of colonialism was not simply the ability to coerce submission but, perhaps more deeply and longer lasting, to shape the very knowledge about their own nation that Koreans developed in these years.

While this may, in part, have been the result of the influence of the powerful Japanese publishing empire, it was also a development following the specific pattern of Japanese colonization. In world historical terms, both Koreans and Japanese were latecomers to the modern knowledge subsumed under the calls for "civilization and enlightenment." Unlike in many colonies of the West, where nationalist ideologies developed in formal colonial settings, in Korea the potential of *munmyŏng kaehwa* was first explored in the years before the imposition of the Protectorate in 1905. For roughly a decade after the conclusion of the Sino-Japanese War in 1895, *munmyŏng kaehwa* seemed to offer the best means of bringing the nation into line with the principles of global capitalist modernity as a way of preserving the sovereignty that had only recently been won. Rueful as their recognition may have been, Korean nationalists acknowledged that the commitment to "new knowledge" developing in Japan, both inside and outside government, was far deeper than in Korea. Exchanges in these areas followed. But the consequences of appropriating what at first appeared to be benign forms of "civilized" information became more apparent by the conclusion of the Russo-Japanese War. The nationalist press had intended to protect the autonomy of the nation, but after 1905, Korean writers faced the dilemma that the knowledge they had worked so hard to produce might, in fact, be facilitating the colonization of the peninsula.

The range of interactions with Japan can be seen in the widespread presence of Japan in the Korean nationalist press, whether they were reports on Japanese reforms, historical features, or the translation of speeches and essays. This presence indicates not only the powerful function of Japan in the formation of East Asian modernities but also the willingness of Korean intellectuals before 1905 to grant Japan this role in the belief that it simultaneously served their own nationalist ends. From the earliest days of the press, the "lessons" of the Sino-Japanese War emerged as a prominent subject of editorial comment. "How could such a small country beat such a large country?" the *Tongnip sinmun* asked. The paper found the answer in Japan's education policies and its understanding of the ways of the West. The result was "out of a one-story wood hut, [Japan] built a three- or four-story brick house."[11] The war provided a study in contrasts: a Japan united in purpose and harmonious versus a China in disarray,[12] a Japan with a committed public bureaucracy versus a China with officials who abused its people,[13] a Japan with mothers who understood how to rear warriors versus a China with a feckless military,[14] and underpinning most of these comparisons, a Japan energized by embracing the "new knowledge" at all levels and a China still clinging to the "old knowledge," where many scholars still stated that "for venerable China, learning from foreign barbarians is a shame."[15] Such comparisons were widely accompanied by a surge in a "How did they do it?" style of writing that dissected the efforts of the Japanese government and the people. Some papers serialized histories of the Meiji program, while others reprinted the famous clauses of the Charter Oath.[16] "In just thirty years of reform" became a stock phrase that at once indicated amazement at the changes in their island neighbor while insinuating that if only Koreans would listen to the enjoinments of these enlightened newspapermen, they could also reach that level in three decades.

By the last year of the nineteenth century, Japan was frequently being equated with the West. It was not catching up but had already caught up. No longer did Japan "lag behind the countries of Europe and America,"[17] since after several decades of change, "its reputation and abilities" ranked alongside those of Europe and America.[18] It had been "accepted" by the West[19] and was "an equal that will never again fall behind."[20] Japan's relations with Western nations were the best testament to its new status, whether it was because in 1898 Japan had successfully renegotiated its unequal treaties with the West[21] or was participating in international conferences.[22] The Japanese handling of pesky Westerners inhabiting their islands also impressed the editors of the *Tongnip sinmun*. At the beginning of 1897, it reported that the German consul in Japan had struck a student, causing such a public outcry that Germany had been forced to apologize officially.[23] Less than one and a half years later, the differing status of Japan and Korea became manifest in the actions of yet another German diplomat, this time one residing in Seoul. When a Korean official from the Foreign Ministry arrived at the

German consulate, he was greeted not with diplomatic courtesy but by an irate consul who physically confronted him, pushed him out the door, and threw ministry documents at his feet. Enraged by what they saw as an insult to the nation, the newspaper's editors could not help but draw a comparison with Japan, concluding that only when the nation was reformed could such shameful abuses be avoided.[24]

The observation that Japan was the equal of the West did not need to be made so explicitly, since the very style of writing about examples of enlightenment often grouped Japan with the West. "Europe, America, and Japan" and "the West and Japan" emerged as standard expressions for the top rungs of the civilizing hierarchy.[25] At times Japan received lead billing, so that the advocacy of a particular reform could begin, "If one looks at Japan and other enlightened countries."[26] Although this particular piece concerned education, such clauses could and were followed by a myriad of examples, spreading across the full range of reforms, such as the improved management of national currency,[27] the advancement of women's education,[28] the dispatch of students overseas at government expense,[29] and its successful promotion of commerce.[30] Even a description of that peculiar modern institution, the zoo, in Tokyo's Ueno Park was deemed deserving of a front-page spot.[31] Firsthand observations by reporters traveling in the islands were reported as lead stories. Letters from students studying in Japan who wrote home about conditions in that country found their way into newspapers.[32] For newspapers struggling to keep their operations financially solvent, the literacy of the Japanese population, together with the high circulation rates of newspapers, was regularly — and wistfully — noted. Newspapers, after all, were for these writers a crucial indicator of a country's level of civilization, a fact they regularly tried to impress on their readers.[33] With thirty-six different papers printed in the morning in Tokyo and distributed by the evening throughout the country, one report explained, newspapers had become part of the social fabric of everyday Japanese life. Everyone — from the emperor and leading officials at the top, down to the average person in factories and farms, children, women, and imprisoned criminals — read the papers. Marveling at this wide readership, it remarked at how even Japanese rickshaw haulers pulled out a newspaper and read by the side of the road when waiting for customers.[34]

Observations of Japan were regularly accompanied by a more direct Japanese presence, such as reprints of speeches made by Japanese experts and translations of editorials from Japanese newspapers. The comments of foreign affairs specialists were approvingly printed as a way of discussing the problems faced by China, one expert explaining the reasons for Italy's attempt to acquire concessions in Zhejiang Province.[35] Visiting Japanese were welcomed to the capital and invited to give speeches. In the *Tongnip sinmun*, Itō Hirobumi's remarks on the importance of such civilizing institutions as universal education — "the basis for building the nation," as he stated — were substituted for the usual editorial.[36] Although women writers appeared only infrequently in newspapers of that time, the *Hwangsŏng sinmun* did print on its front page a short letter from an anonymous Japanese woman extolling the importance of orphanages, citing her donation to a newly opened foundling home as a testament to her commitment.[37] To be sure, editors quoted those speeches and cited examples related to their own concerns. In representing Japan as a success and reprinting the speeches of Japanese specialists, editors borrowed Japanese authority to reinforce points and issues that, in most cases, the editors had already made and were likely to repeat again in the future in another form.

This use of Japan was a strategy that cut across the Korean political spectrum. Almost anyone interested in reform could find something in Japan that could be cited in support of a particular cause or position. Even for those advocating a style of reform Confucianism, Japan could be invoked to make their case. As one writer pointed out, the rush for new learning had led Koreans to abandon their own national inheritance. But in Japan, where the "new learning is as high as anywhere," they could learn the new while maintaining the old. To support his case, the writer noted that Japanese scholars continued to revere the famous Korean Confucian thinker and teacher Yi Toegye, even though in Korea, as he bemoaned, no one studies his works anymore.[38] The authority of Japan was such that it could even be invoked to urge Koreans to embrace more fully their own heritage.

This offered a powerful strategy to garner support for reform in Korea, yet it was not without a certain reservation and ambivalence that writers associated Japan with the highest levels of civilization. Accompanying these representations of a Japan more enlightened than Korea was the memory of an earlier age when these roles were reversed, when in areas as diverse as "Japanese religion, literature, clothing, architecture, medicine, and tools," according to one commentator, Korea had been the teacher.[39] Such writing was more than nostalgia for better times. In their contrasts of a brighter past with a dismal present, these self-critical pieces confirmed just how far the country had slipped, decrying the course of events that led to the current disparity with Japan. One especially galling case was porcelain, since as the editors of the *Hwangsŏng sinmun* claimed, Japan originally had no porcelain of its own, having learned the art from Korean craftsmen. The irony for the editors was that Japanese porcelain was currently displayed in museums and exhibitions around the world, receiving such acclaim that a porcelain industry had arisen with exports reaching 165,000 pieces a year. That Korea was the ancestral home of this art was forgotten, but in their opinion, even more troublesome was the sobering fact that over the years Korean porcelain had lost its luster. "How is it that with the same original roots, Japanese porcelain has thrived, whereas Korean porcelain has receded?"[40] The answer to this question ruefully confirmed Japan's function as a hortatory example: the Japanese nurtured their artisans which, when extended to the national level, explained why they had become rich and strong. Causal theories abounded for the disparity — the inability to promote talent, to maximize the natural resources of the land, or to build an effective education system — but that Japan had waxed while Korea had waned confirmed one of the key suppositions of *munmyŏng kaehwa*: there was nothing essential or fated, nothing due to national character, that underlay the current differences between the two countries. In short, the former status of Korea could once again be achieved. This version of the past ensured that writers could always find refuge in a type of historical disdain for Japan. In the words of the *TaeHan maeil sinbo*, since "Japan is a country that in the past was enlightened by Korea, no matter how awesome its military power, Koreans in their hearts look down at Japanese."[41]

Others combined recollections of Korean superiority with a perfunctory dismissal of the Meiji reforms. This critique stressed that there was nothing special about Japan, since everything it had accomplished came from either the West or Korea. "The material civilization of Japan, which it boasts leads the East, all came with the arrival of Western ships. And what Japan boasts to the world as its own unique culture was all once imported from our country."[42] While its newly gained status offered the best proof that a non-Western nation could in fact climb the hierarchy of civilization, advocates of this style of critique were quick to point out that those things that were most frequently accepted as universal could be made particular to the West as long as they served to denigrate Japanese accomplishments.

This conclusion did not diminish the interest of students in going to Japan. Their numbers rose fourfold, from 187 in 1897 to 739 in 1909.[43] But this was mainly a question of proximity and frugality. Students did not go to

study what they perceived as specifically Japanese forms of knowledge but those truths of enlightenment that they somewhat paradoxically accepted as universal yet Western. Yu Kilchun explained that even though it had taken only thirty years for Japan to build its strength and wealth, eight or nine out of ten of the policies and institutions were little more than imitations of Western styles.[44] Yu was in the first group of foreign students in Japan studying at Fukuzawa Yukichi's Keio Academy and, for a short time, was even billeted in Fukuzawa's house. But this was not enough for Yu.[45] He left Japan for the West to verify "with his own eyes," he explained, what he had learned in Japan, as though he did not quite trust it as genuine.[46] At a later date, other Koreans residents in the United States urged Korean students not to go to Japan but to cross the Pacific. Writing in the early twentieth century, the editor of one overseas Korean newspaper told prospective students that what Japan had learned was only a "shadow" of the Western original. All they could hope to create by studying in Japan, he warned, was "a shadow of a shadow"—so why not travel to the United States, where they could study the original and, at least, form their own "shadow?"[47] In this way, although the blanket assertions about "Europe, America, and Japan" or "the West and Japan" filled the press, suggesting equivalence, the status of Japan was also rendered that of a surrogate, merely a derivative of what had already been achieved elsewhere.

What this overt downplaying of Japan and the emphasis on direct links with the West concealed was the important function of Japan as the primary mediator through which Korean writers learned about the West and its supposed universal civilization. After spending a little more than a year as the first Korean student in the United States, at Governor Dummer Academy outside Salem, Massachusetts, Yu returned to Korea and wrote his famous work *Sŏyu kyŏnmun* (*Observations of a Journey to the West*) that he had printed in 1895. In this widely circulated and highly influential work, his descriptions of the mansion of a New York merchant, Western education systems, the disinclination of "gentlemen" to smoke in front of women, and the variety of governmental forms bore witness to his assertion that the locus of civilization lay in the West. But what was not made explicit to the reader was the book's relation to the seminal Japanese work by Yu's former teacher, Fukuzawa Yukichi, entitled *Seiyō jiji* (*Conditions of the West*). Although the accounts of his journey to the United States, France, Germany, and other countries in *Sŏyu kyŏnmun* were Yu's personal observations, the first four-fifths of the book, which related more general information on topics as vari-

[handwritten margin note: most of Yu's accts based on his former teacher's experiences— yukichi]

ous as the races of the world, the basics of currency, the history of Western religions, and the format of fairs and exhibitions, owed much to Fukuzawa's work.

In a careful comparison of these works, Yi Kwangnin noted that roughly 50 percent of the two main sections of Yu's book were copied directly from the *Seiyō jiji*, sometimes with a few explanations or some elaboration added.[48] Most of the remainder was Yu's own, yet even in these sections the conceptual vocabulary did not veer significantly away from that in Fukuzawa's work. Fukuzawa also had a direct hand in the publication of the work. In Korea at this time, there were no modern printing presses with Korean script capabilities, but such presses did exist in Japan. As Yi Kwangnin has shown, Fukuzawa not only provided Yu with a subvention of 450 yen for the work but also had his publishing house produce the volume.[49] One thousand copies were published, which Yu promptly distributed to high government officials and influential reform advocates. Appearing one year before the establishment of the first newspaper, *Sŏyu kyŏnmun* was the first widely circulated didactic work introducing the West and enlightenment to Korea. It had an immense impact. Often used as the basis for later editorials and essays, *Sŏyu kyŏnmun* became a key reference for explaining the new conceptual vocabulary from abroad.[50] This book on the West with ostensibly no connection to Japan was, in its content and form, shaped by Yu's experience in Japan; indeed, his ties with Japan enabled its very production.

[handwritten margin note: printing press in J not K]

[handwritten margin note: book on West ties to J]

The conceptual vocabulary that Yu used in his work reflected what over the next fifteen years emerged as a shared lexicon for much of East Asia. In Korean newspapers at the turn of the century, one of the primary didactic functions of editorials was defining terms. "What is this thing called money?" began an editorial in the *Cheguk sinmun* in typical fashion for the era.[51] Whether defining currency, international law, or welfare houses, such pieces introduced the new concepts that were to frame the nation and the project of reform within the ideologies of capitalist modernity. Behind these terms, derived from the West, stood the mediating function of Japan, where most of these neologisms had first been created.[52] If Yu's *Sŏyu kyŏnmun* was one source for the dissemination and definition of these terms, so too were Japanese dictionaries. During these years, no modern Korean-language dictionaries had yet been produced. Not until 1920 did the first modern Korean-language dictionary appear. Until that time, however, anyone wanting to understand new terms could purchase a Korean-Japanese dictionary at most Seoul bookstores.[53] It was through these types of reference works that writers

[handwritten margin note: no K dictionary]

were literally coming to terms with the new international order and notions of enlightenment. This was true even of the two main editors of the *Tongnip sinmun*, Philip Jaisohn and Yun Ch'iho, who had the rare opportunity to spend more time in the United States as students than in Japan. Despite its editors' direct access to the West, its status as the first newspaper in Korea, and its position as the first to abandon the use of characters, the *Tongnip sinmun*'s calls for reform were not expressed through its own idiosyncratic neologisms but were lexically little different from what was appearing in newspapers in Japan or China.[54]

The remarkable consistency in the formation of a shared vocabulary for nationalist reformers across East Asia had much to do with the growth of newspapers in all three countries at the end of the nineteenth century.[55] Indeed, it is arguable that a transnational newspaper culture, centered in Japan, emerged. Key to this newspaper realm was the shared use of characters in all these countries, enabling translated concepts to be immediately incorporated by writers across the region. For Korea, this was certainly ironic, since this was precisely the historical moment when Koreans were calling for the expurgation of characters as a premise for establishing an authentic national culture. Yet these new terms, rooted in characters, were now shaping conceptions of the nation. This common newspaper culture also depended on the regular exchange of newspapers across national boundaries. As Chŏng Chin-sok has argued, few newspapers could afford to send correspondents to cover news in their neighboring countries. It was far cheaper to subscribe to foreign newspapers and to reprint, whether attributed or not, stories from that paper.[56] This was especially necessary when Western wire services did not carry the detailed coverage of Asian affairs that editors wished to pass on to their readers.[57] In Korea, papers regularly quoted and sometimes engaged in heated arguments with their counterparts from around the region. From China came the *Zhongxi ribao* and *Wanguo gongbao*, and from Japan came the *Tōkyō Asahi shimbun*,[58] *Jiji shimbun*,[59] *Ōsaka Mainichi shimbun*,[60] *Nichinichi shimbun*,[61] *Taiyō*,[62] and *Yorozo chōhō*,[63] among others. On the peninsula, the Japanese resident press was always ready for an editorial debate with its Korean counterparts, particularly in the cases of the Seoul-based *Kanjō shimpo* and the Inchon-based *Chōsen shimpo*.[64] The *Qingyibao*, published in Japan by the exiled Liang Qichao, had an especially wide readership, with two distribution offices on the peninsula, one in Seoul and one in Inchon. The *Qingyibao* reached out to many of Liang's contemporaries, particularly those transitional elites who were trained in the classics but were now struggling with new forms of knowledge. Like so much of his other writing, Liang's pieces in the *Qingyibao* were often précis of Japanese articles. They had immense influence in Korea, where they were frequently translated in journals and further circulated in a multivolume collection of selected works.[65]

Only rarely did a newspaper bring the otherwise transparent process of translation to the attention of their readers. Even rarer was the choice of a specific term challenged. One letter writer to the *TaeHan maeil sinbo* did just that, however, questioning the Japanese neologism for "protectorate." In Japanese, what had been rendered *hogokoku* or, in Korean, *pohoguk*, was a two-character expression consisting of "protect" and "nation," implying that the object being protected by foreign rule was the nation itself. He argued this term had been deliberately chosen so as to conceal the true nature of Japan's actions.[66] Despite this challenge, the paper continued to use the term, indicating how difficult it had become to move outside this powerful shared lexicon even with a critical understanding. Thus, as a consequence of these interactions, the conceptual vocabulary of the modern Korean nation was fashioned by this shared East Asian lexicon. The fact that Korean editors could decide to incorporate a Japanese speech or essay into their own newspapers reflects the degree of lexical commensurability between their nationalist project and the reform endeavors undertaken in Japan. With a shared vocabulary and working within the common framework of *munmyŏng kaehwa*, Korean and Japanese reform intellectuals spoke the same language.

That these terms were shared, however, does not mean that they were always equivalent. In their didactic function of explaining these neologisms, newspapers regularly returned these universal terms to a national context, often pushing the nuances and uses of a term in new and unusual directions.[67] Indeed, part of the contest between colonialists and nationalists was over the meaning of this shared vocabulary, as each tried to define the terms in ways that would buttress their conflicting political goals. The struggle between nationalism and colonialism was often one of definition.

A Nationalist Dialogue

Interactions with Japan were not restricted to the possibilities of the "new knowledge" and the exchange of vocabulary. The same Meiji publications from which editors extracted commentary and news reports also carried a wide variety of articles about Korea. The peninsula was headline news in these years, as Japan's political and economic interests became deeply enmeshed with Korea's fortunes. Much recent scholarship has shown how European powers built their empires not only with superior weapons and elaborate administrative infrastructures but also with the efforts of experts and nonspecialists whose knowledge of the colonies both enabled and supported the construction and maintenance of metropolitan rule.[68] Similarly, the growing presence of Japan on the peninsula provided opportunities and stimulated new endeavors to investigate and write about Korea.

Just as Korean newspapers were producing knowledge about Korea as part of their nationalist commitment, so was knowledge about the peninsula integral to the growing Japanese dominance. Featured in the same newspapers and intellectual journals as the other expert Japanese opinions used by Korean editors, these articles were also grounded in the universals of "civilization and enlightenment," only now these concepts and terms were being applied to Korea. These pieces used Korea as an illustration for further articulating the principles of civilization, and conversely, these principles were used to frame public representations of Korea. At times, especially before 1905, these Japanese writings about Korea were often cited by Korean writers as outside authorities to confirm their own judgments and arguments. But around 1905, it became increasingly clear to many Koreans that Japanese representations of their country were supporting the colonization of their country. Consequently, the principles of civilization that underlay both Korean and Japanese writing — principles that had enabled the earlier interchange — began to be viewed with growing cynicism.

Japanese writing on Korea could be put to good effect by Korean newspapers. An editorial in the *TaeHan maeil sinbo* in 1907 captured one common way in which Japanese authority on civilization as expressed vis-à-vis Korea could be used by Korean writers. Written as a fictitious conversation between a Korean and his close Japanese friend, the editors granted the Japanese figure the enlightened ability to discern the reasons for Korea's plight. The piece begins with the Korean character asking his friend why Japan has trampled over the rights of Koreans, leaving them "hardly a spot to make a living," especially since in the past Japan had announced to the world that it supported Korean independence. "This is what the Russians have done to the Polish and what the French have done to Vietnam," the Korean accuses, "How could you have so profoundly abandoned humanitarian ways [*indo*]?" The Japanese companion immediately responds that his interlocutor has missed the crux of the dilemma: "People must first humiliate themselves before others can humiliate them. A country must destroy itself before others can destroy it." He follows up on the offered historical analogies, arguing that Poland and Vietnam caused their own ruin, just as Korea was currently doing. Shifting to his diagnosis of Korea's situation, he focuses first on the holders of power. The people in office "know only themselves, not the country; know only their families, not the people" he begins, and because of their fear of Japan, there was "not a single right they were unwilling to hand over." Moving on to satirize the Confucian elite (*sarim*), the Japanese points out that all they do is read old books and dismiss newspapers as heterodox. Finally, taking a broader look at society, he criticizes the people for being willing to sell their homes and lands to foreigners. He concludes, "You cannot turn your anger against others but must reflect on yourselves." In this exchange, the Korean figure is not so much upbraided than taught by the Japanese figure that the dilemma of his nation is internal, one that cannot be resolved by blaming others. The Japanese figure's voice is that of an astute adviser, aware of the ways of the world and able to recommend the proper ways of extricating the nation from its predicament.

In contrast, the Korean figure is depicted as less worldly. His response is to sigh deeply and maintain a long silence as he contemplates these remarks, as though they came as a surprise. Finally, he admits that there were indeed self-inflicted reasons for Korea's predicament. But despite granting the Japanese figure authority over matters of enlightenment, the editors reserve for the Korean character a superior moral sensibility. With his final parry, the Korean figure counters his Japanese friend's attempt to rest the blame solely on Korea. He states, "It is not only a question of our country but also a question of your country . . . [because Japan is] seeking petty profits and has abandoned a deep sense of what is right." At this point, it is the turn of the Japanese figure to sigh and wipe away his tears in what amounts to the ultimate redemption of the deeper meaning of the otherwise hapless Korean character.

The effect of this dialogue was to present two different views, when in fact both voices were that of the editor. To a regular reader of the *TaeHan maeil sinbo*, there was little new in what the Japanese character had to say about Korea: the selling of land had been a controversial issue since the early days of the *Tongnip sinmun*; criticism of officeholders and concession politics was a mainstay of editorial writers; denunciations of conservative elites were a favorite of progressives; and the analogies of Poland and Vietnam had been widely bandied about in the type of comparative history that could slide past Japanese censors. Yet assuming a Japanese voice at a time when Japan was widely seen as having accomplished what Koreans wished to do was an effective rhetorical technique for acquiring more authority for arguments already made in the past and to be repeated in the future. The Korean character, with his assent to the gist of the Japanese character's position, both reflected and affirmed this authority and the logic of his analysis. But just as important, the Japanese companion was used to show that Japanese authority over matters of enlightenment did not necessarily transfer to a parallel ethical authority, an authority allocated to the Korean figure who could castigate Japan for the impropriety of its interference with Korean sovereignty.

To conclude the piece, the editors assumed their own voice to address the reader directly. Noting that the conversation had served "to awaken these two gentlemen," they explained that they printed the piece in the hope it would have a similar, wider impact.[69] Regardless of this one editorial's effect, the two voices captured the ways that the *TaeHan maeil sinbo* and other papers employed Japanese writing and speeches about Korea. As in the dialogue, certain Japanese were granted the authority to speak on Korean matters, and Korean readers were advised to heed their words. Whether in the voice of a fictional character or in the reproduction of a real Japanese speech, it was the editors' decision to deploy Japanese authority to support the reforms of their own choice. Editors of the *Hwangsŏng sinmun* urged Korean capitalists to pay careful attention to the speech by the consultant to the Kyūshū Enterprise Group, entitled "The Wealth of the Country Lies in the Wealth of the People," in which he offered paths that Koreans could follow to richness and strength while pointing out weaknesses in the nation's trade infrastructure and financial institutions.[70] A Japanese expert's essay on Korea's finances stressed frugality for the state at a time of reform when matters such as hiring foreign advisers put a strain on financial resources: expenditures must meet revenues, he urged, so that debt is not incurred.[71] An official from the Japanese Daiichi Bank was interviewed about the Korean currency over six issues.[72] Summaries of essays written about Korea by Japanese travelers who ventured on inspection tours also were printed, as in the case of Matsumiya Haruichirō, whose critique of the Korean government, especially the power of translators, appeared in the *Hwangsŏng sinmun*.[73] Again, these pieces were carefully selected to fit the particular points the editors chose to make, largely concerning those "civilized" reforms in which Japan had been so successful that individual Japanese had earned the authority to speak or write on such matters to a Korean audience about Korean affairs.

Beyond these areas of supposed universal expertise, however, Korean writers did not hesitate to challenge Japanese views. Replicating the function of the Korean character in the dialogue, editors could easily assume the moral imperative to condemn Japanese views. Just as commonly, Japanese commentaries were reprinted so as to set them up as targets for scathing criticism. The *Tongnip sinmun* took issue with a Japanese newspaper's characterization of Koreans as intemperate and unable to sense humiliation.[74] More typically, Japanese suggestions of the possible diminution of Korean rights received anything but a welcoming response. Well before 1905 and before being subject to Japanese censorship, the *Hwangsŏng sinmun* reprinted Japanese criticisms of the Meiji government for not being sufficiently aggressive on the peninsula. The next day it followed with a long list of powers already wrested away from the Korean government: Japan, it asked, has "taken over more than half of Korea's important powers — how is this not enough?"[75] The Japanese-language press in Korea, often far more jingoistic than its counterparts on the home islands, frequently became the object of scorn. The *Hwangsŏng sinmun* scolded the *Kanjō shimpo* for urging censorship of Korean-language papers, lecturing its Japanese counterpart that diversity of opinion and debate were essential to freedom and progress.[76] Like writers in other colonial settings, these writers trod a careful line, granting Japan an authoritative function in their own attempts to use *munmyŏng kaehwa* to frame the nation while resisting any implications that reform in the name of enlightenment and as recommended by these outside observers might undermine their own nationalist goal — full sovereignty.

This dilemma worsened as Japanese actions on the peninsula became more aggressive, showing *munmyŏng kaehwa* as able to support both nationalizing and colonizing projects. The double nature of *munmyŏng kaehwa* had always been apparent to Korean writers. But as intellectuals who saw themselves belonging to the forces of progress in Korea, it had not always been apparent that the notions of civilization in which they framed their conceptions of the nation would actually be used to rationalize its usurpation. The press's treatment of worldwide colonialism before 1905 reflected this disassociation. Although some sympathy was expressed for the aspirations of colonial peoples to free themselves of external rule, colonialism per se did not emerge as a target of criticism. Indeed, the opposite held: writers tended to identify with the claims of the imperialist powers to be spreading "civilization," a goal that they saw as part of the same historical processes that were shaping their own enterprises in Korea. The *Tongnip sinmun*, with its Anglophile tendencies, repeatedly praised Britain for a wide variety of accomplishments, among which was always listed its expansion of empire.[77] On the occasion of Queen Victoria's sixtieth year of reign, it marveled at the immense advancements during that time, pointing to the fact that Britain now controlled 27 percent of the world's total area. "Every year its national flag is raised over barbarous countries and now is even in Africa." Without any hint of the inherent incongruity, the *Tongnip sinmun* commented that Britain was the teacher of freedom for the rest of the world.[78] In India, it explained, the British had used the country's rich resources, which, because of internecine disputes, had been allowed to lie idle and go to waste. Only when India became a colony (*sokpang*) of Britain, were its riches properly exploited.[79] The *Tongnip sinmun's* English-language edition spoke more generally of the link among the West, civilization, and colonialism. "History tells us that wherever Western civilization has made its appearance, the place was transformed into a new country altogether . . . many places of the tropical coasts of India and Africa have been changed into abodes of some of the most enlightened races of man."[80]

Although not in the same category as Britain, the nascent Japanese empire also received the plaudits of the *Tongnip sinmun* and other papers. Specifically, they admired the amount of capital and manpower Japan was investing in civilizing endeavors in Taiwan, the island "stolen from China."[81] The *Cheguk sinmun* devoted an entire editorial to the finances of the Japanese project in Taiwan, recording the enormous expenditures on schools and sanitation and the encouragement of commerce and agriculture.[82] This admiration was extended to Japan's internal colonization of the Ainu, who were repeatedly treated with scorn. The editors of the *TaeHan maeil sinmun* regularly held up — with little sympathy — the Ainu as a counterexample of what happened to a people who did not reform.[83]

Known for its nationalist editorial policy, the *TaeHan maeil sinbo's* attitude toward colonialism was ambivalent. In an editorial published during the Russo-Japanese War, the paper took up what was to become a common and much debated comparative case of colonialism, the British rule of Egypt.[84] The piece set out to measure British colonial practices in Egypt against Japanese involvement in Korea, two cases that it concluded were somewhat similar but ultimately were incommensurate. This appraisal did not rest on the fact that Japan had not yet annexed Korea formally but centered on the paper's view of the comparative benefits of colonialism. In Egypt, the British had invested immense capital, built up the infrastructure, and transformed a country that had been poor into one "just as rich as India." Crucial to the paper's argument was the belief that these advancements had been for the benefit of the people. In this way, the *TaeHan maeil sinbo* linked colonialism to development, leading it to condone British rule in India and Egypt. This same logic had the paper dismissing a comparison with Japan's actions in Korea, for the Japanese were neither developing Korea nor pursuing any policies for the benefit of the people. As it concluded, "Japan says that it will modernize Korea, but it is clear that it will work for the benefit of its own country." This distinction, more than any ideological opposition to colonialism itself, had the paper at this stage rejecting the legitimacy of Japanese rule. At a later date, the editor expressed his amazement when looking at a world map at the ability of certain strong countries to spread their rule around the globe. Writing in 1909, well into the Protectorate period, the editor's point in mentioning these empires was not to question their morality or legitimacy. Rather, in a statement reflecting the powerful logic of the civilizing endeavor, he wondered when Korea would be able to establish its own realm around the world.[85]

Such comparisons were nevertheless tempered by a warning. It might be proper, in the case of Britain's occupation of India, that idle resources were finally used, but the example was a cautionary tale designed to incite Koreans into properly exploiting the peninsula's riches before a country like Britain could come along and do the same to Korea.[86] They could commiserate with colonial peoples, wishing that people like the Filipinos could reform themselves as an independent nation, but again never questioning the priority they granted to *munmyŏng kaehwa*.[87] For readers, a list of all the colonies in the world, "covering two-thirds of the globe territory," could be enumerated, emphasizing the ability of Europe, "the smallest continent," to conquer all these countries and contrasting Western abilities with the "ignorance and weakness" of the colonies.[88]

As Japan extended its reach into peninsular affairs, however, faith in notions of "civilization and enlightenment" was replaced with cynicism as writers became aware that Korea's lot would more likely rest with the colonized than the colonizing. There had always been some doubt about the claims of the powers to be both civilized and civilizing, a skepticism that owed much to social Darwinism. But now the earlier cynicism came to be more widely and, in some cases, more vehemently expressed in a steady stream of pieces satirizing Japan's civilizing claims.[89] Because of its experiences with the Japanese censor, the *Hwangsŏng sinmun* was forced to employ indirect, but nonetheless effective, means. In a four-day serialized editorial published in 1907, "The New Ways of Destroying Countries" (Myŏlguk sinbŏmnon),[90] past and recent tactics of vanquishing countries were compared. Whereas in earlier days, one court might replace another court, as Koryŏ (A.D. 918–1392) replaced Silla (57 B.C.–A.D. 935), and Chosŏn replaced Koryŏ, the country itself was never obliterated. Today, it warned, the country was not the property of a single person or family, so destroying the country now would mean not replacing the court but destroying the people. Such a method might be much slower but would be possible through the use of techniques like advancing loans, providing replacement soldiers, appointing advisers, stirring up factional strife, or constructing roads. Parodying the rhetoric of the Resident General Office without actually naming it, the editorial elaborated:

> [When a] civilized country is extinguishing your country, it must say, "I am reforming your politics," as an excuse for interfering in your internal affairs; it must say, "I am rectifying your currency," as a verbal cover for grasping control of your finances, or it falsely invokes threats to the public order in order to restrict your right to expression, or claim to be repressing internal disorder . . . or it moves its own country's people [into your country] to exploit your resources, or it secretly stirs up unreliable and shameless followers to serve as its leading puppets, or it establishes educational organs aimed at making the people ignorant.

Although the editorial discussed in detail the history of such techniques in Poland, Egypt, India, and Persia, it did not extend the discussion to Korea itself. Instead, it merely asked who was "to blame for Korea's fall." The answer to this question, after all the attention to the problems created by the new forms of colonization, could be found by turning inward: "The first reason is our own fault. The second reason is also our own fault." Two years into the Protectorate, during which many of these new methods had been already been deployed in Korea — especially for the editors, the restrictions on the right to expression — the Japanese could not be mentioned. Over the next few years, the paper covered other colonial situations, often using these cases for the opportunity they offered for veiled criticism of Japanese policy. Increasingly, such pieces exhibited a sense of solidarity with other colonized peoples.[91]

The *TaeHan maeil sinbo*, free of the heavy hand of the Japanese censor, could be more direct. Its editors complained that Japanese always talked about how they had to lead the Koreans to advance their civilization. But through the example of a recent loan that had been extended for the purpose of "developing Korean education" and a proposal to use Japanese-language books in the schools, they argued that these policies were little different from methods used by Russia to "swallow" Poland. This was a "hidden poison" that Japan extended at the same time as it claimed to "nurture civilization and develop education" — a tactic, it charged, that "couldn't fool the smallest child."[92]

To be sure, the editors of these two newspapers were not fooled. But to acknowledge and satirize the self-serving uses of *munmyŏng kaehwa* did not translate into its complete disavowal. Korean nationalists could hardly abandon this notion, since it offered the higher conceptual framework in which their reform agenda, fundamental conceptions of the nation, and even their own self-perception as a leading force of change were positioned. *Munmyŏng kaehwa* so deeply shaped their sense of self and nation that even though they had become cynical about its application, it was difficult to move outside its conceptual parameters. What had been seen as a mutual enterprise, in which Japan provided a hortatory example, promised by 1905 a much more ambiguous future. Consequently, the idealistic appeals to *munmyŏng kaehwa* receded in these two papers, but its logic, however implicit, continued to shape their discussion of the nation, particularly in regard to cultural self-representations.

Images of the *yangban*

With a mutual commitment to capitalist modernity, as captured in their calls for civilization and enlightenment, nationalist and colonial thought shared similar assumptions about the relationship among nation, culture, and progress. For both, the teleology of history was relentlessly progressing toward the modern, in which culture was measured for its contribution to this advancement. In the early twentieth century in Korea, one of the main

areas in which this relationship was articulated was in representations of the
yangban, the traditional hereditary elite that emerged as metaphorical per-
sonification of the Chosŏn dynasty. As one of the most dissected, vilified,
and satirized groups in these years, the *yangban* was prominent in both
nationalist and colonial writing as a convenient shorthand for representing
the Korean past and, to varying degrees, Korean national culture. And as an
icon of national culture, the *yangban* offered a means to account for the
country's political, economic, and social conditions. Despite some significant differences in tone, both colonial and nationalist writing treated the
yangban in similar ways, although their representations were put to different
purposes. How these differences played out — with one using the *yangban*
as an example to exhort reform and the other using them to assert the im-
possibility of change — affected the disposition of power on the peninsula.

In Japanese newspapers, the *yangban* became a stock character for representing Korea. With his black horsehair hat, flowing white robes, and
traditional shoes, the figure of the *yangban* delighted cartoonists with possibilities for caricaturing the Korean people. Annexation could be captured
in the image of a helpless-looking *yangban*, his hat and robe discarded in
the background, as a robust-looking Japanese helped him put on a kimono
in front of an applauding foreign audience.[93] A *yangban*, bent on his knees,
gnawing on and desperately hanging on to the leg of a hardworking Japanese
worker expressed fears about the costs of colonial rule to Japan.[94] And a
yangban waving a Japanese flag signified the supposedly exuberant Korean
celebration of annexation.[95]

Besides mocking and belittling, such images represented Korea as backward. Sonia Ryang has explained how travel writers like Itō Sadagorō could
write, "White clothes and a long pipe — these seem to reveal a cultural backwardness and primitiveness."[96] Whether the faults of the *yangban* were re-
deemable was a point of contention among Japanese writers, with some
arguing that this backwardness was part of an immutable heritage and others
suggesting that Japanese guidance could overcome the problems.[97] Generally they agreed that because of one or another feature — and here authors
could place onto this useful figure their individual diagnosis of his sickness — the *yangban* as a group was one of the root causes of Korea's dilemma.
The *yangban*'s responsibility for what was seen as the country's internal political turmoil was perhaps the most prominent theme.[98] So, too, was their
so-called social uselessness, as *yangban* had no particular military or learned
skills, in the opinion of one commentator, and merely occupied a privileged

social position while living and eating off the labor of the commoners.[99] The *yangban*'s greed as officials knew few bounds, according to many, causing the people to be naturally suspicious.[100] In short, writers identified their various causes for Korea's problems and, by linking them with notions of "enlightenment," found an embodiment of their causes in this white-robed, black-hatted figure.

In Korea, the *yangban* assumed an even more prominent position in nationalist writing, although the disparagement and ridicule never reached the degree in those pieces written by Japanese authors. In much of Korean writing, the *yangban* was a convenient target because, again, many of Korea's ills, about which so much had been written, could be attributed to them. This form of self-criticism also was part of the process of decentering China, since the *yangban*, as the elite of the Chosŏn dynasty, could be held responsible for a history of cultural and political subservience to China. Implicit in these discussions was an interpretation of the past that provided a historical context for the nation's current dire straits. At a time when comprehensive national histories had not yet been written, the *yangban* emerged as the single most potent historical image, through which the earliest efforts to interpret the national past in light of new theories of progress were made. A number of themes linked the various newspapers' treatment of the *yangban* — in particular, their lack of practical knowledge, laziness, corruption, and tendency toward factionalism — all themes that also were featured in Japanese writing about Korea.

The *Tongnip sinmun*, the earliest and most zealous proponent of "civilization and enlightenment," took special aim at the unwillingness of Confucian scholars to refurbish their learning in accordance with this new era of change. Their adherence to outmoded styles of thought, a spring editorial noted, was like wearing your winter clothes in the summer.[101] Editorials written in a conversational style imitated the questions of a conservative scholar, ignorant of the ways of the world, to a recently returned traveler from abroad. In one, the scholar begins by noting that newspapers have begun to appear in Korea, only to complain that all they do is "print useless rumors and circulate them in the world." The traveler counters, "Newspapers are just as critical to enlightenment as schools." To this, the scholar takes umbrage, pointing out that schools teach the Four Books and Three Classics along with the composition of poetry, odes (*pu*), memorials (*p'yo*), and essays, so "How can you compare them with newspapers? What a strange thing to say!"[102] The editorial reflected the *Tongnip sinmun*'s emphasis on knowledge (*hangmun*), whereas the fundamental "sickness" of the nation, as best illustrated by the *yangban*, was the lack of it. Because of this absence, Korea had not progressed and was not treated by foreign powers as an equal.[103] The editors of the *TaeHan maeil sinbo* also used this line of criticism, indicating their amazement that as late as 1910, a group of 150 scholars could petition the government for a subsidy to publish the massive *Complete Works of the Song-Dynasty Philosophers* — "of all the books urgently needed in Korea these days!"[104]

Unlike the *Tongnip sinmun*, the *TaeHan maeil sinbo* did not so lightly or polemically dismiss what it called "Confucian circles" (*yugye* or *yurim*). This was partly a question of strategy, since in one editorial entitled "What to Do with the *Yangban*?" the editors estimated that one of three people fell into this category — a number, they argued, that could not be discounted if the country was to reform.[105] Admitting that answers to the question were not easy, they repeatedly announced that because *yangban* had been leaders in the past and remained so today, the future of reform and hence the country rested in their hands.[106] This did not mean that the *yangban* did have not serious problems. Picking up on a theme popular in all the media, the editors contended that the past veneration of literary learning had made scholars passive and indolent.[107] Most of them did not grasp the value of time, even though its proper use was what distinguished "the strong from the weak, the courageous from the cowardly." Instead, too many were content to stay at home in bed and read the same books over and over again.[108]

For the *Hwangsŏng sinmun*, the *yangban* was a much more complicated figure. Committed from its beginning in 1898 to joining Confucian values to notions of civilization and, in the last three years of its run, going so far as to advocate a revitalized Confucianism as critical to the nation, the editors refrained from sweeping statements that condemned the group as a whole. For a newspaper that continued to write in an opaque style full of classical allusions and Chinese characters, it was the traditionally trained elite who provided the main market for their product and the target audience for its exhortations to change. Appropriately, the editors adopted a time-honored Confucian strategy of exculpating what they defined as the core of Confucian teaching while berating those who, they claimed, had abandoned these principles. For those delinquents — those who "close their ears and eyes and seal their minds" and do not "breath the air of civilization"[109] — the editors reserved a special term, "corrupt Confucians" (*puyu*) and, like other newspapers, did not hesitate to criticize them.[110] Most notably, these people resisted change because "regardless of the issue, they revered what the ancients did and looked down on the accomplishments of their contemporaries."[111] What they valued was nothing more than "frivolous and empty" literary writings.[112] They provided the source for officials even today, even though their "custom of idleness had become a sickness," a custom that "inevitably would lead to disaster."[113] Many *yangban*, the editors accused, do not work for the country and want only to become officials for selfish reasons, without learning what is necessary to fulfill their duties at this special time.[114]

As part of their attempt to limit these problems to those "corrupt Confucians" while salvaging what they saw as the core of Confucianism, the editors specifically contrasted the recent past with the earlier years of the dynasty. The problems of the nation were traced to the late Chosŏn dynasty, when the elite lost the commitment of their predecessors. The ancestors of today's *yangban*, the editors maintained, had pursued the principles of the classics, had loyally built the country, and had established a great peace for the people. But after several hundred years, their descendants no longer were learning the appropriate knowledge and technologies, no longer serving the monarch loyally, and no longer protecting the people with a loving heart. "They have not prevented the foundational achievements of their ancestors from collapsing, so should they still be called the *yangban* descendants of *yangban*?"[115] In this vision of what was tantamount to a "fall" in the last half of the Chosŏn dynasty, ease of living and idleness were again offered as reasons.[116]

So too the change in dynastic fortune and the character of the *yangban* were linked to what became the main issue of governance in the period, factionalism. Divisions among officials from the sixteenth century onward had beset the court politics of the Chosŏn dynasty. Nationalist writers highlighted this disunity and squabbling, citing it as an explanation for the nation's misfortune and blaming it for establishing patterns of political conduct that continued to shape the current administration. Linking the notion of scholarly *ki* (vitality) to the nation's prosperity, one editorial noted that at the beginning of the dynasty, *ki* enlivened the country but that since the outbreak of factionalism, this *ki* had been squandered.[117] Using factionalism to link a disputatious elite to poor government was nothing new. During the Chosŏn dynasty, Confucian writers blamed factions for putting the petty interests of inferior men (*soin*) ahead of those of the greater, moral good — an argument with a long history in East Asia.[118] The *Hwangsŏng sinmun* revived this style of critique to show how the ills of the past had led to the current political turmoil dividing officeholders, who they called the "criminals of society."[119] The vocabulary of the past — the old and the new factions, the north and south parties versus the Way of Kings — was fused with notions of "civilization and enlightenment" — efficient, stable, and centralized government as necessary for reform — to formulate appeals for good governance. Both conventional and new critiques were fused, offering a critique of the political elite and a bleak assessment of the late Chosŏn dynasty.[120]

In these many ways, the *yangban* came to personify the problems that writers, sometimes with divergent political goals, identified with Korean society and politics. As a repository for the country's various ailments, the *yangban* served as a negative model, used to admonish the past for setting the course that had led to the current predicament. As a form of cultural representation relating the current nation to the past and offering a target for cultural critique, Koreans' representations of the *yangban* were not unlike their depiction in the Japanese media. In theme if not in tone, writers in both countries focused on similar issues, such as factionalism, laziness, bookishness, or a lack of originality. These derived from the common usage of "civilization and enlightenment" with its emphasis on economic efficiency, unity in government, emphasis on action, and privileging of "practical" knowledge. All the people should be disciplined in this fashion while the culture of the nation should be judged by its contribution to or detraction from these ideals.

Despite this resonance, significant differences also separated Japanese and Korean writing on the *yangban*. Most notably, they differed on the question of reformability. At the core of all reform agendas — whether nationalist or colonial — was the need to guide the population into the kinds of activities that would both enable and spur change in desired directions. Self-strengthening, as editorial after editorial in the full range of publications from the period explained, began with the individual — his or her outlook as captured in issues such as valuing time, taking the initiative, and helping oneself. Slothfulness, laziness, and idleness — these were the obstacles to change. On this point, both Korean and Japanese writers might agree, but as applied to the *yangban* — and often extended to the entire population — they differed in their emphasis. Korean condemnations tended to underscore the *need* for disciplining the population, whereas Japanese reproaches highlighted the *lack* of disciplining. The former, written from an activist position, had much to do with the self-identity of the reformers, who viewed themselves as models for the rest of society, in opposition to the conservative

yangban circles. Through such a view, they allocated to themselves the role
of leaders who, with their newspapers, could properly enlighten their readers
about what constituted the necessary disciplining. This also meant that Korean editors were quick to combine their critical assessments of the *yangban*
with evidence of successful change in the country, however insufficient they
believed it to be. Accounts of collecting funds to create private schools were
frequently printed together with the charters of newly established agricultural, commercial, or workers' night schools.[121] A song celebrating the opening of a school in Hamgyŏng Province was deemed worthy of publication.[122]
In 1909, the *TaeHan maeil sinbo* reported the happy sounds" (*pogŭm*)
emerging from Confucian circles as more and more scholars were "awak-
ening" and participating in the new education movement.[123] Six months
later the "happy sounds" had crescendoed into what they now called a "revolution" in Confucian intellectual circles.[124] The need for discipline came
with the *possibility* of disciplining and all the consequences that it entailed.
The conservative *yangban* were an obstacle and the late Chosŏn dynasty
might have been a bleak era, but already in areas as diverse as the construction of schools in the countryside, the opening of a new pottery factory, and
the establishment of the first public library, there were promising signs of
change. In this way, the minatory was accompanied by the hortatory, as
editors warned their readers against the complacency of the *yangban* and
the late Chosŏn past while offering encouraging models in the present that
illustrated how the legacy was indeed already being overcome.

In contrast, much Japanese writing downplayed the potential for Korean
reform and ignored the changes already under way in the country. Especially
before 1905, when most writing took the position of an external observer,
often in a self-congratulatory vein comparing Korean and Japanese social
customs, little heed was paid to the changes made by Korean reformers.[125]
This was the reason why Kim Okkyun, a would-be reformer with close connections to Japan, was — more than twenty years after his attempted putsch
in 1884 — still widely remembered in the Japanese press. He alone was considered to have tried to separate himself from the legacy of the *yangban*. For
many Japanese, his failure stood as the loss of opportunity and the end of
the possibility for autonomous change in Korea. His assassination in 1893
by a Korean who was, in turn, rewarded for his actions by the government,
only confirmed this assessment. Thus, the lack of discipline embodied by
yangban as represented in Japanese texts was just that — an absence that few
writers questioned and even fewer refrained from presenting as an essential

national character.[126] Unwilling to see the changes already achieved in Korea, Japanese reports tended to suggest that reform would result only from external impetus or foreign guidance.

The common themes in Japanese and Korean representations were also partly due to direct exchanges. Korean writers, well versed in Japanese newspaper culture, were aware of the Japanese characterizations of *yangban*, however uncomfortable it was for them to read the same criticisms in foreign papers. The editors of the *TaeHan maeil sinbo* worried about the effect of Japanese media depictions on Korea's international reputation. The problem was that although they realized Japanese reports ridiculed Koreans as always smoking tobacco or enjoying afternoon naps, as if they were "cold-blooded animals," the portrait was sufficiently close to their own complaints that it was difficult for them to refute it. The only way to stop such shameful writing, they charged, was to "put an end" to these customs, a response that, in not opposing the representation, indicated their concurrence.[127] They might regret Japanese attention to such matters, but they did not challenge the depictions themselves. Other Koreans used these less than salutary Japanese representations. The *Hwangsŏng sinmun* summarized the contents of an article appearing in the *Nihon shimbun shūhō* (*Japanese Newspaper Weekly*), entitled the "Diseases of Korea," in which the Korean elite were described as those who "don't do anything to clothe or feed themselves and only form factions" — an account, according to the Korean editors, that characterized them "quite appropriately."[128] In an essay on the need for unity, Chang Chiyŏn cited five "sicknesses" that divided the Korean people, one of which was laziness. In explaining his reasoning, Chang turned to a Japanese observer, invoking his assessment that "the laziness of Koreans cannot be seen elsewhere in the world."[129]

While no doubt lending the representations a sense of veracity by a foreigner's confirmation, such exchanges were not the sole reason for the thematic similarities in colonial and nationalist writing. This was less a question of Japanese influence on nationalist writers — images originating in Japan and spreading to Korea through the media — than the logical consequence of these writers sharing the same ideological framework. The impulse of nationalism to articulate the nation's uniqueness, accompanied by the evaluative criterion of *munmyŏng kaehwa*, caused national culture to be judged in terms of compatibility with reform and ideals of an economically and politically defined citizenry. This impulse led to the overlap in not only the strategies but also the content of cultural representation. Despite the opposing goals of nationalist and colonial writers, the *yangban* served as a locus for writing about Korean culture and exploring the connections between that culture and the sovereignty of the peninsula. Although both nationalists and colonialists condemned the *yangban* for a variety of features that seemingly interfered with the progress of the nation, the different ways in which these representations were invoked supported different goals and actions. One sought self-strengthening through *munmyŏng kaehwa*, in which the legacy of the *yangban* was to be overcome in order to protect national sovereignty. The other privileged *munmyŏng kaehwa* as the ultimate goal, even if achieved through external stimulus and regardless of sovereignty.

The Dangers of *Sadaejuŭi*

The congruency of colonial and nationalist representations carried significant political ramifications. For nationalists, there was the danger that these shared assumptions and cultural characterizations, developed and disseminated before 1905 for their own political objectives, would be linked to colonial goals after 1905. The overlap and similarity, despite differences in tone and intent, meant that nationalist representations intersected with colonial ideology. This threat was evident in a topic often related to the notion of the lazy *yangban* too comfortable with traditional knowledge to pursue national ends, namely, dependence on foreign powers. Anyone treating early Korean history had to deal with Sino-Korean relations, a situation no less true of colonial than nationalist writers. If the move to decenter the "Middle Kingdom" entailed a sustained critique of Korea's historical relationship with China, one that juxtaposed a past dependence with a contemporary independence, then so too did colonial writing discuss Sino-Korean ties, highlighting Korea's historical reliance on China as an indication of the lack of national will and the absence of the potential for self-rule.

As Hatada Takashi has observed, from the 1880s, Japanese historians underplayed Korean subjectivity, reducing the peninsula's cultural, political, and economic history to one of external forces.[130] Hayashi Taisuke's important *Chōsenshi* (*History of Korea*), the first comprehensive Japanese history of Korea, published in 1892, reflected this approach. In the first page of his preface, Hayashi wrote about the early extension of Japanese rule over the southern portions of the peninsula, following these comments with discussions of Korea's reliance on China.[131] External dependence was twofold: in the earliest ages, on Japan, and, afterward, on China until the end of the nineteenth century. At the time of annexation, the Japanese media repeatedly raised the issue of dependence, using it as a departure point for countless articles explaining the train of events, whether long term or short term, that had led to the annexation treaty. After all, since "dependence" identified the Korean national character and since for "two thousand years of history, [Korea] frequently relied on and followed other countries," most Korean phenomena could be related to this central stereotype.[132] Shortly after annexation, the *Tōkyō Asahi shimbun* published an article describing Korean customs and institutions that it characterized as reminiscent of earlier Japanese ages. Immediately equating the Korea of today with the Japan of yesterday, the article depicted Korea as backward and unchanging. The reason that current Korean items like food implements, the wearing of white clothes, and the three divine implements resembled their past Japanese counterparts, the article continued, was because both countries borrowed heavily from the Tang dynasty. What distinguished the two, it concluded, was the Japanese ability to develop subsequently its own distinctive customs while, even after the Tang dynasty, Koreans continued to imitate Chinese style. The article emphasized the cultural aspects of "dependence" to show Koreans had little originality and no ability to develop their own national customs. Everything, it insinuated, was derived from other cultures.[133]

The official propaganda after 1910 continued to emphasize "dependence." The Governor General's Office publicly claimed that it was part of the national character (J. *kokutai*, K. *kukch'e*), making every dynasty submit to China from the Han dynasty onward. In the eyes of this official publication, *sadae* allowed Korean history to be divided into two periods: all of Korean history until annexation was marked by evil, despotic governments that submitted to China, versus "Chōsen," the new Japanese colony, which was reaping the benefits of "civilized law and benevolent administration."[134] Whether used to make such a bald link to the reasons for annexation or, as in the case of the *Asahi shimbun* piece, used to disparage Korean culture, the various ways of explaining "dependence" made this concept central to the Japanese production of knowledge about Korea, both in public and state-sponsored writing.

Again, as in representations of the *yangban*, the colonial and nationalist writing on "dependence" sounded similar themes. From the earliest days of the nationalist press, "dependence" had been key to contemplating Korean sovereignty and its relation to national culture. But by 1905, as it became apparent that this concept was being used to legitimize the Japanese presence on the peninsula, the question confronting nationalist writers was to what extent they could continue to use this concept effectively when the colonizing state and its supporters were using a very similar version. Japanese public and private usage threatened to arrogate the concept and make it less viable for Koreans to use for a radically different purpose: reform in pursuit of sovereignty. This was one of the most powerful consequences of the colonial production of knowledge about Korea. As writers became aware of the double nature of *munmyŏng kaehwa*, they could take pleasure in satirizing its use by the resident general. But although the direct, more vulgar invocations of "civilization" were easy to scorn, it was less simple to dismiss the many ways that the powerful standards of *munmyŏng kaehwa* had been used to represent and evaluate various aspects of Korean culture. It was precisely these more subtle articulations of this overarching framework, as captured in the type of cultural representations that by 1905 had already shaped Korean self-understanding, that Japan was now effectively employing for its own political objectives.

This threat was manifested in the gradual shift in the Korean terminology for "dependence." In early nationalist texts, this historical phenomenon had largely been designated as a question of reliance and dependence (*ŭibu* or *ŭiroe*) or slavishness (*nobisŏng*). But after 1905, the term began to shift toward a Japanese expression. By the mid-colonial period, "dependence" had gradually become more or less fixed on various forms of the Japanese term for the phenomenon — *jidai* or, in Korean, *sadae*, used in a compound form as *sadaejuŭi*, literally the "ism of serving the great," or *sadae sasang*, "the ideology of serving the great."[135] Even in essays by some of the most famous nationalist polemicists writing in exile, outside the immediate colonial setting, this lexical shift can be observed.[136] The power of Japan to determine even the vocabulary of nationalist versions of "dependence" threatened to blur the division between nationalist and colonial usage, rendering nationalist meanings less effectual. By 1905, nationalists had so widely promoted the notion that "dependence" was a deep-seated feature of Korean national character that any reader of the Korean press would be quick to point to this problem as in urgent need of reform if the nation was to be saved. But now Japanese colonial officials were invoking similar notions of dependence. What nationalists had so authoritatively disseminated over the preceding ten years as a new historical understanding crucial to the future of their nation was now being wielded for a very different objective. It was a powerful strategy, one that threatened to make amenable to colonization a major trope in nationalist conceptions of history and identity. This overlap, in turn, compelled some nationalist writers to readjust their own uses of "dependence" so that despite the lexical and representational similarities, it could be conceptually fine-tuned in order to retain its nationalist potential.

The danger of co-option was not lost on the editors of the *Hwangsŏng sinmun* and *TaeHan maeil sinbo*. Both sought to preserve nationalist uses of "dependence" by denying the equivalence of the Korean and Japanese uses of the term and highlighting their differences. In so doing, the earlier, more polemical critiques of reliance on China that had served such an important function in decentering the "Middle Kingdom" were adjusted to counter the potential encroachment of Japanese definitions of *sadaejuŭi*. As many Japanese claimed, if Korea's relationship with China demonstrated a lack of ability for self-rule, thereby justifying Japanese governance, these two papers responded by defining more narrowly their account of past Sino-Korean relations at the same time as they contrasted that relationship with Protectorate rule.

The editors of the *Hwangsŏng sinmun* admitted that for more than five hundred years since the founding of the dynasty, Korea had submitted to China, receiving their patents (*komyŏng*) and engaging in the rituals of conferring tribute.[137] But as for the administration of internal and external affairs, "there was nothing that we did not control ourselves [*chaju*] and administer exclusively. Never did we endure even an iota of interference." Using contemporary terminology for past practices, they insisted that although "nominally we were a vassal state, in actuality we were an independent [*tongnip*], self-ruling [*chaju*] nation." The oppositional character of this piece took on special importance, since it followed by one day the paper's summary of a Japanese legal expert's opinion, entitled "The Future of Korea," in which he offered a classic justification for colonial rule: Without the wherewithal for independence, Korea would be protected and eventually guided toward sovereignty by Japan.[138] Under the gaze of the censor, the editors could not directly challenge this argument, but because *sadaejuŭi* was inherently a historical issue, a reinterpretation of history offered a means of debunking the Japanese position by underscoring the self-autonomous features of the dynastic past. This reinterpretation denied Japanese claims that past practices demonstrated a lack of Korean experience in self-rule, showing instead that they did have the wherewithal — in fact, had been autonomous for more than half a millennium.

The piece next went beyond this point to contrast tribute relations with the Protectorate. Arguing that since the Sino-Japanese War, Korea had been nominally independent, the editors pointed out that it was precisely because of Japan that Korea had been unable to substantiate this status and instead had been declared a protectorate. Looking back over recent affairs, they noted that in internal and foreign affairs, "the right to self-rule has been completely lost." Reversing the phrasing for Sino-Korean relations, they wrote, "Although nominally we are independent, in actuality, we are an example of a vassal state. Even protectorate nations should not be [treated] like this. Is there any greater shame for the nation than this?" What earlier nationalist and Japanese colonial writing had castigated as historical was now rendered contemporary — and blamed as the doing of Japan. The vocabulary of dependence — before 1905 the province of nationalists — was here confirmed, only they now sought to reverse its meaning against Japan.

With its more protected political position, the *TaeHan maeil sinbo* did not need to shy away from more explicitly barbed comments. It, too, offered a reinterpretation of past Sino-Korean relations, only more narrowly directed toward Japan and its allies on the peninsula. "In the eyes of Japanese," it began, "Korea had already been oppressed by the Yuan, the Ming, and the Qing dynasties, so that for six or seven centuries since the time of the Koryŏ dynasty, it had lost its independence."[139] That many Koreans had made similar arguments in the past was not pertinent to the editors, who now realized annexation was imminent and sought to undermine some of its ideological underpinnings. "Because of this, they [Japanese] hold Koreans in contempt." As the article went on to contend, the times had changed. In the past, Koreans had considered China the ancestral country of Confucianism. Now that this "period of religion" had been supplanted by a "period of the nation," Koreans would never submit to Japan. Moreover, taking up the argument offered by the *Hwangsŏng sinmun*, the editors maintained that the earlier submission to the Ming and Qing dynasties had been superficial, little more than forcing the government to offer some gold and some ginseng under the guise of "tribute nation." Suggesting that Korea in fact received more in return than they gave and noting that neither the Ming dynasty nor the Qing dynasty "dared usurp the people's rights," the editors argued that their status as a "tributary nation" was nothing but an "empty name" and that the people suffered no hardships. Again, a contrast was drawn to delegitimate the Japanese assertion that the past *sadae* relationship was part of Korean nature and thus amenable to colonial rule: "Koreans do not consider what the Japanese are doing as the same as the Ming and Qing."

The *TaeHan maeil sinbo* moved further away from earlier nationalist usage in order to tie "dependence" to the present problem of how individual Koreans related to the Japanese presence on the peninsula. As with earlier usage, this shifting definition had both a political and a cultural dimension. The editors redefined *sadae* away from what had been a historically oriented concept directed at past attitudes toward China to a more contemporary usage, targeting followers of Japan. What had been seen as a traditional style of behavior, blamed for leading the peninsula into its current predicament was now seen as a contemporary problem. Both were traditional behaviors, reinforcing the notion that this was part of the national character, but one was in the past, whereas the other marked the continuity of this traditional behavior in the present. People of this "slavish ilk" (*nobae*), began one description, have the "vile tendency to believe blindly in the ancients, to be locked in old habits, pander to the prevailing power of the time, and worship foreign countries." While this description fit neatly into earlier nationalist writing concerning dependence on China, to the point that such behavior would "lead to the destruction of the nation," the cases that followed looked in a different direction. Instead, the writer described walking along a street in Seoul where he noticed on the lintel of a prominent Korean home a name board that imitated Japanese-style names. It combined the name of a Korean town famous for its Confucian scholarship, Andong, with a typical Japanese ending for personal names. This produced a hybrid name that, in Korean, would be pronounced "Andong ch'anang" or, alternatively, in Japanese, "Andōjirō." In short, powerful Koreans were of their own accord taking on Japanese-style names. The article next complained about Koreans who constantly had the name of Itō Hirobumi on the tip of their tongue, venerating him as though he were a teacher or father figure. Making a comparison with another colonial situation, the editors pointed out that even though Gladstone was generally considered to be a great person, Egyptians certainly did not think of him in this way. But Koreans, the editors warned, were willing to worship the very people who were destroying their nation. They also took offense at a recent letter by a local government official who, against all protocol, had used the Meiji reign dates rather than Korean ones.[140] Thus, much to the chagrin of the editors, in terms of names, heroes, and even the recording of time, Korean were already aping Japanese ways.

Earlier worries about the obsession with Chinese characters and classical texts were now being supplanted by the fear of Japanese cultural forms — with the cultural and temporal gap between these two explained by the same concept of *sadae*.

"Dependence" also came to be redefined as a strategy for subverting pro-Japanese groups in Korea. "Japan's Three Great Loyal Slaves" was the title of one editorial that accused a trio of leading public figures of activities that threatened the nation's vitality.[141] Japan might use *sadae* to rationalize its presence on the peninsula, attempting to co-opt the concept from the na-tionalist arsenal of rhetorical weapons by rendering it supportive of coloni-alism. But nationalists could, in turn, also redirect the concept's use toward Japan's own allies in Korea, deploying the same negative meanings used by the Office of the Resident General for this concept to delegitimize the of-fice's own allies. The historical tendency of Koreans to rely on others was seen by the editors of the *TaeHan maeil sinbo* as having been transferred to Japan. Just as reliance on China in the past had weakened the nation, de-pendence on Japan in the present, they warned, would make sovereignty unattainable. As in Japanese definitions of *sadae*, the division between past and present remained central to this formulation, but rather than attributing to the Japanese Protectorate the current freedom of Korea from China, past and present were linked, bridged by the same concept of *sadae*, only here the temporal division was interpreted as a shift in the recipient of Korea's dependence, from China to Japan.

In these ways, "dependence" came to be further articulated and, ironi-cally, by widening the scope of the concept, ensured its entrenchment in Korean political culture. Yet the genealogy of this term so central to the nationalist movement cannot be seen as merely the autonomous outgrowth of a burgeoning sense of nation. Rather, its meaning came from within the colonial context, through various interactions with and against Japanese co-lonial discourse. Japanese colonial power extended well beyond the reach of their policemen with the samurai swords. With both colonizer and na-tionalists embedding their knowledge of Korea in "civilization and enlight-enment," nationalists struggled to preserve a discursive space for the nation that could not be co-opted into supporting, directly or indirectly, the colonial enterprise. One of the ultimate powers of the colonizer is to define the terms and representations in which the colonized articulate their own sense of self. But the slipperiness of the terms, together with the multivalences of representations, offered much latitude for Koreans to continue to work with the concepts and forms of knowledge that they had explored for their own purposes before 1905 but that thereafter Japan threatened to arrogate for its own purposes.

Colonial Denouement

Although the editors of the *TaeHan maeil sinbo* and the *Hwangsŏng sinmun* made a number of efforts to contest various aspects of colonial ideology in the last few years before annexation, the establishment of formal colonial power in 1910 ended the possibility of further public exploration of these possibilities. The day after announcing annexation, the colonial authorities shut down both papers. The *TaeHan maeil sinbo*, with its unsullied nationalist reputation, was quickly transformed by the new Governor General's Office into its official mouthpiece. With *TaeHan* struck from its title, it became simply the *Maeil sinbo*, or *Daily News*. As the only Korean-language daily newspaper, the *Maeil sinbo* became the most important voice for explaining colonial policy during a time when the majority of Koreans still could not read Japanese.[142] Many prominent staff members, like Sin Ch'aeho, resigned from their positions with the paper, but others such as P'yŏn Il, Sŏnu Il, Yi Haejo, and Cho Chungnae stayed in the paper's offices after 1910, easing the transition between a paper that was once the most prominent critic of Japanese policy to one that legitimized colonial rule.[143] To be sure, the takeover of the paper, now under the official guidance of the famed Japanese newspaper entrepreneur Tokutomi Sohō and grouped together with the *Keijō nippō*, the official Japanese-language organ of the Government General, resulted in wrenching editorial change. Any treatment of sovereignty, so central to the earlier nationalist newspapers, became taboo. Now readers were told that their goal should be to behave like good imperial subjects by properly celebrating the emperor's birthday and commemorating annexation as the day when "doubt and hate between the two Korean and Japanese peoples was abandoned."[144]

The replacement of calls for independence with the promotion of imperial ideologies was nevertheless still expressed within the parameters of "civilization and enlightenment." Although there was certainly a rupture with earlier editorials on the nation, those Koreans who continued to work in its offices likely found some solace in the continuity in other areas of the paper's editorial positions. This continuity, both lexical and thematic, could be seen in cultural representations and the calls for reform. The figure of the *yangban* as a conservative scholar once again appeared prominently in the early pages of the *Maeil sinbo*. Again he was depicted as always committed to "an old form of knowledge" consisting of the words of the sages and the "Way of Kings" while dismissing all alternative forms of knowledge as "heterodox."[145] Using a rhetoric reminiscent of earlier nationalist papers, the editors warned "corrupt Confucians" of their insensitivity to the demands of a new era:

> If their thought is corrupt, then even if they have ears they cannot hear, and even though they have eyes they cannot see, and even if they have mouths they cannot taste. They have no sense whatsoever of changes. When they sit, they are little more than statues, and when they walk they are nothing more than moving flesh — how can they be called living people?[146]

Such passages could have been lifted from the pages of the *TaeHan maeil sinbo* or the *Hwangsŏng sinmun*. Although the standard of critique had changed little, now missing was any linkage to sovereignty. The attitudes and activities of these scholars might need to be improved, but now this reform was an end in itself, in service to *munmyŏng kaehwa* and not the nation.

Clearly, the *TaeHan Maeil sinbo* had been stripped of its nationalist goals. However, many of the assumptions and representations that underpinned nationalist writing were still held with conviction by its successor, except that now the higher authority that had once framed the definitions of the desired nation — civilization and enlightenment — had become the ultimate goal. As seen in editorials treating topics as diverse as the enlightening function of newspapers,[147] early marriage,[148] laziness as the cause of corruption,[149] hygiene and sanitation,[150] standardizing measurements,[151] and the harm of superstition,[152] the agenda of reform had changed little. In this way, the nationalists' dilemma of what took precedence — the nation or civilization? — was resolved by colonialism in favor of the latter. The nationalist attempt to come to terms with their participation in a global capitalist modernity through *munmyŏng kaehwa* had unraveled — and the nation was left out.

Here lay the conundrum of a nationalism that appealed to the higher authority of the universal principles of "civilization and enlightenment" and the natural laws of social Darwinism. Nationalist interpretations of *munmyŏng kaehwa* did buttress a program of self-strengthening: only reform enabled a nation to survive and to receive equal treatment from the community of "civilized" nations. But the double nature of *munmyŏng kaehwa* was that it could also be used to promote acceptance of colonization, whether it was the permanent loss of independence or its postponement to a future date. Natural laws taught, after all, that the strong *should* conquer the weak, and the progressive vision of history demonstrated that the less civilized *needed* the guidance of the more civilized. To oppose these conclusions was to oppose the natural laws of society and the proof of history. While many Korean nationalists were eager to stake out such a position, others, like the Korean staff of the *Maeil sinbo*, found the commonalties between colonial and nationalist thought sufficient grounds to work within the strictures of colonial rule. Their commitment to capitalist modernity remained, only now rather than being channeled through a sovereign Korean nation, it was to be achieved through colonial subordination.

4   Spirit, History, and Legitimacy

These days in Korea, everyone talks about "love of country,
love of country," but finding just where the spirit of patriotism resides
is difficult.
        — *Hwangsŏng sinmun,* April 25, 1908

In March 1910, the editors of the *TaeHan maeil sinbo* asked its readers how foreigners viewed Korea. "Is the image of Korea in the eyes of Europeans and Americans a true view of Korea," it asked, "or is the image of Korea in the eyes of Japanese a true view of Korea?" The stimulus for this query came from an editorial in the Seoul-based Japanese paper, the *TaiKan Nippō,* which in its own way was also worried about representations of the peninsula. In the estimate of this Japanese paper's editors, however, the problem lay with Americans and Europeans, who misunderstood Japan's policy in Korea. They charged that foreigners were sending erroneous views back to their home countries, leading their readers to believe, for example, that "Koreans are a people that have the wherewithal for independence." The *TaiKan Nippō*'s accusations of muddled understanding tried to claim that the paper had a deeper and truer insight into Korean affairs than other newspapers did. By reprinting parts of this editorial in their own newspaper, the editors of the *TaeHan maeil sinbo* hoped to undermine that claim, showing just who, in fact, had a more muddled understanding.[1]

The Japanese editors' sensitivity to Western criticism and the eagerness of the *TaeHan maeil sinbo*'s editors to play on these fears reveal the concern in the early years of the twentieth century about images of Korea, past and present, true or false. Japanese colonial authorities and Korean nationalists fully realized that cultural representations were an integral part of their contest over the peninsula's political future. Both expended much energy disseminating those visions of Korea that supported their political goals to counter the efforts of their opponents to offer dissenting images. For Korean nationalists, much of this activity after 1905 extended beyond representations linked to self-strengthening reform to issues of national spirit and essence. This area offered the potential for rethinking the nation in ways not informed by *munmyŏng kaehwa* while presenting an alternative site and tactics for resistance. Articulated in conjunction with key events during the period — in particular, the suicide of Min Yŏnghwan and the threat posed by Japanese textbooks — these representations were explored most often through studies that tried to locate Korea's national spirit in history.

Although national spirit offered one motivation for exploring history, early Korean research was being published at the same time that modern histories of the peninsula written by Japanese were being introduced. One of colonialism's most powerful ways of dominating Korea was controlling the ways that the Korean past could be mobilized for political purposes. How Korean historians dealt with these colonial histories — absorbing them, confronting them, or some combination of the two — emerged as a crucial issue in the development of modern Korean historiography. Moreover, as the exchange between the *TaeHan maeil sinbo* and the *TaiKan Nippō* disclosed, the concern about representing the Korean past and present moved beyond these two countries onto the international stage. Both colonized and colonizer understood that the late historical development of Japanese colonial rule meant that public opinion in the West could determine the fate of Japanese colonial efforts. Consequently, their contest moved onto the international stage, ensuring that not only the self-knowledge of Koreans but also the international knowledge of Korea were shaped by the politics and aesthetic strategies of colonialism.

A Spirited Nation

In 1915, five years after annexation, Pak Ŭnsik published his famous work on recent events in the peninsula, entitled *The Agonizing History of Korea* (*Han'guk t'ongsa*). Published in Shanghai so as to avoid censorship, his narrative began with the nation's emergence from isolation, recounted the severance of ritual tutelage ties to China, and traced the nation's slide from its recently won position as an independent nation into colonial status. In the closing pages, Pak employed a dualism to highlight the predicament of the colonized nation yet open the possibility for national salvation. "Alas!

The body of Korea has already died," he lamented, but "will its soul survive?"[2]

This dualism — a national body versus a national soul, the material contrasted with the spiritual — offered Pak a means of recounting the vagaries of all nations. As he went on to explain for the case of China, the Chinese soul rested in literature. Although China had been invaded by countless nations over the course of its history, he argued that the five-thousand-year-long tradition of literature had remained intact, always preserving the soul of the nation. In contrast, the Mongols, able to conquer enormous territories and instill terror in the hearts of all under Heaven, had a strong body but a weak soul. Mongol rule was short-lived, he concluded, and like many of the peoples who had occupied, rather than changed, China, they came to be transformed in its image.[3] Korea's soul now faced a similar dilemma: the body of the nation had been stolen by the Japanese, but would colonialism lead to the outright destruction of the Korean nation, the annihilation of the Korean soul?[4]

The Agonizing History of Korea was intended to create a record of the recent past that would engender a popular memory of the nation — preserve the "soul," in Pak's words — while enlisting others to participate in this resistance through conservation. If the nation's soul survived such collective efforts, Pak believed that the body itself might be resurrected. Such a strategy was a culmination of more than a decade of writing that had explored various ways of conceiving the nation as a spiritual entity. The emergence of these new ways of writing about the nation had much to do with the circulation of nationalist ideas throughout East Asia. In both Japan and China, writers similarly employed this type of essentialist vocabulary in their newspapers and history books for the national soul (*kukhon*), the national essence (*kuksu*), and the national spirit (*chŏngsin*). To be sure, some of these terms had ancient precedents, as Sin Yongha has shown in a study tracing Pak Ŭnsik's term for "soul" back to the earliest classics of the Confucian canon.[5] Yet the reemergence of this term and its particular linkage to the nation in roughly the same period in all three East Asian countries shows how useful these concepts were for rethinking the nation during an era of massive regional change, when intellectuals in all three countries struggled to come to terms with global capitalist modernity. At a time when the urban setting and material lives of many of these writers were rapidly changing, such terms offered a conceptual space in which they could talk about an inner core for the nation untainted by either modernity or the West, even though the stimulus for this rethinking accompanied Korea's incorporation into the global system.[6] In each national context, although these concepts acquired different meanings, they did share a desire to define the nation in ways that no longer centered on the state.

In the specific context of early-twentieth-century Korea, this move away from state-centered definitions of the nation offered an alternative strategy for resistance, as Pak suggested in his history. Since Japan had extended its control over an ever increasing sphere of state functions and had implemented select political and economic changes to expedite its control of the peninsula, Korean advocates of education and reform were confronted with the dilemma of dealing with the very power that had violated their sovereignty. *Munmyŏng kaehwa* might offer a way to independence, but its Japanese analogue — *bunmei kaika* (civilization and enlightenment) — was being used to rationalize the Japanese usurpation of the Korean state. Until the establishment of the Protectorate in 1905, the nationalist movement had been dominated by calls for self-strengthening as a means of recovering full national rights. But with its focus on the material, institutional, and organizational aspects of the nation-state — railways, defense systems, local government, schools, and the like — self-strengthening directed all energies to bear on precisely those areas over which Japanese officials were tightening their grip. Now that the state and territory had been taken over, national survival could be redefined through more spiritual concepts, less as an effort to civilize and progress until the criteria for sovereignty were achieved and more as a collective effort to sustain a sense of self by nurturing those facets of the nation such as history, language, and religion — areas that were less accessible to the soldiers and bureaucrats of the colonial state. If self-strengthening meant training in the requisite forms of civilized knowledge that led to equality, this new venue was rooted in cultural knowledge, knowledge less of the new international scene than of the past reorganized into a new nationalist framework. Resistance did not mean the disciplining reform of the population but memory — and befitting such a conception, historians were at the forefront of producing this spiritual knowledge.[7]

The shift toward a more spiritual vision of the nation that was rooted in Korea's overall political situation after the Russo-Japanese War was worked out over specific, highly charged public issues. In particular, the suicide of Min Yŏnghwan and the controversy over a proposed plan to use Japanese-language textbooks in Korean schools incited a widespread usage of spiritual conceptions of the nation, which eventually culminated in Pak Ŭnsik's du-

Min yŏnghwan suicide

alism of national soul and national body. In 1905, Min Yŏnghwan, a high official who had frequently served as his country's ambassador, submitted a memorial to the Korean emperor protesting the Protectorate Treaty and demanding that it be rescinded. When the memorial had no effect, Min returned home, wrote a testimony to his countrymen, and, with a short dagger, took his own life. News of his patriotic act quickly spread, as did his message. Writing that he was "dead but has not died," Min promised to help his compatriots in their struggles from below the Nine Springs, a classical allusion to the afterworld.[8] This hint of an existence after death on behalf of the nation gained immediate attention, emerging as one of the primary tropes for interpreting Min's suicide.

The *TaeHan maeil sinbo*'s editorial announcing Min's "sacrifice for the 20 million people" of the nation asked its readers to memorize the text of his suicide note. Focusing on the note's approach to the relation between life and death, the editorial referred to examples of other people who, like Min, believed that only through death could life be gained. Here the life of the nation and the individual were conflated, the sacrifice of the latter making possible the existence of the former. The editorial quoted Min's words about his death's not being a true death, elaborating on the brief passage to argue that it was only his body that had passed away while his spirit continued to fight for the nation.[9] This interpretation of Min's suicide gained momentum five months later, when reports spread that a clump of bamboo had sprouted on the very spot where Min had fallen.

At the time of Min's suicide, the *Hwangsŏng sinmun* had been unable to cover the story because it had been shut down by the Japanese immediately after publishing its famous editorial against the Protectorate Treaty.[10] But with the discovery of the bamboo, the editors received an opportunity to revisit the event — and explore the spiritual interpretations of Min's actions.[11] At first, the paper merely confirmed that bamboo had grown on the spot of his suicide, limiting itself to reporting the bedlam outside Min's home, where a sea of people struggled to see the bamboo. It recounted the reactions of the "astounded" crowd, quoting conversations: one person noting how Min's righteous conduct was "as bright as a star," another remarking that "having seen this bamboo, I cannot but look up to him," and others so deeply moved that they emerged "sobbing and crying."[12] The next day the paper's tentative tone changed dramatically as the perspective of the editor moved from the position of an external observer to one enthralled by the experience of his own visit. In an editorial more personal than usual and written in the

first person, he admitted doubting these reports that had "sped through the
nation like thunder." But when he, too, saw the bamboo, he "raised his head
and shouted to the sky, 'This is not bamboo, this is blood!'" Making the link
to the nation, he wrote how Min's act "expelled the evil airs that filled the
sky, shook away the evil spirits, and represented the spirit of independence
of our 20 million people." Playing on the wording in Min's testament, he
exclaimed, "Alas! Min has died, but our Korea has not died, and so long as
our Korea is not dead, Min is not dead."[13]

The notion that Min had not truly died became an especially lyrical
theme in the flood of poetry that followed these stories for months. The
opening line of one piece asked, "Who says that Min has passed away?"[14]
The "blood bamboo" (*hyŏlchuk*), as it quickly came to be known, was described as the "spirit that over one thousand autumns does not die."[15] The
TaeHan maeil sinbo actively pursued these themes as well, dwarfing its report
of the bamboo with a long stream of poems that for several months explored
Min's sacrifice and spirit.[16] Advertisements bought by individuals moved by
his sacrifice and eager to commemorate his soul also appeared in its pages.[17]
The paper even offered a full-page illustration of the bamboo, the only time
in the paper's entire run that a whole page was devoted to a drawing.[18] Thus,
in papers that over the years had devoted considerable editorial space to
railing against various superstitions as inimical to the nationalist project, the
"blood bamboo" came to be accepted with an ardor that moved beyond the
metaphorical to the literal resurrection of Min's spirit. Nation and loyalty
were captured in these sprigs of green, and his spirit was the medium of
rebirth.

At roughly the same time, a controversy arose over reports that the Ministry of Education was planning to introduce Japanese-language textbooks.
Although this event involved different people in a different sphere, it also
came to be interpreted as an issue of national spirit. In October 1905, a letter
sent to the *TaeHan maeil sinbo* describing the opposition of teachers and
students to the Ministry of Education policies noted that Shidehara Hiroshi,
a Japanese adviser who had served in the ministry for two years, had suggested that Japanese books be adopted. The minister of education, Yi
Wanyong, did not oppose the proposal, an action for which he was branded
a "traitor" by the paper — the first in a long line of such accusations against
Yi.[19] By March, the paper reported that Shidehara's proposal had been completed and would soon be implemented, leading to another onslaught of
editorials and letters. Over the next two years, the paper sought to discredit
such proposals in its editorials and questioned the very need of foreign ad-

visers who, it charged, accomplished nothing and just wasted tax dollars with
their expensive salaries.[20]

Textbook compilation had long been an issue for nationalist reformers.
From the earliest days of the press, editors had constantly called for revamping teaching materials, in part to distance students from former modes of
learning no longer considered relevant and also to teach students the new
knowledge being produced about their country. As the school movement
expanded, dramatically increasing the number of teaching facilities around
the country, schools and teachers were confronted with a dearth of teaching
materials. Without the institutional infrastructure of universities and professional academic or teaching associations, new textbooks were slow to
emerge, as the responsibility devolved to a few devoted scholars who sought
to gain the Ministry of Education's approval for their individual, often idiosyncratic, efforts.[21] Although the new schools were intended to teach "civilizing knowledge," instructors often had little choice but to turn to the
pedagogical materials used in the Chosŏn dynasty, such as the *Ch'ŏnjamun*
(*Thousand-Character Classic*) and the *Tongmaeng sŏnsŭp* (*Primer for Ignorant Children*).[22] Others opted for Japanese books. Shidehara's plan may
have shared nationalist concerns about the lack of texts, but the two hardly
agreed on what constituted an appropriate choice.

From the outset, Korean critiques of Shidehara's proposal moved beyond
earlier injunctions about the need for schoolchildren to know their country.
The plan was quickly interpreted as a threat to the national spirit. In the
words of the *Hwangsŏng sinmun*, the possibility of instruction in Japanese
at the lowest levels of the school system betrayed the goal of lower education
in all countries of the world to "nurture the spirit of one's own nation."[23] As
the *TaeHan maeil sinbo* editorialized, Shidehara's plan was an attempt to
"transform Koreans into Japanese."[24] Textbooks, only a few years ago seen as
an instrument for decentering the Middle Kingdom and instilling nationalist
thought, now threatened to be the main source for what critics saw as an
attack on their national character. One letter writer highlighted the dualism
by confessing that when the 1905 treaty with Japan had established the
Protectorate, he had not shared the angst and anger of his countrymen. He
had reasoned that a treaty was "dead writing on paper" that had little relation
to whether or not the nation would be independent.[25] Distinguishing between "material invasions" and "spiritual invasions," he described the former
as being a "substantive" (*yuhyŏngjŏk*) but temporary occupation of the national land and a theft of national political rights. It was the spiritual, not
the material, invasion that should be feared, he warned. In case of the latter,

eventually a day would come when the nation could be resurrected, but in
case of the former, there would be no future, an argument that foreshadowed
the central theme in Pak Ŭnsik's history.[26] Japanese-language textbooks,
then, were a greater danger than the Protectorate Treaty because they would
quickly destroy the national character (kuksŏng), and "if there was no national character, you could have a nation but be without the nation."[27]
Although conceptual terms such as national essence, national spirit, and
national soul existed well before the establishment of the Protectorate, it was
largely due to the political consequences for reform in the context of the
Protectorate that specific incidents like Min Yŏnghwan's suicide and
Shidehara's proposal could stimulate these spiritual ways of thinking about
the country. They offered writers a way of distancing themselves from the
modern, capitalist ideologies captured in munmyŏng kaehwa without rejecting them outright. The same newspapers used both ways of writing about
the nation, but in the five years after the Protectorate Treaty, the spiritual
side of the nation seemed to offer greater possibilities in a time when self-
strengthening reform required working with Japan. In these five years, the
usage of spiritual concepts increased in frequency and became a major subject of inquiry.[28]

Although this spiritual realm offered a site of resistance less penetrable to
the technologies and bureaucrats of the colonial state, it was not an untouch-
able zone. Its emergence as a prominent way of thinking about the nation
ensured that it would become another contested realm, one that would
continue to explore the knowledge produced about Korea, particularly the
writing of history. As became clear to many Korean writers, the spirit of
the nation might be located in history, but since Japanese authors had, by
the turn of the century, already developed a number of modern theories
about the Korean past that served their own colonial interests, new Korean
histories might dampen that spirit unless they treated Japanese historical
interpretations circumspectly. If resistance in the spiritual realm was less a
matter of self-strengthening and more one of remembering, the colonial
authorities were more than willing to assist Koreans in the ways they recalled
their national past.

From Ancient Imperial Myths to Modern Colonizing Myths

Shidehara's proposal to use Japanese-language textbooks was only the first
in a long line of disputes concerning textbooks. In the next few years, the

controversy was extended to history texts, focusing on the difficulties of re-counting early Japanese-Korean relations. As Korean scholars tried to answer the calls for a new curriculum and identify the locus of national spirit through history, various individuals — with or without the sponsorship of the Ministry of Education — responded by writing books intended for the class-room. Most turned to Confucian historiographic conventions of the late Chosŏn dynasty, modifying them in various ways to suit what they saw as the needs of a sovereign nation.[29]

Others were attracted to the new histories of Korea that had been written in Japan since the mid-Meiji period. Whether through the brief treatments of Korean history that regularly appeared in the Japanese media or through the detailed academic studies of the peninsula's history, historians in Korea were coming into contact with fresh historiographic techniques and empir-ical sources that offered new avenues for early Korean history. Many were intrigued. The same authority that had been invested in Japan in issues concerning *munmyŏng kaehwa* now spilled over into Japanese historiogra-phy, which because of its use of novel conventions and fresh narrative forms appeared decidedly modern to these aspiring nationalist historians. More-over, in their early calls for a new national history, many Korean historians bemoaned the dearth of sources for writing the early history of the peninsula. The "newly arriving Japanese histories," as one observer described them, accordingly were heralded also for the empirical sources they offered for filling in the lacunae of early Korean histories.[30]

Japanese historians had a long tradition of treating relations with the peninsula in their annals of the Japanese islands. The earliest book, the *Kojiki (Record of Ancient Matters,* 712), established a number of story lines that continued to be resurrected over the next millennium, often further elaborated and used for various historiographical and political ob-jectives. The primary purpose of this historical work was the consolidation and legitimization of the imperial house and its key supporting families. As has often been noted, this was accomplished by using various myths to link imperial rule to a purported age of the deities, when such events as the formation of the Japanese archipelago and the unification of the islands were undertaken by a succession of emperors depicted as descendants of the gods.[31] In this context, myths concerning Korea served a useful purpose.

The centuries preceding the compilation of the *Kojiki* had witnessed many interactions between the kingdoms on the peninsula and those on the islands. But the *Kojiki* omitted many of these events, since some of them, like the defeat of the Japanese navy by the combined efforts of the Korean Silla and the Chinese Tang dynasties, hardly served the work's aim of enhancing imperial authority. Instead, in a passage that acquired a significance remarkably out of proportion to its brevity, the *Kojiki* recounted how the gods had presented Emperor Chūai with a divine oracle to gain the lands to the west, Korea. For doubting whether such lands existed and refusing to undertake the expedition, the emperor died prematurely.[32] Only then did Empress Jingū lead armies across the sea to subjugate Silla, making the country her "royal stable groom" and setting up "offices" on the peninsula.[33] Few scholars today recognize Jingū as a historical figure or vouch for the accuracy of this account of Japanese actions on the peninsula, yet this version of relations with the peninsular kingdoms served the compiler's purpose well: here was a Japanese ruler with the military might to strike fear even in her neighbors across the sea.[34]

Jingū's mythical ventures were taken up in the later, more widely circulated historical work, *Nihon shoki* (*Chronicle of Japan*, 720). A much more detailed work than its predecessor, the *Nihon shoki* often offered multiple versions of the same events. It provided a richer account of the myth of Jingū, stating that after Emperor Chūai died for refusing to conquer the "Land of Treasure," Jingū dressed in the attire of a man, trained three divisions of an army, and, with battle-ax in hand, headed across to the peninsula.[35] The Silla king was depicted as so overwhelmed by the force that he offered no resistance. Instead, he recognized the divinity of Japan, took it upon himself to act as her "forage provider," promised in fulsome language to send tribute every spring and autumn, and provided hostages for the Japanese. The kings of Paekche (18 B.C.–A.D. 660) and Koguryŏ likewise swore to deliver annual tribute, promising that their "lands shall be styled thy western frontier provinces."[36] After instituting "interior governments" supported by her armies, the empress returned to her islands. In the *Nihon shoki*, these events not only were presented as the first extensive contact between the islands and the peninsula but also set the standard for the expected form of relationship between them — in short, submissiveness on the part of peninsular kingdoms as an indication of their recognition of Japanese superiority. For the remainder of the work, Silla is represented largely as a miscreant kingdom, frequently seeking to shirk its duties and repeatedly having to be persuaded to pay tribute, through the judicious use of threatened attacks or actual invasions.[37]

While many of these early myths were included in subsequent histories,[38] it was with the rise of nativist studies during Japan's Edo period (1600–1868) that the myths of the divine emperors, including the exploits of Jingū, attracted renewed attention. This movement is generally regarded as having begun with the scrutiny of ancient Japanese poetry as a way of uncovering a lost Japanese sensibility, but by the latter half of the eighteenth century, historical texts were being examined as well. The leading figure, Motoori Norinaga (1730–1801), attempted to eliminate in his commentaries on the *Kojiki* what he saw as the tendency of Confucian scholars to neglect and denigrate the ancient myths, myths that he believed demonstrated the superiority of Japan.[39] For Norinaga, Jingū's subjugation of Korea was nothing more than a historical fact, so that the subsequent submission of tribute by the Korean states was inevitable.[40]

This resurrection of imperial mythologies helped lay the intellectual foundation for the Meiji Restoration and the subsequent development of the modern emperor system. By the 1880s, when scholars were ready to write new national histories, the introduction of Rankian-style empiricist historical methodology cast a critical eye over many features of the accepted mythology, only this reconsideration did not extend to accounts of early relations with the Korean kingdoms.[41] In formative works such as *Kokushikan* (*A National History*), leading historians like Shigeno Yasutsugu, Kume Kunitake, and Hoshino Hisashi embraced the fundamental claims made about Korea in the early Japanese histories, making them into cause-and-effect national history.[42] Stripped of some of its more dramatic details, the myth of Jingū's conquest of Silla was featured in a section entitled the "Era of the Submission and Vassalage of Korean Lands" (Hanto fukuzoku no sei).[43] This piece concentrated on the imposition of an official administration over the peninsular kingdoms, claiming that they were directly controlled by what was to become known as the "Japanese government of Mimana." The establishment of Japanese rule over part of the Korean peninsula demonstrated the power and the prestige of the imperial line even in this distant time. These images of relations had first been used to consolidate the claims of the imperial line; now, more than a millennium later, they again proved useful in a new form of history in which a national narrative traced the deeds of the emperors. Thus from the earliest moments in modern Japanese historiography, representations of Korea were important as elaborations of the myths that became central to the imperial system and Japanese national history.

The treatment of Korea in these early national histories was based largely on Japanese sources, with an occasional addition of references to Chinese sources. But as Hatada Takashi has noted, the field of *tōyōshi* (Eastern history) began in the 1880s with studies of Korea, creating a separate field of inquiry that explored Korean sources for their material about both Japan and Korea. Led by Shiratori Kurakichi, scholars filled the Meiji period's historical journals with comparative studies of Japan and Korea as well as articles focusing exclusively on the peninsula.[44] The rise in studies of Korea, Hatada has pointed out, accompanied the increasingly close political and economic ties between the islands and the peninsula. These links were apparent in the newspapers and journals of that time, which placed current events into a historical framework that reflected many of the conventional ways of viewing Japanese-Korean relations. Although leading academics like Shiratori sometimes ventured into these more public venues, more often than not the nuances and complexities of the academic debates were overlooked by the media, which in most cases were eager to use versions of the ancient myths as a precedent for more intrusive involvement in Korean affairs.[45] The title of an article in a leading journal, *Taiyō (The Sun)*, bluntly described the annexation: "The Unification of Japan and Korea Is a Proposal for Resurrecting the Ancient."[46] A short version of Korean history appeared in the *Tōkyō Asahi shimbun*, in which a Confucian-style tracing of court history was supplemented with comments about the various Japanese conquests (including Jingū's), the rise of kingdoms that various Japanese had supposedly helped establish on the peninsula, and those Japanese who supposedly reached high levels of power at the court of Silla.[47] Historical Japanese activities in the peninsula, it insinuated, were therefore consistent with current colonial interests in Korea.

By the early 1900s, this version of the ancient relationship between Korea and Japan was so widely and unquestioningly accepted that articles in leading newspapers no longer needed to explain the mythical precedents, since their readers shared their understanding of them. Indeed, it was often from this shared departure point that newspapers launched more detailed treatments of other Korea-related topics. The *Tōkyō Asahi shimbun* could begin an essay on the history of art in Japan and Korea by simply repeating the suppositions, as though they were incontestable, that Jingū had conquered the three Han, setting up the administrative unit of Mimana. Koreans had accepted Confucianism to the degree that *sadaejuŭi* had become the national character (*kunigara*), so that "even in art it [Korea] imitated China, not having the originality to express its national character."[48] Or in a speech on annexation, Matsuda Masahisa could begin a talk on the "Korean problem" by noting that it extended back to the ancient history of two thousand

years ago and continued until today, as though the two were directly interlinked.[49] What had begun as a few lines in a book intended to legitimize
one family's claim to a throne had been transmogrified into a dominant,
widely espoused rationale for colonization.

The versions of the Korean past offered in these Japanese histories gained
a fairly large audience on the peninsula. Advertisements in the press show
the *Nihon shoki* for sale in eight Seoul bookstores in 1908.[50] For some, the
use of Japanese sources introduced by these works was simply good evidential
history: perusing and comparing different, often contradictory, sources in
order to discover the historical truth. Moreover, at a time when even history
was seen as a universal enterprise, employing Japanese sources gave the
authors a degree of cosmopolitanism, something they were eager to cultivate.
One textbook writer, Kim T'aegyŏng complained that earlier Korean historians referred only to Chinese works, but now in an age when "ten thousand
countries" were communicating and exchanging ideas, the abundant Japanese works on Korean history should be consulted.[51] They were. History
became one more item of exchange, as authors, ranging from little-known
textbook editors to some of the most prolific writers of the era, began to
select information from Japanese works relating to Korea for incorporation
into their own studies.

In some cases, the stories about Jingū were incorporated without question
into new Korean accounts. A good example is Kim T'aegyŏng's textbook for
schoolchildren, first printed in 1902 under the title *Tongsa kyeryak* (*A Concise Korean History*), then republished in an edited form in 1906 under the
slightly modified title of *Yŏksa kyeryak* (*A Concise History*). Although intended for the schools, Kim's *Yŏksa kyeryak* must have been tough slogging
for students, as it was written in classical Chinese and dealt with many of
the historiographical principles that had interested late-Chosŏn-dynasty
scholars. Nevertheless, this "compass to the past," as one reviewer termed
the earlier edition,[52] followed, in the words of its preface, "the recent examples of national histories for countries around the world."[53] Besides including a second preface to the volume by Shidehara Hiroshi, the Japanese
adviser to the Ministry of Education who had caused an uproar over his
textbook plans, Kim cited Japanese primary sources and secondary sources
in his bibliography and text. Based on these sources, Kim offered a typical
account of Jingū's exploits. In a rather matter-of-fact manner, he described
how Jingū dressed in male attire, picked up a battle-ax, and led three armies
across to the peninsula. He recounted how the Silla king, fearing the might

of these armies, immediately petitioned for peace, whereupon Jingū installed some military commanderies and returned to the islands.[54] Later, Kim again wrote about Japanese activities on the peninsula. This time, in an alliance with Paekche, Japan attacked Silla. Emerging victorious, Japan was credited with establishing a separate realm on the peninsula called Great Kaya (TaeKaya), its administration ruling a portion of the southern peninsula where soldiers were garrisoned.[55]

In a few areas, however, Kim did disagree with the version of events recorded in the *Nihon shoki*. In particular, he added an editorial comment disputing the constant references to the envoys of various Korean kingdoms who traveled to Japan to offer tribute. Contrary to the Japanese accounts, Kim stated that Koguryŏ and Paekche instead took the initiative to send emissaries to Japan in order to establish good relations.[56] Such quibbles did not detract from the main consequence of his version of early Korean-Japanese relations: he had accepted the fundamental Japanese historical claim that in an earlier age Japan had ruled part of the Korean peninsula. Indeed, insofar as Kim challenged a number of minor points presented in the Japanese records, the effect of his evidential approach was to confirm those features of the story that he did not question. Thus, the *Yŏksa kyeryak* reproduced to a remarkable degree one of the central Japanese myths about early relations with the peninsula, making it part of the new national history taught to Korean schoolchildren.

The claim that Jingū extended Japanese rule — in either the form of a government or merely a military garrison — over sections of the peninsula was an issue that historical geographers also addressed. Again, as in the case of creating new histories, while there were constant calls for new geographies, it was easier to demand them than to produce them. Chang Chiyŏn, one of the most widely published writers of the period, responded by revisiting an earlier geographical work written in 1811 by Chŏng Yagyong, *An Investigation of Our Nation's Territory (Abang kangyŏkko)*. Chang amended this work in various spots so as to serve his nationalist purposes better and had it published and distributed by his newspaper house.[57] But as Chang noted, Chŏng Yagyong wrote the book at a time when he had no access to Japanese histories, meaning that issues like Mimana that today "could not be overlooked" in the study of territory were left out of the work — an indication of just how deeply these questions had penetrated scholarly circles by Chang's time.[58] To compensate, Chang appended a section entitled

"Imna" — the Korean pronunciation of the two characters making up the Japanese term Mimana — in which he dealt with these questions more fully than did any other work of the period.

Unlike Kim Taegyŏng, Chang offered Japanese records as a "supplement" to Korean records, approaching them with skepticism. In the seven pages devoted to this question, Chang constantly compared Japanese sources with Korean ones to verify dates and events in an attempt to sort out conflicting versions. Alternative primary sources were included side by side, followed in the end with Chang's own opinion.[59] Imna, identified as an alternative name for what in Korean records had been more conventionally known as Tae-Kaya, was depicted as having been squeezed between its more powerful neighbors, at times submitting to Silla and at other times resorting to assistance from Japan. The Jingū story found its way into Chang's work as a précis of the *Nihon shoki* version of the story, but Chang followed the account with expressions of doubts about Japan's claims that it had ruled substantial portions of the peninsula. That Korean kingdoms regularly offered tribute to the Japanese court was little more than the "self-conceit" of the *Nihon shoki* compilers, for which, Chang concluded, there was insufficient proof. Paekche, he asserted, certainly had relations with Japan, but as the strongest of the Korean kingdoms, these ties were based on an equal exchange, not the submission of tribute. Change admitted that in an earlier period, before Silla had developed into a strong kingdom, Jingū may have attacked the peninsula and set up an armed garrison, but he dismissed the possibility that this meant all of Imna had submitted to or was controlled by Japan. Moving to restrict the spatial scope of this Japanese control, Chang was willing to allocate only a small enclave to Japanese control, one that he likened to the three ports in the southeast opened in 1426 to Japanese traders.[60] Although Chang, like Kim T'aegyŏng before him, challenged certain aspects of the Japanese accounts, he retold the story of Jingū, thus opening the possibility of Japanese rule, however limited in area, on the peninsula. One of the most widely read nationalist monographs of the period — and one that continues to be translated into modern vernacular Korean to this day[61] — again conveyed a fundamental myth of Japanese history to its Korean readership. By the end of 1906, any widely read student of Korean history would likely have been familiar with the outlines of the Jingū myth. Ironically, unsustainable myths that offered a rationale for resurrecting a modern version of the ancient Japanese rule had gained a foothold in the writings of nationalist scholars, all in the name of a new national history and geography.

Contentious Histories

By 1908, alternative ways of employing Japanese histories of Korea emerged that demonstrated their usefulness while underscoring their political delicacy, even danger, to the nation's spirit. In this year, the textbook writer Hyŏn Ch'ae published the third edition of his translation of Hayashi Taisuke's 1892 *Chōsenshi* (*A History of Korea*) and his 1901 *Chōsen kinseishi* (*A History of Modern Korea*) under the title *Tongguk saryak* (*A Brief History of the Eastern Kingdom*).[62] Hyŏn noted in the preface that Hayashi had "put great effort into our country's history" and, in a style of admission common to the period, lamented, "Alas! Not being able to write the history of the country one lives in, to the point that foreigners do it in one's place — is this not humiliating?"[63] However humiliating it may have been, Hayashi's work appealed to Hyŏn because of its strong evidential approach to both new and old sources. In addition, its organizing principles moved away from Confucian conventions to offer a Korean history arranged for the first time under such non-court-centered subjects such as customs, manufacturing, institutions, literature, and the arts.

What Hyŏn identified in the preface as a "translation" was in fact a substantially modified version of Hayashi's work.[64] It is possible that Hyŏn was appealing to Japanese sensibilities so as to get the work by the censors with a minimum of fuss. By this time, historians in the peninsula had become well aware of what some plainly called "mistakes" in Japanese works and what others realized were their self-serving aspects.[65] Hyŏn seems to have tried to take advantage of fresh Japanese approaches to Korean history while expurgating those sections that offended his nationalist sensibilities. Most notably, this meant reinterpreting the myths surrounding Jingū, which had appeared in the first lines of Hayashi's preface and were featured prominently in the body of the text. Hyŏn instead chose to contextualize Jingū's attack on the peninsula as one of the many battles among the Korean kingdoms as well as between them and Japan. The only consequence of Jingū's attack was that the younger brother of the Silla king was offered as a hostage, although his return was arranged shortly afterward. As a textbook intended for middle school students, Hyŏn presented this history without referring to any problems in the sources or any of the controversies. His brief treatment of Jingū did not extend beyond this mention of an attack and never raised the issues of garrisons or tribute that were central to the myth in Japan.[66] Indeed, he reversed the question of tribute, noting that it was Japan, specifically the people of Ezo, that had dispatched tributary missions to Korea, an event not covered in Hayashi's work.[67]

In his treatment of the Chosŏn dynasty, Hyŏn closely followed Hayashi's *Chōsen kinseishi*, frequently using the same headings in Hayashi's work for his own subtitles. Hyŏn did make strategic changes, however. Most notably, in the section on Hideyoshi Toyotomi's invasion of the peninsula at the end of the sixteenth century, Hyŏn answered the calls for a remembrance of past heroes by describing the officials who sacrificed their lives in combat. Without drawing explicit parallels to the events of his own time in the countryside, Hyŏn devoted much space to detailing the many victories won by the sixteenth-century *ŭibyŏng*. What in Hayashi's version amounted to a Japanese defeat at the hands of overwhelming Chinese forces — another example of *sadaejuŭi* in the Japanese author's eyes — in Hyŏn's hands became a victory not by the Ming armies but by the Korean fighters in the countryside together with Yi Sunsin and his turtle boats on the seas.[68] Such shifts in content were numerous, giving this so-called translation an interpretation very different from that of the original work.

The divergent political motives of these two works were most noticeable in their final sections. Both authors depicted the last years of the Chosŏn dynasty, especially after the arrival of the West, as an era dominated by two major, related, themes: national sovereignty and reform. For Hayashi, this was manifested internally in a struggle between two parties, what he called the "sadae party" and the "independence party." Using common tropes for the peninsula, his narrative showed that the strength of the former combined with the inability of the latter prevented any progress, serving only to create chaos. The very last sentence of the work asserted that it was only through Japanese power (*Nihon no chikara*) that Korea "completely cast off the despotic fetters of the Qing and became an independent country."[69] This, then, was the culmination of Hayashi's two-volume narrative of the entirety of Korean history: a feckless Korea that was unable to master its own affairs and could reach the teleological goal of national history — sovereignty — only with the help of its neighbor. In short, a Korea that was saved from its own history by Japan.

Hyŏn did not feel compelled to alter all aspects of Hayashi's account of

the late Chosŏn period. Hyŏn's account, like Hayashi's, was concerned with
Korea's dependence on China. He wrote about the political schisms caused
by factionalism, emphasizing foreign invasions. That these historiographic
tendencies did not offend the sensibilities of a nationalist writer in the first
decade of the century indicates just how much congruency there was between the nationalist and colonialist approaches to the peninsula's past, despite their divergent political ambitions. Reflecting their common commitment to capitalist modernity, colonial and nationalist history often evaluated
the past according to the same criteria. As seen in Hyŏn Ch'ae's account,
the result was that a nationalist diagnosis of the historical reasons for Korea's
crisis shared much with their colonial opponents, even though their descriptions of the past ended with conflicting conclusions: Japan rescuing Korea
versus Japan crushing Korea.

As was common among Korean writers, Hyŏn acknowledged that Korean
independence had been achieved only through the Treaty of Shimonoseki,
although he did expunge Hayashi's point about the role of Japanese power.
But unlike Hayashi, Hyŏn did not make this the single, final statement of
his history. In a forty-four-page addendum, he continued Korea's national
story until his own time, thereby providing a broader context for the Treaty
of Shimonoseki. Noting that Korea had been moved by Japan's righteousness
at the conclusion of the war, Hyŏn traced in more detail than had any other
source available at the time the subsequent Japanese violation of what he
called the "deep trust" in which Koreans held their neighbors.[70] What had
been the culmination of Hayashi's narrative, the Shimonoseki treaty, was
overshadowed by Hyŏn's exhaustive treatment of the 1905 Protectorate
Treaty, a very different end — both metaphorically and teleologically — of
Korea's national history. The Treaty of Shimonoseki was no longer presented
as a move toward the peninsula's freedom, as it was in Hayashi's work, but
just one more step leading toward protectorate status. The Chosŏn dynasty
may not have been able to protect its independence, but whereas in the past
it had been a problem vis-à-vis China, Hyŏn now showed that it was the
activist Japanese policy, goaded by the lingering legacy of the "ideology of
dependency" (ŭiroe sasang) that had led to the Protectorate.[71] While Hyŏn's
work both appropriated and, in its judicious changes, took a stand against
certain tendencies in Japanese scholarship, it did so in a subtle fashion designed more to get the revamped history past the textbook inspectors than
to disparage openly Japanese versions of the past. Although the changes
reflected a nationalist orientation, they were made in such a way that only

those few readers familiar with Hayashi's original work could detect the shifts and their ideological significance. The significance of his alterations even escaped his later nationalist critics.[72] This was a new Korean history in the guise of a direct translation of an eminent Japanese scholar, discreetly slipping into the voice of Japanese authority a nationalist version of the past that questioned the motives and directions of Japanese policy toward the peninsula. It was anything but a confrontational approach, yet when the creativity of Hyŏn's translation came to the attention of the Resident General Office in 1909, the book was quickly banned — always an indication of the subversive nature of the offending piece.[73]

Others, however, were less reluctant to take an openly adversarial stance. At the opposite end of the spectrum from Kim T'aegyŏng was the *TaeHan maeil sinbo*. With writers like Sin Ch'aeho working under the protection of the paper's British owner, it was free to identify and attack Japanese colonial myths, which it did on a regular basis.[74] In one highly polemical editorial, entitled "Absurd Passages in Textbooks," it scornfully dismissed Japanese claims about early relations between the two countries.[75] It pointed out that in an age when Korea had established its first kingdom but "Japan had yet to come up with a national name" and an era when there was a flourishing culture on the peninsula but Japan did not even have a writing system, there was no possibility that Japan could have dominated any part of Korea. That such a history supported Japanese political goals was a point not lost on the editors, as they accused Japanese historians of deliberately manipulating the past in order to bolster Japan's political position on the peninsula:

> Since the Meiji Restoration, Japanese have waited for the opportunity to extend their reach to Korea. At first they used their pens and tongues to vilify and humiliate [Korea], so as to drum up the feeling of foreign competition [*oegyŏng sasang*] among their own people, saying that "since ancient times, Korea has been a vassal state under Japan, that Empress Jingū conquered Silla, that Sŏkt'arhae[76] was a Japanese person, and that the majority of Koreans were the descendants of Japanese." Never before in history have events been fabricated to this extent.

This editorial implicitly acknowledged a link between national interests and histories, indicating a certain sympathy for the duty of their Japanese counterparts to create the myths the editors so eagerly wished to debunk.

But such an admission could not be reserved for the Korean historians who accepted these myths. The editorial's wrath came down most harshly on those Korean textbook writers who did not investigate the past on their own but "crazily believe the words of others, commonly incorporating them into their own textbooks." Ultimately, it was these writers, not the original Japanese authors of these theories, who posed a danger, since it was their books that were shaping the self-knowledge of Koreans. Reverting to the language of the spiritual nation, the editorial castigated the writers for ruining the country's future by confusing "the thoughts of our youth." These books, the editorial concluded, were destroying "our national soul."

The year 1908 was crucial to the development of Korean history writing. By the end of the year, a whole range of written materials were available to those interested in the early history of the peninsula. On the politically sensitive issue of early Korean-Japanese relations, the uncritical incorporation of the myths of Jingū and her peninsular garrisons coexisted with the anticolonial editorials of the *TaeHan maeil sinbo*, which tried to dismiss these myths. Between these two poles lay various other interpretations, including the more skeptical work of Chang Chiyŏn and the "translation" by Hyŏn Ch'ae of Hayashi Taisuke's work. Besides these four, other alternatives appeared in this year, but all had a short publication life span.[77]

Two years later, when Korea was annexed into the Japanese empire, all possibilities of republishing these works or printing new ones ended. Upon annexation, the colonial authorities immediately moved to control the press, either shutting it down or, as in the case of the *TaeHan maeil sinbo*, turning this staunchly anticolonial paper into the main Korean-language publication of the Governor General Office. Careful attention was given to textbooks. Some were banned outright, while teachers were informed by early 1911 what sections of particular textbooks could be taught in what fashion.[78] Paralleling official efforts to control textbooks already in circulation was a surge in writing — both officially sponsored and private — on the historical background of annexation.

Both in the home islands and on the peninsula, commentators regularly returned to early history as the context for explaining recent political events. Annexation was an unprecedented event that now had to be woven into the seamless web of Japanese national history, as suggested by the title of an article in the *Tōkyō Asahi shimbun*, "The Annexation of Korea and National History." As was common during these years, annexation was incorporated by denying its novelty, thereby making annexation the final resolution of a two-thousand-year-old problem in Japanese history.[79] Korea was presented as a historical part of Japan, a "branch family"(*bunke*) of the Japanese "main family" (*honke*), which, if somewhat wayward for a couple of thousand years, was finally returning to the fold. Jingū's conquest featured prominently in this narrative. The inconvenient fact—one that doggedly accompanied this line of reasoning—that after the defeat of Mimana, Korea and Japan had anything but intimate ties was shunted aside by means of a simple strategy: because distances were far and communication inconvenient, it was claimed, Koreans had been able to rebel. Thereafter, "Japanese and Koreans forgot they had the same ancestors and were of the same country. Ultimately, they ended up developing a sense of being separate countries." Over time, Koreans had also been imprisoned in *sadaejuǔi* thought, continuing this separation. Annexation, then, would excise this sense of separateness that had been allowed—improperly, it was suggested—to develop over the past centuries.[80]

In the newly annexed colony, similar views became part of the official voice of the Governor General Office as expressed in the *Maeil sinbo*. The office quickly moved to present these myths as part of the historical basis for annexing the peninsula to the islands. Six months into Japanese rule, a speech by a foreign affairs official, Komatsu Midori, on Korean-Japanese historical relations was translated and reprinted on the front page of the *Maeil sinbo*.[81] As Komatsu asserted without elaboration, the ancient Japanese histories were most reliable, and the stories of Chūai and Jingū, even if not corroborated by equivalent accounts in Korean records, could be confirmed by archaeological evidence. What the story of Jingū showed, according to Komatsu, was that "Japanese power extended to the greater part of the Korean peninsula."[82] He glossed over the irksome problem that even in his own interpretation, the number of years of division far exceeded the number of years of unity, with the same explanation that because of communication and transportation difficulties, relations were "not constant" over the years. Nevertheless, "the recent amalgamation of Korea and Japan is not the first integration of two peoples and two countries but, rather, is nothing more than the resurrection of the same related people with ancient roots who were temporarily separated."[83] This, then, was to be the official version of the past, one of the mainstays of Japanese colonial ideology for the next thirty-five years. Over this time, many other ways of presenting annexation as the "return of a separated family" emerged. Racial theories, often buttressed by physical and cultural anthropology, abounded, as did various hypotheses based on archaeological work on the peninsula.[84] Despite the further and more diverse articulation of colonial ideologies, history—in particular, the myth of Jingū's subjugation of the peninsula — always remained central to the legitimization of Japan's presence.

Japanese Colonialism on the International Stage

How Korea, past and present, was to be represented was a struggle that extended beyond the Japanese islands and the Korean peninsula to the wider international stage. From the imposition of the Protectorate in 1905, the Japanese colonial leadership carefully cultivated Western public opinion about their activities in the peninsula. As one Western observer of Japan commented later, "Few nations have striven so manfully to create a pleasant impression upon foreigners as have the Japanese"[85] — an effort that in the first two decades of the century extended to its colonial record. As a late colonizer, Japan remained vulnerable to the competing interests of the Western powers. Bitter memories still lingered of the 1895 Triple Intervention, in which Germany, Russia, and France had forced the return of one of the most valuable spoils of Japan's victory over China, control of the Liaodong peninsula. Ten years later, Japan's newfound status as a regional power still remained dependent on an intricately woven set of diplomatic arrangements.[86] Its 1902 alliance with Britain together with the 1905 agreement recognizing American interests in the Philippines in favor of a reciprocal recognition of its own status in Korea is what had given Japan, at a diplomatic level, a free hand on the peninsula. Gaining the support of public opinion in the West and deflecting any criticism of its Korean policy protected these diplomatic arrangements and safeguarded them against a repeat of a Triple Intervention kind of external interference. Such sensitivity and vulnerability were reflected in the extraordinary efforts by Japanese officials and private newspapers to reassure Western diplomats, businessmen, and missionaries that Japanese domination would not endanger their own interests in Korea.[87] Newspapers such as the *Asahi shimbun* regularly featured reports on foreign reactions to Korea policy. In the days immediately following annexation, there was more news in its pages about Western newspapers' responses and politicians' speeches than treatment of public opinion within Korea.[88]

Moreover, just as Japan's earlier renegotiations of its unequal treaties with the West at the end of the nineteenth century had entailed a revamping of many social and political institutions to prove that Japan merited treatment as an equal, so too did its rise to colonizer status require that Japan exhibit the proper requisites of a civilized empire builder. Japan was now not only the prodigal student who had reformed itself to the point that it could vanquish a major power, it could now also reform others, participating in the global project of civilizing the noncivilized. As Alexis Dudden has shown, the mastery and manipulation of international diplomatic conventions and language were integral to gaining the West's approval.[89] Equally important was the production and dissemination of knowledge about Korea that configured the Japanese-Korean relationship as one of colonizer to colonized, a knowledge that rationalized the usurpation of another nation's sovereignty and granted, however begrudgingly, legitimacy to the brutal tactics that such action sometimes entailed. In short, the colonial authorities sought to disseminate to the West the rationale for their growing Asian empire — originally developed domestically during the Meiji period and then, after 1905, extended into Korea.

To this end, an elaborate propaganda campaign was launched by the Resident General Office and, after 1910, continued by the Governor General Office. For a Japanese-speaking colonial administration seeking to gain the West's support for its endeavors in Korea, this plunged the office into the task of preparing foreign-language materials about its endeavors. Its premier series, begun in 1907, was a glossy yearbook written in English entitled *Annual Report on the Progress and Reforms in Korea,* a less than subtle promotion of colonialism. During the first decade of publication, the yearbooks' format was a "before and after" presentation offering explanatory, pictorial, and statistical evidence of the changes Japan had made on the peninsula since establishing the Protectorate. This approach could be applied to almost any topic, from hygiene to road systems, with the contrast achieved through the judicious choice of adjectives. Accordingly, the peninsula's financial condition before annexation was in the "wildest confusion," and expenditures were "wasted to no purpose." But after Japan's reforms, the foundation of Korea's finances was "firmer," and details of how these achievements had been accomplished were buttressed by reams of statistics.[90] This contrastive effect was also captured in photographs, as in the case of two pictures of the Han River south of Seoul. A photograph of a bridge built under the new Japanese administration was placed next to a second photograph showing a few boats moving back and forth across the river, labeled "before the construction of the Iron Bridge."[91]

The prose of these reports was not always even this subtle. As one historical account opened, "For many centuries . . . her [Korean] people did little towards development as a nation." All the standard reasons were trotted out—reliance on China, corruption, factionalism, and inability to reform. "All culture was lost; industry was at its lowest ebb; and the life and property of the people was in constant danger."[92] The editor of 1917–18 annual report wrote an especially enthusiastic description of subsequent changes: "It appears as though the entire Peninsula, for the first time in its modern history, has been blessed with the dawning of prosperity and has recovered from the unspeakable poverty and depression to which its people had been subjected for many a century past." Japanese education policy, it explained, "is making a favorable impression upon the natives, and is aiding wonderfully in the promotion of the standard of civilization in both town and country."[93] While the emphasis was on material additions—road systems, sanitation facilities, modern buildings, and the like—the editors were careful to make sure that material progress could not be interpreted as leaving moral well-being behind. They may have claimed to be modernizing Korea, but their efforts left no room for the malaise of modernity. "Though the progress of material civilization is apt to induce moral relaxation," one volume stated, "the public morality of the Koreans is in general steadily improving."[94] These volumes were powerful testaments to Japan's colonial efforts. Individually, they served to publicize Japanese enterprises on the peninsula during the latest year, and together, they sought to offer a sequential record of—as the titles suggest—progress over time. These presented the public face of colonialism, frequently acting as a source of information for Western writers about Korea.[95]

Besides such official publications, individual colonial officers frequently arranged for articles to be published under their own names in Western mainstream publications. In his position as resident general, Itō Hirobumi explained in 1908 to the readers of *Harper's Weekly* the reasons for Emperor Kojong's abdication, assuring them that "sincerity was the key note of all that I have tried to accomplish in Korea on behalf of the Korean Imperial family and of the people."[96] His assistant, Motosada Zumoto, wrote an article for the influential American news weekly *The Independent* that presented annexation as "the most unique opportunity ever offered her [Korea] for her regeneration and advancement along the line of modern civilization."[97] Terauchi Masatake, the governor general notorious for his comment about whipping Koreans with scorpions, submitted eleven chapters under his name for a collection of writings on Korea, published in 1910 by a Boston publishing house. The chapters treated such subjects as "industrial encouragement," "sanitation" and "trade conditions," the type of topics found in the annual reports, without any hint, of course, of either scorpions or whips.[98] Another governor general, Saito Makoto, also published an article in *The Independent*. Entitled "A Message from the Imperial Japanese Government to the American People," it was intended to dispel any disquiet that may have arisen among Americans about Japan's Korea policy from reports about "recent disturbances," Saito's euphemism for the massive March First demonstrations of 1919.[99] Such pieces appeared in magazines as diverse as the *Atlantic Monthly*,[100] *Review of Reviews*,[101] *Missionary Review*,[102] and *Outlook*.[103] Written by a variety of officials, from the head of water engineering to statesmen like Count Okuma, these articles tended to present the individual officers of the colonial state as dedicated to the cause of "civilization," eager to make personal sacrifices to help Koreans develop.[104] They highlighted the paternalistic side of their colonial efforts while concealing the harsher aspects — always phrased in the language of enlightenment and appealing to Western sensibilities about the rationality and advisability of colonial rule.

Far more effective than these obviously self-serving pieces by colonial officials was the writing of Western travelers. Many Western observers of Japan, impressed by Japan's defeat of China in 1895 and Russia in 1905, were willing to accept Japan's decision to play a larger role in Asian affairs. Japan's imitation of Western colonial rhetoric, moreover, struck a chord with a public that more often than not was enthusiastic about their own nation's colonial entanglements. When Western travelers came to Korea, often via Japan, they were often already well disposed toward Japan's involvement in Korea. The Japanese colonial authorities built on this disposition, often targeting influential travelers and appealing to these sympathies in the belief that they were potential shapers of public opinion back in their home countries. Some individuals were invited to the peninsula with the express purpose of having them write about colonial policies. George Trumbell Ladd, a Yale University professor of philosophy and self-professed "friend of Japan,"[105] was approached during one of his lecture tours in Japan by Itō Hirobumi, the current resident general, to visit Korea. In the volume based on this trip, *In Korea with Marquis Ito* — which Ladd, in somewhat of an understatement, confessed was of an "apologetic character"[106] — he bluntly described the purpose of his visit. Itō was concerned with the "exaggerations and falsehoods" about his administration that had been circulating among Westerners and "thought that I might assist his administration if I would spend some time upon the ground as his guest."[107] Ladd was given special access, as he repeatedly pointed out, and "the purpose of the visit was to be in full accord with that of the Resident General Office — to help the Koreans, and to convince all reasonable foreigners of the intention to deal justly with them."[108] Itō's strategy worked wonderfully, as Ladd became a leading supporter of Japan and proponent of what he called the "benevolent assimilation" of Korea into the Japanese empire.[109]

Other visitors to Korea, although not expressly invited by Japanese authorities, were nevertheless often hosted and guided by Japanese officials. Important foreigners were the most common targets of these efforts. They often were granted visits to the highest levels of Japanese administrative circles, and their itineraries were frequently arranged by resident Japanese. Such was the experience of the British officer Herbert H. Austin, who during seven days spent "scampering" around Seoul was accompanied by Japanese interpreters, called on leading officials in the administration for tea, and toured such Japanese institutions as schools, prisons, and military barracks. For the duration of his trip, Korea remained comfortably on the outside, only occasionally seen through the prisms set up by his Japanese handlers.[110] F. A. McKenzie, a reporter for the London *Daily Mail*, who originally was sympathetic to the Japanese project in Korea but quickly became critical of their tactics and methods, wrote in 1908:

> Foreign visitors of influence were naturally drawn to the Japanese rather than to the Koreans. They found in the officials of the Residency General a body of courteous and delightful men, who knew the Courts of Europe, and were familiar with world affairs. On the other hand, the Korean spokesmen had no power or skill in putting their case so as to attract European sympathy. One distinguished foreigner, who returned home and wrote a book largely given up to laudation of the Japanese and contemptuous abuse of the Koreans, admitted that he had never, during his journey, had any contact with Koreans save those his Japanese guides brought to him. Some foreign journalists were at first blinded in the same way.[111]

The advantages that this approach gave Japan in influencing Western public opinion did not escape Korean scrutiny. The *TaeHan maeil sinbo* made just this point in an article discussing the published writings of George Kennan, after his fact-finding tour to the East on behalf of the American president. In particular, the paper took umbrage at his recommendation that the United States not interfere with Japanese actions on the peninsula. "What qualifications does Kennan have to speak about Japanese behavior in Korea?" it asked. His reports, it argued, were little more than the repetition of arguments found in Japanese newspapers and heard in Tokyo. Speaking more broadly, the paper noted that the Japanese deliberately manipulated visiting foreigners, offering Kennan as a prime example of their success. "Mr. Kennan is a naive child on a theater stage," it concluded.[112]

By 1910, having repeatedly seen this style of exchange and read the results in foreign newspapers, the *TaeHan maeil sinbo* suggested that in an era of international exchange when Korea was "sitting in a deep bitter prison," there was still one way for Koreans to bypass Japan and have direct interchanges with the world's peoples — through one-on-one exchanges with European and American tourists.[113] The paper told its readers that any foreigners coming this far to Korea were not there just to gaze at the beautiful scenery but wanted to know about the people and its customs, were curious about how widely the "flag of civilization" had been planted since the opening of the ports, and were keen to find out whether Korea since 1905 "had climbed to pleasurable heights or plunged into the water and fire." Complaining that when foreigners actually came to the peninsula, Korean faces were as seldom seen by them as "stars on a bright day," it noted that all their dealings were with Japanese, so that they believed the Japanese were virtuous and good and that Koreans were ignorant. Urging Koreans to engage in this style of private diplomacy (*sagyo*), the paper concluded that "this seems like a trifling matter, but the extent of its influence is truly great."[114]

Urging individual diplomacy was not enough for the editors of the *TaeHan maeil sinbo*. The problem of Western misperceptions of Korea, they argued, was exacerbated by the deceit of the Japanese media. "Japanese newspapers make great efforts to conceal from the world Japanese behavior in the peninsula, deceiving them [about the situation]." It accused the Japanese newspapers of distorting facts when it suited their purpose and failing to report controversial matters that undercut their objectives. Countering such false reports, the paper announced, was a major objective of the paper.[115] To this end, in both its Korean- and English-language editions, the *TaeHan maeil sinbo* regularly took Japanese papers, in both Korea and Japan, to task for what it perceived as insults to Korea or inaccurate reporting. Not surprisingly, Japanese officials moved to muzzle the paper.

Ever since its owner-publisher, Ernest Bethell, had come from Japan to cover the Russo-Japanese War for the *London Daily Chronicle* and ended up establishing the bilingual newspaper, Japanese officials had tried to encourage the paper to take a pro-Japanese editorial stance. But Bethell's initial enthusiasm for Japanese involvement in Korea turned into disillusionment as he witnessed the unveiling of specific policies that, he felt, violated Japanese responsibilities as colonizers by advancing their own interests at the expense of Koreans.[116] Japanese expectations that this Englishman would provide an independent vehicle promoting the virtues of their efforts on the peninsula turned into outright alarm as Bethel veered in the opposite direction to articulate an anti-Japanese position. Because of his extraterritorial status, his criticisms could be bolder than the censored, Korean-owned papers. Japanese officials immediately began to pressure their British ally to rein in Bethell's editorial pen. At this time, the activity of all British journalists in Asia was controlled by ministerial orders in council, which could decide the fate of any newspaper. However eagerly British officials wished over the next few years to remove what was proving an irritant in their relations with Japan, they were more worried that any action on their part might have consequences for the principle of extraterritoriality and the management of other British papers in Asia. As Britain procrastinated, the influence of the paper expanded. Japanese intelligence reports showed that the paper's influence and reputation now outstripped all others.[117] Moreover, its reports were frequently being reprinted in other Asian newspapers, and according to some foreign observers, the Japanese authorities were worried about the effect of the Korean-language editions on the growth of anti-Japanese sentiment.[118]

British indecision led the colonial authorities in 1906 to pursue a second strategy. They set up a rival English-language newspaper, the *Seoul Press*. As one observer wryly commented, "Here we have had and have the amazing journalistic situation of two daily papers being published in the English language in a city containing probably not more than a hundred white men."[119] Commercial viability aside, the *Seoul Press* attempted to undermine the reputation of the *Korea Daily News*. It accused the paper of duping Koreans into believing that independence was a possibility, thereby encouraging Koreans to oppose Japan.[120] The paper presented itself as the true friend of Korea, taking swipes at unnamed newspapers, asserting that "gar-

bled half-truths and grotesque falsehoods can never serve any good purpose."[121] Continuing this theme, it noted that

> these "friends" of Korea of course avow a consuming and disinterested
> desire to do service to Korea and her people. If so, it must be observed
> that they are going about it in a wrong way. Instead of serving the
> Koreans, they are only doing their best to inflict incalculable injury
> upon their "beloved" people.[122]

These people were in fact "the worst enemies Korea ever had." True friends,
it insisted, should persuade Koreans that the only sensible course of action
was cooperation with Japan.[123]

While *The Seoul Press* railed, Japanese diplomats continued to work for
a more conclusive settlement. In mid-1907, when the Japanese threatened
to use their police powers to shut down the paper or deport Bethell, the
British finally succumbed. Bethell was brought to court in November 1907
under an order in council prohibiting newspapermen "to produce or to
excite a breach of the public order."[124] He was found guilty and placed on
a six-month pledge of good behavior against three hundred pounds sterling.
But the colonial authorities, dissatisfied that the paper was still publishing
and realizing that at best, its editorial platform would be muted for only six
months, continued to urge Britain to remove Bethell from the country. Succumbing once again to this diplomatic pressure, the British put Bethell on
trial for a second time in June 1908. This time his punishment was more
severe: sentenced to three weeks' imprisonment, Bethell was forced to pledge
his good behavior for six months under the threat of deportation. He died
shortly thereafter. The paper, sold to Alfred W. Marnham just before the
second trial, continued to publish its critical views, though in a somewhat
more subdued tone. The most dogged critic of Japanese policy in Korea had
succumbed.[125]

Countering criticism and promoting their efforts as a *mission civiliatrice*
were not the only ways that Japanese colonial theory came to be disseminated in the West. Although Western writers' primary interest in Korea was
comparative colonialism, their interest extended to Korean history as a way
of contextualizing recent events. But because Koreans were still developing
new approaches to national history and because there was little available
in English about Korean premodern history, it was the Japanese versions
of the Korean past that tended to shape foreign commentary on Korean

history.[126] This can be seen in the widely read work of Joseph Longford. Author of one of the best-selling popular histories of Japan in the early twentieth century, entitled The Story of Old Japan, Longford capitalized on this success by turning his attention to Korea, publishing The Story of Korea one year after its annexation.[127] Like many other writers about Korea in these years, Longford had strong Japanese connections. Having served as the British consul in Nagasaki, Longford was a professor of Japanese at King's College, and as he explained in the preface to The Story of Korea, he consulted with the embassy's Japanese staff when clarifying points about Korean history.[128] Devoting an entire chapter to early Korean-Japanese relations, Longford provided one of the most detailed accounts about early Japanese myths relating to Korea available at the time in a popular English-language work. Longford's treatment of these accounts delighted in the mythical aspects of the story at the same time as he quickly dismissed their historical value. Citing the work of W. G. Aston on the myth of Jingū, he noted that European scholars, "unbiased by the national vanity and prejudices of the descendants of these invaders," had "cast a deep shadow of scepticism on the whole of the romantic story."[129] He also referred to Korean historical records, which he felt were far more credible than their Japanese counterparts, noting that they did not mention Jingū.

Although Longford ostensibly rejected these myths, in his actual account of the peninsula's history, he merely discounted the way in which the story was remembered in the Japan of his day. He noted the pride the Japanese people felt in this myth:

> All Japanese . . . to the present day hold firmly to the belief that the whole of the peninsula of Korea submitted to their great Empress, that the three kingdoms bound themselves by similar vows, and thenceforth became the vassals of Japan, and Jingo's [sic] conquest was the remote foundation of every claim which Japan has since made on Korea down to the present generation.[130]

Where Longford disagreed with the myth and its current usage in Japan was in not accepting that the entire peninsula had succumbed to Japan. Regardless of the fantastical claims made in the early histories about Jingū, Longford willingly accepted the basis of these events as denoting a defeat of the kingdom of Silla. "It is not difficult to understand," he wrote, why an "unwarlike" kingdom like Silla might fall to a Japanese attack, but "faith is sorely tested" by the subsequent stories of Paekche and especially Koguryŏ voluntarily submitting to Japan without a single battle. Without clearly explaining why one part of the story was rejected while the other was preserved, Longford accepted the mythical victory over Silla as the origin of a Japanese presence on the peninsula — one that he called Mimana. Mimana, he later pointed out, using a vocabulary that presaged the events of his own day, "bore some resemblance to a Japanese colony, so much so, at least, that a Japanese resident and a garrison of Japanese troops were always stationed there."[131] Like some of the Korean writers discussed earlier, by rejecting certain aspects of the myths, Longford's treatment of these theories served only to confirm those other parts that he did not jettison from his own account of the peninsula's history. Later, in the contemporary section of the work, Longford expressed his support for Japanese annexation — what he called "another great step in her [Japan's] national career"[132] — reassuring the reader of Japan's civilizing power. In choosing to insert the myths of Mimana into his Korean history and specifically referring to it as a colony, Longford's early history foreshadowed the events of the twentieth century, reproducing key ideological tenets of a colonial project that he supported.

On this issue, Longford was hardly alone. Often without attempting to examine the problems inherent in Japanese histories, many popular writers incorporated, in a variety of ways, these accounts into their writing. For a country like Korea, which at the end of the nineteenth century had attracted neither as much Western media attention nor the interest of academic Orientalists as much as its two neighbors had, it was mainly through Western attention to the effects of the Japanese presence after 1905 that the peninsula began to gain a more prominent profile. At a time when its officials and media were both celebrating and legitimizing the colonization of the peninsula, Japanese representations of and theories about Korea became accessible sources of information to Western writers. Whether they were historians of early Japan, who were interested in Mimana as an indicator of the degree of centralization achieved by the Japanese state, or travel writers who blithely used these myths as historical background for the events they were reporting, the myth about a historical Japanese presence in the Korean peninsula was prevalent in Western writing on Korea.[133]

When the *TaeHan maeil sinbo* asked about foreigners' impression of Korea — "Is the image of Korea in the eyes of Europeans and Americans a true view of Korea? Or is the image of Korea in the eyes of Japanese a true view of Korea?" — it assumed the former was independent of the latter. But just as with Korean self-knowledge, Western understanding of Korea was also engaged with Japanese colonial discourse. Although these theories were variously, even critically, treated in some Western accounts, the fact that the principal subjects such as Jingū and Mimana came to be reproduced shows how Japanese colonial discourse had insinuated itself into Western knowledge about Korea. Such was the power of Japanese knowledge on Korea. Able to shape Korean nationalist self-perceptions, Japanese colonial writing also was the source of information for much Western writing. Knowledge about Korea — whether inside the peninsula, in Japan, or in the West and whether about the peninsula's present or its past — came to be deeply informed by the politics of colonialism.

5   Narrating the Ethnic Nation

In my observation, among the history textbooks used in today's
schools, there are absolutely none with any value.
— Sin Ch'aeho, "A New Reading of History," 27 August 1908

In the summer of 1908, a self-described history buff — "Who
loves history more than I?" he asked — sent a letter to the editors of a daily
newspaper describing his passion for the past. He admitted that previously
his understanding of history did not extend beyond works from China and
that he "had not given the slightest glance to histories of my own country."
Now, a convert to the cause of promoting Korean history, he lamented,
"Who was more ignorant of history than I?" What most befuddled this new
aficionado of the Korean past was, in a sense, the most basic of questions.
"What," he asked, "is the name of our nation [*pon'guk*]?" He surveyed the
possibilities used by earlier historians. "Is it Chosŏn or Sam Han? Is it Koguryŏ? Or is it even Silla, Paekche, or Parhae?" All these he rejected. As
individual titles that had been used for previous dynastic houses, they were
too narrow in scope, too brief in duration, and did not represent his sense
of the nation. He next considered the possibility of the name used by foreigners, what he transliterated as the *K'orian* nation, but this was equally
unsatisfactory to him, since it was just a foreign rendition of Koryŏ, another
dynastic title. "What about calling it *Tongguk* [Eastern nation]?" he finally
asked, only to conclude that this hoary name was unacceptable, because
Korea was not the sole nation in the East. Empty-handed, he could do little
else than to ask, "Where should we now look?" and conclude that historians
had to give this dilemma serious consideration.[1]

What proved so vexing for this student of the Korean past was the unset-
tled state of national history at the outset of the twentieth century. That there

was no clear-cut answer to the question "What is the name of our nation?" reflected the shifting definitions of the subject of history, as earlier dynastic annals written in a Confucian style were deemed irrelevant and new conceptions of the purposes and modes of history were still being explored. Just what the nation was and how its history should be written were still open questions. The critique of China-centered history had led to a surge in empirical works on the Korean past, especially biographical writings. Some nationalist writers had warned of the dangers posed by Japanese histories of Korea. Yet as the letter writer had discovered, these specific historical circumstances could lead to a shift in historical consciousness without immediately producing alternatives to these Confucian and colonial histories. It was not until two crucial elements in what emerged as a new form of national history were fused together that an answer to these questions was formulated.

One of these elements was a neologism for the ethnic nation, minjok, which when combined with a second element, an age-old myth about the progenitor of the Korean people, Tan'gun, offered new historiographical opportunities. The result was a radically new vision of the past, which in presenting an ethnic definition of national subjectivity was the ultimate step in decentering the Middle Kingdom, countered colonial versions of the Korean past, and even offered an alternative to enlightenment-style accounts of time as progress. It was a definition of the historical subject that engaged the efforts of historians for years to come.

National Etymologies

The term minjok was part of the new lexicon that accompanied the rise of nationalism in East Asia. Pronounced minjok in Korean, minzu in Chinese, and minzoku in Japanese, the two characters of this neologism had strong resonances with ancient terms for ethnic or racial groupings. The first character, min, appeared in the most ancient texts as a term for "people," whereas the second character, also present in classical texts, denoted the "clan," "tribe," or "family." Both terms were separately combined with other characters to designate a variety of social groupings, variously translated in English as "ethnicity" or "race." However, it seems that in none of the premodern writings of Korea, China, or Japan were these two characters regularly linked as a single compound to designate large collectivities.[2] This very combination — two venerable characters traditionally used to denote various types of social groups — served to blur the term's recent origins, suggesting an etymology that, like the claims being made for the nation, stretched into the distant past. Moreover, with its individual components giving the term a somewhat organic touch through its intimation of a popular (*min*) and familial (*jok*) derivation, it proved most useful for intellectuals writing about the nation as a natural entity.

The term quickly became current among nationalist writers throughout East Asia. While its precise origins remain obscure — a testament to the term's ability to conceal its newness — the consistent use of *minjok*, like so many other terms relating to modernity and the nation, first appeared in Japan,[3] although it quickly became popular in China as well.[4] The appearance and usage of the word *minjok* in Korea have been subjected to relatively little scrutiny, with some historians deeming the novelty of the term to be irrelevant.[5] The term rarely appears in the canonical texts of various streams of the Korean nationalist movement in the ten years before the Protectorate Treaty of 1905. Works as diverse as Yu Kilchun's *Observations of a Journey to the West* (1895), Chu Sigyŏng's essay "On National Language" (Kungmunnon, 1897), Min Yŏnghwan's testimony before committing suicide in protest against the Protectorate Treaty (1905), the more than two years of daily editions of the *Tongnip sinmun* (1896–98), and the prison interrogation records of Chŏn Pongjun, leader of the Tonghak peasant armies (1895) all were completed without the use of *minjok*, even though each of them dealt extensively with national concepts. As in the cases of Japanese and Chinese intellectuals, most Korean intellectuals did not employ the word *minjok* in the early stages of the nationalist movement because it had not yet found a conspicuous place in their conception and definition of the nation.

The appearance and dissemination of *minjok* can be traced in one of the longest-running newspapers of the period, the *Hwangsŏng sinmun*. An editorial dated January 12, 1900, contained one of the earliest public uses of *minjok*, a fitting opening for a century that was to witness the concept's rise to prominence.[6] The editorial used *minjok* several times, on each occasion to indicate a racial unit transcending Korea to incorporate all the peoples of East Asia. Combined with either the terms for "eastern" (*tongbang*) or "white" (*baegin*), *minjok* at its inception reflected a social Darwinian scheme of competing races, the eastern *minjok* pitted against the onslaught of the white *minjok* — a usage that otherwise was more regularly denoted by the term *injong* (race). Although the editorial marked one of the earliest appearances of *minjok*, the editors were still groping for a definition of a term whose conceptual bounds had yet to be fixed. A few years later the meaning of the term had markedly changed.

In the interim, however, *minjok* cropped up only sporadically in the pages of the *Hwangsŏng sinmun*, often not appearing for months on end. Its infrequent use hardly presaged its eventual eminence, but gradually and without fanfare the editors increasingly incorporated the term into their paper. As it came to be used more commonly, so, too, did the limits of its meaning come to be more rigid. *Minjok* soon lost any connotation of a supranational racial unit and began to be restricted to denoting only the people inhabiting the Korean peninsula. In June 1907, in a four-part editorial entitled simply "Minjok-ism" (Minjokchuŭi), the editors for the first time consciously invoked the term at a conceptual level, arguing that the *minjok* was the basis of the state (*kuk*) and that all the people must work together for the benefit of the *minjok*.[7] By this time, the term had already become a regular feature of editorials in the *Hwangsŏng sinmun*.

The advent of *minjok* can also be detected in the works of individual writers. At the beginning of his career, in his famous *Observations of a Journey to the West*, Yu Kilchun wrote a great deal about nations, both Korean and foreign, without ever once referring to *minjok*. But a little more than a decade later, in the preface to his *Korean Grammar* (*TaeHan munjŏn*), he defined his project of rectifying grammar as one task in preserving the "unique language" of the *minjok*.[8] Between 1895 and 1909 Yu had learned, adopted, and begun to wield this neologism.

The appearance and spread of *minjok* offered writers a powerful conceptual tool to reconsider the nation in multiple ways. The same term served intellectuals in all three countries of East Asia, giving to nationalist writing in East Asia a shared vocabulary and, through this common usage, reinforcing the naturalizing claims of the term to universality. Yet the power of *minjok* was found less in this common usage than in the term's flexibility. The etymology of the terms' two characters may have suggested approximate directions for definition and exchanges among writers in different countries led to a number of common uses. But divergent local contexts shaped the meaning and use of the term such that there was often great variance both between these countries and within any single one. In Korea, it was largely after the imposition of the Protectorate that *minjok* became more widely deployed. Like the expressions that had given the nation a spiritual character—*kuksu* (national essence), *kuksŏng* (national character), and *kukhon* (national soul)—*minjok* similarily offered a locus for the nation independent of a state that had come increasingly under the control of a foreign power. But because *minjok,* unlike the spiritual conceptions, was construed as an objective entity, it could be infused with those criteria and features — territory, people, language, and the like — that were seen internationally as determining nationhood. With the state stolen, the *minjok* presented an alternative locus for national existence and autonomy, an existence that was defined historically.

Legitimacy as a National Narrative

As the usage of *minjok* became more widespread, the term's bounds came to be set largely by historians, who rewrote the past with this new subject for their national narratives. In so doing, *minjok* came to be linked with a centuries-old mythical figure, Tan'gun, who emerged as one of the premier nationalist symbols through efforts to flesh out the meaning of this neologism in a Korean context. The earliest account of the Tan'gun myth appears in the *Samguk yusa* (*Memorabilia of Three Kingdoms*), a compilation of tales and myths recorded by the Buddhist monk Iryŏn. Written in the thirteenth century, more than three thousand years after the purported date of these events, the *Samguk yusa* recounts how Tan'gun descended from Heaven in the year 2333 B.C. and landed under a sandalwood tree on Mount Paektu.[9] According to this account, Tan'gun taught the people more than 360 arts, such as agriculture, medicine, and law, as well as offering them a new set of moral principles. Tan'gun also appeared in the mid-Koryŏ-dynasty work *Chewang ŭngi* (*Songs of Emperors and Kings*), written by Yi Sŭnghyu as a history in verse of rulership on the peninsula. Placed at the beginning of both these works, the Tan'gun story offered a foundation myth for the oldest of the peninsular kingdoms, Old Chosŏn.

The Tan'gun myth was not without rivals, however. In 1145, the famous scholar-official Kim Pusik submitted to the Koryŏ king the officially sponsored *Samguk sagi* (*History of the Three Kingdoms*), a long work without even a single mention of Tan'gun. Instead, Kim presented a different pedigree, one more befitting his status as a leading proponent of Confucianism, in which precedence was given to another legendary figure, Kija (Ch. Jizi). A virtuous official of the Shang dynasty in China, Kija had been unwilling to serve the newly established Zhou dynasty. According to this myth, Kija fled with his retainers to the East, reputedly arriving on the peninsula as a

Tangun or Kija?

refugee in 1122 B.C., and carrying the knowledge of civilized norms that he used to establish a new kingdom, supplanting Old Chosŏn.

Since the inception of these two distinct legends, all histories of the peninsula have, in one way or another, had to sort out these two competing claims. No archaeological or contemporary documentary evidence concerning these two figures has ever been discovered, so historians have only vague, fragmentary, and often contradictory references to the legends that were made well after the reputed events occurred — providing just the right combination to enable writers to produce a host of conflicting interpretations of the two figures' roles.[10] More often than not, the relative position ascribed to these two men in any single historical work reflected the political and ideological disposition of the period or of the writer. During the nearly one millennium that historians have been mulling over the Tan'gun-Kija relationship, the original versions of the myths have gradually accumulated a startling number of additions. In the case of Tan'gun, what in the *Samguk yusa* was little more than a few paragraphs has burgeoned today into a field of study producing works that fill entire shelves in bookstores.

Beginning with Kim Pusik's history, Kija's eastward journey came to represent for a long line of Confucian scholars the inception of civilized culture in their part of the world. Tan'gun may have been first, but it was Kija who offered a connection to the golden age of the sages. During the Chosŏn dynasty, this connection was especially valued, since the chief historical narrative device was legitimacy (*chŏngt'ong*), a venerable Confucian concept associated with the Mandate of Heaven. As first proposed and developed by the likes of Ouyang Xiu and Zhu Xi, this notion of history rested on the assumption that only a single court, the legitimate court, could hold the Mandate of Heaven at any one time. The task of the historian was thus identifying the legitimate ruler — a contentious task in periods of rival regimes — and then describing, through a moral appraisal of their actions, how the rulers of this court attained, maintained, and lost the Mandate of Heaven. Sinocentric in origin and intended to legitimize China's claim to status as the "Middle Kingdom," such narratives recognized only Chinese courts. There could only be one emperor, the Chinese emperor; all foreign rulers, including the Korean monarch, were merely kings, subordinate to the Chinese "Son of Heaven."

By the seventeenth century a number of Korean scholars, like Yi Ik, began to appropriate these same conventions, turning them around to challenge certain aspects of their Sinocentric foundation. Employed by the authors to assert a sense of Korean autonomy vis-à-vis their larger neighbor, they deliberately violated certain conventions so as to imply an equality with China and downplay any connotations of Korean subordination. It has been argued that the very appropriation of the concept of legitimacy for Korean history served such a purpose, since in theory, the only legitimate court necessarily resided in China.[11] By appropriating this concept for their own history, Chosŏn scholars were assuming that not just China but Korea, too, could have a legitimate court. In this way, they undermined the Sinocentrism of conventional legitimacy theory, suggesting that the Korean court was an equal of its Chinese counterpart. Kija played a seminal role in this style of historiography, for ultimately the lineage of the reigning king could be traced back through Kija to the great sages themselves, a very useful means for establishing a dynasty's legitimacy through history. By the latter half of the Chosŏn dynasty, after the Manchus had conquered the Ming dynasty, such a pedigree could be invoked as evidence that the "Eastern Kingdom," not the new Qing dynasty, was the legitimate heir to the mantle of "Middle Kingdom" and that it was Chosŏn, not the Qing dynasty, that was superior.[12]

At the beginning of the dynasty, officials vehemently debated the status and position of these two figures in state rituals.[13] Eventually both Tan'gun and Kija were featured in state ceremonies. But as the state relentlessly implemented a self-styled Confucian rule, Tan'gun's standing weakened as Kija's role as the original carrier of culture was highlighted.[14] By the latter half of the dynasty, Tan'gun was removed from official state rituals. Similarily, as Han Yŏngu has shown in his survey of key historical works in the Chosŏn dynasty, Kija was favored in mainstream histories, although during the late Chosŏn period, an increasing number of scholars granted more attention to accounts of Tan'gun.[15]

With the call for new history textbooks in the first years after the Kabo reforms, the question arose of how the relationship between these two mythical figures should be treated in a history ostensibly supporting the nation's recently recognized but still shaky independence. Calling for a new history was much easier than writing it, however. As the demand for textbooks to serve the burgeoning school movement grew, the quickest response for historians — all of whom had impeccable classical training — was to turn to histories written in the late Chosŏn dynasty. Although some of the writers made substantial adaptations, most of the books published in the ten years after 1895 closely followed the narrative approaches of conventional Chosŏn histories, hardly fulfilling the expectations of the "new history" and ensuring that Confucian historiographical conventions would continue to be taught in these new schools.

In particular, these textbooks centered on the royal court, using theories of legitimacy to follow the succession of dynasties. This association was made in the preface of A Concise History of Chosŏn (Chosŏn yŏktae sayak) published by the Ministry of Education in 1895. As the preface carefully explained, the narrative traced Kija's mantle as it was passed down to the southern court of Mahan, explicitly following the precedent set by Zhu Xi in using legitimacy theory to explain the Shu kingdom's inheritance of the Han dynasty's mantle in third-century China.[16] Several centuries after being first laid out by Zhu Xi, this solution to the problem of identifying the moral court was still finding a place in the history textbooks used in Korean schools, only now the notion of legitimacy was linked to concepts of national sovereignty — a development that no doubt would have befuddled Zhu Xi but that indicates the adaptability of received historical narratives.[17] Although not always so open about the source of their narrative techniques, most other textbooks from these years, whether published by the Ministry of Education or edited by private individuals, adopted the same narrative device. The authors differed on exactly where the line of descent should be drawn in the ancient period — some promoting what has been called the Three Han Legitimacy Theory, and others using the rival Three Chosŏn Legitimacy Theory[18] — but whatever the differences in the particulars of these accounts, they all were based on theories of legitimacy.

Consequently, the tendency to privilege Kija over Tan'gun continued. Textbooks as various as the Ministry of Education's A History of Chosŏn (Chosŏn yŏksa)[19] adopted Confucian historiographical conventions when dealing with Tan'gun and Kija, in almost all cases providing a more detailed treatment of Kija. In some books, such as An Elementary History of the Great East (Ch'odŭng Taedong yŏksa), the author even supplied a drawing of Kija traveling with his retainers, ostensibly on his eastward journey from China to the peninsula. He did not include a picture of Tan'gun.[20] Even when some of the textbooks from this period did begin to give equal space to Tan'gun — in his 1908 book, Chŏng Inho did, after all, pair his portrait of Kija with one of Tan'gun[21] — the narratives nevertheless continued to follow the same legitimacy-generated method. These textbooks still depicted a Kija who had brought civilized culture to the peninsula. At a time when the critique of past Chinese cultural influence was emerging as part of the effort to recover Korean authenticity and when, as part of this critique, editorials regularly stressed the urgency of learning Korean history, these textbooks served an ambiguous role. To be sure, they discussed Korean history, fulfilling one recent demand. But because they used a legitimacy theory deeply enmeshed in Chinese imperial claims to superiority, the narratives still positioned China, through Kija's connection to the sages, as the locus of superior culture. And it was from this source, these textbooks implied, that the peninsular kingdoms derived their legitimacy. Thus the empirical knowledge of Korea conveyed in these books remained rooted in a style of history with inherent limits on its use for decentering the "Middle Kingdom."

Within this framework, some writers were able to adapt their predecessors' conventions to better suit an age when history was thought to serve the nation. Following the pattern set by some late-Chosŏn historians, they deliberately violated Confucian terminological conventions in order to make a claim of equality for Korea. References to China as a "neighboring country" (in'guk) — a term that earlier had been used to refer to relations with Japan and that in ritual terminology denoted equality — rather than in terms that implied subordinance were common.[22] Ancient events could also, with the inventive substitution of a key term or two, be used to assert Korean independence. One such example concerns the myth of Punu, the son of Tan'gun, who allegedly traveled to China to meet the Chinese sage Yu. The traditional story was that Punu had come to see Yu in order to pay tribute, the word used to describe the encounter, kong or cho, denoting Yu's superior status. Although a number of the textbook authors still used this ritual language, others deleted the single word that described the event as coming to pay tribute. In explaining this switch, the author of A History of the Great East (Taedong yŏksa) dismissed the subordinating terminology as the "empty boasts and slander of Chinese historians," adding that these characters merely showed that the arrogance and tendency toward self-elevation (hogo) of the Chinese had become a habit.[23] In its place, he inserted a different character, hoe (meeting). What had been interpreted as "tribute bearing" was thus transformed into a "meeting" between two equals. To other authors, not only was this a meeting in which Punu "participated" (ch'am), but appropriate to an increasingly internationalized Korea at the turn of the twentieth century, it also was presented as an international convention, literally a "meeting of ten thousand countries" (man'gukhoe).[24]

As metonyms for their respective nations, Punu's meeting Yu represented a Korea on equal footing with China. Like the adoption of legitimacy theory by late Chosŏn historians, such maneuvers questioned those aspects of the theories supporting Chinese dynastic claims to the status of "Middle Kingdom." But in the new international environment, these historiographical practices took on an added forcefulness as they merged with new concepts of independence. Although in many cases, the practices remained the same, the context — Korea in a world system populated by nations — had changed dramatically. What in the late Chosŏn period had reflected historians' discomfort with Chinese claims of centrality, by the turn of the century was being used to prop up new definitions of Korea as sovereign.

Even here, however, Korean subjectivity was always asserted vis-à-vis China. It was through the creative appropriation of concepts of legitimacy, the artful use of ritual language, and the deliberate violation of certain features of historiographical convention that Korea's autonomy was asserted. None of the textbook authors writing before 1905 seriously challenged this view of history. Their histories were still centered on the court; Kija was largely privileged at the expense of Tan'gun; and legitimacy provided the sole narrative device. However creative their efforts, as long as historians sought to establish Korean autonomy through the manipulation of such conventions, their history was locked in a style of narrative that granted China the principal role in measuring the Korean past, present, and future.

History as Genealogy

As the linchpin in this style of history, Kija was targeted by writers eager to create a more autonomous history. At first, this was only a subtle maneuver. Newspapers and journals gradually began to highlight Tan'gun at the expense of Kija as a way of decentering China. The *Hwangsŏng sinmun,* a paper that as the main advocate of reform Confucianism had the greatest investment in invoking the authority of the Confucian sages, had always grouped Tan'gun and Kija together in a single expression composed of the first two syllables of their names, Tan-Ki.[25] This compound had long been used to express the joint rule of the two figures in establishing the earliest kingdoms. The *Hwangsŏng sinmun* regularly used "since the time of Tan-Ki" as shorthand for the origins of the nation, even though the legends of the two figures were separated by more than a millennium in time. But as Korean history loosened its ties to the Confucian sages, now seen as Chinese, Kija's position in the paper gradually was overshadowed by Tan'gun. "Since the time of Tan'gun" now increasingly became the operative phrase indicating the beginning of the nation. Especially after 1905, this newer form of expressing origins was accompanied by a surge in editorials treating various aspects of the Tan'gun myth and commemorating his birthday.[26] Although Kija did not disappear, he was mentioned less often, and his role was diminished.

This shift was most evident in the growing use of the *Tan'gi*, or Tan'gun calendar, as a means of dating. Calculated from Tan'gun's purported descent from Heaven in 2333 B.C., this calendar appeared on the mastheads of many of the era's newspapers and journals. Even time could be reckoned in relation to Tan'gun.[27] As one letter to the editor pointed out, by abandoning reign titles in favor of the Tan'gun calendar for recording events in Korean history, people would associate events with Tan'gun, see themselves as common descendants, and thereby love their country even more.[28] Tan'gun could serve regional interests as well, since as the journal of one regional education group pointed out with pride, it was in their region, the northwest, that Tan'gun's descendants were said to have first settled.[29] Their monthly organ consequently regularly worked Tan'gun into its articles, in one case setting as the country's most urgent task the preservation of Tan'gun's bloodline (*hyŏlt'ong*) in a time of world struggle.[30] By 1909, Tan'gun appeared in poems and had long odes written about him.[31]

The growing status of Tan'gun paralleled the increased use of the term *minjok*, as the two often were loosely tied together. The first person to join these two elements in an extended treatment of national history was Sin Ch'aeho, an editorial writer for the *TaeHan maeil sinbo*. The widespread use of the new term *minjok*, together with the heightened awareness of Tan'gun — two developments that Sin himself had helped foster as a member of the *TaeHan maeil sinbo* — offered him two powerful instruments for writing a new type of history in line with the period's intellectual shifts and answering the long-standing calls for a new national history. In a serialized article entitled "A New Reading of History" (*Toksa sillon*), published in 1908, Sin provided the first detailed historical treatment of *minjok*. This was a polemical piece, with no documentation, in which Sin organized a conceptual framework for *minjok* that delineated its parameters and identified the main issues with which all subsequent Korean historians would be concerned. Sin's work offered both a fundamental critique of conventional history and, by setting the *minjok*'s bounds, began to create a vision of the nation as a historically defined ethnic entity.[32]

This did not mean, however, that Sin explicitly defined the term *minjok*. None of his writings broaches the issue of the term's newness. From Sin's perspective, the use of *minjok* did not mark a new subjectivity, since he believed that the *minjok* was an objective entity that had existed throughout history, regardless of whether people were aware of it. In this sense, his choice of the word "new" in the title of his essay, "A New Reading of History," did not, in his eyes, signify a new conceptualization of the nation but, instead, marked the rediscovery of an objective unit that centuries of historians preceding him had failed to recognize for various reasons that he explained in the essay. The *minjok* was presented as a natural entity that, through the proper historical perspective, could be identified and traced by empirical inquiry.

Presenting and elaborating such a historical perspective was the essay's central goal. Sin rejected all forms of history that did not place the *minjok* as the central subject. As he explained in his preface, "If one dismisses the *minjok*, there is no history."[33] Other histories — whether of the state (*kukka*) or the court — resulted in what Sin called a spiritless, debilitating history, for they ignored the *minjok*.[34] In this formulation, *minjok* and history were mutually defining: history did not exist without the *minjok*, while the *minjok* could not be understood without history. The task of the historian, then, was newly set as identifying the *minjok* and tracing its fortunes over time. Central to this endeavor, Sin argued, was the correct identification of the *minjok*. Pointing out that in any single country, there could be multiple *minjok*, Sin stressed that historians must not be distracted by minor groups but must concentrate on what he called the main or host group (*chujok*).

> Those who pick up the pen of the historian must first recognize the host people of their nation, and after having made it the subject [of their research], they must narrate how its political rule expanded and receded, how its enterprises rose and fell, how its military prowess advanced and retreated, how its customs changed and shifted, how foreign peoples were absorbed, and how it interacted with other countries. This, then, can be called history.[35]

After stating that the historian's task was to identify the host *minjok*, Sin did not hesitate to undertake the task himself. Choosing the name of an ancient kingdom, Sin called this *minjok* Puyŏ.

In Sin's history, the Puyŏ *minjok* was located by the departure point of his narrative — the birth of the *minjok* as manifested in the appearance of its progenitor, Tan'gun. "A New Reading of History" positioned Tan'gun at the start of history, for if history was a record of the *minjok*, nothing existed before the *minjok*'s appearance, here equated with Tan'gun. In China, if historians were rediscovering Huangdi (The Yellow Emperor), and in Japan, if the Meiji state used the sun goddess Amaterasu to define the imperial line as the basis of official history, then in Korea, Sin could elevate Tan'gun. All history flowed from Tan'gun. The vicissitudes of the past became an account of the fortunes of the descendants of the progenitor traced through Puyŏ, the Three Kingdoms, Unified Silla, and Parhae, and then, though not included in his "A New Reading of History," the Koryŏ and Chosŏn dynasties. Both history and *minjok* were thus defined through the single figure of Tan'gun. It was the bloodline, the genealogy of the ethnic nation that unified Sin's new narrative.

In this detailed attempt to articulate the direction of a national history, Sin made clear that this was a history in which the *minjok* was continually competing with its neighbors, in which "the superior survived and the inferior was destroyed" (*ujŏn yŏlmang*). The social Darwinian nature of Sin's account was both supported by and, in turn, supported an organic, almost biological view of the *minjok*. Social Darwinism in Europe and America as well as in the rest of East Asia had largely been posited in racial terms: history was the record of struggle in which the subjects were defined racially.[36] The most prominent metaphors — most famously, the "weak shall be the meat of the strong" (*yagyuk kangsik*) — exhibited a carnality that reinforced the social Darwinian vision of organisms in conflict. With its emphasis on the rise and fall of the *minjok*, defined by its bloodline and always imperiled by its counterparts, "A New Reading of History" was a clear endorsement of a social Darwinian worldview extended over the nation's entire past. In the history of the Puyŏ *minjok*, five main rivals were listed: the Xianbi, the Chinese, the Malgal, the Jurchens, and local tribes.

Deliberately omitted from this list of protagonists, Japan was instead grouped with the Mongols as insignificant players. Sin reasoned that until the Japanese leader Hideoyoshi invaded in the late sixteenth century, the ties between Korea and Japan had been limited to the comings and goings typical of two countries with coasts on the same ocean. An insignificant number of people had come to the peninsula from Japan — and this included garrisons that Japan might have stationed on Korean shores. "There is no evidence [of Imna] in our histories," he wrote in his introduction, "and there is no reason to rely rashly on what other histories have to say."[37] Later, he returned to the issue of Japanese theories, castigating contemporary textbook writers for accepting what "besmeared our divine and sagely history," making "our four thousand years of recorded history an accessory to Japanese history."[38] To his assertion that there was no reliable evidence for theories of a Japanese domination of the peninsula, he added that these theories simply did not make any logical sense, since in this early time, Korean kingdoms were far more developed than Japan. Japanese believed in the conquest of Jingū simply because these falsehoods had been repeated so many times and written in so many books. As a result, "since ancient times, Japanese believed that Korea was a possession of their own family."[39] Sin went on to dismiss various aspects of these histories, constantly wondering at the ignorance of his compatriots for even considering these theories. Although Sin, like his contemporaries, was quick to bemoan the loss of early records, he at no point regarded Japanese sources as a possible solution to this dearth, never once citing objective empiricism as a reason for considering their veracity. In perhaps the most powerful statements about the validity of these colonial myths that had by 1908 elicited such diverse responses from his fellow historians, Sin simply dismissed their relevance, not even bothering to include them as part of Korean history.

In embracing social Darwinian approaches to the past and framing his history around the *minjok*, Sin was certainly engaging with the prevailing international and regional intellectual currents. But his history also looked inward, toward domestic traditions, particularly in his ordering of time. Indeed, Sin's vision of *minjok* history resonated strongly with one type of record that is not generally recognized as history as such but whose conception of time offered Sin a means of recounting the history of the *minjok* from Tan'gun to the present.[40] This record was the *chokpo*, a family or clan genealogy. Kept by families of *yangban* heritage during the Chosŏn dynasty, the *chokpo* functioned as a means of establishing the pedigree of elite families, maintaining clan consiousness and recording marriage alliances. In a highly segregated class society, these records played the all-important role of marking the bounds of the hereditary elite, and ordering society along patrilineal lines.[41] To have a *chokpo* was to lay claim to *yangban* status; to lack a *chokpo* was to be a member of the commoner or slave classes. During the Chosŏn dynasty, the *chokpo* was perhaps the most common mode of thinking about the past, of recording the succession of time that played a role in the everyday lives of the elite sections of the populace. Its distinct sense of time was measured not by the calendar year but by generational markers, one succeeding the other. A family's past could be traced back to a discrete starting point, a single figure positioned as the ancestral head of the family. In certain cases, this might be a historical figure who had lived several centuries ago, or in other *chokpo*, it might be a putative head, often a mythical figure as in the case of the Kyŏngju Kim clan, who claimed descent from Kim Alchi, hatched out of a golden egg in A.D. 65.[42] If seen as a narrative or a mode of history, the *chokpo* followed the generations descending from the head and extending into different branches. With the clan dispersed over wide areas and containing many members, the *chokpo* was in part an attempt to maintain a sense of clan consciousness. Its mode of time was clearly linear, and insofar as its account ended with the clan members' current status, it was also teleological — two narrative characteristics, as Prasenjit Duara has argued, that were necessary for a modern nation.[43]

The compilers of *chokpo* faced dilemmas similar to those of a writer of *minjok*-centered history like Sin. Tracing the patrilineal descent of a clan from its putative head down to the present was as problematic for the *chokpo* compiler as was Sin's task of tracking the successive generations of Tan'gun. Where the line of Tan'gun's descendants became sketchy, Sin could blame the lack of historical records, just as the compiler of the *chokpo* could complain in his preface about the inability of earlier generations to preserve records in the face of either familial or natural disasters. Still, such inconveniences could not be allowed to break the line of time for either the compiler of a *chokpo* or the writer of *minjok* history. The compiler merely filled in such gaps with a judicious dotted line, while Sin followed his remarks about the dearth of records with an assertion of continuity, despite his inability to fill in the many lacunae. Tracing the pedigree might be troublesome, but as a linear history, it could never be broken, especially if this mode of time was to fulfill its teleological function of showing how the clan or *minjok* descended from a certain point in the past to its status at the time of composition.

Nor was the pedigree to be sullied. Other families were introduced into the *chokpo* only through the surnames and hometowns of the women who married into the clan. "Kim from Andong" an entry might note, showing the alliance by marriage to a woman from one particularly illustrious family of the late Chosŏn dynasty. Even though it was noted, the matrilineal line was tangential to the descent line, which remained undisturbed by this entrance. The *chokpo*'s patrilineal genealogy was not unlike Sin's call for a history focusing on the *chujok* — the host *minjok* — untainted by the other minor *minjok*. Other *minjok* might enter his narrative, but only as vanquished rivals or assimilated others who, like women entering the clan, were absorbed without impeding the focus and momentum of the narrative. In this sense, both were exclusionary, emphasizing the purity of descent. The difference was *what* they excluded, one focusing on the clan, the other on the nation. From this familial record designed to arrange society along patrilineal lines, Sin extracted a mode of narrating time and transposed it onto the nation. In this way, the patrilineal emphasis of the most widely held record of the Chosŏn dynasty was transposed to the new national history. Like the family records of the *yangban*, *minjok* history was patrilineal in conception. Moreover, when combined with the many popular biographies of martial heroes such as Ŭlchi Mundŏk and King Kwanggaet'o — figures who as part of the decentering of the Middle Kingdom were supposed to supplant the supposedly effete legacies of the Confucian *yangban* — the *minjok* emerged as a strongly masculine representation of the nation.[44]

That Sin's historical vision was shaped by the narrative structures and devices of a vision of time like that of the *chokpo* is not surprising given the tendency in these years to equate nation and family. Indeed, the metaphor of the familial nation was unrivaled in this age.[45] Writers consciously invoked the "family" or "household" as a means of trying to teach patriotism to a population that they felt was not sufficiently conscious of the nation. Schoolchildren learned the comparision in their textbooks. The management of the household was equated with that of the nation: if people take care of their household affairs, everything will go well; likewise, if people take care of national affairs, everything will go well.[46] Governance was equated with heading a household: "ruling a country is like ruling a household, so that reforming the nation is like repairing a house.[47] The international stage could be compared to a neighborhood, with each house being a country of its own. Just as the affairs of one's home affect everyone in the neighborhood, so the condition of one's nation influences events beyond one's borders.[48] Expanding a sense of familial bonds to the nation was also an attempt to ensure that commitment to the family did not take precedence over loyalty to the nation, a concern of all nationalists who believed this phenomenon was one of the reasons why nationalist feeling had been so weak during the Chosŏn dynasty. Why, one paper asked, did people feel shame for unjust actions committed against their family but not those against the nation? Their reaction, it argued, should not be any different.[49]

Sin himself made a number of such analogies in editorials that he contributed to the *TaeHan maeil sinbo* shortly after the publication of his history.

Playing off the double meaning of the word *ka*, as both family and house-hold, Sin wrote, "People are born here, they grow old here, they sing here, they cry here, they live together here, they eat and dress together here, they rest together here — so how is the household different from the nation?" As was often his wont, he answered his own question, denying any difference: "The nation is just one large clan [*kajok*]."[50] Later he called on all Koreans to build "the large house called the Great Han Empire."[51] In other editorials Sin went so far as to refer to the relation between family records and national history. As he noted, the last "four thousand years of recorded history is the genealogy of Tan'gun.[52] Or more simply put, Koreans "have a family gene-alogy [*kabŏ*] of four thousand years,"[53] and "history is the genealogy of a people."[54]

Others were even willing to hint at the strategic utility of using the *chokpo* tradition to make people associate with this new unit of subjectivity, the *minjok*. The *Hwangsŏng sinmun* had actively promoted *minjok*-based con-ceptions of the nation since at least 1906, well before Sin's article appeared. By 1910, the editors had already adopted Sin's basic maneuvers in his "A New Reading of History" as part of their own treatment of national history. Moreover, they used the family, with its *chokpo*, and the *minjok*, with its history, as an analogy linking three features of the family — its history, land, and rules — to its national counterparts. The leading families, readers were told, preserved the genealogical records of their brothers and ancestors, the land on which their familial graves rested, as well as their family regulations (*kabŏp*). Only slaves and other base people were ignorant of these things, thus allowing them to be lost. "How is this any different," the editors asked, shifting to the larger unit, "from the situation of our entire *minjok*? Alas! Our brothers and sisters are the descendants of the divine figure who four thousand years ago was born under a sandalwood tree on Mount Paektu." This was a divine pedigree, it continued, but the "spirit of commemorating and preserving" had been lost. Like slaves and beasts, the descendants of Tan'gun no longer remembered the branches of the clan (*ssijok*), the breadth of territory, and his teachings.[55]

The following day the editorial expanded on this connection between the clan and the *minjok*, only here, in a rare occurrence, the editorial hinted that the extension of notions of the family to the nation was a deliberate and useful strategy. In the past, it began, there had been two ways of organizing human society in the East (Tongyang): clan regulations (*chongpŏp*) and village covenants (*hyangyak*). The former played a far more effective role in maintaining social order, in the opinion of the editors, because it relied on "natural" affection and close bloodlines. The purpose of these clan regulations could be very useful, proposed the editors, for if they were to be "expanded," they could unite the spirit and thoughts of the entire *minjok*, leading everyone to celebrate and respect their ancestral origins. "It is the most necessary organization [*kigwan*] for making our sisters and brothers mutually understand and clearly perceive the closeness of their bloodties and their natural affection." Family and nation were linked through a common sense of ancestral beginnings, with history acting as the vehicle for tracing generational descent.[56] This was an explicit statement of what Sin was writing — national history as a form of *chokpo* writ large, or, in short, the *chokpo* of the *minjok*. *Minjok* may have been a new concept and its history may have served new nationalist purposes, but the mode of narration — with its emphasis on the progenitor, patrilineal descent lines, and its sense of time — had a genealogy of its own, stretching well back into the Chosŏn dynasty.

The State of History

In creating a history that privileged the *minjok* as defined through Tan'gun, Sin tried to undermine two features of received Korean histories, what he called the history of territory and the history of the state (*kukka*). It was in response to these two approaches to the national past that Sin articulated his conception of the *minjok* and the proper historical perspective while seeking to decenter China.

Sin rebuked his predecessors who used geography to delimit history. These historians — "territorial historians" in Sin's dismissive parlance — committed the error of privileging geography rather than the *minjok*. According to Sin, they simply accepted the contemporary peninsular boundaries of the Chosŏn dynasty, traced these back in time, and concluded that all peoples living in this realm were ancestors of the *minjok*.[57] He compared this approach with the idea that Americans should erect temples to those he called the "red peoples" (*hong'in*) and worship them as ancestors simply because, at an earlier date, the "red peoples" occupied the areas now inhabited by European settlers.[58] In Korea, Sin complained, previous historians, not aware of the existence of the *minjok*, granted central roles to foreigners for the single reason that they had been living in Korean territory.

This exclusionary history enabled Sin to foreground Tan'gun. If Tan'gun was to define the outset of history and function as the progenitor of the *minjok*, the status of his main competitor for preeminence in previous narratives, Kija, needed to be diminished. In Sin's eyes, his Confucian predecessors, misconstruing the task of history, committed their gravest error in their accounts of this Chinese refugee to Korea by interpreting his arrival as the inception of moral civilization. For Sin, this was unacceptable. Kija's presence in what was understood to be Korean territory was no reason to incorporate him in national history, let alone place him into such a vaunted position: "How could their ignorance reach such levels?" he protested.[59] This historical practice violated Sin's desire to limit Korean history to the account of a single *minjok*, the Puyŏ nation. Furthermore, it diluted the history of the *minjok* by incorporating others into what Sin attempted to define as the history of a national self.

Sin devoted a significant portion of "A New Reading of History" to reversing the centrality of Kija in Confucian narratives. If history meant an account of the ethnic nation, as Sin propounded, Kija, as a foreigner, did not rightfully belong in any account of the Puyŏ *minjok*. By labeling him as a figure from outside the *minjok*, Sin stripped Kija of his formerly privileged position in received accounts. But expurgation alone was insufficient for Sin. He also challenged the approach and conclusions of these earlier narratives, devoting much effort to invalidating his predecessors' numerous historical propositions concerning Kija. As a result, despite his call to exclude Kija from narratives of the Korean past, Sin treated Kija's legacy in far greater detail than he did most other historical characters in his account — if only to dismiss him. In some cases, Sin did this by disputing the conventional readings of accounts relating to Kija. In others, he simply disagreed with those versions of events, for example, pointing out the lack of logic in traditional accounts stating that Tan'gun's descendants had readily offered their kingdom to the Shang refugee: why, he asked, would the Korean people submit at first glance to a stranger who did not even speak their language or know their customs?

In his final evaluation, Sin proposed, though without offering any evidence, that Kija had arrived in Korea at a time when the fortunes of the Puyŏ dynasty were still bright. He did not assume rule of the region; on the contrary, Sin claimed that the Puyŏ king offered Kija an enfeoffment, a territory covering no more than one hundred *li*. The king of Puyŏ was the ruler, Sin insisted, and Kija was only his vassal.[60] This treatment both removed Kija from the narrative and eliminated him as a possible rival to the figure whom Sin placed foremost in his history, Tan'gun. Kija, once a refugee from the political turmoil of China, had now been expelled by Sin from his conventionally preeminent spot in Korean history. A history of the *minjok*, then, meant not only tracing the descendants of Tan'gun but also excluding all individuals or groups that could not claim a consanguineous link with the progenitor, whatever their geographical location.

The second approach to history against which Sin articulated his conception of the *minjok* was that focusing exclusively on the state. In earlier dynastic histories as well as contemporary textbooks, the state, as represented by the court, stood at the center of historical inquiry. But with Sin's vision of the *minjok*, this changed. Sin argued that national history should not be confused, as it had been by so many of his predecessors, with the history of the state. In his narrative, the *minjok* was not only central but also transcendent, existing—though at times precariously—from the beginning of the history to the present, rising above such temporal phenomena as states. Ephemeral and historic, states were "organic bodies composed of the spirit of the *minjok*."[61] History was not one of the state, but of a more fundamental matter, the *minjok*.

Since the time of Tan'gun, Sin bemoaned, the *minjok* had never again been unified into a single state. But even while the many states composed of the *minjok* rose and fell, divided and unified, the *minjok* itself remained untouched by the fortunes of these individual states. Thus, for Sin, Koguryŏ was linked to its southern neighbors, Silla and Paekche, through their common descent from Tan'gun. Despite their internecine wars, the three kingdoms were of the same *minjok* and, consequently, of the same history. Parhae and Koryŏ, too, were in Sin's eyes two parts of the same whole. In this sense, Sin's conception of the ethnic nation superseded state boundaries. The state, although important to locating and tracing the *minjok*, was not the repository of Sin's nationalist ideals. Ideally, the state and *minjok* should be united, although Sin's vision of the ethnically defined national community was independent of the state. Significantly, for an era when Korea was under a Japanese protectorate, the *minjok* was seen as able to exist on its own without a supporting state structure.

This historical vision had important ramifications for the relation between monarch and nation. Only a few years earlier, King Kojong and his officials had been seeking to redefine the throne in such a way as to position it at the center of the growing nationalist movement. Now Sin Ch'aeho was articulating a vision of the nation with little room for a monarch. To be sure, others in the nationalist movement had tried to distinguish king from nation, arguing that the nation was not the king's property, and specific reform efforts had been geared to restricting the power of the monarch, in one case, separating his finances from those of the government.[62] Yet for the most part, these were restrictions on the political power of an institution that for many still remained the premier symbol of the nation.[63] Nonetheless, in Sin's history, the monarch was irrelevant to the *minjok*-defined nation. Like any other member of the *minjok*, the king might prove to be a powerful figure in advancing the nation's interests, but he was no longer fundamental to defining the nation. National history as familial history had supplanted the court-centered history that had dominated for centuries.

In shifting away from the court and jettisoning Kija, Sin's history was the final step in decentering the "Middle Kingdom." Now the nation could be described in historical terms that made no reference to China. Its existence and legitimacy could be determined independently of its larger neighbor. Survival and aggrandizement were the measures of its success. But in creating this autonomous subject that could trace the continuity of its consanguineous line in a social Darwinian world, Sin left little room in his history for enlightenment-style advancement. Whereas such approaches to the past had been typical of much newspaper writing as one way of conceptualizing Korea's participation in the world, notions of progress did not find a place in "A New Reading of History." Despite being teleological and linear insofar as it traced the existence of the *minjok*, it was hardly history as Progress. Progressive visions of time were a staple of the *munmyŏng kaehwa* project, but perhaps fittingly for a nation that had been placed under a protectorate in the name of civilization, the dynamic of Sin's history was a relentless contest for existence, a contest whose viciousness had not been tempered by the advancement of time. The uneasiness with enlightenment underlying much of the work of nationalist intellectuals after 1905 found its expression in this style of history. As articulated through age-old conceptions of familial descent, this social Darwinian framework enabled Sin to offer a history that distanced itself from both the legitimizing claims of the Japanese colonial project as "enlightening" and historical narratives that validated this conceptual framework by equating advancement in time with progress. Nevertheless, this history was still part of the larger project of articulating the uniqueness of Korea as stimulated by its participation in a world populated by nations. "A New Reading of History" did offer history as a site of resistance to Japan, and it did vacate the framework of enligtenment-style history. But in seeking to specify what made this particular nation Korean, the historical work itself marked Korea's engagement with the global ecumene.

In distilling contemporary intellectual trends and fusing two elements — *minjok* and Tan'gun — Sin created a mode of history in which the subject and narrative structures broke from earlier dynastic annals and abandoned the techniques manipulated by textbook writers to claim an independent national subjectivity. The nation stood alone, defined through Tan'gun and, although threatened by external dangers and internal crises, it had never been fully overcome by any external force. The bloodline of the *minjok* prevailed, not just during the tumultuous millennia covered by Sin's narrative but also, the work implied, for a time when Japan had captured both state and territory.

From Man to God

Sin's move to position Tan'gun as the unrivaled source of national history was quickly taken up by his contemporaries. But whereas Sin presented the progenitor of the *minjok* as a historical figure, others were more eager to accept the claims made in the early myths that Tan'gun had descended from Heaven. In the year after Sin published "A New Reading of History," a group led by the nationalist Na Ch'ŏl established a new religion that worshiped Tan'gun.[64] Originally called the Tan'gun'gyo (Tan'gun religion) and then renamed a year later the Taejonggyo (Great Ancestral religion),[65] this organization received the support of many leading Korean intellectuals such as Sin and Pak Ŭnsik. Accepting such mythical accounts of Tan'gun as presented in books like *Samguk yusa* (*Memorabilia of Three Kingdoms*), the organization promoted the worship of Tan'gun as a divine figure. Shortly after its establishment, one of its leaders described the Taejonggyo's tenets in a speech that showed just how closely its religious program reflected contemporary intellectual currents. As part of the group's program, he included such seemingly nonreligious goals as protection of the nation's territory and the stimulation of commerce. Still, Tan'gun lay at the heart of the group's endeavors. Concerned that Kija overshadowed Tan'gun, the leader explained that Kija's arrival in Korea marked the start of "Our people's bedazzlement with the culture of the Han lands and was the initial reason for the gradual forgetting of the divine transformation of our Heavenly Ancestor." The primary task confronting them, he announced, was to reinstill a respect for Tan'gun and his spirit.[66] According to the group's charter, belief in Tan'gun was directly related to the concern that vexed all nationalists at the time, the strength of the nation. Widespread belief in and practice of Tan'gun's teachings were associated with times of prosperity and peace, whereas those periods in which his legacies were forgotten were marked by turmoil and invasion.[67]

Some of the earliest public espousals of Taejonggyo doctrine appeared in the *Hwangsŏng sinmun*, the longtime promoter of decentering China and an early user of *minjok*. Shortly after the religion was founded, the paper began to run editorials embracing the teachings of the "divine progenitor." These were the earliest public forays into national history written from the perspective of the Taejonggyo. "A Divine and Sagely History of Our *Minjok*," as one piece was titled, started with Tan'gun and spoke of the importance of commemorating and revering this history for Korean self-respect and autonomy.[68] Even though it was impossible to ascertain the precise date of Tan'gun's descent — a point it was willing to grant its critics — the *Hwangsŏng sinmun* urged its readers to commemorate the birthday of the founding father on the third day of the tenth month of the lunar calendar — what was to become known as the Day Heaven Opened (Kaech'ŏnjŏl). All civilized countries, they were told, remember their founders. For Koreans to do so "will forever preserve the national character of our *minjok*, lead to harmony and solidarity, and will display our qualities as a civilized people."[69]

Following annexation in 1910, Na Ch'ŏl tried to escape the control of the colonial authorities by expanding his organization into the rapidly growing exile community in Manchuria. According to Taejonggyo's own exaggerated estimates, these efforts to expand its organization were highly successful: between 1910 and 1914, membership jumped from 20,000 to 300,000.[70] As its organization continued to grow, its religious functions became overshadowed by its social and educational role in the expatriate community in Manchuria. Setting up schools and social centers, the Taejonggyo became one of the principal organizational networks for the national independence movement north of the border.[71]

One of the leading figures in this religious organization, Kim Kyohŏn, the man who after Na Chŏl's death became the Taejonggyo's second patriarch, devoted his attention to promoting and standardizing beliefs concerning Tan'gun. In 1914, Kim published the *True Records of the Divine Tan'gun* (*Tan'gun silgi*), in which he collected, edited, and annotated extant historical materials relating to Tan'gun. More important to elaborating a narrative of the national past was Kim's second book, a *History of the Divine Tan'gun's People (Sindan minsa).*[72] This was one of the first independent monographs to be published after Sin Ch'aeho's work that offered a comprehensive approach to the Korean past. Intended as a history textbook and written in a vernacular style without citing historical sources, the *History of the Divine Tan'gun's People* adopted many of Sin's methods for defining history as a project of the *minjok,* a testament to the power of Sin's earlier work in redefining conventional historical narratives.

Unlike Sin's more polemical essay, however, Kim's work was a simple chronological exposition of his version of the *minjok,* now given the name Paedal in place of Sin's Puyŏ.[73] Kim paid special attention to cultural issues, spending entire sections of the work on the development of institutions, changes in technology, and the advent and dissemination of religion. To Sin's use and conception of *minjok,* Kim added a second line of inquiry, one further entrenching the centrality of Tan'gun and offering a historical mission for his church. This inquiry focused on what Kim called *sin'gyo,* or "divine teachings," those practices, beliefs, and customs that according to the early myths, Tan'gun had bestowed on all Koreans as his divine Way. As introduced in the *History of the Divine Tan'gun's People,* these included sacrifices to Heaven every October, the maintenance of temples dedicated to the holy triumvirate, as well as the Nine Oaths and Five Prohibitions that offered a moral guide to the people. The *sin'gyo* was deemed fundamental to the *minjok,* as they were what marked Koreans as different from other people. As Kim explained, the "divine Tan'gun's people are those that live within the culture of the divine teachings."[74] Thus, to the bloodline first offered by Sin, Kim presented a second criterion of the *minjok,* its distinctive culture as originally granted by Tan'gun.

Tracing the "divine teachings" became one of the central narrative lines of the *History of the Divine Tan'gun's People.* The problem Kim faced was that although the early Tan'gun myths identified some of his teachings, there was little evidence to suggest that these teachings had been passed down in a unified form. Identifying their unity and continuity was less than clear-cut. As a result, the narrative of *sin'gyo* began with its identification and then pointed out which practices across the ages resembled its core teachings, with the ultimate purpose of establishing its continuity. This strategy was adopted even for the name of the teachings, since no other period's records gave any indication of a set of practices called *sin'gyo.* Consequently, Kim was forced to make equivalent what he called Puyŏ's "Serving Heaven" religion (Taech'ŏn'gyo), Koguryŏ's "Revering Heaven" religion (Kyŏng-chŏn'gyo), and Parhae's "True Ancestor" religion (Chinjonggyo) among oth-ers. In his hands, all were later versions of sin'gyo.[75] By the Koryŏ dynasty, sin'gyo had been transformed into a religion named after the founder of the dynasty, "Wang Kŏn religion" (Wang Kŏn'gyo), where the famous festival of the era, the Festival of the Eight Vows (P'algwanje), served as a tribute to Tan'gun. What to this point was seen by Kim as the dispersion of sin'gyo now encountered its greatest challenge. For as Kim informed his readers, the "divine teachings" were prohibited during the Mongol occupation of the peninsula.[76] Subsequently, they went underground to be practiced less rigorously and often folded into other belief systems. By the time of the Chosŏn dynasty, Kim claimed, only a few people still knew about these teachings.[77] What this vision of the decline of sin'gyo ensured, of course, was not just the centrality of Tan'gun to the minjok — this time in cultural rather than consanguineous terms — but also a historical rationale for the founda-tion of the Taejonggyo. Only its leadership, as the guardians of a nearly lost sin'gyo, could offer the means to the cultural unity desperately needed in these years of crisis. As Kim suggested in his history, from the time sin'gyo had been prohibited, the minjok had been weak. Resurrecting these forgot-ten "divine teachings" would enable a return to cultural unity and national strength — a return that would be led by his church and understood through his history.

Forgotten or not, these "divine teachings" always followed the descent line of the minjok. On the preeminence of the ethnic nation as the focus of national history, Kim agreed fully with Sin Ch'aeho. But on the details of where the descent lines of the minjok spread, Kim's genealogy — as seen in a genealogical chart at the beginning of the book — resulted in a very dif-ferent final outcome. Whereas Sin's history had been exclusive, carefully excluding any groups that he defined as outside the minjok, Kim drew the boundaries of the minjok much more broadly, incorporating into his version of the past some groups far beyond the reach of Sin's history. The result was a startlingly different account. As Sin did, Kim began with the foundation of Tan'gun's kingdom, what he called Tan'gun Chosŏn, following it to the formation of Tan'gun Puyŏ. At this point, Kim diverged from Sin when he separated the minjok's lineage into two branches, one based in the north and one in the south, a division that was crucial to his narrative. With respect to the lineage of the southern branch, Kim's history differed little from Sin's. From Puyŏ, according to Kim, the southern line was inherited by Mahan and then extended to the kingdoms of Paekche, Kaya, and Silla, followed by the Koryŏ and Chosŏn dynasties.[78]

In contrast, in the *History of the Divine Tan'gun's People* the account of the northern branch offered a dimension to *minjok* history that had been wholly lacking in "A New Reading of History." As in Sin's account, the line of descent at first passed through the various Puyŏ kingdoms in the north to Koguryŏ and then Parhae. Whereas at this point Sin's narrative focused solely on the courts occupying the peninsula, Kim continued to tell the history of those dynasties which, after the fall of Parhae, survived in the north: the Liao, Jin and Qing dynasties. Before the publication of the *History of the Divine Tan'gun's People*, these dynasties had never been considered by any historian to be part of the narrative of the peninsular courts. Conventionally, these kingdoms had been viewed as part of Chinese history. But by following the logic of his definition of the *minjok*, with the central role of Tan'gun, Kim made these three dynasties part of his history of the divine Tan'gun's people.

The incorporation of these three dynasties into his history of the Tan'gun people inspired Kim to reinterpret creatively several other historical events, particularly the relations between the Qing and Chosŏn dynasties. Kim referred to the period before the defeat of the Ming dynasty in 1644 as the Chosŏn period. The beginning of the Qing dynasty served as a marker in his periodization, however. Now that a descendant of Tan'gun occupied the former lands of the Ming, the period after 1644 was designated the Chosŏn-Qing period or, alternatively, the Southern Chosŏn and Northern Qing.[79] In short, these two dynasties represented for Kim the northern and southern branches of the same *minjok*, establishing separate, coexisting regimes.

In this way, the Qing became part of his history of the *minjok*. Kim's rewriting of this period glossed over much of the turbulence between the Qing and Chosŏn courts during the rise of the Qing dynasty. In 1627 and again in 1637, Manchu armies swept into the peninsula, coercing the Chosŏn court to pay obeisance to their newly declared dynasty. The Korean king had been forced to prostrate himself in front of the Manchu leader, Abahai, and declare his loyalty. This event, recorded by the erection of a stone monument — the *Samjŏndo* stele — at the spot where the Korean king had prostrated himself, had been viewed by Koreans as a humiliation. But having included the Manchus in the *minjok*, Kim gave these events a different spin. His version mentioned the fighting in 1627, but its resolution — what his contemporaries viewed as the submission of the Korean court — he simply

termed an oath between brothers (*hyŏngje*).[80] Similarly, Kim briefly described the 1637 battles but, again, recast the terms of the resolution that
caused so much consternation to his contemporaries. Other than noting how
tribute would be annually paid and that hostages were taken, Kim omitted
the king's prostration or the erection of the stele. Instead, he simply referred
to the events as the "peace treaty of Samjŏndo."[81] Such were the narrative
consequences of Kim's distinctive tracing of Tan'gun's descendants. In fore-
grounding the *minjok* as defined through Tan'gun, Kim was able to claim a
more grandiose vision of the national past, but one that asserted the singu-
larity of the *minjok* by downplaying any internal conflicts. In these ways,
Kim answered Sin's challenge to write a new *minjok*-centered history with
Tan'gun as the starting point, yet as his history clearly showed, the parameters
of this historical project were broad enough to produce different narratives.

These two new histories — Sin's "A New Reading of History" and Kim's
History of the Divine Tan'gun's People — typified the direction of Korean
national history for many years to come. Kim, like many who followed him,
unquestioningly adopted the methods first espoused by Sin: in place of the
earlier Confucian-style narratives, the *minjok* became the subject of history,
with its departure point located with Tan'gun, regardless of whether he was
considered a historical figure or deity. In accordance with this assumption
about the historical subject, the problem confronting historians was not
whether the *minjok* existed but how it should be identified. How they should
draw its bounds — who should be excluded and who should be included —
became the preoccupation of many of the subsequent histories. Later historians tended to follow the Sin's narrative more closely than Kim's highly
tenuous exaggerations. However, within these parameters, virtually countless
alternatives could be pursued, allowing much room for debate on both large
and small issues without ever pondering how Sin first developed these very
parameters. Accepting the *minjok* as an objective unit stretching back across
historical time, historians busied themselves with empirical searches of documents believed to be capable of revealing the location and condition of
the *minjok* at any given time in the past. Because the historians were pre-
occupied with identifying the *minjok*, the conceptual foundations on which
the historical project rested remained all but uncontested.

This silence is a testament to the powerful naturalizing tendencies of
minjok-centered history. Its role in radically reorienting history was both
extolled and downplayed. This was the new history that every publication
had been demanding. Yet as spelled out by Sin, Kim, and various newspa-

pers, this history was not the revelation of a new historical subjectivity but the remembrance of a unit that was difficult to locate because of insufficient sources and the absence of proper historical perspectives. As Sin Ch'aeho frequently complained, his predecessors had for centuries forgotten about the *minjok*. The Taejonggyo, too, claimed that its organization's fundamental task was *chunggwang*, "lighting anew" the memories of Tan'gun. History, accordingly, offered a means of recovering what was lost and resurrecting memories of a forgotten entity that maintained a subterranean existence, even when the members that constituted its whole were not conscious of its existence.

Consequently, the very historicity of *minjok* as a concept for rethinking the nation was eliminated as a subject of consideration, let alone research. The *minjok*, so entrenched in the specific milieu of the early twentieth century, was paradoxically presented as an ahistorical entity. The context of its conceptual formation — the intellectual trends of nationalists throughout East Asia, the urge to distance earlier Confucian history and decenter the "Middle Kingdom," the resistance to Japanese colonial history, all occurring in an age when the peninsula had been incorporated into the global capitalist order with its universalizing, modern ideologies — appeared irrelevant to this autonomous subject, which apparently transcended the very history that produced it. Some people may still have been confused that the question "What is the name of our nation?" was still not satisfactorily answered by the likes of Sin and Kim, who referred to the *minjok* by various names.[82] But what they did in fact settle was that the *minjok* was the unrivaled subject of national history.

6 Peninsular Boundaries

Raise the flag on Mount Paektu and fodder the horses by the
    Tumen River
Pull out your long swords and follow me
Everywhere, we will be ferocious, scaring away the spirits of
    our enemies
— "Hurry," anonymous poem, *TaeHan maeil sinbo,* August 8, 1909, *sajo*

In early 1907, the editors of the *Hwangsŏng sinmun* called on their 20 million compatriots to build an eighty-thousand-square-mile fortress of independence. It warned lyrically of the alternative:

> Don't forget your spirit of independence [*tongnipsim*].
> If this spirit is forgotten,
> The fortress of independence will be overturned,
> And if this fortress is overturned,
> To where will our Korean people venture?

Suggesting that they might be forced into the waters of the Eastern Sea or to float aimlessly far from home, the song and the accompanying editorial repeated the image of a fortress as both the refuge of the people and an impenetrable defensive shell.[1] Such a metaphor reflected the sense of siege, which since the conclusion of the Protectorate Treaty had become ever more pervasive.

This poem and editorial also captured the renewed interest in the territoriality of the nation. Crises of the nation, after all, are spatial in nature: *where* events happen determines their national significance or insignificance. Accordingly, the act of delimiting space is fundamental to the nation, since as best shown by modern maps that carve the totality of space into neatly adjacent units, there is little tolerance of territorial ambiguity for nations that are expected to exercise sovereignty over discrete areas. For a

peninsular nation like Korea, the eastern, southern, and western limits of
the nation, with the exception of a few islands, were relatively unambiguous,
leaving the northern frontier the main direction where the identification,
delimitation, and demarcation of territorial bounds became an issue.[2] Precisely where the walls of this "fortress of independence" lay along the Sino-
Korean border in the region immediately east of Mount Paektu became a
heated issue, the "most urgent question" facing the nation, according to one
report.[3] Using the new conceptual vocabulary of territorial sovereignty, both
China and Korea tried to define and defend their conflicting visions of their
shared border, leading to armed skirmishes that after 1905 even embroiled
Japan.

The introduction of new geographical discourses had various consequences for the ways in which territory was understood in early-twentieth-
century Korea. Most studies of the spread of Western geographic knowledge
to Asia have tended to emphasize its disruptive nature, seeing the rise of
some modern Asian nations as an externally produced shift from nonterri-
torially defined polities to the spatially discrete unit of the nation.[4] In such
accounts, indigenous geographical knowledge is supplanted by Western cartographic and surveying knowledge. The boundary controversy over the area
east of Mount Paektu — called Kando (Ch. Jiandao) in the contemporary
press — reveals a more complicated process of appropriation in Korea, one
that does not so neatly match a transition from tradition to modernity as
marked by the replacement of a nonterritorial understanding of space by a
territorial nation.

To be sure, certain forms of geographic knowledge prominent during the
Chosŏn dynasty were to be displaced at the national level. This was especially true of geomantic theories, which had long offered a vision of the
peninsula as a hierarchy of mountain chains that channeled the flow of the
earth's inner energies (ki) through the lands. But in the late nineteenth and
early twentieth century, when the very sovereignty of the nation was so frag-
ile, nationalist writers deemed geomantic theories irrelevant to the task of
firming up the shaky walls of the "fortress of independence." Relegated to
the realm of the individual or family, geomancy came under attack as a
superstitious practice that impeded the advancement of "civilization and
enlightenment" and as something to be erased by the edifying experience
of modern education. Extraneous to the now urgent need to affirm the
nation's territory, geomancy found little place in nationalist visions of the
peninsula.

Geographic knowledge during the Chosŏn dynasty was hardly unitary, however. With a centralized state that, by the early twentieth century, had already ruled a relatively fixed piece of territory for more than half a millennium, geographic writers during the Chosŏn dynasty developed a powerful administrative discourse on space that was not simply erased by the introduction of Western geographic discourses. As the disputes in the Kando crisis reveal, earlier investigations and surveys of the Sino-Korean border, particularly the marking of a section of the border in 1712, created a diverse body of territorial knowledge that was to segue neatly into international conceptions of territorial sovereignty. The same arguments used in the early eighteenth century reappeared nearly two centuries later. But now they were articulated in the vocabulary and conceptual framework of international geographical discourses, which, in turn, shaped memories of the 1712 border activities.

The divergent fates of these two modes of understanding space — a displaced geomancy and a reconfigured administrative discourse — mediated the shifting fortunes of what became one of the nation's preeminent symbols, Mount Paektu. Straddling the border and positioned as one of the principal mountains in geomantic conceptions of the peninsula, Mount Paektu's significance in the years before annexation shifted with the fortunes of the geographic theories that underpinned its various meanings. With geomancy in decline, less value was accorded to Mount Paektu as the top peak in the geomantic hierarchy of mountain chains. But as nationalist writers elevated Tan'gun as the progenitor of the *minjok*, the mountain's position as the mythical spot where Tan'gun descended from Heaven was highlighted, making more urgent the defense of a mountain that was at the literal frontier but the metaphorical heart of the nation.

Bordering China

The turn of the twentieth century was a troublesome time along the northern border. Korean officials and newspapers constantly reported border-crossing incidents, sometimes a group of Russians crossing into Korean territory to cut timber illegally or to map and survey the area.[5] More commonly, reports accused Chinese bandits of raiding Korean homes, killing residents, and kidnapping people for ransom.[6] Nor did Koreans remain untouched by this spirit of cross-border comradery, as evidenced by the large number of protests lodged by the Chinese ambassador in Seoul.[7] For many observers on the southern side, this alarming activity required resolute action. As one newspaper warned, these troubles might appear now as little more than "incursions of mice," but if not dealt with quickly, they would become "disturbances of tigers."[8] Never before had there been so many reports of border violations.[9] The rise in the number of reports of border incidents stemmed in part from the increased flow of both Korean and Chinese migrants into the region during the last half of the nineteenth century, with the denser population leading to more activity along — and across — the frontier. But the greater number of reports was also the result of a greater sensitivity to territorial issues accompanying the emergence of nationalism on both sides of the border, prompting both sides to seal more tightly those borders that in the past had been only loosely supervised. By the turn of the century, the upper reaches of the Tumen River had already been the subject of several decades of dispute between the Qing and Chosŏn states. Consequently, one of the reasons that Korean writers called for more geographic knowledge was to gather the information that would fulfill the Korean requirement of identifying a specific positioning of the border that had a claim stretching back to the early eighteenth century. To the east of Mount Paektu, along the upper reaches of the Tumen River, enforcement remained secondary to the more fundamental issue of the border's actual location.

One of the main authorities on geographical matters in these years was Chang Chiyŏn (1762–1836).[10] As editor of the *Hwangsŏng sinmun* from 1902 to 1905, Chang had promoted the works of a number of Chosŏn-dynasty statecraft reform thinkers, offering their writing as examples of an earlier form of Korean "enlightened" thought that still remained relevant to his own time. More than any other figure, Chŏng Yagyong attracted Chang's attention, in particular because in 1811 Chŏng had written one of the most important geographical treatises of the late Chosŏn dynasty, entitled *An Investigation of Our Nation's Territory* (*Abang kangyokko*). This work was a collection of essays on specific geographic issues that had been long debated, such as the location of ancient Chosŏn, the positioning of the four Han commanderies, and the realm of the kingdom of Parhae. The book emerged out of the statecraft stream of Neo-Confucian thought that dominated intellectual circles in the late Chosŏn dynasty, one school of which devoted considerable attention to geography and cartography. The work also reflected the administrative discourse on space, which focused on shifts in the location and titles of administrative units, as found in many state-sponsored geographical projects. These two trends gave the work a distinct empiricist (*kojŭng*) flavor, as one of the tasks Chŏng set for himself was the investigation and verification of place-names.

Chŏng's treatise was in many ways the culmination of a long tradition of geographic writing that centered on the term *kuk*. The etymology of the term, traceable to bronze inscriptions, signified the dynastic house or state, whether used for a fiefdom or a tributary state.[11] But by the late Chosŏn dynasty, the various meanings of this term had expanded beyond its etymological definition, enabling it to serve as a broader locus for expressions of identity. This broader sense of *kuk* was linked to the fact that the Chosŏn dynasty was a centralized administrative system that had ruled over a relatively stable territory from the late fourteenth to the twentieth century. *Kuk* frequently was thus seen as a territorial entity, one separate from China, that transended any single house of rule. Long-standing metaphorical expressions reflected this sense in both prose and poetry — a mention of "three thousand *ri*," the distance from the tip of the peninsula to the Yalu River, was instantly recognized as the territorial realm. Likewise, the common reference to the "eight provinces" (*p'aldo*) reflected a notion of this expanse, though in a much more administrative sense. This expression could even be the basis of poetry, as seen in the seventeenth- and eighteenth-century examples of *kasa* poetry, which described the eight provinces and the features of local settings.[12]

In the late Chosŏn dynasty, this sense of space was reflected in more detailed studies of territory. In his work *T'aengniji* (*On Selecting a Village*), Yi Chunghwan pondered at length the dilemmas faced when choosing the ideal place on the peninsula to settle. Written in an era when competition at court was fierce, often forcing officials out of their positions, the *T'aengniji* offered a survey of the peninsula as an aid to disfavored officials needing to relocate their homes.[13] All parts of the peninsula received Yi's sometimes biting commentary as he assessed the prospects for living the good life in these localities. Certain areas were obviously more desirable — and where these places were is what Yi pointed out — but the work's underlying assumption was that a person might choose to move to any location in the realm, an assumption that reflects a concept of space remarkably similar to what scholars of nationalism claim to be a requisite feature of the modern nation, that is, a sense of homogeneous space.[14]

During the dynasty, the question of delimitation and demarcation of territory arose. In 1627, as part of the joint oath between the Manchu leader

Nurhaci and King Injo, in which the Chosŏn king recognized the suzerainty of the rising Manchu power, the two courts declared, "We two *kuk* have now established peace. From today onward, let us each respect this agreement, each observe our realms [K. *ponggang*; Ch. *fengjiang*; literally, bestowed lands] and refrain from disputing trifling matters."[15] Even without a distinct division of the entire stretch of the frontier, let alone its demarcation, the two courts could, in principle, recognize the finiteness of their realms. By the late Chosŏn dynasty, travelers to China were quite conscious that, in the words of the famous reform scholar Pak Chiwŏn, "This river [the Yalu] is the point of contact and the boundary between them and us."[16] To cross the Yalu River was to enter into Qing territory. Parts of the frontier, especially the lowest sections of the Yalu River, had long been defined by means of social and administrative practices, creating what Marion Eggert has called a "ritualized space."[17] But along other stretches, particularly the remote, depopulated sections of the upper Yalu and Tumen Rivers, just where the territory of the two dynasties began or ended was less clear.

This understanding of the finiteness of the territorial realm was one of the assumptions underlying Chŏng's *An Investigation of Our Nation's Territory*. In addition, the work offered a narrative of the development of the realm. Divided into topical issues, some of which were restricted to specific centuries in the ancient past, the work sought to show how the current disposition of lands had been directly inherited from the past, both recent and distant. This is most obvious in Chŏng's treatment of the northern and northwestern frontiers. Spending a chapter on each, he traced the events on the frontier from the most remote historical period to his own era. Time and space were linked in this work, by which means dynasties served as a way of periodizing change but territory was given a continuity that transcended any one dynasty. Territorial changes, as Chŏng indicated in the title of his work, were of *abang* — our nation, thus giving the *bang* a spatial character that extended beyond the holdings of any single ruling house. Insofar as Chŏng attempted to understand contemporary Korean lands by charting their evolution from an ancient past to the present, this was a teleological history. The current realm was seen as a product of and contextualized within these historical changes.

The use to which Chang Chiyŏn put *An Investigation of Our Nation's Territory* reveals the ways in which the Chosŏn administrative discourse on space segued into the international conceptual vocabulary of territorial sovereignty. As already suggested, Chŏng's geographical work provided a rough territorial narrative. Although it was not intended for making specific terri-torial claims, it could, with a few judicious changes, be used for this purpose, a strategy quickly undertaken by Chang Chiyŏn. In 1903 Chang arranged for the publication of *An Investigation of Our Nation's Territory* by the pub-lishing house of the *Hwangsŏng sinmun*.[18] The political context of geograph-ical writing had radically changed in the intervening nine decades since Chŏng had completed the book. With territorial questions making headlines in the press and border incidents causing diplomatic rows, geographical inquiries assumed a much more public function than had the solitary work of Chŏng. In this new environment, even without any changes in the con-tent, Chŏng's book could now be seen as containing implicit nationalist meanings.

But Chang, hardly satisfied with the implicit, moved to make the con-nection explicit. He made a number of amendments and additions designed to position its vision of the territorial past in a nationalist framework. Most notably, Chang changed the title. *Abang* (our nation) was replaced with *TaeHan* (Great Korea), the name chosen in 1897 by the court to replace the old dynastic name of Chosŏn as part of its restoration movement. More-over, Chang gave the territorial narrative a visual representation by including a sequence of maps at the beginning of the book. In the introduction, Chang commented on the contemporary relevance of the work: "During these days when there are constant incidents in our lands and our powerful neighbors surround and watch over us, committed patriots will find it useful to place their hearts in this book."[19] He hoped that the book would make readers aware of their "national character" (*kuksŏng*), a term that would have been unknown to Chŏng Yagyong.[20]

On the question of Kando, however, adding a few new terms and phrases was not enough for Chang's purpose. This was because, as he explained, Chŏng Yagyong had been writing at a time when Kando had not yet become controversial, and consequently, Chŏng had not dealt with the issue. But at the beginning of the twentieth century, when Chang was preparing a book on territory written in explicit nationalist terms, Kando could hardly be left out.[21] Consequently, he appended an extra twenty-three-page chapter. Here Chang wrote about two significant moments in the past identification of the border that enabled him to assert a Korean claim on Kando. Arguments proposing a certain dispensation of lands are invariably supported by partic-ular versions of the past, in which the spatiotemporal axis offered by national history is quite literally "grounded" in territorial boundaries. The two moments raised by Chang—the first in the early 1700s and the second in the 1880s—had by this time emerged as crucial points in Korean historical interpretations of the northern limits of their national space. Chang discussed these two moments only briefly, but in presenting them as unproblematic moments in border identification, he succeeded in reaffirming a particular narrative that to this day supports Korean claims on the proper location of this section of its border with China.

The first of these moments highlighted a mission that had long been considered by Chosŏn scholars and officials as identifying and demarcating the final stretch in a border reaching across the northern extreme of the peninsula.[22] The mission had been launched by the Kangxi Emperor, who, having consolidated his reign across the breadth of China, cast a nostalgic eye back on the Manchu homelands at the same time as the appearance of Russians in the northeast presented a new security threat. Gathering information about the topography of the region also served his wish to compile a national gazetteer.[23] After several years of having their requests for information about the frontier rebuffed and their missions to the area rejected by Chosŏn officials, Kangxi finally succeeded in 1712 in getting a Manchu emissary, Mukedeng, into the Mount Paektu area. From the beginning of this mission, records of Chosŏn court debates show that Chosŏn officials assumed that the Manchu emissary would be surveying the region in order to determine the border.[24] They thus decided that those officials accompanying Mukedeng should convince him that the Yalu and Tumen Rivers served as the borders, so that "everything south of the river is our land [aji]."[25] For the area between the two rivers on the top of Mount Paektu, one minister urged that a line be drawn in the area between the two river sources. The king underscored the urgency of this strategy, telling his mission's lead official that "territory is of the utmost significance. You must make great efforts."[26]

According to the reports sent back to the court, Mukedeng was easily convinced of this position, since he knew nothing about the local topography.[27] Nonetheless, the sources of the river still had to be identified. The march up the steep side of the mountain, through the heavy underbrush and forest, was especially arduous. The middle-aged Chosŏn officials, traveling in palanquins, could not keep pace with the younger Manchu and eventually dropped out, agreeing to rendezvous with him on his descent down the other side of the mountain.[28] When Mukedeng reached the summit, his survey quickly located the source of the Yalu River,[29] but the source of the Tumen River was less clear. With several streams heading in various directions, merging and diverging, identification proved more complicated. It took more than a day, but Mukedeng eventually chose a spot. He ordered a stele to be erected there as an indicator of the watershed from where the Yalu River flowed west and the Tumen River flowed east. As he told one of the Koreans in his retinue, "To set the border and erect a [marking] stone was my imperial order."[30] Over the next year, at Mukedeng's request, a fence was built to indicate the border along a certain stretch below the stele where the river went underground for about one hundred ri.

Thus, more than one hundred years before markers and fences were used in Europe to identify and demarcate borders, the border between China and Korea had been determined for the entire northern peninsula, with even its most remote sections in the upper reaches of the Tumen River divided by a fence.[31] This was not conceived as a frontier with buffer zones or transitional areas but understood as a distinct line. Local populations were expected to observe this line: according to the dynastic laws, if you crossed over it, you would be decapitated; your head would be stuck on a pole along the border to dissuade others; and your entire family would be made slaves. Local officials responsible for enforcing the border would be punished with internal exile if they neglected this duty.[32]

Outside official circles, the events of 1712 were not as welcome. Grumblings about the stele's position spread, especially among scholars outside the corridors of power. Over the next century, these men continued to blame Chosŏn officials for dereliction of duty — specifically for not having accompanied Mukedeng to the summit — and their criticism did not stop there. Some, as Cho Kwang has shown, targeted the court's basic policy of proposing the Yalu and Tumen Rivers as demarcation lines. The lands on the northern side of the Tumen River, complained scholars like Sin Kyŏngjun, had been abandoned too quickly.[33] According to Chŏng Tongyu, it was commonly believed that Mukedeng's mission had resulted in "our country losing much of our old land [kugye]."[34] Yi Kyugyŏng wrote, "Setting territorial boundaries is a matter of great importance for the nation . . . so how is it that one can just listen to another's words, withdraw, and sit quietly?" Singling out the Chosŏn delegation's two head officials, he complained that they had allowed Mukedeng to erect the stele single-handedly "without one word of argument" and thus "lost" (shil) more than three hundred ri of land.[35] In the travel account of Sŏ Myŏngan, describing his visit to Mount Paektu in 1766, the lost area grew to seven hundred ri: "What a pity that in one morning we looked on with folded hands and lost it," he wrote.[36] Although these officials were disgruntled with the final disposition of lands, their complaints were based on the same interpretation of the events as that of court officials: that Mukedeng's mission had resulted in the demarcation of a linear border dividing their lands from Manchuria.

The border was not contested again until almost 150 years later — the second moment pointed out in Chang Chiyŏn's work. In the1870s, Qing authorities began to open up Manchuria, which had been shut off from Han Chinese migration since the earliest years of the dynasty. In stages between 1878 and 1906, the entire expanse of Manchuria was opened to settlement, with the Tumen River valley receiving its first legal Han settlers in 1881.[37] When these Qing settlers arrived, however, they quickly discovered that the far more numerous Koreans had already begun farming much of the best land.[38] Many of them had moved into the region in the 1870s to escape various famines in the northern provinces. By 1882 the presence of large Korean communities in the region came to the attention of the official in charge of the region, who lodged a protest with the Chosŏn court, laying down a number of conditions: as long as these Koreans paid taxes to the court, registered their households with local authorities, recognized the legal jurisdiction of the Qing authorities, and shaved their heads in the Manchu style — in short, became Qing subjects — they were welcome to stay; otherwise, they should return to Chosŏn territory. Seoul responded by urging the official not to register their subjects, for within one year they all would return home — an agreement that seemed to accept Qing land claims. For the farmers themselves — the people who had fled the famine and labored for more than ten years to cultivate the land — moving off the lands hardly seemed a favorable option. Few left. By April of the following year, the head of the local Qing resettlement bureau again demanded that by the conclusion of the fall harvest, the farmers return to the other side of the river.[39]

In response, local farmers challenged the assumption inherent in the Qing demand, namely, that the farmers had settled beyond the Chosŏn frontier. Their position centered on an interpretation of the stele erected by Mukedeng more than two centuries earlier. The farmers contended that they had never crossed any boundary and were in fact *within* Chosŏn territory. Their argument skillfully played off the ambiguity surrounding the character engraved in Mukedeng's stele to represent the first syllable in the name of the Tumen River. They maintained that the Qing officials had failed to distinguish between two different rivers, both called Tumen but written with two different characters for the first syllable — the first, the character carved into Mukedeng's stele, indicating "earth," and the second, a character not on the stele and signifying what today is considered the "tu" for Tumen River, meaning "diagram." The river behind which the Qing officials demanded the farmers withdraw was the latter. As the farmers pointed out, even though the pronunciation was nearly identical, the different characters signified two distinct rivers. The first Tumen River marked the northernmost point of the Chosŏn jurisdiction, while a second Tumen River flowed inside Chosŏn territory. Qing authorities mistakenly believed that the two rivers were one and the same, the petition contended, only because Chinese settlers had falsely accused the Korean farmers of crossing the border. In fact, their homes were *between* the two rivers, meaning that they lived inside the boundaries of Chosŏn. The way to substantiate their claims, they urged, was to conduct a survey of the Mount Paektu stele, for in their opinion, only the stele could determine the boundary.[40] The stele erected in 1712, thus became a central point of contention for local land disputes that were soon to expand into an issue for nationalist camps on both sides of the border.

At this time Ŏ Yunjung, who later became a famous reform official, was appointed as special inspector for the northwest. Upon receiving his appointment, Ŏ informed the king in wonderful Confucian rhetoric that the farmers would "naturally return" as soon as they learned of the king's sagely virtue, but when he arrived at the frontier, he quickly discovered that sagely virtue was no match for land. He immediately learned about the farmers' situation.[41] In response, Ŏ undertook two investigations, the first to verify the position and text of the Mount Paektu stele and the second to ascertain the sources of the river. The results of both sufficiently confirmed the farmers' position that Ŏ, in an audience at court, confidently eased any royal doubts about their claim to these lands. "That these lands are not the lands of China," he stated, "is most clear."[42] From this time, Ŏ's support for the farmers' claim became the position of the Chosŏn government. The consistency of its position was tested in a series of negotiations, first in 1885 and then again in 1887, when Chosŏn representatives met their Qing counterparts along the frontier. The large number of border incidents in the early 1880s, combined with the fact that the Qing had recently participated with the Russians in a joint survey to establish the precise location of their common border in the east, led to the first attempt since 1712 to conduct a joint examination of the Sino-Korean border in the Mount Paektu area.

These negotiations were a fascinating example of how spatial issues could be contested within the tributary relationship, without explicit refence to Western discourses on space. Both sides constantly invoked the vocabulary of tribute, regularly referring to the "superior" (*taeguk, daguo*) versus the "inferior" country (*soguk, xiaoguo*). But this attention to the formalities of subordination did not restrain the Chosŏn negotiators, led by Yi Chungha, from taking an aggressive approach toward their Qing opposites. As the verbatim accounts of some of the negotiations show, Yi constantly rebuked his Qing counterparts, pointed out contradictions in their arguments, and demanded that they produce evidence to support their statements. The Qing negotiators, perhaps caught off guard by the incongruence between tribute formalities and the adamancy of the Chosŏn position, were often frustrated by their counterpart's refusal to accept their land claims, frequently losing their tempers.[43] Despite the subordinate position of the Chosŏn court and the unconventional influence wielded by Yuan Shikai, the Chinese emissary to Seoul, the Chosŏn negotiators steadfastly advanced the argument that the Chinese continued to confuse the two rivers.[44]

The basic difference in the two sides' position rested on divergent interpretations of the stele. The Chosŏn delegates arrived at the frontier steeped in a long history of writing and debate about Mukedeng's mission of 1712 and the meaning of the stele. Although it is not clear from the 1885 or 1887 discussions how detailed the Chosŏn negotiators' knowledge was of the 1712 mission, it is clear that the basis of their territorial claim rested on this memory of Mukedeng's mission as an exercise in border identification and demarcation.[45] If any ambiguities in the border remained, their position was that the stele provided the basis for clarification. Accordingly, in both sets of negotiations, they argued that the survey mission should begin from the stele and then follow the flow of water that had been demarcated as the dividing point. What had served as a point of demarcation in 1712 still served the purpose in 1885 and 1887. The Qing efforts to undermine this position were interpreted by Korean officials as attempts to expand southward into Korean land. As the Korean negotiator, Yi Chungha, dramatically declared during the 1887 negotiations, "You can cut off my head, but you can never carve away our territory."[46]

The Qing representatives, however, refused to concede the centrality of the stele to the border. Unlike in Korea, in China the erection of the stele in 1712 had received little more than cursory attention from the court and had elicited little comment from scholars interested in imperial geographies. Moreover, as the Qing delegates sheepishly admitted in 1885, even the official documents relating to the mission had been either lost or rotted with time. In comparison to the Chosŏn delegates, who had come armed with material and documentary evidence to support their position, the Qing delegates knew little about the stele.[47] Consequently, their response was to undermine the stele's relevance to the border dispute. They argued that the border should be clarified by a reverse procedure. That is, the survey should be started at the mouth of the river, which they recognized as the only Tumen River, and head upstream through the river's main channel until reaching the headwaters. If this happened to be where the stele was located, fine, but if not, then the stele was irrelevant to the mission.[48]

During both negotiations, a number of survey teams were dispatched to map out the terrain and chart the various water flows in the region, in the hopes that this would resolve the dispute, but the accuracy of maps and surveys was not the fundamental issue separating the two parties. Both agreed that a historic border existed and that the task was to identify that border, but just how to identify what had not been an object of official scrutiny for one and half centuries and had been patrolled in only the most desultory sense remained in contention. The issue was not resolved, and with the outbreak of the Sino-Japanese War, the issue was placed on the back burner.

A Public Border

Not long after the termination of hostilities and the renewal of Sino-Korean relations as equal sovereign nations, the Kando question began to make headlines in the presses of both countries. In 1898, Ŏ Samgap, a minor Korean military official in the border region, memorialized the emperor, complaining about Qing officials' encroachments on what he viewed as Korean territory and requesting that an official be appointed to protect Korean residents in the region from future Qing depredations. Ŏ did not write this memorial for an audience larger than the emperor and his bureaucracy. But it circulated much more widely when the *Hwangsŏng sinmun* reprinted it in a condensed, partially vernacular version on its front page.[49] That a daily newspaper reproduced the memorial and in future issues repeatedly wrote editorials on the Kando issue marked an important shift away from the dynastic monopoly over territorial issues in the Chosŏn dynasty. No longer an affair solely of the state, the border became an affair for a growing reading public.

Chang Chiyŏn's 1903 publication of the *TaeHan kangyŏkko* was part of this broadening participation. He worked the events of 1712 and the 1880s into his section on Kando by simply noting how the 1712 mission had demarcated this stretch of the border and how the Qing had "mistakenly recognized" the two rivers as one for the next 170 years. These two lines of argument — the first one offered in the eighteenth century, the second one raised by local Kando residents, and both part of the official government position since the 1885 negotiations — were now made nearly canonical by this widely disseminated and authoritative text. The argument of local residents, subsequently adopted as government policy, also became a central contention in nationalist writing on the nation's spatial limits.

Chang was not shy in seeking publicity for his reprinted version of Chŏng Yagyong's work. In addition to advertisements featured on the back page of the *Hwangsŏng sinmun*, Chang used his position as editor in chief to print a serialized summary of the *TaeHan kangyŏkko*'s contents in place of the regular editorials.[50] In the summaries, he further highlighted Chŏng's teleological narrative, linking it directly to the Kando question. These editorials dispensed with the compartmentalized essays on single topics that had characterized the *Abang kangyŏk ko*, weaving the various topics on territory into a unilinear narrative stressing the gradual diminution of Korean lands.[51] In a postscript, Chang extended the theme of loss to contemporary times by linking the longer historical trend to the Kando issue through the 1712 mission. Emphasizing the importance of geographical knowledge (and indirectly plugging his book), Chang blamed the Korean officials who had accompanied Mukedeng for their "thin knowledge" and inability to "consider larger issues": if they had known more about the history of Korean territory, they would have resisted Mukedeng's decision and not have abandoned six hundred to seven hundred *ri* of fertile lands so quickly.[52] The list of territorial losses and the invasions of foreigners were now captured in this unresolved question. Chang linked Kando to the pressures of the powers in northeast Asia, tying historical to contemporary dilemmas, especially the struggle for power in Manchuria. He admitted that the comparative strength of China and Korea would likely determine the issue but that "clarifying the dividing line was the way to self-strengthening and self-protection."[53]

That Chang presented this more overtly nationalist reading of the *Abang kangyŏkko* in a newspaper was fitting. All the leading dailies had written about Kando even before Chang's more scholarly treatment of territorial history appeared. In their format, the newspapers could link separate nationalist stories simply by placing them on the same page or in the same issue. The Kando question was presented — and read — on the same pages as other contemporary issues, whether it was a strictly territorial grievance — an island in the middle of the Yalu River,[54] the Tokto Islands in the Eastern Sea,[55] or extraterritoriality — or a more abstract question relating to space such as the problem of Japanese immigration[56] and the circulation of Japanese coinage on the peninsula.[57] And in putting Kando into their headlines, newspaper editors were able to express their claim on the lands more fully in the language of the modern nation. Whereas Chang had inserted a few nationalist terms and added a few sections to position Chŏng Yagyong's *Abang kangŏk ko* in a nationalist framework, most newspaper writers distanced themselves more deliberately from the late-Chosŏn lexicon. The various stories on territorial issues were given a further degree of commonality by a shared vocabulary. Seen as part of the national crisis, the sale of land to foreigners,[58] the use of Japanese place-names in Korea,[59] and the bad behavior of Japanese individuals[60] were linked to Kando through the nation's new terms. These all were questions of "national rights" (*kukkwŏn*) "independence" (*tongnip*), and "international law" (*man'guk chi pŏp*).

These concepts also began to influence the form of historical narratives used to make the case for a Korean Kando. Increasingly used anachronistically, the terms shaped the historical memory of the 1712 mission. Authors continued to rue the results of 1712, but the stele and fence were now presented as material proof of not just a two-hundred-year-old demarcation but an act that had established what was now a two-century-old sovereign jurisdiction over Kando. "Sovereignty" and "national rights," two terms that needed to be explained to readers at the end of the nineteenth century, were now being used as powerful conceptual weapons to reinterpret history. This very modern concept of inalienable sovereignty came to be grafted back on time, becoming the central interpretative framework for signifying events in 1712.

The various writings on Kando available to the Korean public in the early years of the twentieth century — from Chŏng Yagyong's empiricist arguments to the highly emotional rhetoric about protecting Kando for the nation's honor — certainly lent a degree of incongruity to the ways that Kando was claimed for the nation. Nevertheless, the themes and issues that the authors used to make their arguments were remarkably similar, a similarity at least partly derived from their inheritance of late-Chosŏn spatial discourse. Key to these writings was their interpretation of the 1712 mission. They shared the assumption that the mission's function was the delineation and demarcation of the frontier. Regardless of whether one was content with the result, the stele and the fence were regarded as markers of a line of division. That this demarcation represented a loss of land was a central theme and that this loss could be blamed on the perfidy of geographically ignorant officials unable to carry out their responsibilities were issues also continually raised. To a scholar from the late Chosŏn dynasty interested in geography, none of these issues would have been unfamiliar. As a means of conceiving the delimitation of national space, the vocabulary of sovereignty — though linked to a new discourse on space — repeated old arguments and conceptions of the bounds of the nation. Nationalist ideology was used to retool, reinforce, and rearticulate a territorial conception that had existed for centuries. In these ways, there was a mutual interpenetration of discourses as modern concepts of sovereignty were cast back onto past events and as themes and issues first raised in late-Chosŏn administrative discourse became embedded in the framework of nationalist ideology.

The Kando crisis was rooted in more than just a shifting conceptual vocabulary regarding national space, of course. Borders, as dividers of space that must be identified and demarcated as a sharp line, need also to be patrolled and enforced. The border had already been conceptualized in the Chosŏn dynasty, but it had not been rigorously enforced. Laws did exist during the Chosŏn dynasty prohibiting "illegal crossings" (pŏmwŏl), and strict punishments were meted out to violators, but given the limits of state power in many of these remote regions, it was only the truly misfortunate who was unlucky enough to be apprehended. Despite the attempt to mark off the territory with fences, there is little evidence to suggest that the central state's conception of the border helped shape the contours of frontier society, especially given the local economy's dependence on ginseng gathering and hunting, two activities not known for their restricted spatial scope. With the advent of notions of territorial sovereignty in the late nineteenth century, the tolerance of porous boundaries rapidly declined, and the effective control of territory became one of the criteria for judging nations' abilities. Sovereignty was something to be performed, and borders were to be implemented. This need to exercise jurisdiction — whether over taxation, population registration, law enforcement, or even dress codes — is what eventually led to the friction between the Chosŏn and Qing states, as each tried to outperform the other in establishing their claims. Ŏ Samgap's memorial requesting that the central government appoint officials to Kando, together with the media's supportive response, reflected the heightened sensitivity to these issues. The desperation of Kando farmers, often pressured to pay taxes to both states, reflected the very real consequences of the impasse.

The Chosŏn court made various attempts to exercise its jurisdiction, most famously with the appointment in 1902 of Yi Pŏmyun as the overseer of the region. In this capacity, Yi tried to register the population and enforce a tax regime. He also recruited his own army for skirmishes against the Qing police. After repeated protests by the Qing representative in Seoul, his aggressive tactics eventually lost him his government position and support. He nevertheless continued on his own to recruit a private army and taxed the population in order to deny Qing jurisdiction over the region. With the establishment of the Japanese Residency General in 1905, any possibility that Chosŏn officials could negotiate a settlement of the border dispute with their Qing counterparts ended, as the Japanese now controlled Korean foreign affairs. At first, the Resident General's Office pursued the Korean claim, going as far as dispatching Japanese police to Kando, thereby causing a number of diplomatic rows and some rather alarming military engagements in the contested region. But in 1909, the colonial authorities suddenly reversed this aggressive stance. In exchange for concessions in Manchuria, Japan signed a treaty with the Qing dynasty that abandoned Korea's position on the border and recognized the Qing's claims. This treaty established what today is generally understood as the border between the peninsula and Manchuria, putting the heavily Korean-populated prefecture of Yanbian (Yŏnbyŏn) under the jurisdiction of the People's Republic of China. In the end, the limits of Korean territory were in this instance determined by the politics of the Japanese empire.

From this point on, the border became one more issue used by the Governor General's Office to articulate its colonial ideology. In its standard "before and after" mode, colonial authorities used the border as an example of the administrative competence it was now spreading through its newly annexed territory. Their reasoning downplayed the Chosŏn state's attention to the border, both in the long term stretching back to 1712 and, more recently, before 1905 in its efforts to settle the issue with the Qing and perform the duties of a sovereign power. Instead, the border was presented as a source of chaos, where people — whether refugees, criminals, or Chinese opium smokers — had crossed without problem.[61] The open border had also been the conduit for diseases entering the country from China, it was claimed.[62] But since 1910, under colonial rule, the situation along the frontier had changed. Overstating their ability to seal off a border that for much of the remainder of the colonial period was regularly penetrated by nationalist forces and that today, despite its best efforts, has not been effectively sealed even by Democratic People's Republic of Korea, colonial authorities presented themselves as performing the acts of sovereignty that the Korean state had been unable to exercise. People could no longer cross without approval, and the border was now a barrier to disease. Korea's inability to patrol its space was contrasted with the colonizer that was able to seal the border. Territory was one more way to claim Korea as unfit for self-rule and, thereby, to arrogate responsibility for that territory. With territory considered basic to any definition of the modern nation, colonization as the regulation of territory could be presented as modernization, even though colonial policies resulted in a smaller territorial unit for Korea.

The Decline of Geomancy and Mount Paektu

Not all ways of conceptualizing space in the late Chosŏn dynasty could be fused so neatly with Western notions of territorial sovereignty. Equally as venerable as the administrative discourse on territory was an understanding of space based on geomantic principles. But geomancy, as a series of practices that also offered individuals a means of enhancing their personal fortunes through the propitious location of various sites, ran afoul of the self-help ethos underpinning the nationalist reform agenda. Despite its prominence during the Chosŏn dynasty, geomancy's differences with the "civilization and enlightenment" program, together with its disregard of spatial issues such as borders, led it to a fate quite unlike that of administrative discourse, a fate that shaped the significance of the mountain intrinsic to its principles, Mount Paektu.

Geomancy has long been practiced in Korea. As Gari Ledyard has observed, the conception of the peninsula as a space defined by its mountain networks had developed as early as the eighth or ninth century.[63] According to the geomantic thought dominant in the Chosŏn dynasty, mountains were arteries that conducted the inner energies of the earth, what in Korean is called *ki*, through the lands of the peninsula. Depending on the specific topography of any given spot — Was the shape of a hill like that of a dragon's back? Which direction did the site face? — the distribution of *ki* determined the benevolence or malevolence of a site. With its emphasis on auspicious locations, geomantic theory spurred families to build their homes, institutions to center their buildings, and even dynasties to place their capitals on auspicious sites — a desire that offered much employment to the experts with the skills and facility to read the land.[64] Despite this localized impetus — Where best to live? Where best to locate ancestral graves? — geomantic thought linked auspicious spots to the broader layout of the mountain chains that determined the geography of the peninsula. In this sense, a specific site derived its attributes through its connections upward through various mountain complexes offering a macrotopographic understanding of the peninsula and even extending into Manchuria, a vision that transcended the northern border, making the very concept of boundaries superfluous to this theory.

This geomantic conception differed markedly from administrative notions of space. Instead of the measurable distances showing jurisdiction, geomantic theories created hierarchies. In privileging *ki* networks, geomancy shunned a vision that organized space uniformly, regardless of the terrain's vagaries and distinctions. It was an understanding that tried less to separate constituent units from their counterparts and more to trace a web of topographical relations that channeled the flows of *ki*. Moreover, as Ch'oe Ch'angjo has proposed, geomantic theories created an integrated approach to physical and human geography, the two related by principles of how local topography directed *ki* to influence human behavior, a relationship not present in the administrative approaches to space.[65]

Despite the differences, these various visions of space were by no means mutually exclusive. In depictions of the peninsula, cartographic traditions from the Chosŏn dynasty commonly combined both administrative and geomantic understandings. As early as the 1530 *Palto ch'ongdo* (*Comprehensive Map of the Eight Provinces*), the most prominent features on Korean maps were administrative zones, mountains, and rivers. The more detailed maps of the seventeenth and eighteenth centuries offered both fuller coverage of administrative units down to the county level and a more detailed treatment of mountain chains. In brightly colored maps such as the *Haedong P'aldo ponghwa san'ak chido* (A Map of the Mountains of the Eight Provinces of the East), the result is a peninsula covered in bright green streaks marking the mountain chains. Even in local maps of counties and cities, great attention was always given to tracing mountain connections. Kim Chongho's *Taedong yŏjido* (*Territorial Map of the Great East*) carried this tradition into the 1860s when his map, which according to legend was drawn by pacing out all the distances in the peninsula, again portrayed the peninsula as a mixture of administrative districts and mountain ranges.

This combination of administrative and geomantic conceptions of space received its most elaborate written expression in Yi Chunghwan's *T'aengniji* (*On Selecting a Village*). In this book, which assessed the various areas of the peninsula in search of the ideal place to settle, local topography was judged according to geomantic theories.[66] Yi laid out the principles of these theories in a separate chapter, explaining the importance of *ki* and showing its relation to the peninsula's mountain ranges. He described the peninsula as defined by its mountains, beginning with Mount Paektu and extending southward.[67] In Yi's actual descriptions, the administrative jurisdictions provided the organizing principle. Instead of following each mountain chain and describing landmarks along its natural course, Yi divided the peninsula into its eight provinces and then discussed each county, always returning to the geomantic principles as they related to the mountains. In this way, both spatial visions were mutually supporting, offering a hybrid approach to both the entire peninsula and individual localities.

As Yi's work showed, the key mountain in these geomantic conceptions of the peninsula was Mount Paektu, the same mountain on which Mukedeng had placed his marker in 1712. Standing at the top of the peninsula in a relatively unpopulated region and with its mysterious crater lake known as the Heavenly Pond, Mount Paektu had, by the Chosŏn dynasty, long been the source of legends and stories. Indeed, the sense of spirituality and mysticism often attributed to the mountain was already apparent in 1259 when the *Samguk yusa* offered the first recorded version of the Tan'gun myth. In its account, Tan'gun descends from Heaven with his three thousand followers to land on Mount Paektu.[68] The histories that kept the memories of Tan'gun alive during the Chosŏn dynasty highlighted the importance of Mount Paektu as the spot where he appeared. On a number of occasions, officials at court debated the possibility and significance of offering official sacrifices to the mountain.

Mount Paektu's stature in geomantic theory was unrivaled. In the hierarchical ascension from the locality to the mountain chains, it was Mount Paektu that was quite literally conceived as the summit of the system. In theory, this northernmost mountain accumulated its *ki* from Manchuria and dispensed it through the arteries that extended through the peninsula, a status reflected in the cartographic convention of adding various artistic flourishes to Mount Paektu, making it larger and more imposing than other mountains.

But at the turn of the century, as part of their elucidation of the principles of *munmyŏng kaehwa*, nationalist writers began targeting geomancy. Their criticisms were not leveled at geomancy's macroperspective of the peninsula but at its actual practice in the localities. Although conservative Confucians with their "old knowledge" (*kuhak*) may have been the main obstacles to enlightenment, in the eyes of many reformers, "old knowledge" remained an enemy restricted to the educated elite. Geomancy, however, penetrated all levels of society, particularly, as the editors of the *Tongnip sinmun* pointed out, as an "old custom" (*kusŭp*) among "people without learning."[69] Described as an "old custom," as opposed to "old knowledge," geomancy was grouped with shamanism and fortune-telling — all of which were derisively labeled "superstitions" (*misin*).[70] As the *Hwangsong sinmun* warned, geomancy was "a type of tremendously corrupt superstition that does not exist in the other countries of the world and is unheard of in ancient and modern history."[71] Others pointed to its simultaneous existence in China, citing it as the reason that these two countries were "the weakest and most corrupt."[72]

The alleged dangers of geomancy were many, but the most prominent was its association with burial practices. Back in the late Chosŏn dynasty, such scholars as Pak Chega and Chŏng Yagyong condemned the self-serving desires that motivated the choice of auspicious grave sites, a practice they believed violated standards of filial piety.[73] Resuming this line of attack, the editors of the *Hwangsŏng sinmun* complained that people would move a grave in order to find a more beneficial site, even though they risked losing or damaging the "white bones" of a mother or father.[74] As some reports indicated, people would go so far as to move a single corpse from grave to grave as many as ten times in search of a more auspicious spot.[75]

Just as commonly, geomancy was censured for its economic inefficiencies. Whether it was the wasteful use of land or the expense of ceremonies, geomancy led to the unproductive investment of resources. Entire mountains and their extensive surrounding lands were taken over by top officials for the burial of family members, sometimes at the expense of forcing the local population off their land.[76] All this geomantic activity, the *Hwangsŏng sinmun* dramatically claimed, meant that "half of the land of the entire country" had been turned into graves.[77] For the editors of the *Tongnip sinmun*, geomantic practices were an utter waste of capital that could be better spent on activities needed by the nation — the construction of hospitals, schools, and manufacturing plants.[78] So expensive were the ceremonies that what people expected to lead their family to good fortune more often than not led to financial ruin, the *Hwangsŏng sinmun* warned.[79]

These were serious charges that took up much editorial space, but the distress of the various editors stemmed less from these specific social abuses than from geomancy's challenge to the very heart of the *munmyŏng kaehwa* enterprise. In promising to offer a way to success and fortune merely by manipulating the location of a grave or moving one's house, geomantic theories encouraged a complacency that discouraged the self-help and activist enjoinments of nationalist newspapers. For the nation to succeed, something needed to be *done*. To this end, the editors cajoled and coaxed the population into certain types of behavior. Although this ability to discipline individuals was linked directly to the strength or weakness of the nation, geomancy offered a way to sidestep this equation. The links between individual success, efforts at self-reform, and the fortunes of the nation were broken. Geomancy threatened to induce an apathy, a denial of the need to struggle against and master those conditions anathema to nationalist reformers.[80] One editorial depicted this dilemma by imagining a conversation between a practitioner of geomancy and his neighbor, a diligent worker. The former derided the latter for working so hard, advising him that the way to make a fortune and expand the holdings of one's ancestors was to find an auspicious grave site, and not by working hard in the fields and studying books.[81] By the end of the editorial, the industrious worker had — not surprisingly — convinced his neighbor of the futility of geomancy, but not before its seductive power to lull people into inactivity had been pointed out. Easy reliance on such practices created, in the words of the *Tongnip sinmun*, "weak hearts" that prevented people from taking up difficult tasks.[82] This was the fear of any true reformer. The focus on geomancy as a corrupt local custom left little room for discussing the spatial theories on which these practices rested. Geomancy eventually was reduced to a private practice that injured the public good and was scorned as little more than a self-indulgent folk practice that should be eliminated.

The displacement of geomancy was manifested by a shift in cartographic conventions. In the maps produced for the new educational textbooks, the Chosŏn dynasty's practice of tracing mountain chains and highlighting prominent peaks became less prominent.[83] Now the new maps were as likely to feature latitudinal and longitudinal lines as to show the location of a few select peaks.[84] In an era when geomancy served as a powerful counterbalance to dominant notions of enlightenment and when questions of territory were posed as questions of sovereignty and defense, there was as yet no attempt to recover geomancy as a marker of the native or a revival of the indigenous.[85]

This did not mean the actual practice of geomancy had receded. Rather, the existence of these antigeomancy polemics indirectly confirmed that in fact, its practice was flourishing, even if there was little place for geomancy in the new ways of thinking about the spatial nation. Instead, notions of territorial sovereignty joined geomancy's Chosŏn-period counterpart, the administrative discourse on space, to supplant geomancy. In a global order populated by nations that defined their sovereignty in territorial terms, geomancy was shunted aside by nationalists anxious to show that Korea could meet the necessary criteria for independence. Now geomancy was regarded as little more than a selfish practice out of sync with its age.

The displacement of geomancy affected the top peak in the hierarchy of mountains, Mount Paektu. In the years just before annexation, this mountain emerged as a salient nationalist icon, but its rise to prominence was not immediate. As the popularity of geomantic theories waned, Mount Paektu lost one of its most important signifiers. New textbooks published in the years immediately after the Sino-Japanese War paid scant attention to the mountain. Despite all the chapters on various geographical subjects and even though these textbooks often dealt with mountains, Mount Paektu was not singled out. None of the textbooks published before 1905 devoted a single lesson to describing, let alone hailing, Mount Paektu. Although the mountain was mentioned, it was usually as a way of describing the northern limits of Korea's territory.[86] Other mountains took precedence over Mount Paektu. A lesson in *An Elementary Primer* describing the nation's principal mountains gave top billing to the nation's tallest mountain, Mount Chiri, before describing three others. Mount Paektu did not make the list and presumably was included in the last line of the lesson, "Besides these, there are many other famous mountains."[87] The most frequently featured mountains in these years were the Kŭmgang Mountains, a scenically renowned series of peaks that had long been featured in poetry, landscape painting, and proverbs. It was touted by the *Tongnip sinmun* as a prospective tourist site.[88] Some textbooks, like *The Essential Reader for Youths*, spent several lessons on describing the beauty and lore of the Kumgang Mountains, again without any mention of Mount Paektu.[89] Clearly, learning about Mount Paektu was not deemed by these textbook writers as "essential" reading for a nationalist curriculum.

This was the state of affairs until another trend again raised the northern mountain to preeminence. After 1907, as tensions in the Kando region continued to rise and interest in Tan'gun surged, Mount Paektu began to appear more regularly in the press, often as a symbol of the pressures placed on Korean territory. Given the vaunted position of Mount Paektu in Korean nationalist iconography today, it is difficult to imagine that the delineation of the northern border could be discussed without much attention to Mount Paektu's value as something more than a chunk of space. Yet in 1712, during Mukedeng's mission, the extensive debates among Korean officials glossed over the legends and lore surrounding the mountain. The same was true of the joint survey missions and negotiations between the Chosŏn and Qing dynasties in the mid-1880s. After the Sino-Japanese War, when the Kando issue reappeared, the more emotional editorials and letters to the newspapers criticized the government for not protecting the citizens and land of Kando, but these comments were not extended to the consequences of the conflict for Mount Paektu.

This connection was not regularly made until 1907 when newspapers such as the *Hwangsŏng sinmun* and *TaeHan maeil sinbo* began to promote Tan'gun as the progenitor of the *minjok*. With Tan'gun attracting so much attention, the mountain to which he supposedly descended also became linked with the *minjok*.[90] Emptied by nationalists of its geomantic meanings, Mount Paektu now came to represent the territorial center of the *minjok*. In so doing, the mountain became a symbol of a sacred national territory extending back into the mists of time, bestowed by Tan'gun to countless generations. Poetry published in the *TaeHan maeil sinbo* captured these new meanings in verse. An ode to Tan'gun had the progenitor descending to Mount Paektu, its "green hills and rivers" part of the glorious gift he bestowed on the brothers and sisters of the *minjok*.[91] Other poetry praised the beauty of the mountain, hoping that in this day and age it would produce heroes as it had in the past.[92] Still other poems offered Mount Paektu as a metonym of the nation. "Look at Mount Paektu," one verse began, "is it not the great ancestor of the East?" Noting that it and the other great Korean mountains were the basis of the empire as bestowed by Heaven, the poem then took a jab at Japan: "Over there, Mount Fuji is no taller, a lone summit on an island."[93]

The growing tendency to romanticize the mountain through its association with Tan'gun resulted in a certain ambiguity about the relation of the border dispute to Mount Paektu. By 1909 the precise location of the boundary had been a subject of dispute between the Qing and the Chosŏn court for more than three decades. In the 1880s, attempts to settle the issue had been conducted through the institutions and with the language of tribute. After the Sino-Japanese War, especially with the recognition of the nation's

independence, the border issue had been transformed into one of two competing states seeking to justify their long-standing rival claims by appealing
to the principles of territorial sovereignty. After 1907, the linkage of Mount
Paektu to the new concept of *minjok* and Tan'gun cast a different light on
the border issue. As a challenge to territorial sovereignty, Kando remained
the customary way of conceiving the border controversy, which was now
accompanied by a second way of conceiving space, one tied less to a history
of boundary fluctuations over time and grounded more in the sweeping style
of *minjok* narrative as articulated by Sin Ch'aeho.

A certain tension existed between these two visions. Straddling the border,
Mount Paektu was partly inside and partly outside Korea. All the debates
about the relevance of the 1712 stele and the exact location of the border
did not resolve the problem that a mountain increasingly seen as the site of
national foundation was not completely inside the current territorial limits.
Appealing to international standards for establishing territorial sovereignty
might have been useful in making claims on the Kando region, but by
definition, this same strategy conceded the partition of Mount Paektu, locating it partly outside the nation. In contrast, the logic of *minjok*-centered
conceptions of space had little to say about borders. Without directly taking
issue with conceptions of sovereign territory, *minjok*-centered conceptions
of national space made an unconditional claim to all of Mount Paektu,
granting borders little relevance in determining the meaning of a sacred
mountain.

This uneasy relationship between the two approaches to Mount Paektu
is captured in the ambiguity of the poem "Hurry," quoted at the beginning
of this chapter. Written just one month before Japan turned over the Kando
area to the Qing dynasty, the call to arms and the reference to the disputed
areas of Mount Paektu and the Tumen River read at one level as a plea to
defend the northern border as defined by the two topographical features. At
a second level is the hint of another motivation. It is not quite clear whether
the foddering of horses and the pulling out of swords are meant to stop at
the northern border or whether these activities are preparations for some
grander enterprise. What can be read as a call to defend the border also
suggests a more expansive realm, one that would include all of Mount
Paektu but might not stop there. As the northernmost limit of the peninsula,
Mount Paektu also reached northward beyond the peninsula. And just as
this mountain extended into Manchuria, many Korean writers began to look
toward the north, questioning the nation's peninsular limits.

7   Beyond the Peninsula

There are many sad things, but not having a country is the
saddest of all. There are many heart-wrenching things, but none more than not
having a home. . . . Where shall we turn?
— *SinHan minbo*, April 14, 1909

The Kando controversy affirmed a spatial vision of the nation
that had been at the forefront for centuries: Korea as a peninsula. Venerable
expressions such as "three thousand *ri*" remained in vogue, often combined
with common peninsular metaphors that now carried a sense of territorial
sovereignty: "the peninsula of the East" (*tongyang ŭi pando*), the "rivers and
mountains of the peninsula" (*pando kangsan*), the "Empire of the Korean
peninsula" (*Hanbando cheguk*), or, most simply, the "peninsular nation"
(*pandoguk*). Images of the peninsula adorned the covers of journals,[1] and
theories on environmental determinism inspired many to question how the
condition of living on the peninsula shaped national character.[2] Odes to
"our Korean peninsula that juts out into the Eastern Sea" appeared in daily
newspapers.[3] By the early twentieth century, the peninsula had become the
preeminent spatial metaphor for the nation.

Nonetheless, a number of developments in these years led some writers
to move beyond the peninsula in their spatial conceptions of the nation.
Whether gazing north to Manchuria or examining the growth of organized
diasporic communities as far away as San Francisco, some writers went so
far as to suggest that the locus of the nation had rested beyond the peninsula
in the past and might very well shift abroad again in the future. Featured in
the same pages of the same media, these alternative but not exclusive visions
vacated the conceptual vocabulary of territorial sovereignty that so dominated debates about Kando to speak instead about national space as it related
to spirit, character, and *minjok*. The memories of the past and the politics

of the present caused writers to make the seemingly paradoxical proposition that the spirit of a unit that was generally defined territorially could, in fact, be located beyond its boundaries. In so doing, they began to tease apart one of the foundational assumptions made about the nation: that territory and cultural identity were isomorphic.

With regard to Manchuria, this meant building on the new style of *minjok*-centered history to assert an irredentist claim to the northern lands as the rightful domain of the Korean people. This perspective remembered a grander national realm when past Korean dynasties occupied Manchuria. Using these past ages as a standard to measure subsequent periods, these authors, led by Sin Ch'aeho, blamed the loss of Manchuria on an earlier attenuation of national spirit, which, when traced down to the current times, explained the dire situation of the peninsula. Infused with a deep sense of loss, these writings saw Manchuria as a central stage of the Korean past that offered the key to the present crisis.

But Manchuria was not the only location outside the peninsula from which to reconsider spatial assumptions about the nation. At the very time that the peninsula was being conceived in terms of territorial sovereignty, Koreans were separating themselves from the finite limits of that territory by migrating abroad. With a population now scattered beyond national boundaries, writers needed to conceptualize the relationship of their deterritorialized compatriots to their peninsular definitions of the nation. Stepping outside national boundaries, as Liisa Malkki has argued, is often seen to imply losing touch with one's national identity or culture, an assumption made by some contemporary Korean observers of the diasporic community. However, as Japan encroached on Korean sovereignty, the peninsula's role as a homeland for distant nationalist communities became increasingly problematic. Koreans writing in Seoul as well as those writing in San Francisco saw the peninsula as tainted by the Japanese Protectorate. With varying degrees of certainty, writers in Seoul and San Francisco began to suggest that only those areas beyond the peninsula were viable redoubts of the nation. Under colonialism, they suggested somewhat paradoxically, the nation could exist only outside the nation.

The articles on Manchuria and the reports on the San Francisco-based diasporic community had little in common on a thematic level. The former dealt with land, and the latter was concerned with people. One location was adjacent to the peninsula, whereas the other was across an ocean. Concern with Manchuria centered on reinterpretations of the past, while writings on the diaspora issue focused on the consequences of colonization. The former rested largely on a social Darwinian framework, in contrast to the "civilization and enlightenment" approach of the latter. Despite these differences, both shared the same desire to reconsider the relationships of their individual subjects vis-à-vis the peninsula, revealing the multiplicity and fluidity of spatial understandings of Korea. Both moved beyond the peninsula to propose solutions for the national crisis.

A Korean Manchuria

The Kando crisis inevitably drew the attention of Korean newspaper readers toward the north. With the announcement in the early years of the century of some significant archaeological discoveries relating to dynasties that had occupied Manchuria in the past, some writers became less content to restrict their northward gaze to the border.[5] These archaeological relics, in some cases removed and exhibited in Tokyo, stimulated a nostalgia and romantic yearning for a stronger, more ancient Korea when the lands to the north were not occupied by others. They also raised the question of the role of Manchuria in the Korean past and the relationship of these lands to the peninsula. One of the leading students of this relationship was Sin Ch'aeho, who in various essays and editorials complained that the existence of a Korean Manchuria had been forgotten, relegated to the early pages of Korean history. He lamented his compatriots' indifference to the lands north of the Yalu River, wondering how many people in the past several hundred years truly comprehended the importance of Manchuria to the peninsula.[6] The answer for Sin, of course, was far too few.

If Sin was looking for people who were pondering the significance of this territorial relationship, he could very well have looked across the sea to historians in Japan. By the turn of the century, as part of the institutional and scholarly matrix that developed the discourse on Tōyō, the East — or what Stefan Tanaka has termed "Japan's Orient"[7] — Japanese historians had already begun to write Korean history not as peninsular history but as *Mansenshi*, Manchurian-Korean history. In their spatial approach, Japanese historians had already established the link that Sin and others made.[8] Yet while this connection was shared, the purpose and function of the Japanese versions of the Korean past were decidedly different from those of the Korean writers. As Hatada Takeshi has pointed out, by merging the peninsula and

Manchuria into a single object of history, Japanese writers represented Korea as historically dependent on and indistinct from the continent. At the end of the nineteenth century, when the Japanese state was trying to establish its interests in the peninsula and Manchuria, combining the two as a unified historical region served their imperialist objectives by undermining contemporary Korean nationalist claims of a historical independence.[9] History rationalized a vision of space that countered conceptions of territorial sovereignty.

In the early years of the twentieth century, writers working at both of the principal nationalist newspapers, the *Hwangsŏng sinmun* and *TaeHan maeil sinbo*, also established a link between the peninsula and Manchuria. Editorials in the *Hwangsŏng sinmun* were regularly about the importance of Manchuria, a geographical relationship that they characterized as "a pillow for the head of the peninsula"[10] and two pieces of land so close that the "dogs and chickens could hear each other."[11] The editors stressed the economic potential of the north, suggesting that its future disposition would determine the fate of the peninsula and that Koreans should participate in its development.[12] But it was Sin Ch'aeho who articulated this relationship most forcefully in an editorial for the *TaeHan maeil sinbo*:

> How intimate is the connection between Korea and Manchuria? When the Korean *minjok* obtains Manchuria, the Korean *minjok* is strong and prosperous. When another *minjok* obtains Manchuria, the Korean *minjok* is inferior and recedes. Moreover, when in the possession of another *minjok*, if that *minjok* is a northern *minjok*, then Korea [Han'guk] enters into that northern *minjok's* sphere of power. If an eastern *minjok* obtains Manchuria, then Korea enters that eastern *minjok's* sphere of power. Alas! This is an iron rule that has not changed for four thousand years.[13]

Japanese historians belonging to the Mansenshi school of history would no doubt have found little objectionable in this appraisal's assumptions. But the conclusions that Sin drew — and the history he wrote — worked at cross-purposes to those of his Japanese contemporaries. Although *Mansenshi* had tied the peninsula to Manchuria so as to downplay Korean autonomy, Sin claimed Manchuria for Korea in order to create a usable past that would resist the very imperialism that Japanese scholarship supported. For Japanese historians, the Manchurian connection constituted a critical move in the creation of a colonizing discourse, but for Sin, Manchuria became the key to constructing a powerful nationalist history. Differing in purpose, function, and content, both these versions of the past nevertheless depended on establishing a link between the peninsula and Manchuria and presenting a vision of space that did not use the language of territorial sovereignty.

Reinterpreting territorial history was not an enterprise undertaken by Sin alone. As in his promotion of *minjok*-centered history, Sin capitalized on intellectual trends that had been developing since the imposition of the Protectorate. In 1907, an anonymous article in the journal *Sŏbuk hakhoe wŏlbo* (Northwest Educational Monthly) entitled "Speaking to a Child About History" (Tae tongja nonsa), enunciated some of the main points about territory that Sin later featured in his more elaborate work.[14] In this piece, a writer describes a child reading a classical history of the peninsula. The child extols the greatness of the early kingdom, Silla, only to find the writer anxious to set his misunderstanding straight. He points out to the child that Silla had succeeded only by pandering to external powers, a policy that led to a long legacy of slavish behavior in Korea. The writer then tells the child that Koguryŏ, Silla's rival to the north, should be held up as an exemplar. It alone, he explains, had stood steadfast as an independent country and, most significantly, possessed and defended the lands of Manchuria. By highlighting the importance of northern kingdoms and valorizing the possession of Manchuria, this short piece foreshadowed some of the key developments in Sin's own work, as he spelled out in the piece that also offered his vision of the *minjok*, "A New Reading of History."

In "A New Reading of History," Sin's vision of the *minjok* and Tan'gun presented a history that retrieved a former greatness for the present, a greatness that he measured in part by the standard of Manchuria. A new history, Sin argued, would reveal the central role of Manchuria in Korean history and, by prodding historical memories and encouraging pride in the past, could also help recreate the glories of that past in the future. If the loss of Manchuria was the cause of Korea's weakness, he reasoned, then its retrieval would ensure Korea's future. As only a historian could so confidently assert, the solution to the crisis Korea faced in the early years of the twentieth century was history, a new history that would help recover Manchuria. Not content with reclaiming Manchuria in the historical past, Sin also desired it in the present—and he even hinted at a plan.

The notion of legitimacy against which Sin developed his conception of the *minjok* also served as the foil against which he articulated his territorial vision. In "A New Reading of History," he wrote with great dissatisfaction about his predecessors, reserving his greatest disdain for those historians who had accepted the nation's current boundaries — in other words, the peninsular limits — and carried them back in time.[15] In this type of history, territory functioned as the backdrop for a moralistic account of kings and courts, in which Manchuria was relevant only in the early periods from Tan'gun to the fall of Koguryŏ. Thereafter, such histories concluded with accounts of either the Koryŏ or Chosŏn dynasties, courts firmly entrenched on the peninsula. Without making any explicit claims about territory and by conferring legitimacy on those dynasties whose northern frontiers did not extend beyond the Yalu or Tumen Rivers, these histories in Sin's eyes effectively delineated the northern extent of the nation's territory. Such history, he argued, restricted the spatial scope of Korean history to the peninsula. In fact, Sin's critique of his predecessors overstated their lack of attention to Manchuria, neglecting to mention people like Yu Tŭkkong, who in his eighteenth-century work *Parhaego* (*An Investigation of Parhae*) made claims on Manchuria by contending that the kingdom of Parhae should be included in their history.[16] It was also common in the late Chosŏn dynasty to write about the "old lands of Koguryŏ," an expression of nostalgia for the north.[17] Sin nevertheless did offer an original means of thinking about Manchuria by linking it to the *minjok* while presenting it as an expanse that had not just once been held by Koreans but that had also functioned as the central stage of Korean history.

It was through his interpretation of Tan'gun that Sin began to reconsider the relationship between the peninsula and Manchuria. As historians today know only too well, no records from this mythical period exist. This did not stop Sin, however. He lamented that the ravages of time and warfare as well as the indifference of later historians to preserving materials from the era of Tan'gun had resulted in enormous gaps of knowledge such that even the names of Tan'gun's descendants had been lost. Nevertheless, Sin claimed that by perusing extant materials — sources that he never specifically cited — certain information could be gleaned, including (most conveniently) the dimensions of ancient territorial holdings. Accordingly, the *minjok*'s territorial history could be recounted as beginning with Tan'gun's appearance in the Changbaek mountain region, followed by a move to the basin of the Yalu River where his people had spread out. As his descendants continued to multiply, they branched off in two directions, one group moving northward into the Liaodong peninsula and Manchuria and the other heading southward into the Korean peninsula. Sin concluded that this early realm stretched from the Amur River in the north to the Choryŏng Mountains in the south (roughly halfway down the peninsula), east to the great ocean, and west to the Liaodong peninsula.[18] In the parlance of Sin, this expanse was the birthplace (*palsaengji*) of the *minjok*, the ancient lands of Tan'gun, which, as his narrative progressed, served as the central stage of Korean history.

Manchuria represented much more than the rediscovery of a birthplace. It also functioned as a means of measuring and narrating the history of the *minjok*. In examining the several millennia of the *minjok*'s history, Sin judged the degree of its success by the vicissitudes in territorial holdings. Losing or gaining land determined victory and defeat, grandeur and disgrace. A major criterion for appraising an individual's contribution to the historical record was his role vis-à-vis Manchuria, luster shining on those who preserved or extended Korean control over Manchuria and shame heaped on those who settled for a peninsular claim. In this way, through his focus on the *minjok* and privileging of Tan'gun, Sin established an implicit territorial standard — Manchuria — to measure the minjok's position in a world of social Darwinian struggle.

Writing at the beginning of the twentieth century, Sin found few moments in recent history that could be termed by this standard as "successful." As a result, "A New Reading of History" was an account of antiquity when the *minjok* was still strong and glorious deeds could still be recounted. It was a history that, beginning with Tan'gun and ending with the loss of the "ancestral lands" upon the fall of Parhae in A.D. 926, asserted a claim to Manchuria in the distant past, demonstrated how the territory was squandered, and showed how the memory of its possession erased. With the resplendence of history located in the distant past, recent history in this narrative became one of ignominy, of losing Manchuria to others, with the *minjok* being separated from what Sin regarded as its natural territory.

Consequently, Sin's narrative was infused with an accusatory tone as he groped for an accounting of the loss of Manchuria and indicted the culprits he found. High on this list was Kim Ch'unch'u (King Muyŏl), the leader of the kingdom of Silla, who in defeating his two neighbors, Paekche and Koguryŏ, abandoned the lands of Manchuria. Having beaten these regimes by A.D. 668, the kingdom of Silla could claim — and, with few exceptions, historians granted — an undisputed and undivided legitimacy for its rule. In Sin's interpretation of previous historical annals, Silla's victory had been depicted as an event that had unified the nation, a unity that had been transmitted intact to the Chosŏn dynasty. In his scathing critique of these earlier accounts, Sin underscored his ideal vision of the *minjok* unified in a single state, stretching from the peninsula to Manchuria. In his view, anything short of joining the peninsula with Manchuria could hardly be deemed a "unification" (*t'ongil*). Such an approach to history meant that there had in fact been very little unity since the outset of the *minjok's* history. Why is it, Sin wondered, that since the era of Tan'gun, no single person had been able to unify the Korean people?[19]

Sin proceeded to answer his own question with a quick synopsis of the history of the Manchurian and peninsular regions from the perspective of (dis)unity. His account was one of disintegration: from the decline of Tan'gun's dynasty, multiple kingdoms constantly vied for ascendancy. Then, with the fall of Parhae, the event that to Sin symbolized the loss of Manchuria, the lands north of the Yalu River finally were relinquished to foreign races like the Khitan and the Mongols. Because of the inability to reverse the fortunes of Parhae, "half of our ancestor Tan'gun's ancient lands have been lost for more than nine hundred years."[20] According to such logic, Sin was able to argue that what Silla had accomplished was actually nothing more than a "semi-" or "half-unification" (*panp'yŏnjŏk t'ongil*). Extending the argument to the founders of the Koryŏ and Chosŏn dynasties, Sin again found reason to object: "It is also said that the first king of Koryŏ unified the East and that the opening of this dynasty likewise unified the East, but these were only half-unifications not full unifications. . . . If we are searching for a full unification, it cannot be found after Tan'gun."[21] By giving up Manchuria and being satisfied with the lands south of the Yalu River, Kim Ch'unch'u and all succeeding dynastic leaders failed to realize Sin's conception of the *minjok's* territorial realm. Not achieved since Tan'gun, unification, in Sin's view, was still a task to be carried out.

While Sin did berate Kim Ch'unch'u for abandoning Manchuria, his harshest accusations were reserved for Kim Pusik, author of the historical annals *Samguk sagi* (*History of the Three Kingdoms*, 1145).[22] Rather than the physical loss of Manchuria itself, it was the effacement of any consciousness of a Korean Manchuria that Sin found to be the greatest travesty. As the historian who eventually set the pattern for the theories of legitimacy, Kim became the target of Sin's wrath, excoriated as the man most responsible for erasing the memory of Manchuria. Discussing the downfall of the ruling Tae family of Parhae at the hands of the Khitan, Sin wrote,

When the Khitan smashed the Tae clan and occupied all of Manchuria, the birthplace of our Tan'gun suddenly entered the possession of a foreign race. This was a time for each member of the Puyŏ nation to raise his sword and surge forward, but even in such a time, they simply rooted themselves to the south of the Yalu River, not wondering about the grievances of their ancestors or thinking of the resentment of the *minjok*. What was the reason for this? It was because Kim Mun-yŏl [Kim Pusik] did not incorporate Parhae into our history, so it was not known that this land was the possession of our *minjok*.[23]

Perhaps more than any of his other writings, this passage reveals Sin's presumptions about the power of historical writing. Just as history could save the nation, it could also destroy the nation.[24] Kim, "totally lacking in historical knowledge and skills,"[25] had caused a decline in the fortunes of the *minjok* by writing a history book. In Sin's view, by excluding Parhae when writing about Silla's "unification," Kim had wiped from collective memory the idea that Manchuria properly belonged to the *minjok*. In this way, glory and territory were linked. The loss of the latter accompanied the loss of the former. This type of history resulted in a "great country becoming a small country, a great people becoming a small people."[26]

Later generations of historians, charged Sin, continued to perpetuate these misconceptions. Consequently, for the last few centuries, the Korean people had in their "hearts and eyes considered only the land south of the Yalu River as their home" and even in their dreams had not contemplated taking a single step beyond the Yalu River.[27] Thus, by combining three elements — an organizing conception of *minjok*, myths of Tan'gun, and territory as a narrative device — Sin sought to lay claim to Manchuria. Although this claim was extended only to the past, the implication of his history was that as the central stage of Korean history, Manchuria should be Korean once again. Lost centuries before, Manchuria offered Sin the standard for restoring the glory of the Korean past.

Sin was not alone in using history to expand the nation's territorial claim beyond the peninsula. These arguments were take up by the *Hwangsŏng sinmun*, and the growing interest in the northern lands enabled *Parhaego*, the late-Chosŏn book that also emphasized the north, to be published for the first time.[28] One of the more idiosyncratic formulations linking Tan'gun and the *minjok* to Manchuria was elaborated in Kim Kyohŏn's work, *History of the Divine Tan'gun's People*. Indeed, Kim's division of the *minjok*'s lineage into two branches, a northern and southern one, derived from his emphasis on Manchuria. According to his account, the kingdom established by

Tan'gun had occupied both the peninsula and the regions to the north, laying the basis for his assumption that all people coming from Manchuria descended from the same northern line. Unless a group explicitly entered this territorial realm from outside — as in the case of Kija and his followers — the group was treated as descending from Tan'gun and thus as part of the *minjok*. This approach to Manchuria allowed Kim to avoid discussing the lack of unity and the loss of the lands that marked the work of Sin Ch'aeho. After all, according to Kim's own historical logic, Manchuria had never been lost to others. Having defined the northern descendants of Tan'gun as all those peoples who merged in Manchuria, Kim's version of the past incorporated such dynasties as the Liao, Jin, and Qing, suggesting that the descendants of Tan'gun continued to occupy Manchuria until his time.

This perspective led Kim to make a number of claims that, to students of more conventional narratives, appear absurd. In describing the territory of the *minjok* during the Chosŏn-Qing period, Kim noted that the realm included not only the eight provinces of the peninsula and the lands of Manchuria but also all the territory conquered by the Manchus in China proper and beyond, specifically "the land of the Han, Mongolia, the territory of the Hui, and Tibet."[29] Events thousands of miles away from the peninsula now came into the purview of *minjok* history. The Qing military campaigns in Tibet, Xinjiang, and Qinghai were now just as much a part of the *minjok*'s history as were events in the Korean peninsula.[30] For Kim, the *minjok*'s geographic scope stretched from the tip of the peninsula all the way to Burma. This spatial vision of the past dwarfed the peninsula, making it little more than one corner of an immense realm but nevertheless essential to the *minjok*. Such were the consequences of a *minjok* history that allocated a defining role to Manchuria in setting the nation's spatial origins.

Irredentist Voices

In the early twentieth century, these arguments about Manchuria were largely historical. At a time when Korea's strength was anything but overwhelming, there was little hope for Sin Ch'aeho's definition of a unified nation to be realized. Since the conclusion of the Sino-Japanese War in 1895, both Japan and Russia had contended to establish dominance over Manchuria. Korea, Sin complained, was content to "sit on the sidelines happily looking on with folded arms" as others decided the fate of the north.[31] Sin, however, was not content to sit by idly. In a poem he likely wrote, appearing in the *TaeHan maeil sinbo* under the pen name "Student of History" (Toksasaeng), irredentist hopes were given voice. Entitled "When?" it asked,

> *The golden age of Koguryŏ, look at its history,*
> *Thousands of miles of northern Manchuria and seven hundred miles of*
>   *Liaodong*
> *Clearly was our land — when will it be again?*[32]

Published in the year the peninsula was annexed to the Japanese empire, the prospect of reasserting Korean rule over Manchuria was obviously dim. Undaunted, Sin nevertheless managed to detect irredentist opportunities in both his overly optimistic reading of trends in historical geography and the growth of a Korean community in Manchuria.

In a short article published in 1910 on the geographical trends of Korean history, Sin argued that historical momentum pointed to a possible recovery of the Manchurian lands.[33] His analysis located two swings in the geograph- ical history of the *minjok*, the first one to the south as Tan'gun's descendants moved from Manchuria into the peninsula. With the loss of Manchuria after the fall of Parhae, Sin saw the geographical history of the *minjok* re- versing itself to extend the frontier northward. Gains, he admitted, had been few, but small steps such as the recovery of the Kusŏng region showed that the southward trend had been reversed and that a period of northern expan- sion had begun. Predicting the future of the *minjok* from these movements, Sin incredibly suggested that these small gains could be expanded so that by gradually advancing forward, Koreans could regain the former lands of Koguryŏ and "relight" (chunggwang) the lost history of Tan'gun. Even Sin was realistic enough, however, to doubt the likelihood of this scenario. Un- willing to abandon the scenario itself, he was willing to jettison the logic of his geographical argument, resorting instead to the convenient device of an emergent hero, a "great dragon," that would lead and propel the people northward, fulfilling the geographical trends that he had identified. Another poem published in the *TaeHan maeil sinbo* the day after the previous poem, boldly called for a hero to do just that. Though anonymous, the title alone — "Who Will Again?" — reflected Sin's irredentist sentiment by appealing to the memories of two figures who had fought for Manchuria:

> *The vigorous strategies of Sogaemun and the martial prowess of Ŭlchi*
>   *Mundŏk*
> *Shine gloriously over a thousand ancient histories.*
> *Today, these mountains and rivers, who will again?*[34]

Even though Sin resorted to the *deus ex machina* of a hero, his hopes were not high. With his usual confidence sagging at the prospect of once again seeing the fate of Manchuria decided by external powers, Sin wondered in concluding his piece on geographical trends whether the *minjok*, pressured by events, would merely give up with a moan or would "follow the trends in geographical history and, bit by bit, advance?"[35]

Impatient for the day when a great leader might appear, Sin hinted in a separate article at a second possible means of asserting a Korean presence in Manchuria — emigration.[36] Throughout the later years of the Chosŏn dynasty, large numbers of Koreans — whether fleeing excessive taxation, searching for uncultivated land, or escaping rebellion and famine — had been crossing into Manchuria. According to one recent study, by 1910 in the Yanbian area of Manchuria alone, Koreans numbered more than 100,000.[37] Other studies put the number of Koreans in Manchuria as a whole at roughly 238,000 by 1912.[38] Many of them were in the Kando region, the very people on whom the border dispute with China centered, but for Sin these people were not merely to be used as a way of settling a dispute over the northern border. Showing just how far his historical vision was from the conceptual framework of sovereignty, his article presented these people as the vanguard for establishing his Korean unity. It was on these growing immigrant communities that Sin pinned his irredentist aspirations. These two pieces completed the steps that Sin took between 1908 and 1910 to construct a framework for his irredentist arguments concerning Manchuria. Moving beyond his linkage of the peninsula to Manchuria through his historical conceptualization of the *minjok*, Sin had by 1910 begun to offer scenarios for recovery.

What the development of *minjok*-centered history offered was a radically different spatial vision of the nation. Defined by the supposed birthplace of Tan'gun, Sin envisioned a territorial unity that joined Manchuria and the peninsula into a single realm for the *minjok* of the past, present, and future. Both Sin and Kim Kyohŏn treated Manchuria differently in their narratives, yet the implication of both was that Manchuria constituted a central stage in Korean history. As Sin's particular conception of the *minjok* was adopted and disseminated by other writers, so was his approach to Manchuria. The Taejonggyo, located after 1910 in Manchuria and serving as an organizing base for Korean exiles, actively promoted this challenge to earlier views of a peninsular Korea. Most of the central figures in Korean historical circles in the colonial period, such as Pak Ŭnsik and Ch'oe Namsŏn, extended their territorial conceptions of Korea northward into Manchuria and sometimes beyond.[39]

Korean writers have long pondered the realities and possibilities of their northern frontier. Yet just as this northward gaze was not unified in the late Chosŏn period, it continued to offer a variety of possibilities to writers reinvestigating the relationship between the peninsula and Manchuria. Irredentist writing, like that of Sin, was less concerned with the new conceptual vocabulary of national sovereignty, avoiding questions of "national rights" in favor of making claims on the north through new modes of history. This was an expansive history, which questioned the peninsular limits of the nation and, by so doing, sought a solution for the national crisis beyond the peninsula.

The Diasporic Nation

Remembering a lost Manchuria was not the only way that Korean writers questioned the nation's boundaries. The reconceptualization of late Chosŏn conceptions of space was part of the same globalizing process producing the territorial violations that, in turn, were providing the impetus for the spatial redefinition. The two were closely related, but such crossings were not in only one direction. Koreans moved in the opposite direction as well, leaving the peninsula to immigrate to other nations. This outward migration created a number of incongruities for nationalist writers intent on affirming a territorial definition of the nation. At the very moment that schoolchildren were being taught that the nation was a discrete unit of space formed by a people, some of those people were abandoning the territory that, according to this view, defined them. Migration raised questions about the assumed congruency of the customary criteria — territory, people, and identity — that underlay the conventional definitions of the nation so frequently offered in didactic writings. The incongruences resulting from emigration stimulated a great deal of writing in the domestic press about overseas Koreans, as writers conceptualized the relationship of spatially distant compatriots to a territorially defined nation.

This attention resulted from the unprecedented growth of organized Korean communities in foreign countries. With the exception of movement into Manchuria, Korean migration abroad was a new phenomenon. Roughly seven thousand workers went to work in Hawai'i in the first few years of the century, many of whom eventually moved to the West Coast of the United States.[40] In 1905, more than one thousand laborers had contracted their services to agricultural interests in Mexico. By 1908, Koreans in San Francisco numbered just over one thousand. Before annexation, most of the Koreans living in Japan were either students or political exiles, but by 1913 their number had grown to nearly four thousand.[41] These numbers were dwarfed by the size of Korean community in the more accessible Russian city of Vladivostok, which was reported in 1909 to have reached more than twenty thousand.[42] Certainly, as a publicly debated issue that raised the concern and interest of those inside the peninsula, the activities of Koreans outside the peninsula were unprecedented. Such was the novelty of this issue that a front-page piece in the *TaeHan maeil sinbo* contextualized outward migration as part of the nation's integration into the global system, offering it as a marker for the country's opening. The advent of migration divided an earlier age of isolation when "it was believed that if you left the country, you would certainly die" from the present age of international intercourse, when Koreans began deliberately to go overseas "in search of foreign civilization and to see the world with their own eyes."[43] While this new era may have been marked by an increasing willingness to countenance moving abroad, the sense that leaving the country was somehow dangerous did not disappear. Indeed, most writing in the nationalist press about Korean migration was fraught with anxiety about the consequences of movement abroad, an anxiety arising from the ambiguous meaning of displacement from the nation. At the outset, this anxiety was simply a fear for physical safety. But over time, this fear changed into an apprehension of cultural loss, as displacement came to be equated in the eyes of many writers with cultural disinheritance.

Events during the first few years of migration to North America offered plenty of fodder for fears about the physical safety of migrants. Early reports from expatriates back to the peninsula captured the imagination of editorial writers, who summarized them for their readers, perhaps with the goal of expanding their readership with the sensational story lines. This was especially true of the saga of migrants to Mexico. Early in 1905, the type of advertisements now so notorious for luring workers to gamble their futures on empty promises of prospective riches encouraged more than one thou-

sand Koreans to risk traveling to Mexico. What was not apparent at the time
was that the Japanese company enlisting the workers turned to Korean labor
only because its horrific treatment of Chinese migrants had ruined its reputation in China, making it impossible to recruit any more workers.[44] The
company's reputation soon caught up with it in Korea as well. Despite the
company's efforts to suppress information about the departed Korean laborers, reports eventually reached the editors of the *Hwangsŏng sinmun*.[45] A
hue and cry followed the publication of these reports as readers learned
about deaths in the transport ships from which those that did survive
emerged "barely resembling humans."[46] Heart-rending descriptions of the
forcible division of families were passed on with accounts of the horrific
work conditions.[47] People were sold like slaves, and to the editors' further
umbrage, they sold for thirty *wŏn* a person, compared with the market rate
of eighty *wŏn* for a pig.[48] Eleven- or twelve-hour workdays in backbreaking
tasks such as weeding and opening new land were common, as was the
compensation of about thirty-five *chŏn*, twenty-five of which was returned
to pay for inadequate food and clothing.[49] Punishment was harsh: according
to one report, lazy workers were beaten "until their flesh split."[50] Some resorted to self-mutilation so that they would not have to work; others, to
suicide. Still others tried futilely to escape, with half of them dying from
hunger and exposure and the survivors captured by the police. According to
one estimate, possibly as many as four hundred out of the thousand died.[51]
As report after report asserted, these Koreans were treated not like slaves and
beasts, but worse than slaves and beasts.

At roughly the same time as the brouhaha arose over Koreans in Mexico,
a second prominent event underlined the hazards of venturing beyond the
peninsula, the 1906 San Francisco earthquake. At first, there was no specific
information about the fate of the more than one thousand Korean residents
there, but the vivid reports about the earthquake emanating from the city
fueled the imagination and rhetoric of Korean writers. Tales of destruction
and death were passed onto readers, leaving them to conjure up worst-case
scenarios. As one commentator asked soon after the first reports arrived,
"What sin have we Koreans committed against Heaven?"[52] Because there
was no Korean diplomatic representation in San Francisco, the *TaeHan
maeil sinbo* launched an appeal for private donations.[53] Contributions
poured in with letters commiserating with the plight of these immigrants
who, in the words of one donor, had enough trouble making a living and
now faced the "cruelty of earthquakes and the disasters of fire."[54] By the end

of May, more specific reports detailing the damage suffered by Koreans arrived, showing that earlier fears had been highly exaggerated. Not a single
Korean had died, but the meeting hall of one of the main Korean organizations had burned down.[55] This was a less than dramatic denouement for
an issue that had captivated the press for several weeks, yet as many editorials
and letters professed, as difficult as life was inside the peninsula, it could be
much harsher, even dangerous, for Koreans overseas.

Beyond these fears of physical danger, reports about the diaspora also
contained a certain cultural apprehension. Editorial writers, who as self-
appointed nationalist leaders made it a business of decrying the lack of patriotism among the domestic population, assumed the problem could only
be more severe for Koreans beyond the peninsula. Their observations reflected a sense that life abroad was somehow unnatural, carrying consequences for the cultural vitality of those who departed. Historical precedent
offered reasons for these fears. Sin Ch'aeho may have expressed his irredentist hopes that migration would provide the vanguard for a Korean Manchuria, but he was quick to point out one shortcoming in this scenario: there
was a long history of Koreans venturing north, only to be assimilated into
the local population. As Sin complained, they abandoned their customs,
language, and religion, leaving no sign of Korean culture in Manchuria.
Consequently, Sin urged Koreans to preserve their *kuksu* (national essence)
when they moved abroad. In one of the earliest cases of a Korean urging his
foreign compatriots to remain faithful to their homeland and true to their
culture, Sin outlined a series of measures that would ensure the cultural
viability of Koreans in Manchuria. His three-point plan urged them to abandon their selfish desires and nurture their love of country by setting up
schools and newspapers that would disseminate patriotic thought. This
would assist them with a second need, the preservation of religion, customs,
language, and other features that made up the *kuksu*. Finally, he urged them
to develop their political skills so that they could protect themselves and
create "a new country" in the foreign land.[56]

Sin's self-assumed authority to hector his deterritorialized compatriots
appealed to one of the most common claims about the nation. To be inside
the boundaries of a nation defined as a territorial unit was to be closer to
the nation in its other, especially cultural, forms of definition. Space and
identity were deemed isomorphic. The very distance of diasporic Koreans
from their homeland opened their cultural rectitude to challenge by people
like Sin who remained on the peninsula. Such a strategy confirmed the

territoriality of dominant conceptions of the nation while highlighting the supposed cultural frailty of anyone who crossed its borders. To be deterritorialized was presented as an uncomfortable and ambiguous position, in which one's very Koreanness, unless assiduously cultivated, was threatened. Culture, in short, was best rooted in the nation's soil — or, at least, so it appeared to the likes of Sin Ch'aeho.

By the time Sin's injunctions were published in the *TaeHan maeil sinbo* in 1910, this inside/outside dichotomy had already served for many years as a standard means of addressing the relationship between the peninsula and the diasporic communities. It was literally captured in the era's vocabulary. *Oeji*, an adjective combining two expressions for "external" and "land," was regularly contrasted with *naeji*, "internal lands." Both appeared as modifiers of nouns such as *minjok* or, more commonly, *tongp'o* (compatriot, brethren), creating compounds implying unity but also difference on the basis of an individual's location. Whether signifying a Korean in Vladivostok, Osaka, Hawai'i, or San Francisco, all were *oeji tong'po*, "compatriots in external lands," an expression regularly contrasted with its opposite, *naeji tong'po*, an equally homogenous term meaning "compatriots in internal lands." In the case of Sin's warnings about cultural assimilation, this division was necessary for structuring a critique that privileged those in the peninsula.

As Japan trespassed on the sovereignty of the peninsula at the same time as Korean emigration grew, a second strategy also resting on this dichotomy gained prominence. This alternative began to separate those two elements seen as congruent in the dominant understanding of the nation — space and cultural identity — to turn Sin's logic on its head. In the hands of other writers, the inside/outside dichotomy enabled the locus of the nation to be shifted beyond the peninsula to those distant communities that, in Sin's estimation, were threatened with loss of their *kuksu*.

Turning the Nation Inside Out

This strategy first gained impetus as a mode of government criticism. By 1898, the *Tongnip sinmun* had already established its reputation as an eager and fearless critic of officialdom. In this year, the paper was offered a new avenue for expressing its antigovernment position while exploring issues of national character when it received a copy of Isabella Bird's travel account, *Korea and Her Neighbors*.[57] A famous Victorian travel writer, this self-described "experienced muleteer" had traveled on the peninsula, Manchuria, and Russia in 1894.[58] During her travels in the north, Bird observed Korean settlers in Siberia, describing their successes in education, their industriousness, and their "independence and manliness of manner" — characteristics that she noted, in the dubious praise of her age, as "rather British than Asiatic."[59]

In their review of the book, the editors of the *Tongnip sinmun* expressed no offense at these and Bird's many other slights, choosing instead to seize on the short passages in which she praised their distant compatriots. In Bird's brief description, they discovered a group of Koreans that displayed the very features of the "new citizen" that the editors had been urging on their own readers. Expanding on Bird's account, they stressed that the abilities and accomplishments of the Siberian settlers testified to the superiority of the Korean character, proving that the laziness of those at home was not an inherent trait but the product of conditions. It was only after these Koreans left the purview of the government, they pointed out, that they were able to realize their potential: freed from government fetters, the settlers demonstrated their innate Korean nature. Such a line of reasoning served to exculpate national character from criticisms that it alone was responsible for the national situation while offering yet another perspective from which to censure officialdom.[60]

In offering the diasporic communities as a counterbalance for the situation inside the peninsula, the editors implicitly suggested that crossing the border to move beyond the peninsula had merits — if only in the realm of self-improvement. In linking the diasporic communities to the issue of national character, the editors were concerned not with the *kuksu* later emphasized by Sin Ch'aeho but with the relationship between culture and reform. Written at a moment when self-strengthening dominated the nationalist movement and fears about Japanese encroachments had yet to be fully articulated in the vocabulary of spirit and essences, this editorial did not focus on culture as national distinctiveness but as the determinant of reformability. In its structure and use of distant immigrant communities as a counterbalance — where those outside could be represented as superior — this line of reasoning opened the possibility of questioning the isomorphic claims made for the nation, a potential that other writers later pursued.

That this potential was explored had much to do with the growing community of Koreans on the West Coast of the United States, especially around San Francisco. As reports came back to the peninsula after 1906 about the activities of these distant Koreans, editors quickly moved beyond the anti-government strategy of the *Tongnip sinmun*. Instead, they began to look at diasporic communities for their potential contribution to that central endeavor of newspaper production, *munmyŏng kaehwa*. If the locus of civilization had been redefined away from China toward the West, there would be few better ways to approach this learning than, quite literally, to approach it physically. Journeying to the West at a time when there were no large Korean communities in Europe became equated with the United States and was interpreted as entering a more enlightened realm. For the most part, the entrance of Koreans was told as a story of success.[61] As giddily described in one report, Koreans in the United States were "gradually advancing and becoming civilized, so that today the reputation of Koreans is higher than that of Japanese or Chinese."[62] These success stories tended to reflect back on the domestic population. After a report marveling at the accomplishments of the community in San Francisco, one paper commented that "to see them and think of ourselves" should lead readers to consider the relative "levels of civilization and barbarity" — a comparison, it implied, that was not favorable to those in the peninsula.[63] Such comparative pieces expanded the style of critique offered in the *Tongnip sinmun*, moving beyond a means of censuring the government to one chastising the people inside the peninsula for not embracing reform more warmly. No longer was the peninsular population excused by blaming the government, since now diasporic communities offered a counterexample of what appeared to be a lackadaisical effort at home. As the *TaeHan maeil sinbo* argued, people in the peninsula might not be perfectly free, but who was stopping them from building schools and investing in businesses? Only their own hearts, it offered in a condemnation of their determination and spirit.[64] In this way, the diasporic community was increasingly displayed as a model for the domestic population, as editors beseeched their readers to be inspired by the actions of their distant compatriots.

By the time these editorials began appearing after 1906, issues of national spirit, essence, and the *minjok* had become prominent concerns of most newspaper editorials. Reports on the diaspora were filled with this conceptual vocabulary. In some cases, like Sin's regret for the loss of *kuksu*, these reports reflected the anxiety that diasporic communities would be unable to sustain their culture as they struggled to make new lives in faraway lands. Contrasting the supposedly selfish immigrants seeking their fortunes overseas with the sacrifices needed for the nation, the *TaeHan maeil sinbo* urged prospective emigrants, "Don't just think of your livelihood but think of the development of the *minjok*."[65] Such explicit injunctions were surprisingly rare, however, since most descriptions of diasporic communities were more celebratory in tone.

Indeed, the development of diasporic newspapers and associations trans-fixed domestic writers, leading them not to decry the absence of patriotism among overseas Koreans but to revel in its abundant presence. In a descrip-tion of the San Francisco–based newspaper, *SinHan minbo*, the editors of the *Hwangsŏng sinmun* extolled their "brothers" for "cherishing the two words 'Great Korea' [*TaeHan*] and for remembering the single idea of 'an-cestral country' [*choguk*]. Although they stand under the heavens and on the lands of the American continent, their eyes remain fixed on the sun and moon over the green hills [of Korea]."[66] Using a by now common strategy, the editors of the *TaeHan maeil sinbo* argued that the San Francisco com-munity offered a "glimpse at the natural character of the Korean *minjok*." Noting that these Koreans survived "at the ends of the earth" with only their own labor, the editors wondered whether it would be possible for these compatriots to maintain thoughts of their ancestral country if not for the fact that the "fundamental nature of the *minjok* is beautiful."[67] Although the diasporic community in San Francisco was not large, they still "sing songs to the nation and cry for the nation."[68] Domestic newspapers frequently reprinted sections from the overseas presses as textual confirmation of their high standing. Readers learned in the pages of the *TaeHan maeil sinbo* the self-professed goals for immigration. All immigrants, they were told by one San Francisco–based Korean, "when leaving, their fathers, mothers, and siblings told them, 'I am heading to America to get civilized knowledge and make our nation glorious.' "[69]

What gave these celebratory pieces extra force was the tone of astonish-ment underlying the editorial praise. Although it may have been perfectly understandable to these editors to expect a higher level of enlightenment from overseas migrants — they were, after all, living "closer" to the source of civilization — the same could not be said for their patriotism. In fact, the opposite held, for as editors were eager to point out, this patriotism developed *despite* their distant location. This incongruity of location and patriotism translated into the use of metaphorical contrasts that emphasized locality. The United States "was not our soil"; "there are differences in the mountains and rivers"; "they experience the winds and frost of a different land" — all these were nevertheless overcome to develop a love of the nation.[70] Whether in Russia, Japan, or the United States, they lived in a land distinguished by different languages and faces, and "it is not their old land [kot'o]."[71] The contrast with people who actually "live in the land, but forget the country" was starkly drawn, the paradox achieving its effect by appealing to the seemingly commonsense notion that soil, culture, and patriotism were commensurate.[72] What overseas Koreans were doing, in the eyes of the *TaeHan maeil sinbo* staff, was beckoning over the national soul (*kukhon*).[73]

These metaphors of place supported another comparative strategy — again, with the overseas community serving as a counterbalance, only here these migrant communities represented not just patriotic Koreans but Koreans even more patriotic than the home population. The editors of the *TaeHan maeil sinbo* did not mince their words:

> Those people floating overseas love their country, exert great effort in civilized enterprises, and try to establish themselves as complete Korean citizens in this world. In contrast, the people living on the soil inside these lands forget the country, still do not reform their conservative and superstitious thoughts, do not even give a thought to civilizing enterprises, are happily willing to act as the slaves or livestock of others, and are completely absent of any thought of protecting their position as an independent people.[74]

Similarly, the *Hwangsŏng sinmun* praised one diasporic newspaper for its ability "to make people never forget about their ancestral land, even if their bodies are in different lands across the seas." For newspaper men who were struggling to establish the newspaper as an institution, the success of Korean newspapers in distant countries where the number of potential readers was so small was met with a mixture of chagrin and joy. Impressed with the papers that crossed the Pacific, they could not but regret that there were still entire villages of thousands of people on the peninsula who had not read a newspaper.[75] They lambasted those "growing up on Korean soil" for "not knowing what a newspaper is," in comparison to "guests on foreign soil" (*kaekt'o*), most of who read wonderful diasporic newspapers like the *SinHan minbo*. The disparity, the journalists explained, was due to the patriotism of the overseas community and the selfishness of those inside, who could not think of the country.[76]

These were harsh words, their severity derived in part from an incongruence that the editors found difficult to explain. If, according to their fundamental definitions of the nation, territory and culture were isomorphic, how could they explain the heightened patriotism of the foreign communities? They struggled to find answers, offering various hypotheses. In one editorial, the *TaeHan maeil sinbo* explained the lack of domestic patriotism as a result of an absence of opportunities to engage in the type of comparative endeavor with other cultures that made people more aware of themselves. Using the case of households to make their point, they argued that "only after facing another house does one know the existence of one's own house, and only after knowing the existence of one's home can one love one's home." Applied to nations, the lesson was the same. Because of Korea's isolation for centuries, "there was no comparison of our country with other countries. From where were patriotic hearts supposed to emerge?" For Koreans living abroad, it was the opportunity to ask questions like "When will we stand up like them? When will we act like them?" that the editors believed had enabled them to develop a keener sense of nation.[77]

It was far more common, however, to explain the differences by pointing to the freedom enjoyed by diasporic newspapers — an issue dear to the hearts of editors that since the Russo-Japanese War had published under the restrictions of Japanese censorship. Due to this pressure, references to the greater freedom enjoyed overseas had to be made circumspectly, even by the *TaeHan maeil sinbo*, but nearly all the reports on the overseas press hinted at the lack of restrictions, crediting these circumstances not only with the wider dissemination of nationalist ideas but also with a style of explicitly patriotic, anti-Japanese writing not permitted on the peninsula.[78] These conditions gave license to diasporic writers to pursue the very mode of nationalist writing that had become increasingly untenable with the growing pressure of Japan.

In particular, this meant combining patriotic appeals with calls for civilizing reform as a means of protecting, even saving, the nation. Ever since the imposition of the Protectorate, writers on the peninsula had been uncomfortable with appeals to "civilization and enlightenment," since this was the same conceptual framework invoked by the Residency General to legitimize its rule. Generally shying away from its explicit use and even satirizing its most vulgar formations, writers instead created other ways of thinking about the nation, such as notions of *minjok*, appeals to national essence, or territorial conceptions that lay claim to Manchuria. But in conceptualizing the diaspora's relationship to the peninsula, domestic writers found in the overseas newspapers groups of Koreans reveling in the discursive formulations that despite their unease, they had been unable to abandon completely. Notions of civilization still supported, however ambivalently, their self-definition as leaders of the nationalist movement and many of their conceptions of the nation. But now they discovered a place where *munmyŏng kaehwa* could again be celebrated without inhibition, because the subjects themselves, diasporic Korean newspapers, were employing the very ideas that were so troublesome in the political context of the peninsula. When reporting on the overseas community, editors put aside their discomfort with *munmyŏng kaehwa*, unabashedly returning to it as the panacea for the nation's problems. In one report on the community in San Francisco, the *TaeHan maeil sinbo* editorialized, "Their loyal and patriotic objectives and their advance toward civilization has created a *new Korea* in North America" (my italics).[79] This new Korea, optimistically understood as already partly established overseas, was what they hoped for on the peninsula, demonstrating how deeply their hopes for the nation were embedded in notions of civilization.

Whatever the reason offered for the heightened patriotism, the domestic press held up diasporic communities — San Francisco in particular — as exemplars for not only their personal struggles in difficult circumstances or their pursuit of enlightened activities but also for their commitment to the nation. Sin Ch'aeho's complaint about the dangers of assimilation for Manchurian immigrants was reversed: it was actually the patriotism of those on the other side of the Pacific that demonstrated the absence of "thinking about the nation" on the peninsula. What could *not* be achieved inside *could* be realized outside. In this single move, the spatial assumptions of standard definitions of the nation were challenged. Sin Ch'aeho's fears about the loss of *kuksu* in diasporic communities rested on a spatial logic that granted those inside a greater moral authority on national issues, but now this logic was reversed, a reversal that suggested that the people with the authority to speak on national matters — and even lecture others — were Koreans living outside the nation's boundaries.

Custodians of the Nation

The ramifications of this reversal were profound for the leadership of the nationalist movement. If the peninsula was not the best location for preserving the nation, who then would lead the struggle for independence? For the home-front newspapers, the answer to this question was somewhat mixed. The *TaeHan maeil sinbo* had also always been impressed with the activities of overseas Koreans, presenting them as a source of inspiration for those on the peninsula. In showing that the "true nature of the *minjok* had not disappeared," the diaspora offered "a small ray of hope for independence."[80] This nebulous sense of hope was as far as the editors would go, however. Noting that those inside were the majority and those outside nothing more than a small minority, they rejected the idea that the nation could be rescued by the efforts of the minority alone. The question instead, they decided, was how the majority inside the country could become enlightened as well.[81] Willing to position diasporic communities as hortative models, they refrained from suggesting that the leadership of the nationalist movement could shift abroad. Yet by raising the issue, if only to reject it, the editors affirmed that the potential of overseas Koreans and their role in the struggle for independence was a subject of much scrutiny.

While the *TaeHan maeil sinbo* was unwilling to relinquish its self-assumed leadership, the *Hwangsŏng sinmun* was more generous in its assessment. From its earliest days of reading the Korean American press, the editors of the *Hwangsŏng sinmun* had recognized that the overseas communities could serve as the vanguard of the nation. In its own terms, they were "the foundation of a future independence," and their newspapers were the "organs of our Korean independence."[82] Still hesitating to confer outright the responsibilities of leadership on those outside, the editors of the *Hwangsŏng sinmun* nevertheless suggested that the function of diasporic communities had moved beyond the role of exemplars.

The group that most relished the idea that diasporic Koreans might best serve the nation was the subject of these reports themselves, the overseas Koreans. This was especially true of the San Francisco–based community, led by an organization publishing the newspaper that had attracted so much attention on the peninsula. The paper began as the organ of the United Korean Association (Kongnip Hyŏphoe), which was established in 1905 by An Ch'angho with the objective of uniting the more than one thousand Korean laborers and students who had come to reside in California in the early years of the century. With the English slogan "For the Koreans and by the Koreans" on its masthead, the newspaper quickly expanded from a handwritten weekly intended for local consumption to a widely circulating, printed paper that, by 1907, was actively advocating the recovery of national rights. In February 1909, following the organization of the Pan-Korean association that it had helped promote, the paper changed its name from *Kongnip sinbo* (*The United*) to *SinHan minbo* (*New Korea Daily*).[83] It maintained close ties with the underground patriotic association on the peninsula, the Sinminhoe (New People's Association), and after the Sinminhoe's dissolution by colonial authorities in 1911, the paper remained one of the few nationalist voices, continuing to publish until the end of World War II.

Even though published in San Francisco, the *SinHan minbo* was in many ways a transnational paper, written as much for its audience on the peninsula as for the one in the United States. Its own circulation figures show that in 1908, for every five hundred papers distributed in the United States and one hundred papers reaching Hawai'i, three thousand copies reached the peninsula.[84] This transnational status was also reflected in its editorial perspective, which often assumed the readers were residents of the peninsula and addressed them accordingly. The press inside the peninsula regularly acknowledged its influence.[85] Perhaps the highest testament to its power was offered by Japanese officials, who often blamed the *SinHan minbo* and other overseas Korean media for stirring up trouble. Colonial authorities expended much effort to intercept the papers at the border "on the account of injuring public peace and good morals."[86]

It was precisely the freedom from Japanese control that the editors of the *SinHan minbo* invoked to claim a special position for their paper. In its pages, there was no trace of the type of ambivalence found in the *TaeHan maeil sinbo* about the function of overseas Koreans in the nationalist movement. Its editors were keen to take up the hortatory role granted to them by the domestic press, except that they tried to push the bounds of their role even further. Indeed, they championed their function as leaders, an assertion that grew even more adamant as Japan intruded deeper into the affairs of the peninsula. In their eyes, by the end of 1907, Koreans outside the peninsula had become the custodians of the nation. To the paper's editors, this was the direct consequence of publishing in a "completely free world."[87] As even its readers pointed out, "words that cannot be said inside the country" could be said in its pages.[88] Such words might indeed be part of a discussion of such vaunted concepts as freedom and rights, but they were just as likely to be the type of anti-Japanese expressions — referring to Japan as an enemy or, more commonly, as *Ilbonnom*, "Japanese bastards" — that the censorship office in the peninsula would be sure to catch and that, because of its political difficulties, even the uncensored *TaeHan maeil sinbo* dared not utter.

To be sure, the *SinHan minbo* allied itself with the nationalist goals of its peninsular counterparts, frequently reprinting for its American readers re-ports and editorials from the *Hwangsong sinmun* and *TaeHan maeil sinbo*. But the paper nevertheless used its unrestricted status to claim superiority over the domestic papers. The papers inside the country, it charged, could not enrich nationalist thought, raise the spirit of the people, or call for the return of independence.[89] Moreover, its presence in the United States gave it other advantages over their peninsula brethren, it claimed, especially for learning the knowledge necessary to save the country. The editors dramati-cally described how the day that Koreans "breathed this new air, we im-mediately developed a new way of thinking, discarding more than five thou-sand years of corrupt thinking and, in one morning, broke stubborn customs."[90] They urged Korean students to come to the United States, ar-guing that a stay in that country was the best way for "breaking old ways and constructing the new."[91] This ability to express nationalist sentiment, the freedom to criticize Japan, and participate in the new Western learning — in short, the entire realm of knowledge that underlay the nationalist enter-prise — were precisely the reasons that the domestic press had reported so favorably on the diaspora, except that the *SinHan minbo* used them to claim a privileged status for diasporic Koreans. The standards and expectations of the nationalist movement in every way gave the paper a special function, except for one: its distance from the nation itself.

This dislocation was, however, turned to the paper's advantage. Distance itself was to be celebrated insofar as true nationalism now lay only beyond the bounds of an occupied nation. This was a claim the paper made directly and one their readers often took up. In one letter published shortly after Emperor Kojong had been forced to abdicate his throne and the 1907 treaty had been signed, four cosigners wrote, "We ask: Where lies the foundation of Korean independence? We answer: in the United States with the United Korean Association."[92] With a little more than one thousand Koreans in the United States — or only one-twenty-thousandth of the total Korean popula-tion — it would not be easy, they admitted. Moreover, they confessed that in terms of knowledge, those outside the nation were no match for the scholars inside the country, "so how can we be the basis of independence?" Their answer, unlike the *TaeHan maeil sinbo* that had used similar calculations to dismiss the political potential of those outside the peninsula, was to assert that it was not the numbers that mattered but commitment. With their commitment to the nation, despite being thousands of miles away, overseas Koreans served as the representatives of those inside the country.[93] More powerfully, the paper published letters from readers inside the peninsula who were willing, even eager, to relinquish their leadership to those abroad. As one put it, "There is no one other than our overseas compatriots who can strive to save our 20 million compatriots, protect our three thousand *ri* of territory, recover our five-thousand-year-old national rights, wake up our ignorant people, reform our corrupt customs, revitalize our depressed economy, and deal with weakened public spirit."[94] This was a tall order, to be sure, but as the editors repeatedly pointed out in a phrase that sought to confirm the point of all these letters, they were the only "hope" of Koreans on the peninsula.

The high self-appraisal of the *SinHan minbo*'s editors accompanied a growing disdain for Koreans back on the peninsula. Blamed by the editors for losing the nation, the home population became the subject of editorials that shifted away from the usual blandishments about reform to ones that scolded, often in churlish tones, their homeland compatriots for their inactivity. The editors wondered whether it was possible for those on the peninsula to act as a "people" (*kungmin*), since a people was defined by their nation and they had lost their "national rights" (*kukkwŏn*).[95] After listing everything Japan had stolen from them and lamenting the weak response of the population, they asked, "Are you dead, or are you alive? Do you have any spirit, or is your spirit gone?"[96] Increasingly frustrated with the situation on the peninsula, the editors began to question the motivations of the domestic population, "Are these really a people who desire and search for independence and freedom?"[97] In addition, they blamed them for shirking their responsibilities, arguing that independence was "not the responsibility" of only those Koreans in North America, Hawai'i, and Vladivostok.[98]

The editors' concern led them to take the final step in reversing the status of the inside/outside dichotomy that structured so much of the writing about the diaspora: they suggested that overseas Koreans not return home. In its early years, the *SinHan minbo* had always assumed that the presence of Koreans in the United States was for the short term, often referring to themselves as sojourners (*yumin*). In historical accounts of their community's arrival to American shores, the editors explained that people had left Korea for one of two reasons: to make a living or to study.[99] In both cases, the motivation was based on an understanding that their stay in the United States would be brief, lasting only until they accumulated either the capital or the knowledge necessary to return home to help the country. Many early editorials urged people not to forget these objectives, so that they would not return home "empty-handed" before they had the wherewithal to make their individual contributions. Otherwise, they warned, these returned Koreans would be like everyone else on the peninsula, as though they had never been overseas. Better to throw oneself in the Pacific or die in the United States, they commented.[100] In a letter expressing these hopes, one writer imagined how after properly preparing themselves in the United States, Koreans would be able to cross the Pacific, exterminate their enemy Japan (wŏnsu Ilbon), fight the victorious battle in returning to their ancestral country, and hold a great celebration in Seoul.[101] To be sure, these were idealistic and naïve hopes, yet the notion of imminent return to both personal and national fortune initially supported their endeavors. But by the end of 1907, their commitment to this belief began to waver.

As Japan's growing power became evident, such hopes appeared fantastical even to the ever optimistic editorial staff of the SinHan minbo. Less than a year and a half before annexation, they began to question the very idea that people should return home, discouraging their readers from making the journey back. Without a nation, they explained, it was not possible to have a home. Deploring a situation in which "Changgong palace is a prison, our land has been stolen, and they want to kill our people," the editors asked rhetorically, "Do you think you still have a country? Do you think you still have a home?"[102] Linking the individual to the nation, the private to the public, the editors argued that there was nothing to go back to on the peninsula. The goal remained to return — "we want to more than anyone" — but the time was not right. The duration of their stay should now be postponed until their nation and, hence their homes, was returned. This style of editorial was one of the final moves to validate the externalized existence of the overseas community as superior to life on a peninsula under Japanese control, a point that was made repeatedly from this time onward. Addressing those who still contemplated returning home, the editors asked them, "Why not head to Vladivostok?" which housed the largest overseas community and where, as they had reported on numerous occasions, key organizations for national independence had been established.[103] Even though this article urged solidarity among the scattered overseas communities, it again reinforced the understanding that a truer national life could be lived outside the bounds of a peninsula that had been made impure by Japanese occupation. Now even this eastern Russian city offered more promise to these editors, as they went as far as to insinuate that that even people on the peninsula might want to move elsewhere.

The spatial logic that underlay Sin's plea to Koreans in Manchuria to preserve their *kuksu* was completely reversed by the *SinHan minbo*'s editors. The politics of the Protectorate split the basic nationalist assumption that identity and culture were necessarily congruent. Now the peninsula, the ostensible home of the nation, had been made impure, unable to function as a true homeland. Dislocation from the nation was not so much a question of distance but of location. In the perception of writers in San Francisco, it was the domestic population that was being dislocated from the nation, precisely because they lived under an alien regime. Those outside the peninsula could thus position themselves as the nation's custodians, arguing that the locus of the nation had shifted outside the reach of the colonizing power.

Epilogue

By the time the Japanese colonial authorities shut down the main Korean nationalist presses in 1910, Korean writers had spent roughly fifteen years publicly pondering in newspapers, journals, and textbooks Korea's position in a global capitalist order. The result had been an outburst of writing about the nation. But the 1910 suppression of the press meant that for the next ten years, it was impossible for Korean writers to continue publicly with these lines of inquiry or to explore their full potential. Only when the press laws were relaxed after the March First Movement of 1919 did writers have the chance to pursue these avenues again, though always within the constraints set by the Governor General Office.[1] Debates in the 1920s and 1930s on issues as various as language reform, national character, history, and the like continued to bear the mark of preannexation achievements, as some of the same writers, together with a new generation, pushed the bounds of concepts first raised before 1910 and adapted them to new demands. Even after Korea's liberation in 1945, when nationalism was adopted as a guiding state ideology — significantly by both the northern and southern regimes — many of the symbols, concepts, and vocabulary for articulating these statist nationalisms had a lineage reaching back to the early nationalist presses.

The legacies of the writers of the Patriotic Enlightenment Movement have received mixed appraisals from their heirs. Since the division of the peninsula into two independent governments in 1948, both the northern and southern states have been eager to present themselves as the sole voice for a divided nation, appropriating past symbols and conceptions of the nation to create official versions of history that would support their rival bids for legitimacy. For the first time in the twentieth century, the state — with its capital, technology, and bureaucracy — became the dominant producer of national knowledge in Korea. In the south, the Republic of Korea (ROK) was to quick to embrace the memory of the Patriotic Enlightenment Movement, making its writers and reformers part of the state's own nationalist pedigree. Claiming a continuity extending back through the expatriate provisional government in Shanghai, to the March First Movement of 1919, then back to the media and the patriotic associations of the preannexation era, the south Korean state has sought to present itself as the only legitimate descendant of this nationalist movement. This has been especially feasible since the first president, Syngman Rhee, participated in the events of these years, even serving time in prison for participating in Independence Club demonstrations and working as an editor for the *Cheguk sinmun*. This connection was further cultivated by the resurrection of many symbols first promoted in the preannexation era. The name selected for the new state, TaeHan min'guk (Republic of Korea), returned to the expression first used by King Kojong in his ascension to the imperial throne and establishment of an empire, the TaeHan Cheguk (Empire of the Great Han). The *t'aeguk* flag, promoted as the preeminent national symbol by newspapers like the *Tongnip sinmun* but suppressed by Japan for more than three decades, was again hoisted up masts in the south as the national banner. Heroes that had been so widely hailed by the early nationalist press were given new life. Ŭlchi Mundŏk, eulogized by Sin Ch'aeho and the subject of so many biographical articles, had a major street in downtown Seoul named after him. School textbooks and general histories confirmed this genealogy, making it the main narrative of modern national history. This was the history of the Independence Movement (Tongnip undong), one that could be captured in the building of a monumental museum, the Commemorative Hall of Independence (Tongnip ki'nyŏmgwan) — and the south was named its only heir.

There was little public disagreement with this national story in the first three decades of the ROK's existence. But since the 1980s, as the historical profession has expanded and new concerns have animated a younger generation of scholars, more ambiguous appraisals of these early nationalist writers have emerged. Other nationalist groups, like the *ŭibyŏng* ("righteous armies") and the Tonghak peasants, became the focus of much research.

Having picked up not pens but weapons to resist the Japan, the *ŭibyŏng* and the Tonghak peasants offered a different style of resistance, one that has been praised as uncompromising compared with that of contemporary nationalist writers, many of whom later went on to work within the strictures of colonial rule. Writing in an era of democratic movements, these historians were inspired by the mass-based nature of the *ŭibyŏng* and the Tonghak movement. In an approach that has come to be known as *minjung* history (history of the masses), the social basis of all movements and individuals was considered the primary criterion for historical appraisal.[2] Still committed to putting the nationalist movement at the center of modern Korean history, historians shifted their emphasis to different groups whose resistance was rooted in popular conceptions of the nation, usually accompanied by visions of social reform. By the 1990s, the writers of the Patriotic Enlightenment Movement appeared elitist compared with that of the peasants of the 1895 Tonghak peasant war, the *ŭibyŏng*, or the subsequent peasant and labor unions organized under colonial rule.[3] Criticizing their own government's self-legitimizing narratives became a powerful tool for the opposition movement in their calls for democratic reform. While the research results, if not always the politics, of this oppositional history have increasingly shaped mainstream histories, the state's support for its legitimizing narrative has not declined. Indeed, the government-financed Academy of Korean Studies published general histories in the 1980s with the express purpose of countering the growing popularity of the *minjung* school among democratic forces.[4] On a symbolic level, when official ties with the People's Republic of China (PRC) were established in 1993, the ROK government quickly moved to acquire and refurbish the former headquarters of the government-in-exile in Shanghai. Now a tourist location for south Korean visitors to China, this headquarters displays the connection between an earlier moment in the nationalist movement and the current south Korean government.

If in the south the competition for historical legitimacy has led to a history including the Patriotic Enlightenment Movement, the north has looked in different directions. In the official histories of the Democratic People's Republic of Korea (DPRK), the contributions of these early nationalists are largely dismissed. Categorized as bourgeois intellectuals, they are condemned for their ineffective efforts at resisting Japanese annexation.[5] The March First Movement is denigrated as a failure for its naïve belief that foreign powers would respond favorably to demonstrations, an assessment that is similarly extended to the diplomatic activities of the Shanghai government-in-exile.[6] In discounting the Patriotic Enlightenment Movement, the March First Movement, and the Shanghai provisional government, the DPRK rejects the nationalist pedigree of the very people whom Seoul has claimed for its own legitimizing purposes. For its own purposes, the north has invoked the radical revolutionary traditions of anticolonial resistance, a line ostensibly not polluted by these intellectuals. The anti-Japanese fighters in the mountains of Manchuria occupy the center stage in this narrative, in which Kim Ilsung's personal exploits have been made the history of the nation.[7] The result of these uses of history in the contest for legitimacy has been the creation of two startlingly divergent — and antagonistic — state-sponsored histories, each with very different assessments of the Patriotic Enlightenment Movement.[8]

Underlying this historiographical divergence has been the DPRK's desire to present itself as making a break with the past, a necessary task for any regime defining itself as revolutionary. Especially since Kim Ilsung's consolidation of power in the 1950s and his subsequent promotion of an ideology of self-autonomy known as *chuch'e,* the development of this self-proclaimed revolutionary ideology has highlighted his singular contributions at the expense of tracing any influences or connections with earlier movements. These are characterized as feudal or bourgeois, important to the narrative only insofar as they serve as a contrast to the advances made by Kim.

Critiques leveled at *chuch'e* thought from the south accept this notion of a break, although for different reasons. Eager to reserve connections with tradition for the south, these critics point to the novelty of the northern ideology, highlighting its ties with foreign Marxist thought. This indictment, by emphasizing the dearth of connections with tradition, implies a lack of Koreanness, thus an absence of legitimacy. Ironically, both the northern ideology and this southern criticism share the tenet that the Kim's thought has little basis in previous forms of thought — the latter for the purpose of claiming tradition for itself and the former so as to present *chuch'e* ideology as unprecedented and without parallel.

What both these positions overlook, however, is that the nationalist ideologies of both north and south, despite the cold war rivalry, continue to appeal to many of the symbols and concepts first proposed as a way of thinking about the nation in the preannexation period. This is not to suggest that the production of national knowledge has remained static since 1910. There have been immense changes since the early years of the colonial period, and visions of the nation have shifted accordingly. Nevertheless, many of the symbols and concepts used to articulate these shifting national visions can be traced to the early efforts of nationalist writers to reconceptualize the nation's spatial and temporal bounds in a modern global ecumene. The differences between Pyongyang and Seoul — as well as among different groups in the south — are often expressed through these same symbols, now invested with novel meanings. Shared but contested, they mark a common heritage bequeathed by writers at the turn of the century who were coming to terms for the first time with the capitalist modernity that supported an international system based on the nation-state — a system that continues to fashion our world today. The power of the knowledge produced at the turn of the century in areas as diverse as historical narratives, territorial limits, and language policy can be seen in the transmission and rearticulation of these historical yet contemporary issues.

Language Purity

Immediately after the defeat of Japan in 1945, the promotion of the Korean script again became headline news on the peninsula. In these heady postliberation days, the alphabet first invented by King Sejong emerged as one of the most potent nationalist symbols, with the simple act of writing in Korean now seen as repudiating the colonial past and heralding a new beginning.

For more than three decades, Japanese had been called the "national language," part of the policy package designed to assimilate Koreans and convert them into loyal imperial subjects. How much Korean language could be publicly tolerated was always a dilemma for a colonial government that espoused assimilation and development but needed a language with which to rule a population that spoke a different tongue. Policies fluctuated throughout the period, determined by strategic decisions concerning politics on the peninsula, pressures from the home islands, and the changing geopolitical situation of the region. With the intensification of assimilation efforts as Korea was mobilized for Japan's continental war after 1937, the eradication of the Korean language became a higher priority. Earlier, more tolerant policies were reversed, a shift most famously marked by a 1938 directive prohibiting the use of Korean in schools. Four years later, the Society for the Study of Korean (Chosŏnŏ hakhoe), an organization that for more than twenty years had guided research on Korean language and promoted its standardization, was suddenly judged in violation of the Peace Preservation laws. Its leading members were arrested, remaining in prison until Japan's defeat.

Upon their release in 1945, longtime language researchers such as Ch'oe Hyŏnbae and Yi Kŭngno immediately set about promoting the Korean vernacular and compiling textbooks for a school system that for the first time in four decades was under Korean control. The use of Chinese characters quickly reemerged as a contentious issue. In the north, writing became closely connected to the socialist program, in particular the efforts to wipe out illiteracy in the late 1940s. Chinese characters were discouraged. In 1949, as part of a broader attempt to purify the language, a policy of writing exclusively in Korean script was adopted. Chinese characters were abolished outright, a policy that has continued until this day.[9] The name for this script, however, was changed from the colonial-era "Han'gul" (Korean script) which, through its use of the word "Han," evoked the official name of the southern state.[10] In its place, the alphabet was called Chosŏn'gŭl (Chosŏn script), after the north's own official name of state, or, alternatively, in memory of King Sejong's original name for the script, simply "Hunmin chŏngŭm."

As he is in the north, King Sejong has been venerated in the south. His statue stands in front of most primary schools. On the officially declared "Han'gul Day," leading officials congregate to commemorate the promulgation of the alphabet in the suitably named King Sejong Cultural Center on King Sejong Road in downtown Seoul. Their efforts have turned the document of King Sejong's promulgation into a canonical text, one that is learned by every schoolchild and that has become so widely displayed that it is generally recognized by its distinctive appearance alone. But despite this public promotion of King Sejong, the south has not followed the north's lead in eliminating Chinese characters. A sometimes vitriolic debate between advocates of the alphabet and defenders of Chinese characters has accompanied shifts in script policy, with both sides picking up arguments from the early twentieth century. In June 1948, the Ministry of Education launched a "Reclaim Our Language Movement," which culminated with legislation the following month making *han'gŭl* the exclusive language of government. The only problem was that the next day, in reaction to pressures from the characters' defenders, a clause was added to the law stipulating that "for the time being, however, Chinese characters may be used together with *han'gŭl.*"[11] Three years later the Ministry of Education changed its policy again, announcing a list of the thirteen hundred most commonly used characters.

This initial squabble over script reform established a pattern that typified the policy toward eliminating characters. Although powerful leaders like Syngman Rhee and Pak Chŏnghŭi, together with their Ministries of Education, have endorsed the sole use of *han'gul*, powerful interests in the media and universities have successfully staved off elimination of characters.[12] The Republic of Korea is perhaps one of the few countries in the world where script reform is deemed sufficiently important to merit public comments and speeches by its presidents, yet for two leaders not known for brooking opposition, script policy proved an elusive area of control. The shifting interests of the participants in these scuffles have led to an inconsistent approach to the use of characters, as perhaps best exemplified by the changing number of characters deemed by the Ministry of high school Education as the "most common" for curriculum purposes.[13] Playing on the frequency of policy changes, people remark, only half jokingly, that a person's year of high school graduation can be discerned from the number of Chinese characters he or she knows.

As part of these debates, a number of calls were made for a "pure Korean movement." Reviving and extending the demands of their predecessors from the turn of the century, these advocates of *han'gŭl* have called for not just the expulsion of Chinese characters but also the purging of all words whose etymological origins are Chinese. Such words as *kang*, a common expression for "river," they complain, are based on Chinese characters that have ousted indigenous equivalents from the contemporary lexicon, in this case what can be expressed as *karam*.[14] The logic of decentering China still shapes the contours of this debate. For advocates of pure Korean, the language question is more than an issue of convenience and literacy. It lies at the core of national authenticity. One of its more prominent supporters, Hŏ Ŭng, has insisted that language is the basis for developing national culture, which is sufficient reason to speak and write pure Korean.[15] By the early 1990s, when some prominent education experts lamented the ability of university students to decipher even the few characters used in newspapers, pure-language advocates tried to shift the terms of the debate to ask why newspapers were even using characters. Even columnists in specialized sports newspapers set aside their commentaries on the prowess of local teams to make their voices heard on the issue, in one case accusing advocates of Chinese characters of working against the natural expression of the Korean people and the progress of history.[16] For these advocates of pure *han'gŭl*, the dream of creating what they called a sphere of "*han'gŭl* culture" is paramount.[17]

This style of critique has long been accompanied by personal attacks on the advocates of characters. In a fashion similar to the accusation made by Yi Kwangsu in 1910, defenders of characters are charged with being "elitist," interested only in demonstrating their erudition.[18] This accusation took on political overtones during the democratic struggles of the 1970s and 1980s. Opposition groups anxious to offer competing definitions of the nation and history emphasized the non-elite nature of *han'gŭl* as a concrete indication of their populist vision. Banners hoisted by labor and student groups during demonstrations featured antiestablishment slogans written in the native script. In keeping with this trend, many young oppositional intellectuals began to write their names in *han'gŭl* instead of Chinese characters. And in 1989, when the first daily newspaper to emerge out of the democracy movement began publishing, it chose a purely Korean script for its daily edition.[19] In the south, the choice to use *han'gŭl* over Chinese characters was part of the politics of opposition.

Despite their success in thwarting the official abolition of Chinese characters, the opponents of exclusive *han'gŭl* use have always been on the defensive. They have been forced to express their doubts in terms of the excesses of nationalism, arguing for the characters' utility. This has been a delicate balancing act.[20] Consequently, while today characters still appear in the pages of most newspapers and many journals, their frequency of use is declining. The use of the Chinese characters and sentence structure has changed remarkably over the duration of the ROK, let alone the last one hundred years. In terms of the types and quantity of characters, even the prose of the characters' staunchest defenders is far removed from the mixed script of early-twentieth-century newspapers such as the *Hwangsŏng sinmun* or the *TaeHan maeil sinbo*, which today would be unintelligible to most educated Koreans. In the 1950s, an average of 46.16 percent of all newspaper articles consisted of characters, a figure that fell to 28.9 percent in the 1960s, 20.12 percent in the 1970s, and 8.21 percent in the 1980s.[21] Even headline writers have lowered their dependence on characters, from 86.9 percent in 1948 to 24.2 percent in 1988.[22] Despite this steady decrease, these figures still provide ammunition for *han'gŭl* advocates to attack the continued use of characters at all. The project first launched by newspapers such as the *Tongnip sinmun* for a pure Korean written language, though in many ways widely successful, is still continuing a century later.

Toward a Postcolonial History

Language policy resurfaced as the most obvious issue remaining from the turn-of-the-century calls to decenter China. History did not. The fundamental redefinition of historical study away from the court-based legitimacy theory that both derived from and supported Chinese imperial claims toward *minjok*-centered national history left little use for China in appraising the Korean past. With the exception of some Marxist historians such as Paek Namun and Yi Ch'ongwŏn, who used class and materialist forms of analysis, the succeeding generation of nationalist historians continued to make the *minjok* the subject of history.[23] Writers like Chŏng Inbo, Chang Tosik, and Ch'oe Namsŏn, as well as the ever prolific Sin Ch'aeho, continued to explore the possibilities of this mode of history, which offered a site for the nation beyond the reach of colonial power. Throughout the 1920s and 1930s, they further investigated the bounds and location of this *minjok*, producing a wide variety of historical narratives.[24]

Since the early 1960s, the question of colonial legacies in the writing of history has been an unwavering concern of Korean historians. Although this concern captured the imagination of the public over yet another textbook controversy — when reports emerged in 1982 that the Japanese Ministry of Education had forced changes in textbook portrayals of Japanese colonial activities — a lower-profile controversy had been brewing for many years over a different historiographical question.[25] This question had a longer history, tied to some of the foundational moments in the national histories of both countries. Centering on interstate relations between the peninsula and the islands in the third century, a debate emerged over Japanese myths about Jingū's conquest of Korean kingdoms.

After World War II, Japanese scholars began writing new national histories that distanced themselves from the excesses of wartime histories. But with the early history of Japan so deeply enmeshed with events on the peninsula, any history concerned with questions of national origin was bound to reconsider some of the historical material that had earlier been used to mobilize history in service of empire, including Jingū's establishment of Japanese administrative rule over the peninsula. During the colonial period, the Kwanggaet'o stele had played a part in promoting this myth. According to Japanese readings of its archaic and weatherworn inscription, certain phrases could be read as evidence that Japanese had conquered the early peninsular kingdoms. Since the evidence was an artifact discovered on the peninsula,

it seemingly offered outside evidence to confirm the veracity of written accounts, like the stories in the *Nihon shoki* about Jingū, thereby legitimizing
a key myth of colonial rule. After 1945, when the ancient Japanese histories
had been delegitimized in most scholarly circles by their wartime uses, the
stele commanded more attention in Japanese historical circles. Although
the stele's function in offering a historical legitimization of colonialism was
not so explicitly made, it retained its value as evidence of the early centralization of the Japanese state — how else, it was reasoned, could Japan's reach
be extended to the peninsula if there was not a power able to mobilize
resources in a single state?[26] If in the prewar period the *Nihon shoki* had
offered proof for the existence of Mimana, now the onus rested largely on
the Kwanggaet'o stele, less for reasons concerning Japanese policies toward
the peninsula and more for the purposes of making arguments related to the
strength of the early court.[27] Consequently, Mimana still had a place in
Japanese national history; indeed, some of the most detailed studies of Japanese rule over parts of the peninsula appeared just after the war.[28]

Korean historians were well aware of these legacies of colonialism. But
due to the tumultuous political situation after liberation, followed by the
devastating civil war, the revival of anticolonial critiques was not immediate.[29] As professional historians began to set up their institutional bases after
the Korean War, theories about Mimana quickly became a hot issue for
historians on both sides of the demilitarized zone. In fact, criticism of theories about Mimana is one of the few issues that unites historians in the
north and south, an indication of their shared roots in the anticolonial origins of modern Korean historiography.

The first salvo came from the north. Beginning with the historian Kim
Sŏkhyŏng, a number of scholars offered alternative theories based on reinterpretations of the same evidence to assert that the "Mimana" cited by
Japanese historians actually referred to communities of Korean immigrants
that the *Nihon shoki* recorded as having settled on the Japanese islands. This
theory not only dismissed the notion that Japan had ruled parts of the peninsula, but it also turned the notion on its head: it was Koreans who had
established settlements in Japan, if only to be conquered by an expanding
Yamato state.[30] This initial proposal was subsequently taken up by many less
tentative historians, especially in the south, who have offered a variety of
theories claiming an early Korean presence on the islands.

Criticisms of Japanese interpretations gained further impetus in the early
1970s when a Korean resident in Japan, Yi Chinhŭi, published a detailed

study of the various rubbings of the inscription. In an argument that shocked history communities in both countries, Yi contended that its earliest Japanese interpreters, the military historians working for the General Staff Office, had altered the inscription to offer an interpretation more favorable to their militaristic goals.[31] This theory inspired a great deal of research in both Korea and Japan, with some scholars attempting to expand on Yi's postulations and others, remaining more skeptical. Korean historians have tended to be more enthusiastic about Yi's theories than have their more dubious Japanese counterparts. One effect of the research generated by the debates has been to debunk in the eyes of most Japanese historians the myths about a strong Japanese rule on the peninsula, even if they wholeheartedly disagree with Yi's argument. With the exception of some conservatives, most Japanese historians have laid these myths to rest and are developing new hypotheses for early relations between the islands and the peninsula.[32]

In south Korea, Mimana has been but one issue within a more wide-ranging effort to overturn a much broader historiographical legacy of colonialism. A new generation of historians trained after 1945 — including Ch'ŏn Kwanu, Kim Yongsŏp, and Yi Kibaek, to name just a few — started their careers by explicitly directing their research against what they called a "colonial historical perspective" (singminji sagwan).[33] In the preface to his 1961 work that became a standard university textbook, Kuksa sillon (A New National History), Yi Kibaek warned of the specter of colonial historiography, asserting that two decades after liberation, it continued to affect Koreans' understanding of their own past. Part admonishment, part lament, his preface called for a new history that would sweep away the colonial legacies that he claimed had been all too easily absorbed by Koreans, leaving them with a sense of inferiority. Identifying five themes emerging out of colonial history — sadaejuŭi, factionalism, stagnancy, a lack of cultural originality, and an environmental determinism centering on the peninsular shape of the nation — Yi argued that a "proper understanding" (olbarŭn insik) of the past could be achieved only if these influences were purged from Korean history. Yi's maneuver returned Japanese historiography to the top of the agenda for Korean historians, positioning it as the main impediment to a history that could act on behalf of the contemporary and future nation.[34] Throughout the 1970s and 1980s, this definition of the historical project became the standard rationale for writing history. Hardly a historical work was published whose preface did not express the author's desire to set the record straight and overcome the prejudices of Japanese colonial history. In the 1990s, despite the diversification of the field in many new directions, this aim has remained a major commitment for many historians.[35]

Accompanying the revival of anticolonial history was a resurgence in *minjok*-centered history. Historians directed their calls for a new history against the work of their postwar predecessors, who led the early institutionalization of the field, a generation trained mostly in Japanese schools. When creating the first history departments, scholars such as Yi Pyŏngdo at Seoul National University had promoted an empirical approach to the past that, in a country just emerging from a civil war and still divided between two hostile regimes, temporarily vacated the politically sensitive realm of *minjok* history. What had become taboo in the last years of the colonial era remained on the sidelines in the early years after the civil war. The rigidly anti-Communist stance of the southern government rendered the term *minjok* politically less acceptable.[36] Tainted by its association with the left in post-liberation politics, *minjok* was overshadowed by other ways of speaking and writing about the nation, in particular more neutral terms for the nation, like *kukka* (nation-state) and *kungmin* (national citizenry), whose meaning could be restricted to imply loyalty to the southern state alone.[37] In this environment, the newly institutionalized professional historians immersed themselves in projects with no apparent focus on the *minjok*.[38]

Events in the first half of the 1960s reversed this tendency. With the overthrow of the Rhee regime in 1960 and the anti-Japanese demonstrations sparked by the normalization talks of 1965, an environment that encouraged new forms of nationalist expression enveloped the campuses that had played such a crucial part in this train of events. By articulating an anticolonial history, university-based historians simultaneously moved to recover the concept of the *minjok* as a unifying framework to create an autonomous historiography that would overcome the legacies of colonial scholarship. Much of the 1960s and 1970s was devoted to this endeavor.[39] In this way, the challenge to colonial history came hand in hand with the reassertion of *minjok* history. Decades after the initial forays into nationalist history in the early years of the century, conceptions of a *minjok*-based history were again deeply entwined with the writing of anticolonial history, only now rather than written in the presence of a colonizing Japan, it was written to purge the historiographical effects of that past.

This close connection between the *minjok* and anticolonial history raises the question of whether a *minjok* history can be separated from colonial interpretations. Or will *minjok* history, because of its origins in the nationalist movement against annexation, always remain dependent on its pairing with Japanese colonial views? The dilemma lies in part with the style of the anticolonial critique itself. Taking up the struggle of preannexation historians, anticolonial history focuses exclusively on questions of sovereignty: how was it extinguished by Japan and how could nationalists preserve the nation and resist? Yi Kibaek's critique made a salutary move into the realm of representation and raised the question of the postliberation continuity of colonial history. Yet his approach (and those of his followers) is structured around an unproblematized dichotomy of the era's political struggle — colonizer versus colonized and modern versus tradition — creating a definitional dependence between *minjok* history and colonial history. What constitutes minjok history is in part defined as what colonial history is *not*. To discover a true *minjok* history, colonial representations and narratives must — in the language of its proponents — be "overcome" (*kŭkpok*). This process of overcoming, now considered fundamental to the historical enterprise, has a seemingly endless potential to discover more ways and more issues in which earlier understandings of the past have been shaped by colonial ideology.[40] In this way, more than half a century after liberation, colonial history still exists as one of the fundamental parameters of Korean historiography, to the extent that it is difficult to imagine a *minjok* history without reference to its counterpart. The agenda of historians who see themselves as the custodians of the *minjok's* past is greatly shaped by their interpretations of colonial history. The two remain defined against each other and yet, by this very definition, mutually dependent on each other.

In setting up this oppositional dichotomy, this definition of history neglects to explore the close interaction between colonial and nationalist historical writing in earlier periods. For the most part, the insinuation of colonial interpretations into Korean historical understandings is seen as one of Japanese influence, whether because the colonial era's publication laws made it difficult to read anything other than Japanese histories or because the first generation of professional Korean historians had been trained in Japan. This reasoning rightly acknowledges the delicacy of writing history under Japan's rule, but it does not explore other factors that accounted for the historiographical results that have been explained as Japanese influence. The five styles of colonial writing pointed out by Yi Kibaek, for example, were for the most part already part of the repertoire of nationalist self-critiques of Korean culture and history before 1905. It was only after the Protectorate was established and, especially, after annexation in 1910, that these approaches to history were understood on the peninsula as part of an official colonial endeavor. The ultimate power of Japanese colonialism was to co-opt such nationalist self-critiques, making them less serviceable for national recovery. The anticolonial critique developed in the 1960s onward sees this congruency — whether it is Korean historians worried about factionalism or writing about *sadaejuǔi* — as the result of a insufficiently developed national consciousness by historians, one that was ultimately complicit with Japanese colonial rule.

In recognizing this congruency as the product of Japanese influence alone, this style of critique arguably reinforces the power of colonial history, however. Insofar as it continues to cede these co-opted realms as a form of specifically Japanese interpretation, it glosses over the fact that many of its features were wielded by earlier nationalist historians. In this way, the power of Japanese colonial writing to lay claim to certain arguments is confirmed rather than refuted. Rather than explore the more complex genealogy of historical interpretations found in the writing of both groups in order to understand the discursive power of such writing, the task of developing a *minjok* history becomes one of avoiding certain realms of thought instead of critically reclaiming them. Paradoxically, this approach results in a history that tries to escape colonial interpretations but in fact confirms the power of colonial history to direct some of the fundamental lines of inquiry in modern Korean history.

One source of this dilemma is the thematic focus of the anticolonial critique. Tracing similarities in historical themes between Korean and Japanese historians as a way of pinpointing Japanese influence certainly reflects the power of colonial discourse. But again, this methodology refrains from exploring the discursive sources of that power itself. Resting on its oppositional pairing of nationalism versus colonialism, the approach shies away from moving below the level of thematic critique to the shared roots of both these modes of thought in the ideologies of capitalist modernity. The nationalist appropriation of "civilization and enlightenment" as the principal framework for thinking about and reforming the nation spurred appraisals of Korean culture in certain directions, directions similar to what at a later date emerged as powerful parts of a colonial ideology that appealed to the same "civilization and enlightenment," only now to destroy rather than rescue the nation. Both appealed to the higher authority of "civilization," for different political ends, but Korean nationalist uses of "civilization" even before 1905 promoted some of the same assumptions about the nation and history that were featured so prominently in Japan's colonial ideology. Focusing on thematic similarities offers no explanation for the autonomous uses of certain historical arguments by nationalists and, if explained as "influence," gives little accounting for why colonial arguments were so appealing to Korean writers. To ascribe this era's history as a particularly Japanese form of colonial ideology whose agency of change is only "influence" is to miss the ultimate source of colonial power in the same ideologies of capitalist modernity that shaped Korean nationalist thought.

Acknowledging and exploring the sources of these close relationships between nationalist and colonial thought, however, have implications well beyond the formal colonial era. Indeed, the postwar reassertion of a *minjok*-centered history, accompanied by its anticolonial critique, remains tied to the ideologies of capitalist modernity, not to what appears to us today as dated notions of "civilization and enlightenment," but to its conceptual descendants, such as development and modernization theory. The 1970s and 1980s, when this style of anticolonial critique was at its height, was the period when the Korean state led the economy into a period of high growth. The Pak Chŏnghŭi regime paid great attention to and made massive investments in the promotion of a national history that both endorsed the government's claim to legitimacy and supported statist economic strategies. High growth, as many government posters proclaimed in such phrases as *sŏnjin'gugŭro* (toward an advanced country), was the attainment of that universal goal of development that had been long espoused by colonialism but was only now being achieved in the name of the sovereign nation. It was, after all, a *Korean*-style of capitalism. History, again, confirmed the teleology of capitalist modernity, and many historians were eager to offer their services to the state for these ends.

For oppositional historians working in this politically fraught environment, it was most disturbing to discover that their own research results could be contorted to statist ends.[41] The troubled relationship between anticolonial *minjok* history and its use by the state for its own legitimizing purposes was one of the main reasons for the rise of the oppositional *minjung* historiography. *Minjung* scholars tried to maintain their commitment to a *minjok* history while raising concerns about the relationship of history, capitalist modernity, and the state. Such a *problematique* is precisely what the anticolonial critiques on their own could not offer. By restricting its scope to a thematic approach to colonial historiography, historians placed a neat box around colonial ideology. Avoiding and criticizing certain themes became the historian's task, as the interactions between nationalist and colonial thought and the reasons for their similarities were glossed over. In this way, it was not necessary to raise troubling questions about the relationship of history, nation, and capitalist modernity, whether in the work of their predecessors or, perhaps more important, their own generation's work. The cost of such a criticism, of course, has been an inability of Korean history to free itself entirely from its anticolonial roots — or, in the words of these critics, colonial historical perspectives have not been completely overcome. If a postcolonial history is to be written, rather than see these continued colonial legacies as the product of an all-powerful Japanese colonialism, its sources must be found in the conceptual assumptions and bounds of the historiographical project itself.

The resurgence of a *minjok*-centered history, despite its ambiguous critique of colonial historiography, has had other ramifications in both the north and south. Most prominently, it has ensured the continued presence of that figure hailed by Sin Ch'aeho and the Taejonggyo as the progenitor of the *minjok*, Tan'gun. During the colonial period, Japanese scholars disparaged the Tan'gun myth, often excluding it from their histories of the peninsula. The colonial state, anxious to support Japan's own national myths as a way of encouraging its assimilation policy, viewed the Tan'gun myth as a competitor — and one around which the nationalist movement could coalesce. Consequently, colonial-era textbooks omitted any mention of Tan'gun. Nevertheless, with the easing of publication restrictions after the 1919 March First movement, scholars such as Ch'oe Namsŏn and religious groups like the Taejonggyo continued to promote Tan'gun as a focal point for articulating a national identity under colonialism. Tan'gun maintained his premier position in Korean written histories. With the support of some newspapers, civic groups went so far as to urge that historical sites that had become associated with Tan'gun be preserved for posterity.[42] By the time of liberation, Tan'gun had become so closely wedded to nationalist self-understandings that both the DPRK and the ROK incorporated him into their repertoires of symbols wielded to establish their competing claims to historical legitimacy.

In the north, Marxist approaches to history might have been expected to prevent Tan'gun from assuming the role of national father. At first, this was in fact the case. In the 1950s, materialist conceptions of history, as first offered during the colonial period by Paek Namun and Yi Ch'ongwŏn, were adopted in the north, leaving little room for what these early Marxist historians denigrated as the mystical aspects of their nationalist counterparts.[43] They regarded Tan'gun as little more than a legend. Over the last few decades, however, the reversal in Tan'gun's fortunes has been breathtaking. From this early neglected position, Tan'gun has emerged as, if not the premier figure, then second only to the person who has been granted the top billing in north Korean histories, Kim Ilsung. From Tan'gun to Kim Ilsung marks the start and finish of the main narrative line of this version of the *minjok's* past, with Kim's son still waiting to be incorporated in a new comprehensive version of national history. The centrality of Tan'gun to this vision was further accentuated in 1993, when archaeologists in the north announced that they had discovered his preserved remains. Although few people accept this claim, the tomb has become a destination for pilgrimages and has featured prominently in asserting the legitimacy of Kim familial succession in the north.[44]

In the south, the ROK made clear its commitment to the Tan'gun myth by passing as one of its earliest pieces of legislation a law making the *Tan'gi* — or Tan'gun calendar — the official dating system of the government. In its second year, 1949, the government proclaimed Tan'gun's supposed descent to Mount Paektu, the Day That Heaven Opened (Kaech'ŏnjŏl), a national holiday.[45] By the end of 1949, one of the phrases that had appeared in the original *Samguk yusa* passage about Tan'gun, and which in the intervening years had been used to develop a rather loose notion concerning the benevolence of Tan'gun's teachings — *Hongik in'gan*, munificence to the welfare of humanity — was adopted by the Ministry of Education as the nation's foundational teaching.[46] Tan'gun was further subsumed into the new education system in the textbooks that for the first time featured him prominently and were read by students who, in some cases, were studying in schools and even a university named after the progenitor. The Taejonggyo reorganized itself in the south, touting the indigenous roots of its religious beliefs and becoming a powerful promoter of Tan'gun. Tan'gun was still divine in their eyes, a divinity they proclaimed in a growing list of publications. New books and old — including a 1986 reprint of Kim Kyohŏn's *History of the Divine Tan'gun's People*[47] — have been published by the Taejonggyo, joining what in the 1970s and 1980s emerged as a resurgence of popular interest in this mythical figure that turned the original few paragraphs about Tan'gun in the *Samguk yusa* into a mini-industry.

Professional historians have treated the Tan'gun legacy more gingerly, however. Although some still consider Tan'gun the founder of the first Korean state — what they call Tan'gun Chosŏn — most treat the myth as a later creation that in its various and shifting renditions reflects the cultural concerns of different historical eras. For many professional historians, this has meant that Tan'gun has been removed from his ascribed role as progenitor of the *minjok*. National origins are seen less as tracing the ultimate source of consanguineous ties but as identifying the emergence of a number of necessary and sufficient criteria marking the coalescence of the nation. For scholars who emphasize language, the enterprise is identifying just when the Korean tongue first was unified into a single distinct language.[48] For historians focusing on territory, the task is recording the fluctuations in the northern border until the territorial realm now considered Korea first became delineated.[49] Different criteria have produced different interpretations. The result has been a cacophony of voices on the origins of the *minjok*, with perhaps the largest single divide centering on the question of whether Silla's unification of the peninsula in 668 marked the rise of the *minjok* or whether this epochal event would be more appropriately marked by the establishment in 918 of the Koryŏ dynasty.[50] Whatever the answer, this definition of the *minjok* is separate from the link between *minjok* origins and Tan'gun's appearance, as first established by early historians like Sin Ch'aeho.

Nevertheless, these debates still share with their predecessors a key narrative strategy for the *minjok*. With few exceptions, the *minjok* is seen as an objective entity descending from the chosen point of origin down to this day, existing regardless of whether the people were aware of its existence. For the centuries in which there was no consciousness of the *minjok*, it nevertheless survived, waiting to be recognized by nationalist thinkers at the start of the twentieth century. The *minjok* remains an ahistorical subject. The earliest advocacy of *minjok* is understood not as an original way of conceptualizing collective life during a specific historical moment but, rather, as the ultimate recognition of a long-standing subjectivity.[51] Consciousness of the *minjok*, however late in historical time, is but one stage in what is otherwise still largely seen as a transcendent history.

Northward Gaze

The reassertion of *minjok* history, together with the resurgence of Tan'gun, has, in turn, affected the writing of Korean territorial history. With the division of the peninsula into two hostile sides, each vying for historical legitimacy, the locations of the rival regimes have been projected back in time, imposing the politics of division on interpretations of the nation's territorial past. The spatiotemporal axis of national history became a battleground for the divided Koreas, as both regimes have sponsored official histories granting their particular part of the peninsula a special nationalist pedigree. Compared with their competing interpretations of the modern nationalist movement, this is a rivalry that reaches far back into ancient history.

Positioned opposite Manchuria, the DPRK has tended to stress the centrality of kingdoms that, like itself, were positioned in the north. For the Three Kingdoms period, the official history out of Pyongyang has highlighted Koguryŏ, a kingdom that occupied much of Manchuria and the northern part of the peninsula. Moreover, in its elevation of Kim Ilsung as the supreme leader of both the DPRK and the historical *minjok*, few legitimizing devices have been as artfully wielded as Kim's role in the anti-Japanese independence struggle, a struggle that took place in Manchuria. Manchuria thus emerges in northern historiography as the central stage of Korean history and further serves as the geographical locus for the Kim regime's claim to nationalist credentials. Indeed, northern propaganda credits the struggle in Manchuria as the inspiration for much of Kim's ideology, making it the crucible for north Korea's political orientation.[52] Although the politics of division has led Pyongyang to stress a northern-oriented past, the politics of the cold war has ensured that the emphasis on Manchuria has remained a historiographical issue alone. Loosely allied with the People's Republic of China and the Soviet Union during the official articulations of this approach, the northern emphasis has been wielded without any explicit irredentist intentions, useful in the present only insofar as it can be used to claim for itself a mantle of historical legitimacy in its struggle with the ROK.[53]

On the opposite side of the demilitarized zone, the politics of division has bequeathed a more complex legacy for the territorial implications of history. The political changes that from the 1960s enabled a return to a *minjok*-centered history also resulted in a growing interest in Sin Ch'aeho, whose name had been forgotten, according to one of his biographers, but who was now credited anew with originating *minjok*-centered history.[54] By the mid-1970s, entire conferences were held in commemoration of Sin's work.[55] For mainstream historians in south Korea, Sin proved an inspiring figure, since reinterpretations of his work served their own purpose of reconstructing a nationalist history. Although a few writers in the ROK and abroad have pointed to the excesses of Sin's nationalism,[56] most writers have uncritically praised him as the first historian writing from the perspective of the *minjok* who managed to establish an autonomous (*chuch'e*) view of the national past.[57] Moreover, as the first historian to criticize Confucian historical conventions and write a non-court-centered history, Sin has also been praised as the first modern Korean historian.[58] As Henry Em has pointed out, the emphasis on Sin's nationalist pedigree has been so pronounced that historians have long glossed over Sin's turn to anarchism in his later years.[59]

Although these historians styled themselves as the heirs and custodians of Sin's history, in the process of reappraising him, they abandoned his emphasis on Manchuria.[60] The *minjok* was again at the fore, only without Manchuria as the central stage of its narrative. This displacement arose in part from a stricter methodology that quietly undermined the many unsubstantiated assumptions that enabled Sin to assert his claims on Manchuria. This elision was also due to the politics of division. To follow the implications of Sin's privileging of the north was to risk being seen as questioning the legitimacy of the south.

Official interpretations of the *minjok* similarly dismissed Sin's linkage with Manchuria. The same event that in the Sin's "A New Reading of History" underscored his vision of Korean territorial unity — Silla's victory over Paekche and Koguryŏ — became a pivotal point in this official history, only with a different spin. For unlike Sin's account, official history in the south privileged Silla and acknowledged what Sin dismissed as a "semiunification" to have been a full unification. By presenting itself as the descendant of the southeastern kingdom of Silla, the regime could imply that Silla's defeat of Koguryŏ — the northern kingdom that Pyongyang claimed for its own legitimization — foreshadowed a reunification of the minjok at the behest of Seoul as well. The symbolic potency of this historical analogy gained extra power by virtue of the fact that the Silla leadership had originated in the same region of the peninsula that was the home of President Pak Chŏnghŭi and the regional power base of his regime, a congruency that was most convenient for Pak's domestic political maneuvering. The state mobilized massive resources behind this version of history. The editing of textbooks was centralized and standardized with this single historical perspective. The government invested heavily in museums and historical sites in the former Silla capital of Kyŏngju, commodifying this past for the hundreds of schoolchildren who were sent to absorb the spirit of the Silla youth corps (Hwarang) and visit the tombs of figures like Kim Ch'unchu, who, though vilified by Sin, was now vaunted as a national hero. Such a history, useful in its struggle for both domestic and peninsular legitimacy, produced a vision of national space as expressed in Silla's unification — a Korea restricted to the peninsula.

Since the late 1970s, however, a number of groups working in privately funded research institutes on the fringes of the south Korean historical community have attempted to reformulate Sin's linkage of *minjok* and territory through history. Emerging from the extreme right of the political spectrum, these groups have been able to revive the politically sensitive issue of the northern lands under the cover of their rigidly anti-Communist ideology. Although not explicitly writing about Sin, these individuals have applied his views on the centrality of Manchuria to the past as well as the future. Following the successful resurrection of the *minjok* by mainstream scholars, it became a rhetorically simple leap for them to reassert their claims on the *minjok* progenitor, Tan'gun, and his birthplace, Manchuria. It is perhaps ironic that while Sin's acclaimed status as the forerunner of modern history stems largely from the efforts of those mainstream historians who view themselves as the heirs and custodians of his *minjok*-centered history, it is the writers outside the university history departments who, without loudly proclaiming their ties to Sin, more closely follow the territorial implications of his earlier work. What had served for Sin as an important step in creating an anti-Japanese nationalist history has under these groups been reduced to a history with strong irredentist overtones.

In a fashion reminiscent of Sin's criticism of territorial historians, one of the main voices for these groups, the conservative magazine Freedom (Chayu), vociferously criticized academics for what it called their peninsular historical perspective (*pando sagwan*). This "defeatist history," one writer accused, abandons the north, leading Koreans to forget that the *minjok* occupied the northern lands for more than three thousand years and has "retreated" to the peninsula for only one thousand years. As in Sin's early work, the immediate target was none other than history and consciousness: a demand to revise school history textbooks so that the proper historical perspective — what is called the continental historical perspective (*taeryuk sagwan*) — be taught to all schoolchildren. Yet in a tone that abandoned all the subtlety of Sin's work, the author imagines that a twofold task confronts the nation: first, to unite quickly with north Korea and then, from this position of national strength, to deal with the problem of the Manchurian lands.[61]

This issue has moved beyond these small research institutes. With the normalization of diplomatic ties with the People's Republic of China since the mid-1990s, historians and tourists from the south have been able to travel freely to Manchuria for the first time in decades, resulting in a growing interest in the region. Concurrent with a relaxation of state restrictions on publishing houses, this interest has been transformed into a growing number of books dealing with various aspects of Manchuria, including a number that owe much to the irredentism of Sin Ch'aeho.

On the Northern Territories, a study by Yu Chŏnggap, a general in the south Korean army, is a detailed and comprehensive version of this approach to Manchuria.[62] Writing with "a heart that pains at the shrunken size of the ancestral land,"[63] he asserts that for a takeoff (toyak) to occur, it is necessary that a resolute historical consciousness that positions Manchuria at the center be established. In a section entitled "Means of Recovering the Ancient Lands," Yu examines a variety of scenarios for regaining Manchuria. Dismissing the use of force as a last resort, he recommends direct negotiations with the Chinese.[64] Yu maintains that Korea is entering a period during which its power is dramatically expanding, whereas China is heading down the road of disintegration and decline. When conditions become ripe, he asserts, negotiations can be started and the long-cherished desire of the minjok can be realized.[65] Just as for Sin, Manchuria represents for Yu more than a lost ancestral land or birthplace. It is also the source of a stronger Korea.

Such irredentist positions have been incorporated in the domestic politics of the south. Sponsored by right-wing research centers and featuring ties with segments of the military not known for their progressive politics, these views have been attacked by scholars at the other end of the spectrum. In particular, the mystical appeals to Tan'gun that have been widely promoted by organizations like the Taejonggyo and generate this nostalgia for Manchuria have been the subject of much scrutiny. Designed to undermine the logic and empirical support for their positions, this critique is based on a long concern with the consequences of right-wing nationalism.[66] For most people, though, irredentist arguments might sound a wistful note but generally are not taken seriously. As long as the peninsula remains divided, the Manchurian focus of these writers will push them to the margins of public debate, since reunification with the north remains the foremost concern. Nevertheless, it is also unlikely that arguments focusing on Manchuria will vanish entirely from the public forum. With a position grounded firmly in widely recognized minjok-centered views of history and by adopting such potent nationalist symbols as Tan'gun, these writers are able to appeal to widely recognized nationalist conceptions, attracting an audience, if not always support, for their position.

The northern gaze of Korean historical and geographical writing has also come to focus on the Kando region. Since the 1960s, historians in the ROK have written much about the jurisdiction of this land. These articles, often by scholars outside the universities, have reexamined the territorial decisions made in 1712 and in 1909 that led this land, populated by a majority of Koreans, to be folded into the PRC.[67] The closer ties between southern scholars and the Korean community in Jilin Province following the normalization of relations with ROK has increased interest in the origins of the Korean community. Inevitably, much of the research on the region challenges the allocation of these lands to China. Aware of these trends, historians in the PRC have responded in kind. Placed in the difficult situation of defending a treaty signed with imperial Japan in 1909 — precisely the type of treaty their own government long ago rejected as illegitimate — these works offer historical justifications of the current border. In a kind of shadowboxing that attempts to counter the arguments offered by Korean historians without actually referring to them directly, historians in China are again treading on the same territory that was featured in newspaper headlines in the early years of the century.[68] The Sino-Korean border, a source of controversy in the past, remains an issue of contention among historians today.

Attention to the northern border inevitably raises the question of Mount Paektu. Ever since nationalists at the turn of the century criticized geomancy as superstitious, the symbolic meaning of Mount Paektu has largely been separated from geomantic theory in nationalist thought. As a local practice, geomancy continued to be pursued, despite the admonishments of nationalists and its repression by the colonial government. But since the late 1970s in the ROK, there has been a renewed interest in the theoretical side of geomancy. In an age when the Korean economy was rapidly growing, there was little worry that geomancy, as a supposed superstition, would inhibit national development. Touted as a philosophy, and one that encouraged a harmonious relationship between humanity and nature, geomancy was lauded as environmentally friendly, a powerful consideration given the less-than-clean high-growth policies of the era. Most important, however, it was the indigenous nature of geomancy that came to be celebrated. Geomancy deserved to be preserved and promoted, its advocates contended, precisely because it was a form of Korean thought.[69] The connection of geomancy with the nation that early nationalists denied has now been established.

The geomantic meaning of Mount Paektu nevertheless remains overshadowed by a much longer tradition of associating the mountain with
Tan'gun and the *minjok*. The connection was promoted in the last few years
before annexation, but it was not until the 1920s that a variety of writers
working in different genres began to explore more fully the power of Mount
Paektu as a national symbol. A number of highly romantic travel diaries of
trips to Mount Paektu were published. Ch'oe Namsŏn's 1927 *Record of a
Visit to Mount Paektu (Paektusan kŭnch'amgi)* and An Chaehong's 1931 *An
Account of Climbing Mount Paektu (Paektusan tŭngch'okki)* recounted much
of the legend and lore surrounding the mountain, proclaiming it as the
founding site of the Korean people and the locus of their spirit. Historians
participated in the promotion of Mount Paektu as well. Ch'oe Namsŏn was
again active in this area. In a famous study that made Korea the center of
northeast Asian history, Ch'oe used Mount Paektu as the linchpin in a phil-
ological theory that traced place-names with the term *paek* (white) as the
means of relocating a lost culture originally created by Tan'gun.[70]

With such historical theories and literary works, Mount Paektu had, by
the time of liberation, become such a central symbol of the nation that the
northern and southern states alike appealed to its memory. In the north,
Mount Paektu has served as special place in the ways in which Manchuria
has been used in constructing a personality cult for Kim Ilsung. It was here
that his anti-Japanese guerrilla operations were allegedly based. Moreover,
it was on the face of Mount Paektu that his son, Kim Jungil, is claimed to
have been born. Such is the power of Mount Paektu that it has been harnessed to the lineage of the Kim family, serving to validate its nationalist
credentials and legitimate the dynastic succession of the younger Kim. In
the south, where until the government recognized the PRC, division and
cold war had made Mount Paektu unreachable, the mountain became a
symbol of reunification. As seen in the paintings of Mount Paektu hung in
restaurant corners or in photographs in classrooms, the mountain was a
source of nostalgia and desire for unity at the same time as it represented
the shared bonds with the people of the north, despite the country's division.

In both north and south, much of the cultural capital used to appeal to
various national visions — whether Mount Paektu or Manchuria, anticolonial history or script reform — is closely associated with the concept of *minjok*. At the start of the twentieth century, this was a neologism that intellectuals in all three East Asian countries were exploring for the possibility and
potential it offered for reconfiguring their understanding of the nation. Its

fortune in each of these countries has varied. In the PRC, official policies have promoted a vision of China as a multiethnic entity ruled by a single state. In such a setting, the current use of the Chinese analogue, *minzu*, whether used historically or for contemporary purposes, remains politically sensitive. Because *minzu* is equally used by minority peoples, who are often located in strategic outlying areas, the state must ensure that the uses of *minzu* do not devolve into a form of nationalism that is equated with the Han Chinese majority. In Japan, the term was widely used in wartime efforts to mobilize the population. This association has often given the Japanese equivalent, *minzoku*, an ultranationalist meaning, making it unacceptable for many, though by no means all, groups. In Korea, however, the use of *minjok* has not been burdened by such politically loaded meanings. During the colonial period, *minjok* proved a useful conception for locating the nation in a time of alien rule. Today, when the Korean peninsula has been divided for more than half a century, the same reasons that *minjok* proved so useful during the Japanese occupation have ensured its continued utility in calls for reunification.

Indeed, the continued commitment to *minjok* as the primary means of envisioning the nation is in part due to division. Just as the *minjok* offered a locus of national subjectivity when state and territory had been confiscated by Japan, the concept in postliberation Korea has provided the rationale underlying most arguments for reunification. During the colonial period, if the concept of *minjok* provided a means of resistance and extended the possibility of recouping what had been lost, then after 1945, the concept privileged unity as a historical norm, undermining any attempt to view the division as permanent. The definition of the *minjok* as a subjectivity that transcends the ephemeral existence of states remains poignant in a period when two rival states continue to vie for legitimacy, each claiming to speak for the whole nation. The teleology of the naturalized *minjok* is one of unity. Sin Ch'aeho's lament that unity had escaped the Korean people rested on this conception of the nation, as do the calls for reunification in both the north and south.[71] Two states, one *minjok*, describes the current condition of the peninsula. But the *minjok* united as a single state remains the ideal.

That a vision of the nation offered as a means of both separating Korea from a historical China-centered regional vision and preserving a realm of national subjectivity in the face of Japanese aggression should at the beginning of the twentieth-first century provide the fundamental rationale for reunifying the peninsula exemplifies the flexibility of national knowledge produced at the outset of the twentieth century. It is also an indication of the power of these conceptions. In their struggle to come to terms with the shifting regional order and the incorporation and participation of the peninsula in a global capitalist system populated by nations, these writers established many of the concepts and parameters that today continue to shape — whether or not acknowledged — many of the debates about the Korea nation on both sides of the peninsula.

Notes

Introduction: A Monumental Story

1. *Hwangsŏng sinmun*, 31 October–6 November 1905. Unless otherwise indicated, all newspaper citations refer to editorials.
2. This was the famous Chinese scholar Zuo Zongtang.
3. The *Sŏbuk hakhoe wŏlbo* also lamented this means of discovery. See Hwangsŏngja, "Tok Koguryŏ Yŏngnak Taewang mokpibon" (Reading the Inscription of the Kwanggaet'o Stele), *Sŏbuk hakhoe wŏlbo* 9, no. 2 (1907): 23.
4. Interpretations of the Kwanggaet'o stele are as varied as they are controversial. I deal with some of these debates in pages 261–263. For some English summaries of these debates, see William Wayne Farris, *Sacred Texts and Buried Treasures: Issues in the Historical Archaeology of Ancient Japan* (Honolulu: University of Hawai'i Press, 1998), ch. 2; Hatada Takashi, "An Interpretation of the King Kwanggaet'o Stele," trans. V. Dixon Morris, *Korean Studies* 3 (1979): 1–18; J. Y. Kim, "The Kwanggaet'o Stele Inscription," in *Contemporary European Writing on Japan: Scholarly Views from Eastern and Western Europe*, ed. Ian Nish (Kent: Paul Norbury, 1988); Yukio Takeda, "Studies on the King Kwanggaet'o Inscription and Their Basis," *Memoirs of the Research Department of the Tōyō bunko* 47 (1989): 63–78.
5. Anonymous, "Kwanggaet'owang ŭi pŏlyŏn kwaji saron" (A History of Kwanggaet'o's Attack on Yan and Expansion of Territory), *Sŏbuk hakhoe wŏlbo* 9, no. 2 (1907): 28.
6. Hwangsŏngja, "Tok Koguryŏ Yŏngnak Taewang mokpibon," 22–23. This piece was later printed word for word as an editorial in the *Hwangsŏng sinmun* 6 January 1909.

7. *Hwangsŏng sinmun* 31 October 1906.

8. On the question of hero worship in this period, see Yi Manyŏl, *Tanjae Sin Ch'aeho ŭi yŏksahak yŏn'gu* (*Studies of the Historiography of Tanjae Sin Ch'aeho*) (Seoul: Munhak kwa pip'yŏngsa, 1990), 164–75.

9. *Sŏbuk hakhoe wŏlbo* 9, no. 2 (1907): 23. This reference to moving the stele was likely an allusion to the efforts by Japanese scholars, led by Shiratori Kurakichi, to have it shipped back to Japan. See Farris, *Sacred Texts and Buried Treasures*, 61.

10. Hwangsŏngja, "Tok Koguryŏ Yŏngnak Taewang mokpibon," 23.

11. For some of the debates during the colonial period, see Michael Robinson, *Cultural Nationalism in Colonial Korea, 1920–25* (Seattle: University of Washington Press, 1988).

12. Partha Chatterjee, *Nationalist Thought and the Colonial World: A Derivative Discourse?* (London: Zed, 1986).

13. One recent study of Korea has used this approach. See Gi-Wook Shin and Michael Robinson, eds., *Colonial Modernity in Korea* (Cambridge, Mass.: Harvard University Press, 1999). For some overviews of this research, see the introduction by Frederick Cooper and Ann Laura Stoler, eds., *Tensions of Empire: Colonial Cultures in a Bourgeois World* (Berkeley and Los Angeles: University of California Press, 1997); Elazar Barkin, "Post-Anti-Colonial Histories: Representing the Other in Imperial Britain," *Journal of British Studies* 33 (April 1994): 180–203; Bernard Cohn, *Colonialism and Its Forms of Knowledge: The British in India* (Princeton, N.J.: Princeton University Press, 1996); Dane Kennedy, "The Imperial Kaleidoscope," *Journal of British Studies* 37, no. 4 (October 1998): 460–67, and "Imperial History and Post-Colonial Theory," *Journal of Imperial and Commonwealth History* 27, no. 3 (September 1996): 345–63; Anne McClintock, *Imperial Leather: Race, Gender and Sexuality in the Colonial Conquest* (New York: Routledge, 1995).

14. Arjun Appadurai, *Modernity at Large: Cultural Dimensions of Globalization* (Minneapolis: University of Minnesota Press, 1996); Etienne Balibar and Immanuel Wallerstein, *Race, Nation, Class: Ambiguous Identities* (London: New York: Verso, 1991); Prasenjit Duara, *Rescuing History from the Nation: Questioning Narratives of Modern China* (Chicago: University of Chicago Press, 1995), ch. 2.

15. A similar point is made by Roland Robertson, *Globalisation: Social Theory and Global Culture* (London: Sage, 1992), ch. 6.

16. Liisa Malkki, *Purity and Exile: Violence, Memory, and National Cosmology Among Hutu Refugees in Tanzania* (Chicago: University of Chicago Press, 1995).

17. Harry Harootunian, *History's Disquiet: Modernity, Cultural Practice, and the Question of Everyday Life* (New York: Columbia University Press, 2000), 49.

18. The stele could be linked to other material objects, such as the celadon of the Koryŏ dynasty or the turtle boats of Yi Sunsin, all seen as indicative of national character. See *Hwangsŏng sinmun* 6 February 1909.
19. Benedict Anderson, *Imagined Communities: Reflections on the Origins and Spread of Nationalism* (London: Verso, 1991).
20. Duara, *Rescuing History from the Nation*, ch. 2.
21. Chatterjee, *Nationalist Thought and the Colonial World*, 40.
22. Most famously for Europe, see Edward Said, *Orientalism* (New York: Random House, 1978).
23. *Hwangsŏng sinmun* 28 June 1907. Also see *TaeHan maeil sinbo* 4 December 1909.
24. Robert Young, *White Mythologies: Writing History and the West* (New York: Routledge, 1990).
25. This point is further articulated in the introduction to Timothy Brook and Andre Schmid, eds., *Nation Work: Asian Elites and National Identities* (Ann Arbor: University of Michigan Press, 2000), 1–16.
26. Anonymous, "Kwanggaet'owang ŭi pŏlyŏn kwaji saron," 29.
27. *Hwangsŏng sinmun* 10 February 1909.
28. Homi Bhaba, *The Location of Culture* (New York: Routledge 1994).
29. Stefan Tanaka, *Japan's Orient: Rendering Pasts into History* (Berkeley and Los Angeles: University of California Press, 1993).
30. Chatterjee, *Nationalist Thought and the Colonial World*, ch. 1–2.
31. Benedict Anderson, *Imagined Communities*; Eric Hobsbawm and Terence Ranger, eds., *The Invention of Tradition* (Cambridge: Cambridge University Press, 1983).
32. Two excellent studies that share this approach are Thongchai Winachakul, *Siam Mapped: A History of the Geobody of a Nation* (Honolulu: University of Hawai'i Press, 1994); and Mathew H. Edney, *Mapping an Empire: The Geographical Construction of British India* (Chicago: University of Chicago Press, 1997).

1. The Universalizing Winds of Civilization

1. *Hwangsŏng sinmun* 3 February 1899. The sick-body metaphor was especially popular; see also *TaeHan maeil sinbo* 26 July 1908.
2. *Hwangsŏng sinmun* 19 September 1904.
3. *TaeHan maeil sinbo* 18 September 1906.
4. *Hwangsŏng sinmun* 29 March 1899 and 2 August 1904.
5. *Hwangsŏng sinmun* 12 May 1899.
6. *Hwangsŏng sinmun* 16 January 1901. Bad-weather metaphors were a favorite; see also 2 June 1906 and *Tongnip sinmun* 25 March 1899.

7. *Hwangsŏng sinmun* 31 July 1903.
8. *Cheguk sinmun* 24 August 1898.
9. *Hwangsŏng sinmun* 31 July 1903.
10. This socioeconomic analysis of the origins of the uprising is most consistently pursued in Han'guk yŏksa yŏn'guhoe, ed., *1894 nyŏn nongmin chŏnjaeng yŏn'gu* (*Studies of the 1894 Peasant War*), 4 vols. (Seoul: Yŏksa pi'pyŏngsa, 1991–95).
11. Much of the research in this area stems from the pioneering socioeconomic work of Kim Yongsŏp, *Chosŏn hugi nongŏpsa yŏn'gu* (*Research on the Agricultural History of the Late Chosŏn Period*), 2 vols. (Seoul: Ilchogak, 1970–71). This social dislocation is famously satirized in Pak Chiwŏn's "The Story of a Yangban." See the translation in Peter Lee, ed., *Anthology of Korean Literature, from Early Times to the Nineteenth Century* (Honolulu: University of Hawai'i Press, 1981).
12. Han U'gun, *Tonghak kwa nongmin ponggi* (*Tonghak and Peasant Uprisings*) (Seoul: Ilchogak, 1983). Also see Susan Shin, "The Tonghak Movement," *Korean Studies Forum* 5 (1978–79): 1–79. For a dissenting view that speaks about the conservative basis of the peasants demands, see Lew Young Ick, "The Conservative Character of the 1894 Tonghak Peasant Uprising: A Reappraisal with Emphasis on Chŏn Pongjun's Background and Motivation," *Journal of Korean Studies* 7 (1990): 149–80.
13. Most recently, see Peter Duus, *The Abacus and the Sword: The Japanese Penetration of Korea, 1895–1910* (Berkeley and Los Angeles: University of California Press, 1995); and also Hilary Conroy, *The Japanese Seizure of Korea, 1868–1910: A Study of Realism and Idealism in International Relations* (Philadelphia: University of Pennsylvania Press, 1960).
14. Alexis Dudden, "International Terms: Japan's Engagement in Colonial Control" (Ph.D. diss., University of Chicago, 1998).
15. Kim Key-hiuk, *The Last Phase of the East Asian World Order: Korea, Japan and the Chinese Empire, 1860–1882* (Berkeley and Los Angeles: University of California Press, 1980); Martina Deuchler, *Confucian Gentlemen and Barbarian Envoys: The Opening of Korea, 1875–1885* (Seattle: University of Washington Press, 1977).
16. The observation of the proximity of these dates was made by Lew Young Ick in Carter Eckert et al., *Korea Old and New* (Seoul: Ilchogak, 1990), 221.
17. *Tongnip sinmun* 21 June 1896, 9 March 1897, 17 March 1898, and 16 February 1899; and *Hwangsŏng sinmun* 1 August 1899, 13–14 June 1904, and 18 February 1906.
18. For a series of essays pertaining to these events, see Ch'oe Munhung, ed., *Myŏngsŏng hwanghu sihae sagŏn* (*The Assassination of Queen Min*) (Seoul: Minŭmsa, 1992).

19. For a discussion of the intellectual roots of "restoration," see Mary Wright, *The Last Stand of Chinese Conservatism: The T'ung-chih Restoration, 1862–74* (Stanford, Calif.: Stanford University Press, 1957).

20. Yu Yongik, *Kabo kyŏngjaeng yŏn'gu* (*A Study of the Kabo Reforms*) (Seoul: Ilchogak, 1990). See his English-language works, Lew Young-ick, "Korean-Japanese Politics Behind the Kabo-Ulmi Reform Movement, 1894–1896," *Journal of Korean Studies* 3 (1981): 39–82; "Yuan Shi-kai's Residency and the Korean Enlightenment Movement, 1885–1894," *Journal of Korean Studies* 5 (1984): 63–108; "Reform Efforts and Ideas of Pak Yong-hyo, 1894–95," *Korean Studies* 1 (1977): 21–63; "Minister Inoue Kaoru and the Japanese Reform Attempts in Korea During the Sino-Japanese War, 1894–95," *Journal of Asian Studies* 27, no. 2 (1984): 145–86; "An Analysis of the Reform Documents of the Kabo Reform Movement, 1894," *Journal of Social Sciences and Humanities* 40 (1974): 29–85.

21. How thoroughly these were implemented around the country remains a topic for research. For example, slavery, though banned, continued to be practiced. See page 62 in this book. The figure of 660 reform documents comes from Eckert et al., *Korea, Old and New*, 225.

22. For further discussion on how this was also an attempt to place the king at the center of the growing nationalist movement, see pages 72–80.

23. Kim Dongno has argued that most of these reforms were underfinanced. See his "The Failure of State Reform Movements in Early Modern Korea and Its Relevance to the Mobilization of Resources," in *Korea Between Tradition and Modernity*, ed. Chang Yun-Shik et al. (Vancouver: Institute for Asian Research, 2000), 172–83.

24. In English, see Shin Yong-ha, *Formation and Development of Modern Korean Nationalism* (Seoul: Daekwang munhwasa, 1989), ch. 5; Kang Chaeŏn, *Han'guk kŭndaesa yŏn'gu* (*Essays on Korean Modern History*) (Seoul: Hanŭl, 1970); Han'guk minjok undongsa yŏn'guhoe, ed., *Ŭibyŏng chŏnjaeng yŏn'gu* (*Studies of the Ŭibyŏng War*) (Seoul: Chisik san'opsa, 1990). Much of the research on the "righteous" armies has focused on various local struggles, for example, Hong Sungwŏn, *Hanmal Honam chiyŏk ŭibyŏng undongsa yŏn'gu* (*The History of the Ŭibyŏng Movement in the Honam Region During the Hanmal Period*) (Seoul: Sŏul taehakkyo ch'ulp'anbu, 1994).

25. Pak Ch'ansŭng, *Han'guk kŭndae chŏngch'i sasang yŏn'gu* (*Studies of Modern Korean Political Ideology*) (Seoul: Yŏksa pip'yŏngsa, 1991); Kim Tohyŏng, *TaeHan chegukki ŭi chŏngch'i sasang yŏn'gu* (*Essays on the Political Ideology of the TaeHan Empire*) (Seoul: Chisiksan'ŏpsa, 1994); Cho Hangnae, ed., *1900 nyŏndae ŭi aeguk kyemong undong yŏn'gu* (*Studies of the Patriotic Enlightenment Movement of the 1900s*) (Seoul: Asea munhwasa, 1992).

26. This was especially true for the editors of the *Hwangsŏng sinmun*, who in their

editorials frequently referred to these earlier thinkers and called on their readers to be more aware of great thinkers and books of the Korean past. See pages 80–86.

27. Kang Chaeŏn, *Han'guk ŭi kaehwa sasang* (*Korea's Enlightenment Thought*), trans. Chŏng Ch'angnyŏl (Seoul: Pibong ch'ulp'ansa, 1981); Yi Wanjae, *Pak Kyusu yŏn'gu* (*Studies of Pak Kyusu*) (Seoul: Chimmundang, 1999).

28. Most recently and thoroughly in Kenneth Wells, *New God, New Nation: Protestants and Self-Reconstruction Nationalism in Korea, 1896–1937* (Honolulu: University of Hawai'i Press, 1990). In Korean, see the work of Yi Manyŏl, *Han'guk kidokkyo wa minjok undong* (*Korean Christianity and the Nationalist Movement*) (Seoul: Chongno Sojok, 1986).

29. See Conroy, *The Japanese Seizure of Korea*; and Duus, *The Abacus and the Sword*.

30. *Hwangsŏng sinmun* 6 March 1908, *kisŏ*.

31. The editors of the *Cheguk sinmun* were quite conscious of the fact that in the future their paper would act as a historical record, remarking that even foreigners would look back at its pages. See 12 August 1898.

32. For just a few examples, see *TaeHan chaganghoe wŏlbo* 1 (1906): 160; *Hwangsŏng sinmun* 23 May 1899; *TaeHan maeil sinbo* 19 August 1906 and 30 September 1906.

33. As recorded in Hwang Hyŏn, *Maech'ŏn yarok* (*Maech'ŏn's Unofficial History*) (Seoul: Kuksa p'yŏnch'an wiwŏnhoe, 1961), December 1894. On the Sŏnggyungwan, see Kuksa p'yŏnch'an wiwŏnhoe, ed. *Kojong sidaesa* (*History of the Kojong Era*) (Seoul: Kuksa p'yŏnch'an wiwŏnhoe, 1969), 4: 167.

34. For medicine, see *TaeHan maeil sinbo* 9 November 1909; for milk, see *Hwangsŏng sinmun* 5 November 1907.

35. *Hwangsŏng sinmun* 2 April 1906.

36. Norbert Elias, *The Civilizing Process: The History of Manners*, trans. Edmund Jephcott (New York: Pantheon Books, 1978), vol. 1.

37. Gerrit W. Gong, *The Standard of "Civilization" in International Society* (Oxford: Clarendon Press, 1984); and Hans Haferkamp, "From the Intra-Society to the Inter-Society Civilizing Process," *Theory, Culture, and Society* 4 (1987): 545–57.

38. Yu Kilchun, *Sŏyu kyŏnmun* (*Observations of My Travels to the West*), in *Yu Kilchun chŏnsŏ* (*The Complete Works of Yu Kilchun*), ed. Yu Kilchun chŏnsŏ p'yŏnch'an wiwŏnhoe (Seoul: Ilchogak, 1996), 1: 375.

39. *Tongnip sinmun* 30 June 1896.

40. *Tongnip sinmun* 25 July 1896.

41. *Hwangsŏng sinmun* 14 August 1905.

42. Yu Kilchun's *Sŏyu kyŏnmun* is perhaps the best example of an extended work structured in this way.

43. *Hwangsŏng sinmun* 8 March 1905.

44. *Tongnip sinmun* 25 July 1896.
45. This was a common advertisement; for one example, see *Hwangsŏng sinmun* 3 May 1908.
46. *Tongnip sinmun* 11 August 1896.
47. *Tongnip sinmun* 30 June 1898.
48. *Hwangsŏng sinmun* 12 May 1899, *chappo*. For another galloping-horse anecdote, see 11 September 1899, *chappo*.
49. *Hwangsŏng sinmun* 10 February 1900.
50. Yu Kilchun, *Sŏyu kyŏnmun*, 377. See also *Tongnip sinmun* 26 January 1897. The latter also offered a four-tier classification, 23 February 1899.
51. *Tongnip sinmun* 23 February 1897.
52. *Hwangsŏng sinmun* 18 March 1905.
53. See my discussion in chapter 3 on attitudes toward Western colonialism.
54. Ernest Gellner, *Nations and Nationalisms* (Ithaca, N.Y.: Cornell University Press, 1983).
55. A group that consisted largely of butchers, leather and wicker workers, and the handlers of corpses.
56. As recorded in Chŏng Kyo, *TaeHan kyenyŏnsa* (*History of the Waning Years of the TaeHan Empire*) (Seoul: Kuksa p'yŏnch'ansa, 1956), 1: 282.
57. Han'guk yŏsŏng yŏn'gu hoe, ed., *Han'guk yŏsŏngsa, kŭndae py'ŏn* (*Korean Women's History, Modern Volume*) (Seoul: P'ulpit, 1992). For extracts from writing dealing with women in these years, see Ihwa yŏja taehakkyo Han'guk yŏsŏng yŏn'guso, ed., *Han'guk yŏsŏng kwan'gye charyojip* (*A Collection of Materials on Korean Women*), 2 vols. (Seoul: Ihwa yŏja taehakkyo ch'ulp'anbu, 1980).
58. A good example can be found in the speech of Yun Hyochŏng, as reprinted in the *Hwangsŏng sinmun* 22–23 May 1906.
59. *Hwangsŏng sinmun* 25 May 1906.
60. For example, see *Cheguk sinmun* 24 February 1899 and *Tongnip sinmun* 26 May and 21 September 1899. No Inhwa, "Hanmal kaehwa chagangp'a ŭi yŏsŏng kyoyukkwan" (Self-Strengthening Reformers' Views on Women's Education in the Hanmal Period), *Han'guk hakpo* 27 (1982): 84–119.
61. *Cheguk sinmun* 27 April 1899.
62. *Hwangsŏng sinmun* 9 May 1908. Whether this charter was actually written by a woman is another issue.
63. *Tongnip sinmun* 13 September 1898.
64. *Tongnip sinmun* 12 May 1897; see also 5 September 1896.
65. For example, *Kajŏng chapch'i* (*Household Magazine*).
66. On the question of heroes, see my discussion of Ŭlchi in chapter 2, and on the question of masculine history, see my discussion of history as genealogy in chapter 5.
67. All newspapers featured letters by women, though none more than the *Cheguk*

sinmun, which set them off with the title "A Letter Contributed by a Woman" (Yŏin kisŏ). See 10 November 1898 and 12 February 1900; *Hwangsŏng sinmun* 30 March 1907; and *TaeHan maeil sinbo* February 29 1908.

68. Yu Kilchun, *Sŏyu kyŏnmun,* 377–78.

69. *Tongnip sinmun* 29 December 1898.

70. Kim Sŏnghŭi, "Munmyŏngnon" (On Civilization), *TaeHan chaganghoe wŏlbo* 6 (1906): 9.

71. Yu Kilchun, *Nodong yahak tokpon (A Reader for Worker's Night School),* in *Yu Kilchun chŏnsŏ (The Complete Works of Yu Kilchun),* ed. Yu Kilchun chŏnsŏ p'yŏnch'an wiwŏnhoe, 2: 261–358 (Seoul: Ilchogak, 1996).

72. *Tongnip sinmun* 24 September 1896.

73. Yi Kijun, *Hanmal Sŏgu kyŏngjehak toipsa yŏn'gu (The History of the Introduction of Western Economics in the Hanmal Period)* (Seoul: Ilchogak, 1985).

74. This was a favorite theme of the *Tongnip sinmun* 30 July 1896 and *Cheguk sinmun* 12 August 1898.

75. *Tongnip sinmun* 11 April 1899.

76. For other examples, see *Hwangsŏng sinmun* 6 April 1905; and *Tongnip sinmun* 2 February 1897 and 7 February 1899.

77. For a description of a journey into the territories controlled by the *ŭibyŏng,* including accounts of villages burned by the Japanese, see F. A. McKenzie, *The Tragedy of Korea* (London: Hodder & Stoughton, 1908), chs. 15–16.

78. Eckert et al., *Korea Old and New,* 244.

79. Japanese censorship interfered with these reports, except for the case of the *TaeHan maeil sinbo.* In the case of the *Hwangsŏng sinmun,* even its watered-down reports did not always get by the censor. See the censored report on the testimony of the captured general Wŏn Yongp'al (11 October 1905) and the editorial of 12 December 1907. The *Hwangsŏng sinmun* regularly reported on engagements in the countryside, but with few details, as can be seen in its "News from the Localities" columns at the end of 1907. An internal gazetteer of the Police Bureau lists a number of censored stories relating to the *ŭibyŏng,* including the reproduction of a call to arms in northern Kyŏngsang Province and a report "without basis" on Min Chŏngsik. See Andre Schmid, "Censorship and the *Hwangsŏng sinmun,*" in *Korea Between Tradition and Modernity: Selected Papers from the Fourth Pacific and Asian Conference on Korean Studies,* ed. Chang Yun-shik et al., 158–71 (Vancouver: Institute of Asian Research, 2000).

80. Yi Manhyŏng notes that this sympathy arose only after 1905 in the *TaeHan maeil sinbo.* Before this, they were uniformly critical. Yi Manhyŏng, "Ku-Hanmal aeguk kyemong undong ŭi dae Ŭibyŏnggwan — TaeHan maeil sinborŭl chungsim ŭro" (The Patriotic Enlightenment Movement's View of Ŭibyŏng — Centering on the *TaeHan maeil sinbo*), *Haesa nonmunjip* 18 (1983): 87–117.

81. *Hwangsŏng sinmun* 29 May 1906.
82. The contrast with the duty of the newspaper was made explicit in *Hwangsŏng sinmun* 22 May 1906.
83. *Hwangsŏng sinmun* 22 May 1906.
84. *Hwangsŏng sinmun* 29 May 1906.
85. *Hwangsŏng sinmun* 19 September 1907.
86. *Hwangsŏng sinmun* 12 December 1907; Kim Tohyŏng has shown how one prominent opponent of the *ŭibyŏng*, Yun Hyochŏng, used such criticisms in the *TaeHan chaganghoe wŏlbo*; see his *TaeHan chegukki ŭi chŏngch'i sasang yŏn'gu*, 88–93. For other pieces in the *Hwangsŏng sinmun*, see 13 October 1905, May 31 1906, 31 August 1907, 10 September 1907, 22 October 1907, 12 December 1907, 19 December 1907, 20 December 1907, 26 December 1907, 12 January 1908, *kisŏ*.
87. *TaeHan maeil sinbo* 30 May 1906.
88. *TaeHan maeil sinbo* 30 March 1906.
89. *TaeHan maeil sinbo* 30 May 1906.
90. *TaeHan maeil sinbo* 1 September 1907.
91. For a translation, see "Thirty Demands Addressed to the Japanese Resident General," trans. Han-Kyo Kim, in *Sourcebook of Korean Civilization*, ed. Peter Lee (Berkeley and Los Angeles: University of California Press, 1994), 2: 406–7.
92. Sin Yongha has argued that while no formal alliance was made between these two streams of the nationalist movement, the *ŭibyŏng* delayed annexation, allowing the intellectuals more time to raise national consciousness with their newspapers; see Shin Yongha, *Formation and Development of Modern Korean Nationalism* (Seoul: Daekwang munhwasa, 1989), ch. 6.
93. For examples of *tanhap*, see *TaeHan maeil sinbo* 26 August 1909; on *hapsim*, see *Tongnip sinmun* 6 March 1899; and on *kun*, *Hwangsŏng sinmun* see 30 November and 1 December 1904 and 23–24 July 1906. Also see the reprint of a *Kongnip sinbo* editorial on this issue in *Taehan maeil sinbo* 7 May 1907, *pyŏlbo*.
94. There was the *Kwanbo*, a government gazette which published official appointments and directives, and the *Hansŏng sunbo* and *Hansŏng chubo*, government-sponsored organs with a didactic purpose which were published between 1883 and 1888. See Ch'oe Chun, *Han'guk sinmunsa* (*A History of Korean Newspapers*), rev. ed. (Seoul: Ilchogak, 1991). There was also an active Japanese-language press serving the expatriate residential community. See Albert Altman, "Korea's First Newspaper: The Japanese *Chōsen Shimpo*," *Journal of Asian Studies* 43, no. 4 (August 1984): 685–96.
95. The "eyes and ears of the nation" was a common expression in this period. For one usage on how it could be expanded to the world, see *TaeHan maeil sinbo* 22 May 1906.
96. His Korean name was Sŏ Chaep'il, but following Chu Chino, I use his English

name, since Jaisohn used his English name on all occasions, even on his epitaph.

97. This is one of the more studied papers of the era. The classic study is by Sin Yongha, *Tongnip hyŏphoe yŏn'gu (Essays on the Independence Club)* (Seoul: Ilchogak, 1976). See also Chu Chino, "Tongnip hyŏphoe ŭi daeŏe insik ŭi kujo wa chŏn'gae" (The Formation and Development of the Independence Club's View of Foreigners), *Hangnim* 8 (1987), and Tongnip hyŏphoe ŭi sahoe sasang kwa sahoe chinhwaron" (Social Thought and Social Darwinism in the Independence Club), in *Sun Pogi paksa chŏngnyŏn kinyŏm Han'guksa nonch'ong (Essays in Commemoration of the Retirement of Sun Pogi)*, ed. Sun Pogi paksa chŏngnyŏn kinyŏm wiwŏnhoe (Seoul: Chisiksanŏpsa, 1988). In English, see Vipan Chandra, *Imperialism, Resistance, and Reform in Late Nineteenth Century Korea: Enlightenment and the Independence Club* (Berkeley: Center for Korean Studies, University of California, 1988); and Wells, *New God, New Nation*.

98. Yi Kwangnin, "*Hwangsŏng sinmun* yŏn'gu" (On the *Hwangsŏng Sinmun*), in Yi Kwangnin, *Kaehwap'a wa kaehwa sasang yŏn'gu (Studies of the Enlightenment Party and Enlightenment Thought)* (Seoul: Ilchogak, 1989), 155–95; Kang Mansaeng, "*Hwangsŏng sinmun* ŭi hyŏnsil kaehyŏk kusang yŏn'gu" (A Study of the *Hwangsŏng sinmun*'s Reform Thought), *Hangnim* 9 (1987): 63–120. For a useful survey of reform Confucianism in the period, see Yu Chun'gi, *Han'guk kŭndae yugyo kaehyŏk undongsa (A History of the Confucian Reform Movement in Modern Korea)* (Seoul: Tosŏ ch'ulp'an sammun, 1994).

99. *Cheguk sinmun*, 10 August 1898. Ch'oe Kiyŏng, *TaeHan cheguk sigi sinmun yŏn'gu (Essays on the Newspapers of the TaeHan Empire Period)* (Seoul: Ilchogak, 1991), 11–65; Yi Hyŏnhi, "Yi Tongning ŭi *Cheguk sinmun* chŏnnon hwaltong" (The Editorial Activities of Yi Tongning at the *Cheguk sinmun*) (Seoul: Minjok munhwasa, 1993), 654–66.

100. Yi Kwangnin, Yu Chaech'on, and Kim Haktung, *TaeHan maeil sinbo yŏn'gu* (On the *TaeHan maeil sinbo*) (Seoul: Sŏgang taehakkyo ch'ulp'ansa, 1986); Chŏng Chin-sok, *The Korea Problem in Anglo-Japanese Relations: Ernest Thomas Bethell and His Newspapers, the Daehan Maeil Sinbo and the Korean Daily News* (Seoul: Nanam Publications, 1987).

101. One local newspaper, the *Kyŏngnam ilbo*, is the subject of a study by Ch'oe Kiyong, *TaeHan cheguk sigi sinmun yŏn'gu*, 143–94.

102. For one example, see No Yidan, "Kukka ŭi yaksan" (The Nation's Medicine Mountain), *Sŏbuk hakhoe wŏlbo* 11 (1909) 35.

103. *Hwangsŏng sinmun* 25 February 1908.

104. Yi Sŏnghŭi, "Sŏ-u hakhoe ŭi aeguk kyemong undong kwa sasang" (The Ideology and Patriotic Enlightenment Movement of the Sŏ-u Educational Association), in *1900 nyŏndae ŭi aeguk kyemong undong yŏn'gu (Studies of the*

Patriotic Enlightenment Movement of the 1900s), ed. Cho Hangnae (Seoul: Asea munhwasa, 1992), 301.

105. For example, Pak Ŭnsik was schooled in a *sŏdang*, a type of traditional rural Confucian school, until the age of seventeen. Sin Ch'aeho served as an official in the Sŏnggyungwan. Yang Kit'ak received a Confucian education, as did Yu Kilchun and Namgung Ŏk.

106. Kyung Moon Hwang, "Bureaucracy in the Transition to Korean Modernity: Secondary Status Groups and the Transformation of Government and Society, 1880–1930" (Ph.D. diss., Harvard University, 1997). Although Hwang also includes military yangban in this category of secondary-status groups, none of the biographical data concerning writers and editors from the period that I have examined include military background.

107. Chandra, *Imperialism, Resistance, and Reform*, ch. 2.

108. *Hwangsŏng sinmun* 24 December 1906, *chappo*.

109. Han Yŏngu, "1910 nyŏndae Yi Sangyong, Kim Kyohŏn ŭi minjokchuŭi yŏksa sosŏl" (The Nationalist Historical Narratives of Yi Sangyong and Kim Kyohŏn in the 1910s), in *Han'guk minjokchuŭi yŏksahak* (*Nationalist Historiography in Korea*), ed. Han Yŏngu (Seoul: Ilchogak, 1994), 94–96.

110. Pak Ch'ansŭng, *Han'guk kŭndae chŏngch'i sasang yŏn'gu*, 47–68.

111. Yi Kwangnin, "*Hwangsŏng sinmun* yŏn'gu," 169–72.

112. On the *Cheguk sinmun*, see Ch'oe Kiyŏng, *TaeHan cheguk sigi sinmun yŏn'gu*, 31.

113. *Hwangsŏng sinmun* 8 July 1899.

114. *Tongnip sinmun* 26 July 1898.

115. *Hwangsŏng sinmun* 16 February 1906.

116. For the *Hwangsŏng sinmun*, see its *sasŏl* for 12 January 1899, 10 September 1899, September 10, 1902, 1 December 1908, and 17 February 1909. For the *Cheguk sinmun*, see Ch'oe Kiyŏng, *TaeHan sigi sinmun yŏn'gu*, ch. 1.

117. Chandra, *Imperialism, Resistance, and Reform*, 105–10.

118. Chŏng Kwŏn notes that circulation was at first 3,000 and then dropped to 2,000. See Chŏng Kwŏn, "Kyonam kyoyukhoe ŭi hwaltong kwa sŏnggyŏk" (The Activities and Nature of the Kyonam Educational Association), in *1900 nyŏndae ŭi aeguk kyemong undong yŏn'gu* (*Studies of the Patriotic Enlightenment Movement of the 1900s*), ed. Cho Hangnae (Seoul: Asea munhwasa, 1992), 443; Yi Hyŏnjong notes a constant circulation of 2,000 in "Kiho hŭnghakhoe ŭi chojik kwa hwaltong" (The Organization and Activities of the Kiho Society for the Promotion of Education), in *1900 nyŏndae ŭi aeguk kyemong undong yŏn'gu* (*Studies of the Patriotic Enlightenment Movement of the 1900s*), ed. Cho Hangnae (Seoul: Asea munhwasa, 1992), 417.

119. Chŏng Chin-sok, *The Korean Problem in Anglo-Japanese Relations*, 178–81.

120. Ch'oe Kiyŏng, *TaeHan cheguk sigi sinmun yŏn'gu*, 35.

121. This figure of U.S. $176,417 was requested by the American consul, Horace Allen, from the foreign minister on behalf of Philip Jaisohn after his return to the United States. The document suggests that the Home Ministry ordered the *Tongnip Sinmun* to send copies to all magistrates in the country. See document #2098 in Koryŏ Taehak Asea Munje Yŏn'guso, ed., *KuHan'guk oegyo munsŏ* (*Diplomatic Documents of Old Korea*) (Seoul: Koryŏ taehakkyo ch'ulp'ansa, 1967), 11: 688–91.

122. Sin Yongha notes that in the capital, the *Tongnip sinmun* used street vendors (Sin Yongha, *Tongnip hyŏphoe yŏn'gu*, 34).

123. *Hwangsŏng sinmun* 2 November 1906, *kisŏ*.

124. *Hwangsŏng sinmun* 26 December 1906, *kisŏ*, and 13 April 1907, *chappo*.

125. Yi Kwangnin, "*Hwangsŏng sinmun* yŏn'gu," 175.

126. Chŏng Chin-sok, *The Korean Problem in Anglo-Japanese Relations*, 67–81.

127. For these lists, see from 1 August 1906.

128. This was the *Hwangsŏng sinmun*'s tribute to the *Cheguk sinmun*, after one of the latter's temporary closings; 17 October 1904.

129. See the letter from readers describing one such case in Kangwŏn Province, *Tongnip sinmun* 9 November 1898.

130. *Korean Repository* 4 (1897): 473.

131. 10 February 1903, as quoted in Yi Kwangnin, "*Hwangsŏng sinmun* yŏn'gu," 167.

132. Philip Jaisohn, as quoted in F. A. McKenzie, *Korea's Fight for Freedom* (New York: Fleming H. Revell, 1920), 67.

133. Isabella Bird, *Korea Among Her Neighbours* (London: Routledge & Kegan Paul, 1897), 440.

134. The *Hwangsŏng sinmun* reported that these laws were basically a translation of Japanese press laws; see 3 March 1899; and Ch'oe Kiyŏng, *TaeHan cheguk sigi sinmun yŏn'gu*, 246–52.

135. This event was reported in the *TaeHan maeil sinbo* 23 August 1904. On the question of censorship, see Ch'oe Kiyŏng, *TaeHan cheguk sigi sinmun yŏn'gu*, 245–94; O Chuhwan. "Ilche ŭi taeHan ŏron chŏngch'aek" (Japanese Media Policies During the Korean Colonial Period), in *Ilche ŭi munhwa ch'imťalsa* (*A History of Japanese Cultural Imperialism*), ed. Han Kion (Seoul: Minjung sŏgwan, 1970), 373–492; Ch'oe Chun, *Han'guk sinmunsa*; and Schmid, "Censorship and the *Hwangsŏng sinmun*."

136. For some of the ways this was achieved, see Schmid, "Censorship and the *Hwangsŏng sinmun*."

137. *TaeHan maeil sinbo* 12 February 1907, *chappo*.

138. I deal with these events in chapter 4.

139. Ch'oe Chun, *Han'guk sinmunsa*, 172–80.

140. Frank Baldwin Jr., "The March First Movement: Korean Challenge and Japanese Response" (Ph.D. diss., Columbia University, 1969), app. 2, 228–31. Baldwin, however, excludes women from his calculation.

2. Decentering the Middle Kingdom and Realigning the East

1. Ministry of Education, *Kungmin sohak tokpon* (*An Elementary Reader for Citizens*) (Seoul: Ministry of Education, 1895), in *Han'guk kaehwagi kyo'gwasŏ ch'ongsŏ* (*A Collection of Textbooks from the Korean Enlightenment Period*), ed. Han'gukhak munhŏn yŏn'guso (Seoul: Asea munhwasa, 1977), 1: 24.
2. For shifting attitudes toward China on the part of early enlightenment thinkers, see Yi Wŏnjae, *Ch'ugi kaehwa sasang yŏn'gu* (*Studies of Early Enlightenment Thought*) (Seoul: Minjok munhwa sa, 1989), 145–77.
3. *Hwangsŏng sinmun* 29 July 1899.
4. *Tongnip sinmun* 5 June 1899.
5. *Tongnip sinmun* 28 December 1897.
6. *Hwangsŏng sinmun* 10 April 1899. A similar editorial concerning Italy can be found on 25 March 1899.
7. *Hwangsŏng sinmun* 20 January 1900.
8. *Cheguk sinmun* 3 December 1902 and 5 July 1900.
9. *Hwangsŏng sinmun* 21 June 1900.
10. *Hwangsŏng sinmun* 30 June 1900.
11. *Hwangsŏng sinmun* 17 May 1901.
12. *Hwangsŏng sinmun* 25 June 1900.
13. *Hwangsŏng sinmun* 12 September 1898.
14. *Tongnip sinmun* 25 August 1899.
15. *Hwangsŏng sinmun* 9 October 1899.
16. *Hwangsŏng sinmun* 13 May 1899.
17. *Hwangsŏng sinmun* 25 January 1900; for another comparison with Britain but concerning newspaper readership, see *Tongnip sinmun* 10 January 1899.
18. *Tongnip sinmun* 2 September 1897.
19. *Tongnip sinmun* 21 May 1896.
20. *Tongnip sinmun* 20 June 1896.
21. *Hwangsŏng sinmun* 6 August 1900.
22. *Kungmin sohak tokpon*, in Han'gukhak munhŏn yŏn'guso, ed., *Han'guk kaehwagi kyo'gwasŏ ch'ongsŏ*, 1: 25.
23. For some comparisons with Japan, see Donald Keene, "The Sino-Japanese War of 1894–95 and Its Cultural Effects," in *Tradition and Modernization in Japanese Culture*, ed. Donald Shively (Princeton, N.J.: Princeton University Press, 1971), 121–75; and Stefan Tanaka, *Japan's Orient: Rendering Pasts into History* (Berkeley and Los Angeles: University of California Press, 1993).

24. For one survey of this literature, see Bill Ashcroft, Gareth Griffiths, and Helen Tiffin, eds., *The Empire Writes Back: Theory and Practice in Post-colonial Literature* (London: Routledge, 1989).

25. For two explicit examples of this comparison, see *Hwangsŏng sinmun* 7 December 1898 and 14 January 1909.

26. *Tongnip sinmun* 15 July 1898; also 16 February 1899. Chang Chiyŏn uses the same point as one of the five sicknesses of Korea, "Tanch'e yŏnhu minjok kabo" (After Uniting, the *minjok* Can Be Protected), cited in *TaeHan chaganghoe wŏlbo* 5 (1906): 5–6.

27. *Hwangsŏng sinmun* 3 June 1907; also see 14 January 1909.

28. This estimate is from *Hwangsŏng sinmun* 12 February 1908; also see the call on the front page for manumission, *Hwangsŏng sinmun* 16–17 July 1910.

29. *Hwangsŏng sinmun* 12 February 1908.

30. The power of this rhetoric of slavery can also be seen in a letter to the *Hwangsŏng sinmun* on 29 July 1906 complaining of the slave-like conditions of Korean workers in Mexico.

31. *Hwangsŏng sinmun* 3 June 1908.

32. *Hwangsŏng sinmun* 19 May 1899.

33. On the general question of hero worship, see *TaeHan maeil sinbo* 4 January 1908, 9 February 1909, 9 April 1909, 15 and 26 June 1909, 2 February 1910, and 24 July 1910; and in the *Hwangsŏng sinmun* 29 July 1909. On the surge in interest on hero biographies, see Yi Manyŏl, *Tanjae Sin Ch'aeho ŭi yŏksahak yŏn'gu* (*Studies of the Historiography of Tanjae Sin Ch'aeho*) (Seoul: Munhak kwa pip'yŏngsa, 1990), 164–75.

34. Yi Kich'an, introduction to "Ŭlchi Mundŏk" (Ŭlchi Mundŏk), by Sin Ch'aeho, in *Tanjae Sin Ch'aeho Chŏnjip* (*The Complete Works of Sin Ch'aeho*) (Seoul: Hyŏngsŏl ch'ulp'ansa, 1997), 2: 259.

35. Even some contemporary textbooks were criticized for not having information about this hero. See the *TaeHan maeil sinbo*'s critique of the *Sohak tokpon* (*An Elementary Reader*), 24 December 1909.

36. Hwang Hyŏn, *Maech'ŏn yarok* (*Maech'ŏn's Unofficial History*) (Seoul: Kuksa p'yŏnch'an wiwŏnhoe, 1961), 534. Also see *Hwangsŏng sinmun* 20 May 1910.

37. *TaeHan maeil sinbo* 22 September 1909.

38. Sin Ch'aeho, "Ŭlchi Mundŏk," 2: 251–351.

39. *Hwangsŏng sinmun* 4 June 1908.

40. An Ch'angho, introduction to Sin Ch'aeho, "Ŭlchi Mundŏk," 266.

41. Yi Kich'an, introduction to Sin Ch'aeho, "Ŭlchi Mundŏk," 257–58.

42. *Hwangsŏng sinmun* 14 January 1909.

43. Yu Kilchun, *TaeHan munjŏn* (*Korean Grammar*), in *Yu Kilchun chŏnsŏ* (*The Complete Works of Yu Kilchun*), ed. Yu Kilchun chŏnsŏ p'yŏnch'an wiwŏnhoe (Seoul: Ilchogak, 1996), 3: 2.

44. See a standard version of this account in Koryŏ Taehakkyo minjok munhwa yŏn'guso, ed., *Han'guk munhwasa taegye* (*Cultural History of Korea*) (Seoul: Koryŏ Taehakkyo minjok munhwa yŏn'guso ch'ulp'anbu, 1967), vol. 5.

45. For general histories of language reform in these years, see Yi Kimun, *Kaehwagi ŭi kungmun yŏn'gu* (*National Language Research During the Enlightenment Period*) (Seoul: Ilchogak, 1970), and "Kaehwagi ŭi kungmun sayong e kwanhan yŏn'gu" (Research on the Use of National Writing in the Kaehwa Period), *Han'guk munhwa* 5 (1984): 65–84.

46. Peter Lee, ed., *Sourcebook of Korean Civilization*, vol. 2: *From the Seventeenth Century to the Modern Period* (Berkeley and Los Angeles: University of California Press, 1994), 295.

47. As translated in Gari Ledyard, "The Korean Language Reform of 1446: The Origin, Background, and Early History of the Korean Alphabet" (Ph.D. diss., University of California at Berkeley, 1966), 106.

48. Ibid., 105.

49. *Hwangsŏng sinmun* 28 September 1898.

50. This was a standard argument in the pages of the *Tongnip sinmun* from its inception, see 16 May 1896, 25 July 1896, and 22 December 1896.

51. The four tones were key to rhyming patterns in following poetic conventions, and the eight styles were formal essay-writing formats. See Han Hŏnggyo, "Kungmun kwa hanmun ŭi kwan'gye" (The Relation Between National and Chinese Scripts), *TaeHan yuhaksaeng hakpo* 1 (March 1907): 29.

52. Yi Pogyŏng, "Kungmun kwa hanmun ŭi kwado sidae" (The Period of Transition Between the National and Chinese Scripts), *Taegŭk hakpo* 21 (March 1908): 17.

53. Sin Haeyong, "Hanmunja wa kungmunja ŭi sŏni yŏha" (What Are the Advantages of Chinese and National Scripts?), *TaeChosŏn tongnip hyŏphoe hoebo* 15 (June 1897).

54. Ibid.

55. Chu Sigyŏng, "Kugŏ wa kungmun ŭi p'iryo" (The Need for National Language and Writing), *Sŏu* 2 (January 1907): 33.

56. Chu Sigyŏng, "Kungmunnon" (On National Writing), *Tongnip sinmun* 24 April 1897. For a similar piece, see Yi Chongil, "Kungmunnon" (On National Writing), *TaeHan hyŏphoebo* 2 (25 May 1908).

57. *Hwangsŏng sinmun* 28 September 1898.

58. Yu Kilchun, *TaeHan munjŏn*, preface.

59. Chu Sigyŏng, "Kugŏ wa kungmun ŭi p'iryo" (The Need for National Language and Writing), *Sŏu* 2 (January 1907): 31–34.

60. *Hwangsŏng sinmun* 28 September 1898.

61. Chu Sigyŏng, "Kungmunnon" (On National Writing), *Tongnip sinmun* 24 April 1897.

62. For two examples, see *Hwangsŏng sinmun* 7 September 1906; and Yi Sŭnggyo, "KukHanmunnon" (On National and Chinese Scripts), *Sŏbuk hakhoe wŏlbo* 1 (1 June 1908): 20–22.
63. *Tongnip sinmun* 7 April 1896.
64. Yi Pongun, *Kungmun chŏngni* (*National Language Standardization*) (Seoul: Hakpu p'yŏnjipkuk, 1897), preface. Also see Chu's reference to the "politics of civilization," in "Kungmunnon" (On National Writing), *Tongnip sinmun* 24 April 1897.
65. Yi Sŭnggyo, "KukHanmunnon" (On National and Chinese Scripts), *Sŏbuk hakhoe wŏlbo* 1 (1 June 1908): 21.
66. Chu Sigyŏng, "Kugŏ wa kungmun ŭi p'iryo" (The Need for National Language and Writing), *Sŏu* 2 (January 1907): 32.
67. *Hwangsŏng sinmun* 7 September 1906.
68. Yi Chŏng'il, "Non Kungmun" (On National Writing), *TaeHan hyŏphoebo* 2 (25 May 1908): 11–14.
69. Yi Sŭnggyo, "KukHanmunnon" (On National and Chinese Writing), *Sŏbuk hakhoe wŏlbo* 1 (June 1908): 20.
70. *Hwangsŏng sinmun* 28 September 1898; and Yi Pogyŏng, "Kungmun kwa Hanmun ŭi kwado sidae" (The Transition Period of National and Chinese Languages), *Taegŭk hakpo* 21 (May 1908): 18.
71. Yi Pongun, *Kungmun chŏngni*, preface.
72. Chu Sigyŏng, "Kugŏ wa kungmun ŭi p'iryo" (The Need for National Writing and Chinese Writing), *Sŏu* 2 (January 1907): 34.
73. Sin Ch'aeho, "KukHanmun ŭi kyŏngjung" (The Importance of National and Chinese Writing), *TaeHan maeil sinbo* 17–19 March 1908.
74. Yŏ Kyuhyang, (untitled), *Taedong hakhoe wŏlbo* 25 February 1908, 52–53.
75. *Hwangsŏng sinmun* 9 November 1899 and 23 May 1899, *pyŏlbo*.
76. *Hwangsŏng sinmun* 13 February 1902.
77. *Hwangsŏng sinmun* 2 March 1900.
78. *Hwangsŏng sinmun* 5 October 1907; for standardization, especially regarding dialects, see *Hwangsŏng sinmun* 9 October 1900 and 10 June 1901.
79. *Hwangsŏng sinmun* 7 September 1906.
80. *Hwangsŏng sinmun* 5 September 1898.
81. Occasionally, letters to the editor would appear in the vernacular, often those from women readers.
82. Yi Kwangsu, "Kŭmil a Han yongmun e tae hayo" (Concerning the Current Use of Our Korean language), *Hwangsŏng sinmun* 24–27 July 1910.
83. Ibid., 26 July 1910.
84. Ross King pays particular attention to this debate in "Nationalism and Language Reform in Korea: The *Questione della Lingua* in Precolonial Korea," in *Nationalism and the Construction of Korean Identity*, ed. Hyung Il Pai and

Timothy R. Tangherlini (Berkeley: Institute of East Asian Studies, University of California, 1998), 33–72.

85. Benedict Anderson, *Imagined Communities Imagined Communities: Reflections on the Origins and Spread of Nationalism*, rev. ed. (London: Verso, 1991), 83–111.

86. For taboo characters, see Hwang Hyŏn, *Maech'ŏn yarok*, 170 and 196, and for the stele, see 171.

87. For a description of the ceremony, see *The Independent* 1, no. 100 (24 November 1896).

88. *The Independent* 20 June 1896.

89. Hwang Hyŏn, *Maech'ŏn yarok*, 168.

90. Yi Kuyong, "TaeHan cheguk ŭi sŏngnip kwa yŏlgang ŭi panyŏng" (The Formation of the TaeHan Empire and the Reaction of the Powers), *Kangwŏn sahak* 1 (December 1985): 75–98.

91. Hwang Hyŏn, *Maech'ŏn yarok*, 215–17.

92. Hwang Hyŏn, *Maech'ŏn yarok*, 218. My translation has been aided by Yun Ch'iho, "The Whang-chei of Dai Han, or the Emperor of Korea," *Korean Repository* 4 (1897): 385.

93. The Han used by Emperor Kojong was different from that of the Han dynasty. The former is still used by the Republic of Korea, and the latter is still used for the dominant Chinese ethnic group in the People's Republic of China.

94. My thanks to Gari Ledyard for pointing out the significance of these names.

95. Hwang Hyŏn, *Maech'ŏn yarok*, 232–33.

96. Yun Ch'iho, *Yun Ch'iho ilgi (The Diaries of Yun Ch'iho ilgi)* (Seoul: Tamgudang, 1971), 27 May 1897.

97. Yun Ch'iho, "The Whang-chei of Dai Han, or the Emperor of Korea," 387.

98. *Tongnip sinmun* 1 October 1897.

99. *Hwangsŏng sinmun* 21 September 1898.

100. *Hwangsŏng sinmun* 21 September 1898.

101. For descriptions of this event, see Vipan Chandra, *Imperialism, Resistance and Reform in Late Nineteenth Century Korea: Enlightenment and the Independence Club* (Berkeley: Center for Korean Studies, University of California, 1988), ch.8; and Sin Yongha, *Tongnip hyŏphoe yŏn'gu*, ch. 7.

102. For an example, see the *Tongnip sinmun* 1 May 1899.

103. *Tongnip sinmun* 22 September 1896.

104. *Hwangsŏng sinmun* 25 November 1904.

105. *Tongnip sinmun* 22 September 1896.

106. Ministry of Education, ed., *Kugŏ tokpon (A Korean Reader)* (1908, reprinted in *Han'guk kaehwagi kyo'gwasŏ ch'ongsŏ*, ed. Han'gukhak munhŏn yŏn'guso (Seoul: Asea munhwasa, 1977), 6: chŏn 3, 57.

107. "Key" cigarettes were regularly advertised in the *TaeHan maeil sinbo*, see 18 August 1906.
108. Yi Sŏngŭn, "Uri kukki chejŏng ŭi yurae wa kŭ ŭi ŭiŭi" (The History and Meaning of the Making of Our Flag), *Kukkasang ŭi chemunje* 2 (July 1959): 177–220.
109. *Tongnip sinmun* 13 January 1898.
110. *Tongnip sinmun* 27 July 1898.
111. *Tongnip sinmun* 1 March 1899.
112. Tanaka, *Japan's Orient*, chs. 1–2.
113. *Tongnip sinmun* 19 September 1898.
114. *Tongnip sinmun* 10 August 1897.
115. *Tongnip sinmun* 5 June 1897.
116. Yu Kilchun, *Sŏyu kyŏnmun*, 384. This was also true of the *Sŏbuk hakhoe wŏlbo*.
117. 23 September 1898. This was an editorial that produced almost verbatim Yu Kilchun's definition; see *Sŏyu kyŏnmun*, 376.
118. *Hwangsŏng sinmun* 23 September 1898.
119. *Hwangsŏng sinmun* 28 April 1899.
120. *Hwangsŏng sinmun* 25 April 1900.
121. *Hwangsŏng sinmun* 9–12 December 1902.
122. *Hwangsŏng sinmun* 28 June 1899.
123. *Hwangsŏng sinmun* 27 April 1899.
124. *Hwangsŏng sinmun* 27–28 April 1899.
125. *Hwangsŏng sinmun* 27 April 1899.
126. In Chinese pronunciation, "gewu." The source for this expression is found in the opening section of *The Great Learning* (*Daxue*): "The ancients who wished to illustrate illustrious virtue throughout the Kingdom, first ordered well their own States. Wishing to order well their own States, they first regulated their families. Wishing to regulate their families, they first cultivated their persons. Wishing to cultivate their persons, they first rectified their hearts. Wishing to rectify their hearts, they first sought to be sincere in their thoughts. Wishing to be sincere in their thoughts, they first extended to the utmost their knowledge. Such extension of knowledge lay in the investigation of things. Things being investigated, knowledge became complete." As translated in James Legge, *The Chinese Classics* (Hong Kong: Hong Kong University Press, 1970), 1: 357–58.
127. *Hwangsŏng sinmun* 3 April 1899; also 30 January 1900. For the use of a similar expression, *kyŏngch'i*, see 9 September 1898, 15 September 1898, and 18 May 1899.
128. *Hwangsŏng sinmun* 27 October 1898.
129. *Hwangsŏng sinmun* 17 July 1902.
130. *Hwangsŏng sinmun* 3 April 1903.
131. *Hwangsŏng sinmun* 30 May 1899.

132. Most prominently, this was accomplished by drawing attention to many of the scholars that today are often referred to as Sirhak scholars, such as Yi Ik (25–26 June 1903), Pak Chiwŏn (29 June 1901), and Chŏng Yagyong (4 August 1899, 19 May 1903).

133. Franz Dikötter, *The Discourse of Race in Modern China* (London: C. Hurst, 1992).

134. Yu Kilchun, *Sŏyu kyŏnmun*, ch. 2.

135. Ibid., 63.

136. For example, *Hwangsŏng sinmun* 24 May 1899; Hwimun ŭisuk p'yŏnjippu, ed. *Kodŭng sohak tokpon* (*An Advanced Elementary Reader*) (Seoul: Hwimun ŭisuk inswaebu, 1906) in Han'gukhak munhŏn yŏn'guso, ed., *Han'guk kaehwagi kyo'gwasŏ ch'ongsŏ*, 6–29.

137. For one of its more free-ranging uses, see *Hwangsŏng sinmun* 2 January 1900.

138. *Cheguk sinmun* 25 August 1898.

139. *Tongnip sinmun* 7 April 1898. The editorial of 2 March 1899 likewise speaks of Japanese and Koreans as being of the same race (*injŏng*).

140. See Okakura Kakuzo's famous expression of Pan-Asianism in *The Ideals of the East* (Rutland, Vt.: Tuttle, 1970).

141. See Eto Shinkichi and Marius Jansen, trans., *My Thirty Years Dream: The Autobiography of Miyazaki Toten* (Princeton, N.J.: Princeton University Press, 1988).

142. For the most detailed treatment of this aspect of Liang's thought in English, see Philip C. Huang, *Liang Ch'i-ch'ao and Modern Chinese Liberalism* (Seattle: University of Washington Press, 1972).

143. Marius B. Jansen, *The Japanese and Sun Yat-sen* (Stanford, Calif.: Stanford University Press, 1954).

144. On Korean Pan-Asianism, see Yi Kwangnin, "Kaehwagi Han'gugin ŭi asea yŏndaeron" (Korean Theories of Asian Unity in the Enlightenment Period), in Yi Kwangnin, *Kaehwap'a wa kaehwa sasang yŏn'gu* (*Studies of the Enlightenment Party and Enlightenment Thought*) (Seoul: Ilchogak, 1989), 138–54.

145. On the Ilchinhoe and its use of Pan-Asianism, see Vipan Chandra, "An Outline Study of the Ilchin-hoe (Advancement Society) of Korea," *Occasional Papers on Korea* 2 (March 1974): 43–72.

146. *Hwangsŏng sinmun* 24 May 1899. The latter expression, *tongmun*, can be more narrowly interpreted to mean "same script." For its use in China, see D. R. Howland, *Borders of Chinese Civilization: Geography and History at Empire's End* (Durham, N.C.: Duke University Press, 1996), 54–57.

147. *Hwangsŏng sinmun* 12 January 1900.

148. *Hwangsŏng sinmun* 12 April 1899, 24 May 1899, 17 July 1900, and 6 October 1904.

149. *Hwangsŏng sinmun* 12 April 1899.

150. *Hwangsŏng sinmun* 12 August 1903.
151. *Hwangsŏng sinmun* 6 May 1904. A similar editorial used the classical analogy of a three-legged vessel: Cut one leg off and the vessel would fall; only if all three relied on one another could the entire vessel stand on its own (*Hwangsŏng sinmun* 12 April 1899). Using historical allusions from the classics, the paper cited instances in which if several countries had united, they "would have been sturdy and strong, but apart they were divided and isolated." Events that took place nearly two millennia ago, it concluded, offered a cautionary reference for the three countries of the East today.
152. *Hwangsŏng sinmun* 17 May 1899.
153. *Hwangsŏng sinmun* 13 June 1899. Peace was given the topmost priority; see *Hwangsŏng sinmun* 24 December 1898. Both the Sino-Japanese War and the Boxer Uprising were cited as examples of crises disrupting the security of the East; see 24 December 1898, 21 June 1900, and 10 July 1900.
154. *Hwangsŏng sinmun* 12 April 1899.
155. *Hwangsŏng sinmun* 12 April 1899.
156. Other editorials complained of a Japan that protected only itself without thinking of its neighbors (*Hwangsŏng sinmun* 17 May 1899). Reiterating the significance of China's survival, the editors argued that if China were divided, even though Japan was ten times stronger, it would have trouble protecting itself (*Hwangsŏng sinmun* 13 June 1899).
157. For one side of the debate over this issue between the *Hwangsŏng sinmun* and Japanese resident newspapers, see *Hwangsŏng sinmun* 7 October 1901 and 28–31 January 1902.
158. *Hwangsŏng sinmun* 12 January 1900.
159. *Hwangsŏng sinmun* 20 February 1904.
160. *Hwangsŏng sinmun* December 1904, 20 February 1904, 19 March 1904, and 23 June 1904.
161. *Hwangsŏng sinmun* 31 May 1904.
162. *Hwangsŏng sinmun* 23 June 1904.
163. Ibid.
164. *Hwangsŏng sinmun* 12 February 1904.
165. *Hwangsŏng sinmun* 20 February 1904.
166. Ibid.
167. Ibid.
168. *Hwangsŏng sinmun* 19 March 1904.
169. Ibid.
170. *Hwangsŏng sinmun* 12 February 1904.
171. *Hwangsŏng sinmun* 24–27 June 1904.
172. *Hwangsŏng sinmun* 24 June 1904.
173. *Hwangsŏng sinmun* 25 June 1904.

174. *Hwangsŏng sinmun* 28 June 1904.
175. "Si il ya pangsŏng taegok." The title translation is from Yi Ki-baek, *A New History of Korea*, trans. Edward W. Wagner and Edward J. Shultz (Seoul: Il-chogak, 1984), 329. This is not included in the reprint of the *Hwangsŏng sinmun* (Seoul: Han'guk munhwa kaebalsa, 1974), perhaps because it was not officially published. Instead, I have used a copy from Chang's selected works. See Kuksa p'yŏnch'an wiwŏnhoe, ed., *Wiam mungo* (*Writings of Chang Chi-yŏn*) (Seoul: Yuchong-sa, 1956). A slightly different rendition of this editorial can be found in Tan'guk Taehakkyo Pusol Tongyanghak Yon'guso, ed., *Chang Chiyŏn chŏnsŏ* (*The Complete Works of Chang Chiyŏn*) (Seoul: Tan'guk Tae-hakkyo Pusol Tongyanghak Yon'guso, 1979–89), 8: 443–44.
176. This nationalist reading of the editorial can be found in such standard works as Yi Ki-baek, *A New History of Korea*, 329–30; or in recent works on the period by Western scholars, for example, Peter Duus, *The Abacus and the Sword: The Japanese Penetration of Korea, 1895–1910* (Berkeley and Los Angeles: University of California Press, 1995), 185.
177. Curiously, attacks on Itō's trustworthiness regularly made their way through the censors and became one of the few areas of specific, direct criticism of Japan found in editorials. See, for example, 19 September 1906 and a critique of one of his speeches on 14 October 1908, although this didn't stop the papers from publishing an illustrated memorial on behalf of him when he was assassinated (29 September 1909).
178. For an interesting example about not geopolitics but cultural interchange, see *Hwangsŏng sinmun* 8 September 1909.
179. *Hwangsŏng sinmun* 15 January 1910.
180. *Hwangsŏng sinmun* 27 May 1909 and 13 January 1910.
181. *Hwangsŏng sinmun* 7–8 March 1906. Also see 20 September 1906.
182. For one example of a dispute over this issue with the *Kanjō shimpo*, see *Hwangsŏng sinmun* 22 March 1905; with the Inchon-based *Chōsen shimpo* over the National Debt Redemption Movement, see *Hwangsŏng sinmun* 7 March 1907; more generally, see *Hwangsŏng sinmun* 26 November 1906.
183. *Hwangsŏng sinmun* 9 October 1907.
184. On the Ilchinhoe and its use of Pan Asianism, see Vipin Chandra, "An Outline Study of the Ilchin-hoe (Advancement Society) of Korea," 43–72.
185. *Hwangsŏng sinmun* 23 March 1905.
186. *Hwangsŏng sinmun* 26 June 1907.
187. Ibid.
188. *Hwangsŏng sinmun* 1 February 1909. Letters from readers critical of the Il-chinhoe were also published—and partly censored; see *Hwangsŏng sinmun* 13–14 November 1907; and on its suppression, see 25 December 1909.
189. *Hwangsŏng sinmun* 14 October 1908.

190. This particular example is in *Hwangsŏng sinmun* 13 January 1910, *chappo*.
191. *Hwangsŏng sinmun* 9 October 1907.
192. *Hwangsŏng sinmun* 25 December 1909.
193. *Hwangsŏng sinmun* 15 January 1910. For an example relating to censorship, see *Hwangsŏng sinmun* 23 March 1905.
194. *Hwangsŏng sinmun* 3 November 1905.
195. This article was written by Sin Ch'aeho, *TaeHan maeil sinbo* 8–10 August 1909.
196. Sin Ch'aeho, *TaeHan maeil sinbo* 10 August 1909.
197. Ibid.
198. Ibid.
199. See his diary as reprinted in *An Chunggŭn ŭisa chumo charyojip* (*A Collection of Materials by the Martyr An Chunggŭn*) (Seoul: Chŏnjugyo chongui kuhyŏn chŏn'guk sajedan, 1990).
200. For one example of its use by the *Hwangsŏng sinmun*, see 20 September 1906.

3. Engaging a Civilizing Japan

1. *Tongnip sinmun* 9 September 1898.
2. "Aguk ŭi pok" (Our National Wealth), *Sŏbuk hakhoe wŏlbo* 4 (September 1908): 25–27.
3. *TaeHan maeil sinbo* 30 September 1909.
4. *Hwangsŏng sinmun* 28 June 1907. For a complaint about the domestic publishing industry, see *Tongnip sinmun* 2 June 1896.
5. *TaeHan maeil sinbo* 16 June 1908.
6. *TaeHan maeil sinbo* 30 September 1909.
7. Ha Ubong, *Chosŏn hugi sirhakcha ŭi Ilbon'gwan yŏn'gu* (*Sirhak Studies of Japan in the Late Chosŏn Dynasty*) (Seoul: Ilchisa, 1989).
8. *Tongguk sinsok samgang haengsilto* (*A New Illustrated Manual of the Three Relations in Korea*) (1614; reprint, Seoul: Taejegak, 1985).
9. As translated in Peter Lee, ed., *Sourcebook of Korean Civilization*, vol. 2: *From the Seventeenth Century to the Modern Period* (Berkeley and Los Angeles: University of California Press, 1994), 333.
10. For a description of the impact of these events on the liberal community in Japan, see Hilary Conroy, *The Japanese Seizure of Korea: 1868–1910, A Study of Realism and Idealism in International Relations* (Philadelphia: University of Pennsylvania Press, 1960).
11. *Tongnip sinmun* 25 April 1896. Also on the question of comparative size, see 12 April 1899.
12. *Tongnip sinmun* 6 March 1899.

13. *Tongnip sinmun* 21 April 1899.
14. *Tongnip sinmun* 9 January and 30 March 1899.
15. *Hwangsŏng sinmun* 17 September 1898.
16. For the Charter Oath, see *Tongnip sinmun* 6 December 1898. For a more than forty-part serialized piece on the Meiji period, see the *Hwangsŏng sinmun* beginning with the 7 November 1906.
17. *Tongnip sinmun* 6 December 1897.
18. *Hwangsŏng sinmun* 26 September 1906.
19. *Hwangsŏng sinmun* 7 February 1899.
20. *Tongnip sinmun* 17 January 1899.
21. Ibid.
22. *Hwangsŏng sinmun* 17 September 1898.
23. *Tongnip sinmun* 30 January 1897. For other reports on the handling of foreigners, see 23 September and 21 May 1898.
24. *Tongnip sinmun* 2–7 July 1898.
25. For example, *Hwangsŏng sinmun* 28 September 1899 and 7 April 1904.
26. *Tongnip sinmun* 13 September 1898.
27. *Sŏbuk hakhoe wŏlbo* 9 (1907): 124; also *Hwangsŏng sinmun* 7 February 1899.
28. *Hwangsŏng sinmun* 31 October 1905.
29. *Tongnip sinmun* 20 January 1899.
30. *Hwangsŏng sinmun* 9 May 1905.
31. *Hwangsŏng sinmun* 19–21 October 1905.
32. *Hwangsŏng sinmun* 25–27 September 1905. Articles written by overseas students also were common, on topics ranging from self-rule to tree cultivation; see, respectively, *Sŏbuk hakhoe wŏlbo* 11 (1909): 32–34, and 12 (1909): 10–17.
33. For student reports, see *Hwangsŏng sinmun* 13 May 1907, *kisŏ*; and *TaeHan maeil sinbo* 6 June 1907, *kisŏ*.
34. *Hwangsŏng sinmun* 27 September 1905.
35. *Hwangsŏng sinmun* 24–25 March 1899. For a speech by the former prime minister, Ōkuma Shigenobu, explaining Japanese policy toward the Qing dynasty, see *Hwangsŏng sinmun* 28 March 1899.
36. *Tongnip sinmun* 30 August 1898.
37. *Hwangsŏng sinmun* 12 February 1907.
38. "'Toegye sŏnsaeng ŭi hagi haengu Ilbonja kuŭi" (Toegye's Learning Has Long Circulated in Japan), *Sŏbuk hakhoe wŏlbo* 12 (1909): 38–39.
39. *TaeHan maeil sinbo* 18 October 1908.
40. *Hwangsŏng sinmun* 10 April 1900.
41. *TaeHan maeil sinbo* 7 January 1910. Another statement of Korean contempt for Japan can be found in *Hwangsŏng sinmun* 31 March 1904.
42. Ch'usŏngja, "Aguk kodae munmyŏng ŭi yuch'ul" (The Outflow of Our Nation's Ancient Civilization), *Sŏbuk hakhoe wŏlbo* 17 (1909): 6.

43. These figures are from the *Tae'guk hakpo*, 6: 12, as recorded in Kim Kiju, *Hanmal chaeil Han'guk yuhaksaeng ŭi minjok undong* (*The Nationalist Movement Among Korean Students in Japan During the Hanmal Period*) (Seoul: Nut'i namu, 1993).

44. Yu Kilchun, *Sŏyu kyŏnmun* (*Observations of My Travels to the West*). In *Yu Kilchun chŏnsŏ* (*The Complete Works of Yu Kilchun*), ed. Yu Kilchun chŏnsŏ p'yŏnch'an wiwŏnhoe (Seoul: Ilchogak, 1996), 1: preface.

45. Yi Kwangnin, "Yu Kilchun ŭi kaehwa sasang" (The Enlightenment Thought of Yu Kilchun), in Yi Kwangnin, *Han'guk kaehwa sasang yŏn'gu* (*Studies of Korean Enlightenment Thought*) (Seoul: Ilchogak, 1979), 51–53.

46. Yu Kilchun, *Sŏyu kyŏnmun*, 1–2.

47. *Kongnip sinmun* 8 July 1908.

48. Yi Kwangnin, "Yu Kilchun ŭi kaehwa sasang," 70–77.

49. Ibid., 65–66.

50. The *Hwangsŏng sinmun* would occasionally extract passages verbatim from Yu's work, reprinting them as its own editorial without acknowledgment. One example can be found on 23 September 1898 for the paper's definition of *munmyŏng kaehwa*.

51. *Cheguk sinmun* 20 August 1898.

52. Lydia Liu found that some of these neologisms were in fact first created by Western missionaries in China, were picked up by Japanese translators, and then retransmitted back to China. See her *Translingual Practice: Literature, National Culture, and Translated Modernity in China, 1900–37* (Stanford, Calif.: Stanford University Press, 1995).

53. These dictionaries and grammar books were readily available after 1905. Newspaper advertisements frequently announced Japanese dictionaries and grammar books such as the *Japanese-Korean Conversational Dictionary* (*Il-Han hoehwa sajŏn*) in *Hwangsŏng sinmun* 1 August 1906; *A Common Japanese Dictionary* (*Pot'ong Ilbon ŏjŏn*) in *Hwangsŏng sinmun* 24 December 1906; and *A Japanese Grammar* (*Ilbon munjŏn*) in *Hwangsŏng sinmun* 11 June 1909.

54. In a few exceptions, pure Korean words were offered as synonyms for and used interchangeably with a foreign neologism. The term *nara* for "nation" is one such case.

55. There were also remarkable similarities in layout design, the style and use of illustrations, advertising, and other visual features of newspapers.

56. Chŏng Chin-sok, *The Korea Problem in Anglo-Japanese Relations: Ernest Thomas Bethell and His Newspapers, the Daehan Maeil Sinbo and the Korean Daily News* (Seoul: Nanam Publications, 1987).

57. The *Hwangsŏng sinmun* started subscribing to Reuters in 1900.

58. *TaeHan maeil sinbo* 7 July 1906.

59. *TaeHan maeil sinbo* 1 April 1910.

60. *TaeHan maeil sinbo* 22 October 1909 and 23–34 May 1910; *Hwangsŏng sinmun* 24 February 1903.
61. *TaeHan maeil sinbo* 28 December 1909.
62. *TaeHan maeil sinbo* 17 October 1909.
63. *Hwangsŏng sinmun* 27 June 1907 and *TaeHan maeil sinbo* 7 July 1906.
64. For debates with the *Kanjō shimpo*, see *Hwangsŏng sinmun* 22–23 March 1905; with the *Chōsen shimpo*, see *Hwangsŏng sinmun* 7 October 1901, 28–31 January 1902, and 7 March 1907. See the opening of chapter 4 in this book for an example of the *TaiKan Nippo*, *TaeHan maeil sinbo* 10 March 1910. On the *Chōsen shimpo*, see Albert Altman, "Korea's First Newspaper: The Japanese *Chōsen Shimpo*," *Journal of Asian Studies* 43, no. 4 (August 1984): 685–96.
65. On Liang's influence in Korea, see Sin Sŭngha, "Ku Hanmal aeguk kyemong undong sigi Yang Kyecho (Liang Qichao) munjang ŭi chŏnip kwa kŭ yŏnghyang" (The Inception of Liang Qichao's Essays and Their Influence in the Period of the Patriotic Enlightenment Movement During the KuHanmal Period), *Asea yŏn'gu* 41, no. 2 (December 1998): 217–34.
66. *TaeHan maeil sinbo* 25–27 May 1905, *kisŏ*. The difficulty of translating such terms as "rights" is discussed in *Hwangsŏng sinmun* 7 May 1900.
67. One of the best examples of this process is the Korean use of the term *minjok*, as discussed in chapter 5.
68. Edward Said, *Orientalism* (New York: Random House, 1978).
69. *TaeHan maeil sinbo* 10 July 1907.
70. *Hwangsŏng sinmun* 17 July 1899.
71. *Hwangsŏng sinmun* 10 August 1903.
72. *Hwangsŏng sinmun* 15–21 February 1907.
73. *Hwangsŏng sinmun* 1 June 1906.
74. *Tongnip sinmun* 9 January 1897.
75. *Hwangsŏng sinmun* 22–23 May 1899.
76. *Hwangsŏng sinmun* 22–23 March 1905. For the Japanese-language press, see Yi Haech'ang, *Han'guk sinmunsa yŏn'gu* (*Essays on the History of Korean Newspapers*) (Seoul: Sŏngmun'gak, 1971), 279–319.
77. *Tongnip sinmun* 10–11 March 1899.
78. *Tongnip sinmun* 22 June 1897. See also the essay by Mun Ilpyŏng noting how England spread civilization to many countries by colonizing them, as reprinted in *TaeHan maeil sinbo* 9 November 1907, *pyŏlbo*.
79. *Tongnip sinmun* 31 August 1898.
80. *The Independent* 14 November, 1896.
81. *Tongnip sinmun* 28 December 1897 and 28 October 1898.
82. *Cheguk sinmun* 5 December 1902.
83. This was a common theme even well after 1905; see *TaeHan maeil sinbo* 5 September 1909.

84. *TaeHan maeil sinbo* 14 September 1904. The Japanese frequently made this comparison themselves, although after much controversy, they eventually prohibited the Korean publication of a history of Egypt in the belief that it was fanning anti-Japanese sentiment. For Japanese uses of this example, see Peter Duus, *The Abacus and the Sword: The Japanese Penetration of Korea, 1895– 1910* (Berkeley and Los Angeles: University of California Press, 1995), 134– 35. For a brief introduction to some of the controversy regarding Korean histories of Egypt, see Andre Schmid, "Censorship and the *Hwangsŏng sinmun,*" in *Korea Between Tradition and Modernity: Selected Papers from the Fourth Pacific and Asian Conference on Korean Studies,* ed. Chang Yun-shik et al. (Vancouver: Institute of Asian Research, 2000), 158–71.

85. *TaeHan maeil sinbo* 27 March 1909.

86. For a similar cautionary note using the examples of India, Egypt, Vietnam, and Persia, see *Tongnip sinmun* 15 December 1898.

87. *Tongnip sinmun* 30 January 1899.

88. *Hwangsŏng sinmun* 31 August — 3 September 1903.

89. For a wonderful example of this earlier cynicism as it applied to the issue of concession politics and "development," see the *Hwangsŏng sinmun* editorial that recounts the story of a Korean cow owner approached by three different foreigners, each of whom promises that if the owner allows them to use a part of the cow, they all will benefit. Of course, when the parts are taken, the cow dies. Confronted by a distraught owner, the foreigners responded that in harvesting the parts, "we all expended a great deal of capital. *That* is your profit" (my italics), 2 August 1902.

90. This was adapted from an essay by Liang Qichao, in *Hwangsŏng sinmun* 1–4 May 1907.

91. On Vietnam, see *Hwangsŏng sinmun* 18 August–5 September 1906 and 3–4 May 1906; on the Philippines, see *Hwangsŏng sinmun* 1 November 1906; and on Egypt, see *Hwangsŏng sinmun* 6 September 1905.

92. *TaeHan maeil sinbo* 29 March 1906.

93. *Yorozu chōhō* 28 August 1911.

94. *Yorozu chōhō* 7 September 1910.

95. *Tōkyō Asahi shimbun* 30 August 1910. Also see the illustrations in Alexis Dudden, "International Terms: Japan's Engagement in Colonial Control" (Ph.D. diss., University of Chicago, 1998), 134.

96. Itō Sadagorō, *Saikin no Chōsen oyobi Shina* (*Recent News About Korea and China*), as quoted in Sonia Ryang, "Japanese Travellers' Accounts of Korea," *East Asian History* 13–14 (June–December 1997): 133–52.

97. For some of the varieties of Japanese colonial discourse as expressed in travel writing, see Ryang, "Japanese Travellers' Accounts of Korea."

98. For example, the article "Kankoku Seitō no gensetsu" (Thoughts on Korean Political Factions), *Tōkyō Asahi shimbun* 9 July 1910.
99. "Chōsen zatsuwa II" (Desultory Notes on Korea), *Tōkyō Asahi shimbun* 25 August 1910.
100. "Chōsenjin no tokusei" (Special Characteristics of Koreans), *Tōkyō Asahi shimbun* 26 August 1910; also see "Gappeiseraru no Kankoku, IV" (Annexed Korea, IV), *Tōkyō Asahi shimbun* 27 August 1910.
101. *Tongnip sinmun* 10 April 1899.
102. *Tongnip sinmun* 15–17 April 1899.
103. *Tongnip sinmun* 13 February 1898.
104. *TaeHan maeil sinbo* 9 February 1910.
105. *TaeHan maeil sinbo* 22 July 1910.
106. *TaeHan maeil sinbo* 16 January and 25 September 1908.
107. One such editorial in the *Hwangsŏng sinmun* (31 March 1904) compared the passivity of Koreans with the more aggressive character of the Japanese.
108. *TaeHan maeil sinbo* 29 May 1908.
109. *Hwangsŏng sinmun* April 4, 1907.
110. Examples of the use of this term abound, see 21 February 1899 for one usage. Various other terms were used as well by the *Hwangsŏng sinmun* and other groups, such as "old Confucians" (*noyu*), 4 March 1899, *chappo*.
111. *Hwangsŏng sinmun* 26 January 1899.
112. *Hwangsŏng sinmun* 24 January 1900.
113. *Hwangsŏng sinmun* 7 January 1899.
114. *Hwangsŏng sinmun* 17 June 1899. This stress on their duty to the nation can also be seen on 22 December 1899.
115. *Hwangsŏng sinmun* 17 June 1899.
116. *Hwangsŏng sinmun* 30 May 1899.
117. *Hwangsŏng sinmun* 31 October 1899.
118. This tradition of critique had an even more venerable pedigree extending back to the famous essay by Han Yu, "Pengdanglun" (On Cabals). For a copy of this essay, see *Guwen guanzhi*. For a discussion of critiques in the Chosŏn dynasty, see JaHyun Kim Haboush, *A Heritage of Kings: One Man's Monarchy in the Confucian World* (New York: Columbia University Press, 1988), ch. 4.
119. *Hwangsŏng sinmun* 24 April 1906.
120. Other editorials in the *Hwangsŏng sinmun* on this issue appeared on 24 September 1898, 31 May 1899, 18 September 1899, 4 February 1902, 11 July 1902, 18–20 December 1902, and 6–7 August 1906. In the *Tongnip sinmun*, see 15 May 1897.
121. *Hwangsŏng sinmun* 9 January 1907, 20 February 1908, and 4 July 1908.
122. *TaeHan maeil sinbo* 1 December 1909, *chappo*.

123. *TaeHan maeil sinbo* 25 September 1908.

124. *TaeHan maeil sinbo* 23 March 1910.

125. When changes were noted, they often were related to Japanese influence, if not the direct result of the Japanese residential community.

126. For a strong statement about the inability to reform and its direct linkage as a reason for annexation, see *Maeil sinbo* 27 November and 8 December 1914.

127. *TaeHan maeil sinbo* 9 July 1908.

128. *Hwangsŏng sinmun* 20 December 1902.

129. Chang Chiyŏn, "Tanch'e yŏnhu minjok kabo" (After Uniting, the *minjok* Can Be Protected), *TaeHan chaganghoe wŏlbo* 5 (1906).

130. Hatada Takashi, *Nihonjin no Chōsenkan* (*Japanese Views of Korea*) (Tokyo: Keiso shobō, 1969): 125–249.

131. Hayashi Taisuke, *Chōsenshi* (Tokyo: Yoshikawa hanshichi, 1892), 1: preface, 1, and general introduction, 1–8.

132. For a comment on national character, see *Tōkyō Asahi shimbun* 29 August 1910; for the quotation, see "Gōhei seraru no Kankoku" (Annexed Korea), *Tōkyō Asahi shimbun* 24 August 1910. For other articles at this time dealing with *sadae*, see "Gappeiseraru besa Kankoku, VI" (Annexed Korea), *Tōkyō Asahi shimbun* 29 August 1910, and "Kokusai no jidaishugi" (Toadyism in the International Realm) *Tōkyō Asahi shimbun* 31 August 1910.

133. "Ōchō jidai to kyō no Chōsen" (The Dynastic Era and Today's Korea), *Tōkyō Asahi shimbun* 30–31 August 1910. For a similar argument pertaining to clothes, see "Narakō to Fujiwara jidai" (Nara and the Fujiwara Period), *Tōkyō Asahi shimbun* 29 August 1910.

134. *Maeil sinbo* 22 November 1914.

135. That the term *sadaejuŭi*, as opposed to the venerable term *sadae*, was originally Japanese was first pointed out to me by Professor Chŏng Okcha of Seoul National University.

136. This shift in terminology is most evident in the work of Sin Ch'aeho, who in his early years never used the term *sadaejuŭi*, although it appeared prominently in his later works.

137. *Hwangsŏng sinmun* 3 October 1904.

138. *Hwangsŏng sinmun* 1 October 1904.

139. *TaeHan maeil sinbo* 7 January 1910.

140. *TaeHan maeil sinbo* 21 February 1908.

141. *TaeHan maeil sinbo* 2 April 1908. This article was written by Sin Ch'aeho and focused on Son Pyŏngjun, for his activities with the Ilchinhoe; Cho Ch'aŭng, for his activities with the Tonga kaedo kyoyukhoe (Eastern Enlightenment Educational Association); and Sin Kisŏn, for his work with the Taedong hakhoe (Great Eastern Studies Association).

142. The Japanese indirectly gained control of the paper in June 1910, when the

British publisher of the paper, Alfred W. Marnham suddenly returned home, selling the paper to Yi Changhun. For a discussion of this issue, see Chŏng Chin-sok, "A Study of the *Maeil Sinbo* (*Daily News*) — Public Information Policy of the Japanese Imperialists and Korean Journalism Under Japanese Imperialism," *Journal of Social Sciences and Humanities* 52 (December 1980): 59–114. Observers from this time noticed that the critical tone of editorials was blunted thereafter; see Hwang Hyŏn, *Maech'ŏn yarok*, 439.

143. Chŏng Chin-sok, "A Study of the *Maeil Sinbo*," 1: preface, vi–vii.
144. *Maeil sinbo* 23 August 1911.
145. *Maeil sinbo* 25 March 1911.
146. *Maeil sinbo* 2 April 1911; also see 27 November 1914.
147. *Maeil sinbo* 19 February 1911.
148. *Maeil sinbo* 16–19 October 1910.
149. *Maeil sinbo* 16 February 1911.
150. *Maeil sinbo* 7 October 1910 and 18 July 1911.
151. *Maeil sinbo* 21 February 1911.
152. *Maeil sinbo* 3 September 1911.

4. Spirit, History, and Legitimacy

1. The Japanese article was translated as part of the editorial in *TaeHan maeil sinbo*, 10 March 1910. The Japanese article also complained about foreigners who believed that Korea was an ancient independent country and knew nothing about the two thousand years of Japanese-Korean relations. It demanded that "Japanese-Korean relations be clearly resolved and the room for misunderstandings be eliminated," a not so subtle criticism of Protectorate rule, rooted in a desire for formal annexation.
2. Pak Ŭnsik, *Han'guk t'ongsa* (*An Agonizing History of Korea*), in *Pak Ŭnsik chŏnsŏ* (*The Complete Works of Pak Ŭnsik*), ed. Tan'guk Taehakkyo Pusŏl Tongyanghak Yŏn'guso (Seoul: Tan'guk taehakkyo ch'ulp'anbu, 1975), 1: 196.
3. Ibid., 196–97.
4. For a very similar piece published as an editorial in the *TaeHan maeil sinbo*, see 19 February 1910.
5. Sin Yongha, *Pak Ŭnsik ŭi sahoe sasang yŏn'gu* (*Essays on the Social Thought of Pak Ŭnsik*) (Seoul: Sŏul taehakkyo ch'ulp'anbu, 1982), 212–15.
6. Partha Chatterjee, *Nationalist Thought and the Colonial World: A Derivative Discourse?* Of course, as we will see, most Korean nationalists would not agree with Chatterjee's position of the spiritual realm as an inviolable one, impenetrable by outside forces.
7. See *Hwangsŏng sinmun* 3 June 1908.

8. As quoted in Chŏng Kyo, *TaeHan kyenyŏnsa* (*History of the Waning Years of the TaeHan Empire*) (Seoul: Kuksa p'yŏnch'ansa, 1956), 2: 189–90. Also see Hwang Hyŏn, *Maech'ŏn yarok* (*Maech'ŏn's Unofficial History*) (Seoul: Kuksa p'yŏnch'an wiwŏnhoe, 1961), 354–56.

9. *TaeHan maeil sinbo* 3 December 1905.

10. See pages 94–95 for a discussion of this shutdown.

11. Subsequent anniversaries were also the subject of commemorative pieces. See *Hwangsŏng sinmun* 1 December 1906 and 1 December 1907.

12. *Hwangsŏng sinmun* 6 July 1906.

13. *Hwangsŏng sinmun* 7 July 1906. The chief editor at that time was Namgung Hun.

14. *Hwangsŏng sinmun* 17 July 1906.

15. *Hwangsŏng sinmun* 13 July 1906.

16. *TaeHan maeil sinbo* 5 July 1907. For some poems, see 18 July, 20 July, 21 July, 26 July, 31 July, 4 August, 12 August, 15 August, 16 August, and 17 August 1906.

17. See the ad signed by Ch'oe Namsŏn and Ch'oe Ch'angsŏn in *TaeHan maeil sinbo* 3 December 1905; also 5 and 7 December 1905.

18. Back page of the 17 July 1906 issue.

19. *TaeHan maeil sinbo* 1 October 1905, *kisŏ*. Yi is remembered for his notorious role as a leading official in concluding the Annexation Treaty of 1910.

20. *TaeHan maeil sinbo* 5 October 1905 and 8 October 1905, *kisŏ*; this point was also made by the *Hwangsŏng sinmun* 9 May 1906.

21. Some of these are collected in Han'gukhak munhŏn yŏn'guso, ed., *Han'guk kaehwagi kyo'gwasŏ ch'ongsŏ* (*A Collection of Textbooks from the Korean Enlightenment Period*), 20 vols. (Seoul: Asea munhwasa, 1977).

22. *Hwangsŏng sinmun* 17 November 1907.

23. *Hwangsŏng sinmun* 5 April 1906.

24. *TaeHan maeil sinbo* 29 March 1906.

25. *TaeHan maeil sinbo* 12 April 1906, *kiso*.

26. *TaeHan maeil sinbo* 13–15 April 1906, *kiso*.

27. Ibid.

28. For a general treatment, see *Hwangsŏng sinmun* 6 February 1907 and *TaeHan maeil sinbo* 29 June 1910 and 29 July 1910; for *kuksŏng*, see *Hwangsŏng sinmun* 22 August 1909 and *Sŏbuk hakhoe wŏlbo* 18 (1 December 1909): 35–37; for *chŏngsin*, see *Hwangsŏng sinmun* 20 March 1908 and *TaeHan maeil sinbo* 29 April 1909 and 7 February 1909; for *kukhon*, see *TaeHan maeil sinbo* 9 November 1909, 2 November 1909, and *Hwangsŏng sinmun* 31 July 1907 and 20 March 1908; and for *kuksu*, *TaeHan maeil sinbo* see 13 January 1910, 25 October 1905, *kiso*, and 13 February 1908.

29. See pages 77–80 for a discussion of these works as they relate to the concept of legitimacy.

30. *Hwangsŏng sinmun* 24 November 1902.
31. John S. Brownlee, *Political Thought in Japanese Historical Writing: From Kojiki (712) to Tokushi Yoron (1712)* (Waterloo: McMaster University Press, 1991).
32. *Kojiki*, trans. Donald L. Philippi (Tokyo: University of Tokyo Press, 1968), book 2, ch. 92.
33. Ibid., book 2, ch. 94.
34. For a historical overview of research on this myth, see William Wayne Farris, *Sacred Texts and Buried Treasures: Issues in the Historical Archaeology of Ancient Japan* (Honolulu: University of Hawai'i Press, 1998), ch. 2.
35. For this account, see *Nihongi: Chronicles of Japan from the Earliest Times to* A.D. 697, trans. W. G. Aston (London: Allen & Unwin, 1956), 221–53.
36. As quoted in W. G. Aston, trans., *Nihongi*, 232.
37. Ibid., 295–96, 349–50, 353–55.
38. One example is in the twelfth-century *Mizukagami* (*The Water Mirror*), which repeated Jingū's conquest of the peninsular kingdoms in much the same vein as first recorded in the *Kojiki*. See Brownlee, *Political Thought in Japanese Historical Writing*, 52; and Farris, *Sacred Texts and Buried Treasures*, ch. 2.
39. In English, see John S. Brownlee, *Japanese Historians and the National Myths, 1600–1945: The Age of Gods and Emperor Jinmu* (Vancouver: University of British Columbia Press, 1997), 61–70; Bob Tadashi Wakabayashi, *Anti-Foreignism and Western Learning in Early-Modern Japan: The New Theses of 1825* (Cambridge, Mass.: Harvard University Press, 1986), 35–40; and Hatada Takashi, *Nihonjin no Chōsenkan* (*Japanese Views of Korea*) (Tokyo: Keiso shobō, 1969): 229–31.
40. Miyake Hidetoshi, *Ilbon'in ŭi Han'gukkwan* (*Japanese Views of Korea*), trans. Ha U'bong (Seoul: Pulp'it, 1994), 109–12.
41. There was the odd exception, as William Wayne Farris has pointed out. Naka Michio and Tsuda Sōkichi are especially important in this regard, though even Tsuda maintained there was evidence supporting the existence of Mimana in the southern peninsula. See Farris, *Sacred Texts and Buried Treasures*, 60–63.
42. Shigeno Yasutsugu, Kume Kunitake, and Hoshino Hisashi, *Kokushikan* (*A National History*), 7 vols. (Tokyo: Taiseikan, 1890). On the advent of cause-and-effect history, see Thomas Keirstead, "Nation and Postnation in Japan: Global Capitalism and the Idea of National History," in *Nation Work: Asian Elites and National Identities*, ed. Timothy Brook and Andre Schmid (Ann Arbor: University of Michigan Press, 2000), 239.
43. Shigeno, Kume, and Hoshino, *Kokushikan*, 1: 15–20.
44. For Shiratori's work on Korea, see the first and third volumes of his complete works, *Shiratori Kurakichi zenshū* (Tokyo: Iwanami shoten, 1969–71).
45. See Shiratori's article "Wagaga jōko ni okeru Kanhantō no seiryoku o ronzu"

(Concerning Our Power on the Korean Peninsula in Ancient Times) *Chūō kōron* (October 1910): 44–55.

46. Yamaguchi Shōichirō, "Ni-Kan tōitsu fukko no gi," *Taiyō* 16, no. 1 (1910): 74–80.

47. "Chōsen zatsuwa I" (Desultory Notes on Korea, I), *Tōkyō Asahi shimbun* 24 August 1910.

48. *Tōkyō Asahi shimbun* 29 August 1910.

49. "Gappei no seisaku" (Policy After the Annexation of Korea), *Tōkyō Asahi shimbun* 25 August 1910.

50. *Hwangsŏng sinmun* 19 February 1908.

51. Kim T'aegyŏng, *Yŏksa kyeryak* (A *Short History*), reprinted in *Han'guk kaehwagi kyo'gwasŏ ch'ongsŏ* (A *Collection of Textbooks from the Korean Enlightenment Period*), ed. Han'gukhak munhŏn yŏn'guso (Seoul: Asea munhwasa, 1977), 15: 76.

52. *Hwangsŏng sinmun* 25 January 1902.

53. Kim T'aegyŏng, *Yŏksa kyeryak*, 6.

54. Ibid., 75.

55. Ibid., 84.

56. Ibid., 76–77.

57. For further discussion of this work, see pages 202–13. Published under the title *TaeHan kangyŏkko* and reprinted in *Wiam Chang Chiyŏn Chŏnsŏ* (*The Complete Works of Chang Chiyŏn*) (Seoul: Tan'guk taehakkyo ch'ulp'ansa, 1981), vol. 3.

58. *Wiam Chang Chiyŏn Chŏnsŏ*, preface, 6–7, and compilation guidelines, 1.

59. Ibid., 2: 47–54.

60. Ibid., 2: 50. For trade relations and a discussion of the "Japan House" during the late Chosŏn dynasty, see Ronald Toby, *State and Diplomacy in Early Modern Japan: Asia in the Development of the Tokugawa Bakufu* (Princeton, N.J.: Princeton University Press, 1984). For some conflicting interpretations of Chang's work, see P'ae Chahyŏk, "Chang Chiyŏn ŭi sasŏ chŏsul kwa yŏksagwan" (Chang Chiyŏn's Historical Narratives and Perspective), 308–62, and Yi Hunok, "Chang Chiyŏn ŭi yŏksa insik" (Chang Chiyŏn's Historical Understanding), 249–307, both in Chŏn Kwanu et al., *Wiam Chang Chiyŏn ŭi sasang kwa hwaltong* (*The Thought and Activities of Chang Chiyŏn*) (Seoul: Minŭmsa, 1993).

61. For example, Yi Minsu, trans., *Abang kangyŏkko* (*An Investigation of Our Nation's Territory*) (Seoul: Pŏmusa, 1995).

62. Hayashi Taisuke, *Chōsenshi* (*Korean History*) (Tokyo: Yoshikawa hanshichi, 1892), and *Chōsen kinseishi* (*Early Modern Korean History*) (Tokyo: Yoshikawa hanshichi, 1900).

63. Hyŏn Ch'ae, *Tongguk saryak* (A Brief History of Korea) (1908, reprinted in

Han'guk kaehwagi kyo'gwasŏ ch'ongsŏ (*A Collection of Textbooks from the Korean Enlightenment Period*), ed. Han'gukhak munhŏn yŏn'guso (Seoul: Asea munhwasa, 1977), 16: *chŏn* 1, 3. Originally printed in 1905, the 1908 edition is reprinted in this series.

64. Cho Tonggŏl, "Hanmal sasŏ wa kŭŭi kyemongjuŭijŏk hŏsil" (The Strengths and Weaknesses of Enlightenment History Books in the Hanmal Period), in Cho Tonggŏl, *Han'guk minjokchuŭi ŭi sŏngnip kwa tongnip undongsa yŏn'gu* (*Studies of the Rise of Korean Nationalism and the Independence Movement*) (Seoul: Chisik san'opsa, 1989), 190–97.

65. The *Hwangsŏng sinmun* had early on welcomed the "newly arriving Japanese histories" but had warned that they were "full of mistakes." See 24 November 1902.

66. Hyŏn Ch'ae, *Tongguk saryak*, *chŏn* 1, 29. Much later, Hyŏn reversed his position on this issue, writing a serialized history about this myth and its significance for early Korean history in the *Maeil sinbo*. See Chu Chino, "Kim Taegyŏng, Hyŏn Ch'ae," in *Han'guk ŭi yŏksaga wa yŏksahak* (*Korean Historians and Historiography*), ed. Cho Tonggŏl, Han Yŏngu, and Pak Ch'an sŭng (Seoul: Ch'angjak kwa pip'yŏngsa, 1994), 2: 41.

67. Hyŏn Ch'ae, *Tongguk saryak*, *chŏn* 1, 4. Hyŏn also moved to diminish the elements of what Hayashi called *sadae* tendencies in Korean history, doing so at the outset of the *Tongguk saryak* in his section on the origins of Korea. Hayashi had dismissed accounts that located the origins of Korea in the figure of Tan'gun as unbelievable "nonsense" (*kōtō*), choosing instead to follow the pattern of Chinese historical sources which allocated the founding role of the nation to the Shang-dynasty refugee, Kija (Ch. Jizi, J. Kishi). But Hyŏn, contributing to what amounted to a renaissance of studies of Tan'gun in these years, opened by presenting Tan'gun as the figure who first established a kingdom in the East. See *Tongguk saryak*, *chŏn* 1, 1 and 19–20. I treat the question of Tan'gun more extensively in the following chapter.

68. Hyŏn Ch'ae, *Tongguk saryak*, *chŏn* 3, 34–64.

69. Hayashi Taisuke, *Chōsen kinseishi*, 2: 96.

70. Hyŏn Ch'ae, *Tongguk saryak*, *chŏn* 4, 71.

71. Hyŏn Ch'ae, *Tongguk saryak*, *chŏn* 4, 101.

72. For example, Sin Ch'aeho.

73. Chu Chino, "Kim T'aegyong, Hyŏn Ch'ae," 2: 40.

74. For another editorial dealing with Jingū and textbooks, see *TaeHan maeil sinbo* 28–29 January 1909, and on the problem of translations and Korean history, see 9 January 1909.

75. *TaeHan maeil sinbo* 27 October 1908.

76. The fourth king of Silla, ruling from A.D. 57–80.

77. Most important, Sin Ch'aeho's "Toksa sillon," discussed in the next chapter.

78. See these instructions serialized as "Kyosusang ŭi chuŭi" (Points of Attention for Teachers), *Maeil sinbo* 22 February–3 March 1911.
79. "Kankoku no gappei to kokushi" (The Annexation of Korea and National History), *Tōkyō Asahi shimbun* 9 September 1910.
80. For more discussion of these theories, see Peter Duus, *The Abacus and the Sword: The Japanese Penetration of Korea, 1895–1910* (Berkeley and Los Angeles: University of California Press, 1995), ch. 11.
81. *Maeil sinbo* 16–24 March 1911.
82. *Maeil sinbo* 16 March 1911.
83. *Maeil sinbo* 17 March 1911.
84. For a study of the work of some of the cultural anthropologists, see Ch'oe Sŏgyŏng, *Ilche tonghwa idaeollogi ŭi ch'angch'ul (The Emergence of Japanese Colonial Assimilation Ideology)* (Seoul: Sŏgyŏng munhwasa, 1997); and for the work of archaeologists, see Pai Hyung Il, *Constructing "Korean" Origins: A Critical Review of Archaeology, Historiography, and Racial Myth in Korean State-Formation Theories* (Cambridge, Mass.: Harvard University Press, 2000).
85. Harry Emerson Wilde, *Japan in Crisis* (New York: Macmillan, 1934), 201.
86. Bruce Cumings, "Archaeology, Descent, Emergence: Japan in British/ American Hegemony, 1900–50," in *Japan in the World*, ed. Masao Miyoshi and H. D. Harootunian (Durham, N.C.: Duke University Press, 1993), 79–111.
87. This was not a surprising reaction, since most Western powers were concerned about annexation only insofar as it might damage their commercial relations. See "British Fear Loss of Korean Trade," *New York Times* 28 August 1910. Reassurance was one of the primary motives for the English-language yearbooks put out by colonial authorities in the early years. See the various Government General of Chōsen, *Annual Reports on Reforms and Progress in Chōsen (Korea)*.
88. In the *Tōkyō Asahi shimbun* alone, see 25 August for France and China; 27 August for Germany and Britain; 28 and 29 August for Britain and Russia; 29 August for the United States; 30 August for an editorial on British reactions; 31 August for China; 1 September for the United States, China, Britain, Russia, and France; 3 September for Russia and the United States; and 7 September for an editorial entitled "Gappei to rekkoku" (Annexation and the Powers).
89. Alexis Dudden, "International Terms: Japan's Engagement in Colonial Control" (Ph.D. diss., University of Chicago, 1998).
90. Government General of Chōsen, *Annual Report on Reforms and Progress in Chōsen (Korea), 1918–21* (Seoul: Government General of Chōsen, 1922), 32–36.
91. Government General of Chōsen, *Annual Report on Reforms and Progress in Chōsen (Korea), 1917–18* (Seoul: Government General of Chōsen, 1920), between 60 and 61.

92. Government General of Chōsen, *Annual Report on Reforms and Progress in Chōsen (Korea)*, 1918–21, 1–3.

93. Government General of Chōsen, *Annual Report on Reforms and Progress in Chōsen (Korea)*, 1917–18, xi–xiii.

94. Government General of Chōsen, *Annual Report on Reforms and Progress in Chōsen (Korea)*, 1916–17 (Seoul: Government General of Chōsen, 1918), xii–xiii.

95. See H. B. Drake, *Korea of the Japanese* (London: John Lane, The Bodley Head, 1930), 4–5. Other semiofficial institutions also took up this publicity tactic, see the Bank of Chōsen's publication, T. Hoshino, *Economic History of Chosen* (Seoul: Bank of Chōsen, 1921).

96. Itō Hirobumi, "Japanese Policy in Korea," *Harper's Weekly* 11 January 1908, 27.

97. Motosada Zumoto, "The Passing of Korea," *The Independent* 69 (18 August 1910): 448.

98. Viscount Masatake Terauchi, His Imperial Japanese Majesty's Residency General, "Reforms and Progress in Korea," in *Korea: Its History, Its People and Its Commerce*, ed. Angus Hamilton, Herbert H. Austin, and Masatake Terauchi (Boston and Tokyo: J. B. Millet, 1910), 217–309.

99. Saito Makoto, "A Message from the Imperial Japanese Government to the American People: Home Rule for Korea?" *The Independent*, 31 January 1920, 167–69.

100. K. Asakawa, "Korea and Manchuria Under the New Treaty," *Atlantic Monthly* (November 1905): 699–711.

101. Adachi Kinnosuke, "The Japanese in Korea," *Review of Reviews* (October 1907): 472–75.

102. Midori Komatzu, "Religious Liberty in Korea," *Missionary Review* (December 1916): 891–913. This article was commissioned by the journal editors. The author is identified as the commissioner of foreign affairs for the Government General of Chōsen.

103. I. Yamagata, "The Korean Annexation: A Japanese View," *Outlook* 1 February 1922, 185–87.

104. T. Ikeda, Chief Engineer for Water Supply, "Rice in Chōsen," *Far Eastern Review* (July 1927): 313 and 316; Count Okuma, "Japan's Policy in Korea," *Forum* (April 1906): 571–80.

105. A self-characterization made, symbolically, while in Seoul. See his speech as reported in the *Seoul Press*, 20 April 1907.

106. *Seoul Press* 20 April 1907.

107. George Trumbell Ladd, *In Korea with Marquis Ito* (London: Longmans, Green, 1908), 5.

108. Ibid., 14.

109. Ladd's essay, "The Annexation of Korea: An Essay in 'Benevolent Assimila-

tion,'" *Yale Review* (1911–12): 639–56; his letters to the *New York Times*, 5 April, 13 May, and 2 November 1908; and his speeches in Korea, *Seoul Press* 20 April 1907, "Five Elements of National Prosperity," to the YMCA at Independence Hall on 25 April 1907; and to the Ladies Patriotic Association of Japan, 27 April 1907.

110. Major Herbert H. Austin, "A Scamper Through Korea," in *Korea: Its History, Its People and Its Commerce*, ed. Angus Hamilton, Herbert H. Austin, and Masatake Terauchi (Boston and Tokyo: J. B. Millet, 1910), 153–214.

111. F. A. McKenzie, *The Tragedy of Korea* (London: Hodder & Stoughton, 1908), 211.

112. *TaeHan maeil sinbo* 23 October 1906. This editorial also takes Kennan to task for his comments on China.

113. *TaeHan maeil sinbo* 5 April 1910.

114. Many foreign travelers and short-term residents reported precisely this type of experience, as individual Koreans tried to enlist their support to publicize their national case. Yet even with those sympathetic to their cause, such urgings rarely produced unambiguous calls for Korean independence. H. B. Drake describes being approached by three of his students who, in exactly the same way as urged by the *TaeHan maeil sinbo* twenty-odd years before, asked that he write about Korea's predicament in English newspapers. He did, exhibiting a clear fondness for the country, but still writing of the necessity of Japanese colonial control. See *Korea of the Japanese*, preface.

115. *TaeHan maeil sinbo* 14 August 1906.

116. Bethell explained at his later trial that he had been favorably disposed to the Japanese effort but that after seeing self-serving policies such as the Nagamori land deal, he turned against the Japanese presence. See Chŏng Chin-sok, *The Korea Problem in Anglo-Japanese Relations: Ernest Thomas Bethell and His Newspapers, the Daehan Maeil Sinbo and the Korean Daily News* (Seoul: Nanam Publications, 1987), 66.

117. Chŏng, *The Korea Problem in Anglo-Japanese Relations*, 180–81.

118. Ibid.

119. McKenzie, *The Tragedy of Korea*, 214. Another purpose of the *Seoul Press* was to act as a voice of praise and defense for Itō Hirobumi. See the editorials on 9 April, 5 May, and 27 August 1907.

120. "Misguided Patriotism," *Seoul Press* 8 March 1907.

121. "Speak Well of Your Friends," *Seoul Press* 28 May 1907; and "The Sensational Newspaper," *Seoul Press* 4 May 1907.

122. "Korea's 'Friends,'" *Seoul Press* 9 March 1907.

123. "The Test of Friendship," *Seoul Press* 28 July 1907. The *Seoul Press* also regularly disputed specific reports that appeared in the *Korea Daily News*; see 16–

17 July 1907 and 20–24 August 1907. The *TaeHan maeil sinbo* responded by attacking the *Seoul Press* as well; see 18 December 1906.

124. Chŏng, *The Korea Problem in Anglo-Japanese Relations*, 219.

125. There were other critical publications, including Homer Hulbert's English periodical, *Korea Review.*

126. Some missionaries relied largely on Chinese classical sources. See Homer Hulbert, *History of Korea* (Seoul: Methodist Publishing House, 1905); and James Scarth Gale, *A History of the Korean People* (Seoul: Royal Asiatic Society, 1972).

127. Joseph H. Longford, *The Story of Korea* (London: T. Fisher Unwin, 1911), and *The Story of Old Japan* (New York: Longmans, Green, 1910).

128. F. Brinkley also wrote his history of Japan in collaboration with Baron Kikuchi, dedicating it to the memory of the Meiji emperor. See *A History of the Japanese People: From the Earliest Times to the End of the Meiji Era* (New York: Encyclopedia Britannica, 1915).

129. Longford, *The Story of Korea*, 93–94.

130. Longford, *The Story of Korea*, 93–94.

131. Ibid., 100.

132. Ibid., 365.

133. See, for example, James Murdoch, *A History of Japan* (Yokohama: Kelly & Walsh, 1910), vol. 1; Angus Hamilton, *Korea* (London: William Heineman, 1904), 129; and Capt. F. Brinkley, with the collaboration of Baron Kikuchi, *A History of the Japanese People*, 88–91.

5. Narrating the Ethnic Nation

1. *TaeHan maeil sinbo* 17 June 1908, kisŏ.

2. One exception to this has been noted by Peng Yingming. In the classical text the *Liji*, the term *minzu* does appear as a word for a clan or extended family, but never as the national collective. See Peng Yingming, "Guanyu woguo minzu gainian lishi de chubu kaocha" (A Preliminary Investigation of the History of Our Country's Concept of Minzu), *Minzu yanjiu* 2 (1985): 5–11.

3. One important line in the genealogy of this term for East Asia was Kato Hiroyuki's translation of Johann Kasper Bluntschli's *The Theory of the State* (*Allgemeines Staatsrecht*). Published as *Kokuhō hanron*, Kato rendered Bluntschli's threefold distinction of *stat*, *volk*, and *nation* with the character combinations of *kokka*, *kokumin*, and *minzoku*. This was later picked up by Liang Qichao in his translation of Bluntschli's work, although Liang typically does not cite Kato's essay. See Liang Qichao, "Zhengzhixue dajia Bolunzhili zhi xuesho" (The Theories of the Great Politics Scholar, Bluntschli), in his *Yinbingshi wenji* (*Selected Works of Liang Qichao*) (Kunming: Zhonghua

shuju, 1941), 10: 31–49. For Liang's reading of Kato Hiroyuki's work, see Philip C. Huang, *Liang Ch'i-ch'ao and Modern Chinese Liberalism* (Seattle: University of Washington Press, 1972), 56–64. Liang's 1902 essay, "Xinminshuo," made *minzu* a key category in his discussion of citizenship; see *Yinbingshi wenji*, 12–14 *juan*.

4. Peng Yingming has identified the earliest use of the term as being in an essay published by Wang Dao around 1874. Wang was a scholar who worked for many years with Western missionaries. Peng believes that the term may have been a translation from English, suggesting the term was coined independently from Japanese usage. However, as he points out, Wang did not continue to use the term regularly in his later writing, and it did not gain currency in Chinese intellectual circles during these years. See Peng Yingming, "Guanyu woguo minzu gainian lishi de chubu kaocha." Later usages of the term can be found in the Chinese newspaper *Qiangxuebao* in 1895, according to Han Jinchun and Li Yinfun, "Hanwen 'minzu' yici de chuxian ji qichuqi shiyong qingkuang" (The First Appearance of the Chinese Term "Minzu" and Its Early Use), *Minzu yanjiu* 2 (1984): 36–43.

5. Henry Em discusses one famous such passage by Son Chint'ae; see Henry Em, "Minjok as a Modern and Democratic Construct: With a Focus on Sin Ch'aeho's Historiography," in *Colonial Modernity in Korea*, ed. Gi-wook Shin and Michael Robinson (Cambridge, Mass.: Harvard University Press, 1999), 337.

6. *Hwangsŏng sinmun* 12 January 1900.

7. *Hwangsŏng sinmun* 20 June 1907.

8. Yu Kilchun, *TaeHan munjŏn* (*Korean Grammar*), in *Yu Kilchun chŏnsŏ* (*The Complete Works of Yu Kilchun*), ed. Yu Kilchun chŏnsŏ p'yŏnch'an wiwŏnhoe (Seoul: Ilchogak, 1996), 2: 1.

9. For a translation of the *Samguk yusa's* account of Tan'gun, see Iryŏn, *Samguk Yusa: Legends and History of the Three Kingdoms of Korea*, trans. Tae-hung Ha and Grafton Mintz (Seoul: Yonsei University Press, 1972), 32–33.

10. For a selection of some of these disparate views, see Yi Kibaek, ed., *Tan'gun sinhwa nonjip* (*Essays on the Tan'gun Myth*) (Seoul: Saemunsa, 1988); on the treatment of Tan'gun by archaeologists, see Pai Hyung Il, *Constructing "Korean" Origins: A Critical Review of Archaeology, Historiography, and Racial Myth in Korean State-Formation Theories* (Cambridge, Mass.: Harvard University Press, 2000), ch. 3.

11. For a discussion of the origins of this method, see Yi Yusŏng, "Yijo hugi kŭn'gi hakpa e issŏsŏ ŭi chŏngt'ongnon ŭi chŏn'gae" (The Development of Theories of Legitimacy During the Late Chosŏn Dynasty by the Kun'gi Group), in *Han'guk ŭi yŏksa insik* (*Understanding Korean History*), ed. Yi Yusŏng and Kang Man'gil (Seoul: Changch'ak kwa Pip'yŏngsa, 1976), 2: 356–62.

12. JaHyun Kim Haboush deals with this shifting sense of identity after the rise of the Qing dynasty, in *A Heritage of Kings: One Man's Monarchy in the Confucian World* (New York: Columbia University Press, 1988), ch. 1, and "Constructing the Center: The Ritual Controversy and the Search for a New Identity in Seventeenth Century Korea," in *Culture and the State in Late Choson Korea,* ed. JaHyun Kim Haboush and Martina Deuchler (Cambridge, Mass.: Harvard University Press, 1999), 46–90.

13. Han Yǒngu, *Chosǒn chǒn'gi sahoe sasang yǒn'gu (Essays on the Social Ideology of the Early Chosǒn Dynasty)* (Seoul: Chisik San'opsa, 1983), 229–272.

14. For an account of the pursuit of Confucian reform, see Martina Deuchler, *Confucian Transformation of Korea: A Study of Society and Ideology* (Cambridge, Mass.: Harvard University Press, 1992).

15. Han Yǒngu pays careful attention to the role of Tan'gun and Kija in his survey of late Chosǒn historiography, *Chosǒn hugi sahaksa yǒn'gu (Essays on the Historiography of the Late Chosǒn Dynasty)* (Seoul: Ilchisa, 1989).

16. Ministry of Education, ed., *Chosǒn yǒktae sayak (A Brief History of Korea)* (Seoul: Ministry of Education, 1895), in *Han'guk kaehwagi kyo'gwasǒ ch'ongsǒ (A Collection of Textbooks from the Korean Enlightenment Period),* ed. Han'gukhak munhǒn yǒn'guso (Seoul: Asea munhwasa, 1977), vol. 11, 2.

17. A number of historians in Korea have harshly criticized these textbook writers for attempting such a project, arguing that such narratives were inappropriate to the needs of the modern nation and that many of their individual narrative devices were even less progressive than those of their more advanced late-Chosǒn-dynasty counterparts. See Cho Tonggǒl, "Hanmal saso wa kǔǔi kyemongjuǔijok hǒsil" (The Strengths and Weaknesses of Enlightenment History Books in the Hanmal Period), in Cho Tonggǒl, *Han'guk minjokchuǔi ǔi sǒngnip kwa tongnip undongsa yǒn'gu (Studies of the Rise of Korean Nationalism and the Independence Movement)* (Seoul: Chisik san'opsa, 1989), 141–217.

18. The Three Han Legitimacy Theory drew the descent from Tan'gun to Kija and then to the Southern Court of Mahan, whereas the less commonly used Three Chosǒn Legitimacy Theory moved from Tan'gun to Kija to the northern court of Wiman Chosǒn. For uses of the latter, see Hyǒn Ch'ae's *Pot'ong kyogwa Tongguk yǒksa (An Ordinary Textbook History of Korea)* (Seoul: Ministry of Education, 1898), reprinted in *Han'guk kaehwagi kyo'gwasǒ ch'ongsǒ (A Collection of Textbooks from the Korean Enlightenment Period),* ed. Han'gukhak munhǒn yǒn'guso (Seoul: Asea munhwasa, 1977), 14: 1–362.

19. Ministry of Education, ed., *Chosǒn yǒksa* (Seoul: Ministry of Education, 1895), in *Han'guk kaehwagi kyo'gwasǒ ch'ongsǒ (A Collection of Textbooks from the Korean Enlightenment Period),* ed. Han'gukhak munhǒn yǒn'guso (Seoul: Asea munhwasa, 1977), 11: 1–265.

20. Pak Chǒngdong, *Ch'odǔng Taedong yǒksa (An Elementary History of Korea)*

(Seoul: Tongmunsa, 1909), reprinted in *Han'guk kaehwagi kyo'gwasŏ ch'ongsŏ* (*A Collection of Textbooks from the Korean Enlightenment Period*), ed. Han'gukhak munhŏn yŏn'guso (Seoul: Asea munhwasa, 1977), 17: 3.

21. Chŏng Inho. *Ch'odŭng TaeHan yŏksa* (*An Elementary History of Korea*) (Seoul, 1908), reprinted in *Han'guk kaehwagi kyo'gwasŏ ch'ongsŏ* (*A Collection of Textbooks from the Korean Enlightenment Period*), ed. Han'gukhak munhŏn yŏn'guso (Seoul: Asea munhwasa, 1977), 14: 2 and 4.

22. See Ministry of Education, ed., *Kungmin sohak tokpon* (Seoul: Ministry of Education, 1895), in *Han'guk kaehwagi kyo'gwasŏ ch'ongsŏ* (*A Collection of Textbooks from the Korean Enlightenment Period*), ed. Han'gukhak munhŏn yŏn'guso, *chŏn* 1: 24. Such phrases were also used to describe the meeting at Tosan, as in Ch'oe Kyŏnghwan and Chŏng Kyo, eds., *Taedong yŏksa* (*History of the Great East*) (Seoul, 1905), reprinted in *Han'guk kaehwagi kyo'gwasŏ ch'ongsŏ* (*A Collection of Textbooks from the Korean Enlightenment Period*), ed. Han'gukhak munhŏn yŏn'guso (Seoul: Asea munhwasa, 1977), 17: 1–434.

23. Ch'oe Kyŏnghwan and Chŏng Kyo, eds., *Taedong yŏksa*, 44–45.

24. Pak Chŏngdong, *Ch'odŭng Taedong yŏksa*, 2. For the royal house, which, through the Ministry of Education, was sponsoring these textbooks, such histories served its goal of making the court the foremost symbol of the nationalist movement. King Kojong, these all implied, was the legitimate heir of a historical entity that now joined court and nation.

25. According to the McCune-Reischauer romanization, this should be spelled TanGi, but to make it easy to identify the second syllable, I have left it as "Ki."

26. *Hwangsŏng sinmun* 21 April 1909 and 21 November 1909.

27. For one example, see *TaeHan maeil sinbo* 1 January 1908.

28. *TaeHan maeil sinbo* 17 June 1908.

29. No Yidan, "Kukka ŭi yaksan" (The Nation's Medicine Mountain), *Sŏbuk hakhoe wŏlbo* 11 (April 1909): 35. As this article shows, the same claim could be made for Kija, although the journal rarely used this option.

30. Paengnam Sanin, "Kungminhak kwa mujirhak" (Citizenship and Materialism), *Sŏbuk hakhoe wŏlbo* 7 (December 1908): 5.

31. "Tan'gun Ka" (Ode to Tan'gun), *TaeHan maeil sinbo* 6 August 1909, *sajo*; and see the poetry column for 11 January 1910.

32. This treatment of Sin's essay has been helped by Henry Em, "Minjok as a Modern and Democratic Construct: With a Focus on Sin Ch'aeho's Historiography," in *Colonial Modernity in Korea*, ed. Gi-wook Shin and Michael Robinson (Cambridge, Mass.: Harvard University Press, 1999), 336–61; Michael Robinson, "National Identity in the Thought of Sin Ch'aeho," *Journal of Korean Studies* 5 (1984): 121–42; Han Yŏngu, "Hanmal Sin Ch'aeho ŭi minjokchuŭi saron" (Sin Ch'aeho's Nationalist History During the Hanmal Period), in his *Han'guk minjokchuŭi yŏksahak* (*Nationalist Historiography in*

Korea) (Seoul: Ilchogak, 1993), 39–84; Chong Ch'angnyŏl, "Hanmal ŭi yŏksa insik" (Historical Understanding in the Hanmal Period), in *Han'guk sahak yŏn'gu* (*Studies of Korean Historiography*), ed. Han'guksa yŏn'guhoe (Seoul: Ulyu munhwasa, 1991), 187–228; Sin Yongha, "Sin Ch'aeho ŭi ch'ogi minjokchuŭi sagwan kwa hugi minjokchuŭi sagwan" (Sin Ch'aeho's Early and Late Nationalist History) in his *Han'guk kŭndae sahoe sasangsa yŏn'gu* (*Modern Korean Social Thought*) (Seoul: Ilchisa, 1987), 438–81; Yi Manyŏl, *Tanjae Sin Ch'aeho ŭi yŏksahak yŏn'gu* (*Studies of the Historiography of Tanjae Sin Ch'aeho*) (Seoul: Munhak kwa pip'yŏngsa, 1990).

33. Sin Ch'aeho, "Toksa sillon" (A New Reading of History), in *Tanjae Sin Ch'aeho chŏnjip* (*The Complete Works of Sin Ch'aeho*), ed. Tanjae Sin Ch'aeho chŏnjip p'yŏnch'an wiwŏnhoe (Seoul: Hyŏngsŏl ch'ulp'ansa, 1987), 1: 471.

34. Ibid., 472.

35. Ibid., 472.

36. On social Darwinism, see James Pusey, *China and Charles Darwin* (Cambridge, Mass.: Harvard University Press, 1982).

37. Sin Ch'aeho, "Toksa sillon," 474.

38. Ibid., 496. This section runs from 494 to 498.

39. Sin Ch'aeho, "Toksa sillon," 497.

40. Pai Hyung Il has noted this similarity, although she offers a different argument. See her *Constructing "Korean" Origins*, ch. 2.

41. Edward Wagner, "The Korean *Chokpo* as a Historical Source," in *Studies in Asian Genealogy*, ed. Spencer J. Palmer (Provo, Utah: Brigham Young University Press, 1972), 141–52.

42. Ibid., 146.

43. Prasenjit Duara, *Rescuing History from the Nation: Questioning Narratives of Modern China* (Chicago: University of Chicago Press, 1995), chs. 1 and 2.

44. For a discussion of Ŭlchi, see 63–64.

45. Another common, but more organic, metaphor was that of the nation as a body. See *Tongnip sinmun* 3 August 1897 and 10 February 1897.

46. *Tongnip sinmun* 20 July 1898 and 9 May 1899.

47. *Tongnip sinmun* 9 May 1899 and 23 May 1896.

48. *Tongnip sinmun* 20 April 1899. Also see the use of household metaphors by the *Hwangsŏng sinmun*, as discussed in pages 89–91.

49. *Hwangsŏng sinmun* 23 November 1900; also see 31 August 1909.

50. *TaeHan maeil sinbo* 31 July 1908.

51. *TaeHan maeil sinbo* 13 May 1909.

52. *TaeHan maeil sinbo* 31 July 1908

53. *TaeHan maeil sinbo* 13 May 1909.

54. "Yŏksa wa aeguksim ŭi kwan'gye" (The Relationship Between History and Patriotism), *TaeHan hyŏphoebo* 3 (June 1908).

55. *Hwangsŏng sinmun* 9 August 1910. Also see 21 April 1909.
56. *Hwangsŏng sinmun* 10 August 1910.
57. Sin Ch'aeho, "Toksa sillon," 486–88.
58. Ibid., 487.
59. Ibid., 481–82.
60. Ibid., 481–86.
61. Ibid., 471.
62. This was the impetus for the Kabo reforms.
63. This was true of the *Hwangsŏng sinmun* and the *Ŭibyŏng*.
64. In 1905 Na Ch'ŏl set up an organization to assassinate the five Korean officials who had signed the Protectorate Treaty with Japan. Discovered and arrested, Na was sent into internal exile and was finally released by a special royal amnesty. For the details of Na Ch'ŏl's early life, see Pak Hwan, *Na Ch'ŏl, Kim Kyohŏn kwa Yun Sebok* (*Na Ch'ŏl, Kim Kyohŏn, and Yun Sebok*) (Seoul: Tonga Ilbosa, 1992); and Pak Hwan, "Na Ch'ŏl ŭi inmul kwa hwaltong" (Na Ch'ŏl and His Activities), in Pak Hwan, *Manju Hanin minjok undongsa yŏn'gu* (*Studies of the Nationalist Movement Among Koreans in Manchuria*) (Seoul: Ilchogak, 1991), 256–71.
65. This middle character for this religion's name was a neologism with the suggestion of "ancestral."
66. *Hwangsŏng sinmun* 25 May 1910, *chappo*. Also see the report on 3 August 1910, *chappo*.
67. As recorded in Taejonggyo chonggyŏng chŏngsa p'onsu wiwŏnhoe, ed., *Taejonggyo chunggwang yuksimnyŏnsa* (*Sixty Years of Taejonggyo History*) (Seoul: Taejonggyo Ch'ongbonsa, 1971), 83–85.
68. *Hwangsŏng sinmun* 21 April 1910. Also see 9 August 1910.
69. *Hwangsŏng sinmun* 21 November 1909.
70. The Taejonggyo has edited a history of its organization, *Taejonggyo chunggwang yuksimnyŏnsa* (Seoul: Taejonggyo Ch'ongbonsa, 1971).
71. For a discussion of this work, see Han Yŏngu, "1910 nyŏndae Yi Sangyong, Kim Kyohŏn ŭi minjokchuŭi yŏksa sosŏl" (The Nationalist Historical Narratives of Yi Sangyong and Kim Kyohŏn in the 1910s), in Han Yŏngu, *Han'guk minjokchuŭi yŏksahak* (*Nationalist Historiography in Korea*) (Seoul: Ilchogak, 1994), 85–122. A reprint and translation of this work has been published; see Yi Minsu, trans., *Sindan silgi* (*True Records of Divine Tan'gun*) (Seoul: Hanppuri, 1986).
72. Kim Kyohŏn, *Sindan minsa* (*History of the Divine Tan'gun's People*) (reprint, Seoul: Sŏul Kong'insa, 1946). No original copies of this work are extant, and there is some disagreement as to its original date of publication. Han Yŏngu lists it as 1914 in *Han'guk minjokchuŭi yoksahak*, 97, and Pak Hwan points to 1923, in *Na Ch'ŏl, Kim Kyohŏn kwa Yun Sebok* (*Na Ch'ŏl, Kim Kyohŏn, and*

Yun Sebok) (Seoul: Tonga Ilbosa, 1992), 115. Han'guk chŏngsin munhwa yŏn'guwŏn p'yŏnch'anbu, ed., points to a publication date of both 1904 and 1923, though the former date is highly unlikely; see *Han'guk minjok munhwa taebaekkwa sajŏn* (*Encyclopedia of Korean National Culture*) (Seoul: Han'guk chŏngsin munhwa yŏn'guwŏn, 1991), 13: 694.

73. This term can be translated as the "delivered people," suggesting its divine origins. *Paedal* is often explained as having derived from *paktal*, an old term for the tree to which Tan'gun's father descended from Heaven. For a brief discussion of this etymology, see Hyung Il Pai, *Constructing "Korean" Origins*, 58.

74. Kim Kyohŏn, *Sindan minsa*, 1: 9.

75. Ibid., 2: 35.

76. Ibid., 3:32.

77. Ibid., 4: 38.

78. One important difference was that Kim included the state of Mahan into his narrative, whereas Sin did not.

79. Kim Kyohŏn, *Sindan minsa*, 4: 15.

80. Ibid., 18.

81. Ibid., 20.

82. It was also common to refer to the TaeHan *minjok*.

6. Peninsular Boundaries

1. *Hwangsŏng sinmun* 15–16 February 1907.

2. These islands did become an issue in Korea's relations with China. In the case of an island in the mouth of the Yalu River, see *TaeHan maeil sinbo* 25 November 1904, *chappo*, and 24 September 1905, *chappo*. With Japan, the issue of Tokto Island created much controversy; see *Hwangsŏng sinmun* 10 December 1903.

3. *TaeHan maeil sinbo* 23 November 1907.

4. Mathew H. Edney, *Mapping an Empire: The Geographical Construction of British India* (Chicago: University of Chicago Press, 1997); Thongchai Winachakul, *Siam Mapped: A History of the Geobody of a Nation* (Honolulu: University of Hawai'i Press, 1994).

5. *Tongnip sinmun* 9 March 1898.

6. *Hwangsŏng sinmun* 22 October 1902. Documents concerning these incidents are available in the appropriate country volumes in Koryŏ Taehak Asea Munje Yŏn'guso, ed., *KuHan'guk oegyo munsŏ* (*Diplomatic Documents of Old Korea*) 22 vols. (Seoul: Koryŏ taehakkyo ch'ulp'ansa, 1965–73).

7. These are reported in Kuo T'ing-i and Li Yu-shu, eds., *Qingji Zhong Ri Han guanxi shiliao* (*Historical Materials on Chinese-Japanese-Korean Relations Dur-*

ing the Qing Period), 11 vols. (Taibei: Chungyang yenchiuyüan chintaishih yenchiuso, 1972).

8. *Hwangsŏng sinmun* 23 July 1902.

9. For a list of violations reported under the tributary system, see Kuksa p'yŏnch'an wiwŏnhoe, ed., *Tongmun hwigo* (*A Compendium of Diplomatic Documents*), 6 vols. (Seoul, Kuksa p'yŏnch'an wiwŏnhoe, 1978).

10. For a collection of essays on Chang's various interests and activities, see Chŏn Kwanu et al., *Wiam Chang Chiyŏn ŭi sasang kwa hwaltong* (*The Thought and Activities of Chang Chiyŏn*) (Seoul: Minŭmsa, 1993).

11. Bernard Hung-kay Luk, "State, Nation, Country and Fatherland: An Etymology of Patriotism in Modern Chinese," paper presented at the Joint Centre for Asia Pacific Studies Conference on Nationalism and Postnationalism, Toronto, 7 September 1996. For its usage in Korea, Kyung Moon Hwang argues it meant the dynastic government or monarchy; see his "New Conceptualizations of *Kukka* (state) in Korea, 1896–1910," paper presented at the annual meeting of the Association of Asian Studies, Boston, 1999. The term has often been rendered as "kingdom" in English, a translation that faithfully approximates the etymology of a dynastic oriented term, circumvents the implications of using the term "nation" in a premodern context, and allows the lexical transition to the modern to be a move from "kingdom" to "nation."

12. As described in Cho Tongil, *Han'guk munhak t'ongsa* (*A Comprehensive History of Korean Literature*), 2d ed. (Seoul: Chisik san'opsa, 1991), 3: 319–20.

13. Yi Chunghwan, *T'aengniji* (*On Selecting a Village*), trans. Yi Iksŏng (reprint, Seoul: Ŭlyu munhwasa, 1971).

14. Benedict Anderson, *Imagined Communities: Reflections on the Origins and Spread of Nationalism*, rev. ed. (London: Verso, 1991), ch. 1.

15. *Injo sillok* 15:50b.

16. Marion Eggert, "A Borderline Case: Korean Travelers' Views of the Chinese Border (Eighteenth to Nineteenth Century)," in *China and Her Neighbours: Borders, Visions of the Other, Foreign Policy, 10th to 19th Century*, ed. Sabine Dabringhaus and Roderich Ptak (Wiesbaden: Harrassowitx Verlag, 1997), 76.

17. Eggert, "A Borderline Case."

18. Reprinted in Tan'guk Taehakkyo Pusŏl Tongyanghak Yŏn'guso, ed., *Chang Chiyŏn chŏnsŏ* (*The Complete Works of Chang Chiyŏn*) (Seoul: Tan'guk Taehakkyo Pusŏl Tongyanghak Yŏn'guso, 1979–89), vol. 4. This work is the basis of a modern Korean translation using Chŏng's original title by Yi Minsu, *Abang kangyŏkko* (*An Investigation of Our Nation's Territory*) (Seoul: Pŏmusa, 1995).

19. *Chang Chiyŏn chŏnsŏ*, 4: 7.

20. Ibid.

21. This can also be seen in the contents of the *TaeHan sin chiji* (*A New Gazeteer of Korea*) published by Chang in 1907. Moreover, the government-sponsored

Chŭngbo munhŏn pigo (A Revised Compendium of Documents) (Seoul, 1907) included an appended section on Kando. Chang worked on the editing committee and likely was responsible for this extra section.

22. For varying treatments of these events, see Sin Kisŏk, *Kando yŏngyu'gwŏn e kwanhan yŏn'gu* (Research on the Rights of Possession of Kando) (Seoul: Tamgudang, 1979); Yang Zhaoquan and Sun Yumei, *Zhong Chao bianjieshi* (A History of the Sino-Korean Border) (Changchun: Jilin wenshi chubanshe, 1993); Zhang Cunwu, *Qingdai ZhongHan guanxi lunwenji* (Essays on Sino-Korean Relations During the Qing Dynasty) (Taibei: Shangwu yinshuguan, 1986); Yang T'aejin, *Han'guk kungyŏngsa yŏn'gu* (Studies of the History of Korean National Boundaries) (Seoul: Pŏpgyŏng ch'ulp'ansa, 1992).

23. Gari Ledyard, "Cartography in Korea," in *The History of Cartography*, ed. J. B. Harley and David Woodward (Chicago: University of Chicago Press, 1994), 2: 235–344.

24. The following discussion is from Andre Schmid, "Tribute, Frontiers and Sinocentricism: A View from South of the Yalu River," paper presented at the annual meeting of the Association of Asian Studies, Washington D.C., 1998. For these discussions, see *Sukchong sillok* 51: 15b–18a.

25. *Sukchong sillok* 51: 16a.

26. Ibid., 17b.

27. Ibid., 22a, b.

28. This decision to drop out of the mission cost two officials their positions for failing to fulfill their duties.

29. A description of the journey up Mount Paektu can be found in Hong Set'ae, "Paektusan'gi" (A Record of Mount Paektu), in *Kando Yŏngyu'gwŏn kwan'gye charyojip* (Materials Relating to the Rights of Possession of Kando), ed. No Yakhyŏn (Seoul: Paeksan charyowon, 1993), 2: 314–31.

30. *Sukchong sillok* 51: 29a.

31. Peter Sahlins, *Boundaries: The Making of France and Spain in the Pyrenees* (Berkeley and Los Angeles: University of California Press, 1989), 28.

32. Many of these cases are treated in Kuska p'yŏnchan wiwŏnhoe, ed., *Tongmun hwigo*.

33. As quoted in Cho Kwang, "Chosŏn hugi ŭi pyŏn'gyŏng ŭisik" (Border Consciousness in the Late Chosŏn), *Paeksan hakpo* 16 (June 1974): 165.

34. Ibid.

35. Ibid.

36. Sŏ Myŏngan, *Yŏ Paektusangi*, as quoted in Yang Zhaoquan and Sun Yumei, *Zhong Chao bianjieshi*, 205.

37. Robert Lee, *The Manchuria Frontier in Ch'ing History* (Cambridge, Mass.: Harvard University Press, 1970).

38. For one paper on Korean migration patterns and their relation to state policy,

see Kim Ch'unsŏn, "1880–1890 nyŏndae ch'ŏngjo ŭi "yimin silbyŏn" chŏngch'aek kwa Hanin yijumin silt'ae yŏn'gu" (The Policy of "Populating the Border Regions" in the 1880s and 1890s and the Situation of Korean Migrants), Han'guk kŭnhyŏndaesa yŏn'gu 8 (1998): 5–36.

39. Yang Zhaoquan and Sun Yumei, Zhong Chao bianjieshi.

40. Hong Ponghan, et al. Chŭngbo munhŏn pigo (Seoul: Hongmungwan, 1907), 316: 2b.

41. Ŏ Yunjong, "Chongjŏng nyŏnp'yo" (A Chronology of Years in Power), in Ŏ Yunjong chŏnjip (The Complete Works of Ŏ Yunjong) (Seoul: Asea munhwasa, 1978), 151.

42. Ibid., 162.

43. These exchanges are recorded in Shinoda Jisaku, Hyakutosan teikaihi (The Boundary Stele of Mount Paektu) (Tokyo: Rakurō soin, 1938).

44. Yuan Shikai arrived in Korea in 1882 as part of the Chinese contingent dispatched in response to the 1882 military uprising and remained behind as the head of these forces. For his activities in Korea, see Lin Mingde, Yuan Shikai yu Chaoxian (Yuan Shikai and Korea) (Taibei: Zhongyang yanjiuyuan jindaishi yanjiusuo, 1969); in English, see Jerome Chen, Yuan Shi-k'ai, 1859–1916: Brutus Assumes the Purple (London: Allen & Unwin, 1961). Mary Wright has also argued that Qing policy in Korea represented a flexible approach to foreign relations; see her "The Adaptability of Ch'ing Diplomacy: The Case of Korea," Journal of Asian Studies 17 (May 1958): 363–81.

45. Detailed reports of these missions existed in the royal court records, although these generally were not available for perusal, even for officials, until the colonial period.

46. Sin Kisŏk, Kando yŏngyu'gwŏn e kwanhan yŏn'gu, p. 68.

47. This remains a sore point for many historians in China, who when refighting these battles are forced to rely almost exclusively on Korean documents for the 1712 mission. See Yang Zhaoquan and Sun Yumei, Zhong Chao bianjieshi.

48. These negotiations have been the subject of much study; see Akizuki Nozomi, "Chō-Chū kankai kōshō no hottan to kenkai" (The Origin and Development of the Sino-Korean Border) Chōsen gakuho 132 (July 1989): 79–108; Yang Zhaoquan and Sun Yumei, Zhong Chao bianjieshi; sin Kisŏk, Kando yŏngyu'gwŏn e kwanhan yŏn'gu.

49. Hwangsŏng sinmun 20 October 1898, pyŏlbo.

50. An advertisement for the book can be found on the back page of many issues during the following year; for example, see 25 July 1904.

51. See the series of editorials beginning 30 April 1903, also 12–15 January 1903.

52. Hwangsŏng sinmun 7 May 1903.

53. Chang followed this with a discussion of the geopolitics concerning Manchuria

as a whole, a question he believed was larger than Kando, as it would determine the fate of the nation as a whole. See chapter 7 for a more detailed discussion of Manchuria.

54. *TaeHan maeil sinbo* 25 November 1904.
55. *Hwangsŏng sinmun* 10 December 1903.
56. *TaeHan maeil sinbo* 6 April 1910.
57. *Hwangsŏng sinmun* 21 February 1907.
58. *Hwangsŏng sinmun* 4 December 1906.
59. *Hwangsŏng sinmun* 10 October 1906.
60. Stories of this kind were endlessly recounted in the *TaeHan maeil sinbo*. For one example of a man named Nakayama who tried to stake out land in the middle of the Haein monastery, see 14 November 1904.
61. Government General of Chōsen, *Annual Report on Reforms and Progress in Chōsen (Korea), 1910–11* (Seoul: Government General of Chōsen, 1911), 35–36.
62. Ibid., 212–14.
63. Gari Ledyard, "Cartography in Korea," 276–79.
64. On the geomantic questions related to choosing a capital, see Ch'oe Ch'angjo, *Han'guk ŭi p'ungsu sasang (Korean Geomantic Thought)* (Seoul: Minŭmsa, 1984), ch. 4.
65. Ch'oe Ch'angjo, "Chosŏn hugi sirhakchadŭl ŭi p'ungsu sasang" (The Geomantic Thought of Sirhak Scholars in the Late Chosŏn Dynasty), *Han'guk munhwa* 11 (1990): 469–504. Also see his *Han'guk ŭi p'ungsu sasang*.
66. Ch'oe Yongjun, "P'ungsu wa T'aengniji" (Geomancy and the T'aengniji), *Han'guksa simin kangjwa* 14 (1994): 98–122.
67. Yi Chunghwan, *T'aengniji*, 336–56.
68. Other peoples of Manchuria, including the Jurchens, also identified the mountain as their birthplace.
69. *Tongnip sinmun* 15 July 1899.
70. Writings on shamanism and fortune-telling are extensive; see *Hwangsŏng sinmun* 27 June 1900, 16 November 1900, 10 December 1900, 8 May 1901, 21 May 1902, 1, 3, 4, and 7 November 1903; *Tongnip sinmun* 11 November 1896, 14 September 1897, 22 October 1898.
71. *Hwangsŏng sinmun* 28 May 1908.
72. Shamanism already was illegal; see the brief account of the arrest of one shaman for worshiping the Jade emperor, erecting images of gods in her house, and seducing people with fortune theories, in *Hwangsŏng sinmun* 13 May 1899, *chappo*. The *TaeHan chaganghoe wŏlbo* called on the government for tighter implementation and new laws to prohibit geomancy and other practices; see *TaeHan maeil sinbo* 12–13 October 1906, *chappo*.

73. Ch'oe Yongjun gives the examples of Pak Chega and Chŏng Yagyong. Pak found the local implementation of these principles to be silly and motivated by selfish desires. Chŏng took this further, arguing that using geomancers to locate a parent's grave in the hopes of obtaining fortune violated propriety and was hardly proper filial behavior. See Ch'oe Yongjun, "P'ungsu wa T'aengniji," 108.

74. *Hwangsŏng sinmun* 7 April 1899.

75. *TaeHan maeil sinbo* 12 October 1906, *chappo*. This was not a practice restricted to the lower social strata; the activities of wealthy families also were criticized. See *Hwangsŏng sinmun* 31 August 1899.

76. *Hwangsŏng sinmun* 14 October 1899.

77. *Hwangsŏng sinmun* 28 May 1908.

78. *Tongnip sinmun* 7 May 1896.

79. *Hwangsŏng sinmun* 7 April 1899.

80. On the question of "fate," see *Hwangsŏng sinmun* 27 November 1900 and *Tongnip sinmun* 12 May 1899.

81. *Hwangsŏng sinmun* 26 June 1899.

82. *Tongnip sinmun* 7 May 1896.

83. See Hwimun ŭisuk p'yŏnjippu, ed., *Kodŭng sokhak tokpon (An Advanced Elementary Reader)* (Seoul: Hwimun ŭisuk inswaebu, 1906), in *Han'guk kaehwagi kyo'gwasŏ ch'ongsŏ (A Collection of Textbooks from the Korean Enlightenment Period)*, ed. Han'gukhak munhŏn yŏn'guso (Seoul: Asea munhwasa, 1977), 5: 4.

84. TaeHan kungmin kyoyukhoe, ed., *Ch'odŭng sohak (An Elementary Primer)*, in *Han'guk kaehwagi kyo'gwasŏ ch'ongso (A Collection of Textbooks from the Korean Enlightenment Period)*, ed. Han'gukhak munhŏn yŏn'guso (Seoul: Asea munhwasa, 1977), 4: frontispiece.

85. This occurred in postliberation Korea, as I explain in my epilogue, pp. 275–76.

86. See Hyŏn Ch'ae, *Yunyŏn p'iltok (An Essential Reader for Youths)* (Seoul: Chongmungwan, 1907), in *Han'guk kaehwagi kyo'gwasŏ ch'ongsŏ (A Collection of Textbooks from the Korean Enlightenment Period)*, ed. Han'gukhak munhŏn yŏn'guso (Seoul: Asea munhwasa, 1977), 2: *chŏn* 1, 10–11.

87. TaeHan kungmin kyoyukhoe, ed., *Ch'odŭng sohak (An Elementary Primer)* (Seoul: TaeHan Kungmin kyoyukhoe, 1907), in *Han'guk kaehwagi kyo'gwasŏ ch'ongsŏ (A Collection of Textbooks from the Korean Enlightenment Period)*, ed. Han'gukhak munhŏn yŏn'guso (Seoul: Asea munhwasa, 1977), 4: *chŏn* 7, lesson 23.

88. *Tongnip sinmun* 23 September 1897.

89. *Ch'odŭng sohak* explicitly states that the Kumgang Mountains are the most famous. See TaeHan kungmin kyoyukhoe, ed., *Ch'odŭng sohak (An Elementary Primer)* (Seoul: Kungmin kyoyukhoe, 1907), in *Han'guk kaehwagi*

kyo'gwaso ch'ongsŏ (A Collection of Textbooks from the Korean Enlightenment Period), ed. Han'gukhak munhŏn yŏn'guso (Seoul: Asea munhwasa, 1977), *chŏn* 7, lesson 23. See Hyŏn Ch'ae, *Yunyŏn p'iltok*, 2: *chŏn* 1, lessons 11–12. Also see the extensive treatment in Hyŏn Ch'ae, *Sinch'an ch'odŭng sohak (A New Elementary Primer)*, (Seoul: Il-Han inswae chusik hoesa, 1909), in *Han'guk kaehwagi kyo'gwasŏ ch'ongsŏ (A Collection of Textbooks from the Korean Enlightenment Period)*, ed. Han'gukhak munhŏn yŏn'guso (Seoul: Asea munhwasa, 1977), vol. 7: *chŏn* 5, lesson 15.

90. Other mountains associated with Tan'gun, such as Mount Myohyang, gained greater play as well; see *Hwangsŏng sinmun* 3 July 1908.
91. *TaeHan maeil sinbo* 6 August 1909, *sajo.*
92. *TaeHan maeil sinbo* 30 October 1909, *sajo.*
93. *TaeHan maeil sinbo* 11 May 1910, *sajo.*

7. Beyond the Peninsula

1. For example, the cover of the *TaeHan hyŏphoe hoebo.*
2. *Hwangsŏng sinmun* 27 April 1910. This included numerous defenses against Japanese uses of these theories to show how the peninsular shape of the nation had undermined creativity and induced dependence; see the editorial in the *TaeHan maeil sinbo*, credited to Sin Ch'aeho, 28–29 January 1909.
3. *TaeHan maeil sinbo* 18 August 1909, *sajo.*
4. The following section on the Korean diaspora owes much to Liisa Malkki, *Purity and Exile: Violence, Memory, and National Cosmology Among Hutu Refugees in Tanzania* (Chicago: University of Chicago Press, 1995).
5. For some editorials on these discoveries, see *Hwangsŏng sinmun* 22 June 1909 and 18 September 1909.
6. Sin Ch'aeho, "Han'guk kwa Manju" (Korea and Manchuria), in *Tanjae Sin Ch'aeho chŏnjip (The Complete Works of Sin Ch'aeho)*, ed. Tanjae Sin Ch'aeho chŏnjip p'yŏnch'an wiwŏnhoe (Seoul: Hyŏngsŏl ch'ulp'ansa, 1987), 4: 232–34. For a fuller treatment of Sin's writing on Manchuria, see Andre Schmid, "Rediscovering Manchuria: Sin Ch'aeho and the Politics of Territorial History in Korea," *Journal of Asian Studies* 56, no. 1 (February 1997): 26–47.
7. Stefan Tanaka, *Japan's Orient: Rendering Pasts into History* (Berkeley and Los Angeles: University of California Press, 1993), 241–53.
8. For a description of the archaeological approach to Mansenshi, see Pai Hyung Il, *Constructing "Korean" Origins: A Critical Review of Archaeology, Historiography, and Racial Myth in Korean State-Formation Theories* (Cambridge, Mass.: Harvard University Press, 2000), ch. 2 and pp. 251–55.
9. Hatada Takashi, *Nihonjin no Chōsenkan (Japanese Views of Korea)* (Tokyo: Keiso shobō, 1969), 180–98.

10. *Hwangsŏng sinmun* 27 April 1910.
11. *Hwangsŏng sinmun* 30 June 1909.
12. *Hwangsŏng sinmun* 30 June 1909, 30 April 1909, and 20 January 1910.
13. Sin Ch'aeho, "Han'guk kwa Manju," 234.
14. "Tae tongja nonsa" (Speaking About History to Children), *Sŏbuk hakhoe wŏlbo* 1, no. 2 (1907): 1–3.
15. See chapter 5 for a more detailed discussion of "Toksa sillon."
16. Yu Tŭkkong, *Parhaego* (*An Investigation of Parhae*) (reprint, Seoul: Ŭlyusa, 1976).
17. Koguryŏ was an ancient kingdom (37 B.C.–A.D. 668), controlling the northern portion of the Korean peninsula and extending into Manchuria.
18. Sin Ch'aeho, "Toksa sillon" (A New Reading of History), in *Tanjae Sin Ch'aeho chŏnjip* (*The Complete Works of Sin Ch'aeho*), ed. Tanjae Sin Ch'aeho chŏnjip p'yŏnch'an wiwŏnhoe (Seoul: Hyŏngsŏl ch'ulp'ansa, 1987), 1: 478.
19. Ibid., 508.
20. Ibid., 509.
21. Ibid.
22. Ibid., 510–13.
23. Ibid., 511–12.
24. Sin Ch'aeho, "Yŏksa wa aeguksim ŭi kwan'gye" (The Relation Between History and Patriotism), in *Tanjae Sin Ch'aeho chŏnjip* (*The Complete Works of Sin Ch'aeho*), ed. Tanjae Sin Ch'aeho chŏnjip p'yŏnch'an wiwŏnhoe (Seoul: Hyŏngsŏl ch'ulp'ansa, 1987), 2: 343–59.
25. Sin Ch'aeho, "Toksa sillon," 512.
26. Ibid., 511.
27. Ibid., 467–513.
28. See the reaction of the *Hwangsŏng sinmun* to the publication of the *Parhaego*, 28 April 1910.
29. Kim Kyohŏn. *Sindan minsa* (*History of the Divine Tan'gun's People*) (reprint, Seoul: Sŏul Kong'insa, 1946), ch. 4, 15.
30. Ibid., ch. 4, 23–28.
31. Sin Ch'aeho, "Han'guk kwa Manju," 234.
32. *TaeHan maeil sinbo* 21 April 1910, *sajo*.
33. Sin Ch'aeho, "Han'guk minjok chirisang palchŏn" (The Geographical Development of the Korean *minjok*), in *Tanjae Sin Ch'aeho chŏnjip* (*The Complete Works of Sin Ch'aeho*), ed. Tanjae Sin Ch'aeho chŏnjip p'yŏnch'an wiwŏnhoe (Seoul: Hyŏngsŏl ch'ulp'ansa, 1987), 4: 198–99.
34. *TaeHan maeil sinbo* 22 April 1910, *sajo*.
35. Sin Ch'aeho, "Han'guk minjok chirisang palchŏn," 199.
36. Sin Ch'aeho, "Manju munje-e ch'wihayŏ chaeronham" (More Thoughts on the Manchurian Problem), in *Tanjae Sin Ch'aeho chŏnjip* (*The Complete*

Works of Sin Ch'aeho), ed. Tanjae Sin Ch'aeho chŏnjip p'yŏnch'an wiwŏnhoe (Seoul: Hyŏngsŏl ch'ulp'ansa, 1987), 4: 238–43.

37. Pak Ch'angok, "Chosŏnjok ŭi Chungguk ijusa yŏn'gu" (A Study of the Migratory History of China's Korean People), *Yŏksa pip'yŏng* 15 (Fall): 179–97.

38. Lee Chae-jin, *China's Korean Minority: The Politics of Ethnic Education* (Boulder, Colo.: Westview Press, 1986), 20.

39. Chizuko Allen, "Northeast Asia Centered Around Korea: Ch'oe Namson's View of History," *Journal of Asian Studies* 49, no. 4 (1990): 787–806; also see Pai Hyung Il, *Constructing "Korean" Origins*, ch. 3.

40. For a detailed study of the Hawai'ian community, see, Wayne Patterson, *The Korean Frontier in America: Immigration to Hawai'i, 1896–1910* (Honolulu: University of Hawai'i Press, 1988).

41. Michael Weiner, *The Origins of the Korean Community in Japan, 1910–23* (Manchester: Manchester University Press, 1989), 52–53.

42. As reported in the *TaeHan minbo* 9 June 1909.

43. A reprint from the *Kongnip sinbo*, in *TaeHan maeil sinbo* 7 May 1907, *pyŏlbo*.

44. *Hwangsŏng sinmun* 29 July 1905, *chappo*, and 8 June 1907, *kisŏ*.

45. *Hwangsŏng sinmun* 8 June 1907, *kisŏ*. Reports reached the editors of the *Hwangsŏng sinmun* via a circuitous route. Some Korean students in the United States had read an account of Mexico in a Chinese newspaper and received a letter from a Chinese friend with descriptions of the Korean community. They forwarded these accounts to an educational organization in Korea, which then passed them to the newspaper.

46. This account has been pieced together from the following articles in the *Hwangsŏng sinmun* 29 July 1905, *nonsŏl* and *chappo*; 31 July 1905; 8 June 1907, *kisŏ*; 12 June 1907; 17 June 1908, *kisŏ*; 27 April 1909; 11 June 1909; 22 July 1909; and *TaeHan maeil sinbo* 19 April 1906, *kisŏ*.

47. On the separation of families, see *Hwangsŏng sinmun* 17 June 1908, *kisŏ*.

48. *Hwangsŏng sinmun* 29 July 1905, *chappo*.

49. *TaeHan maeil sinbo* 19 April 1906, *kisŏ*.

50. *Hwangsŏng sinmun* 31 July 1905.

51. *TaeHan maeil sinbo* 14 September 1907.

52. *TaeHan maeil sinbo* 29 April 1906, *kisŏ*.

53. *TaeHan maeil sinbo* 27 April 1906. Of course, Japan claimed to represent Koreans in the area. There was a controversy over whether some Koreans had falsely represented themselves to the Japanese consul as leaders of the Korean community in order to coax money out of them; see *TaeHan maeil sinbo* 29 July 1907, *chappo*.

54. *TaeHan maeil sinbo* 5 May 1906, *kisŏ*. For a similar sentiment see 10 May, *kisŏ*. A list of donors was published beginning on 5 May 1906.

55. *TaeHan maeil sinbo* 20 May 1906, *chappo*.

56. Sin Ch'aeho, "Manju munje-e ch'wihayŏ chaeronham," 4: 238–43.
57. Isabella Bird, *Korea and Her Neighbours* (London: Routledge & Kegan Paul, 1897).
58. Ibid., i.
59. Ibid., 235.
60. *Tongnip sinmun* 28 May 1898.
61. Some noted that Americans did not always treat them favorably and urged their overseas compatriots to prove them wrong; see *TaeHan maeil sinbo* 9 January 1909.
62. *TaeHan maeil sinbo* 12 July 1906, *chappo*. This comparison was made frequently; see the editorial comments on the charter of the "Great Eastern Educational Association" (Taedong kyoyukhoe), *TaeHan maeil sinbo* 9 August 1906, *kisŏ*. Diasporic newspapers were always seen as an indication of enlightened success; see *Hwangsŏng sinmun* 15 February 1908.
63. *Hwangsŏng sinmun* 16 February 1906.
64. *TaeHan maeil sinbo* 25 August 1909. For a similar editorial, see the *TaeHan maeil sinbo*, 4 December 1909.
65. *TaeHan maeil sinbo* 14 April 1910.
66. *Hwangsŏng sinmun* 17 December 1906.
67. *TaeHan maeil sinbo* 1 August 1906.
68. *TaeHan maeil sinbo* 14 December 1909.
69. *TaeHan maeil sinbo* 26 October 1906, *pyŏlbo*.
70. *Hwangsŏng sinmun* 17 December 1906.
71. *TaeHan maeil sinbo* 25 August 1909.
72. *TaeHan maeil sinbo* 12 November 1905.
73. This was a common expression; see *TaeHan maeil sinbo* 15 September 1909.
74. *TaeHan maeil sinbo* 12 November 1905.
75. *TaeHan maeil sinbo* 4 December 1909.
76. *Hwangsŏng sinmun* 16 February 1906.
77. *TaeHan maeil sinbo* 4 December 1909.
78. For example, *Hwangsŏng sinmun* 19 September 1909, and *TaeHan maeil sinbo* 4 December 1909.
79. *TaeHan maeil sinbo* 11 April 1907.
80. *TaeHan maeil sinbo* 1 August 1906.
81. *TaeHan maeil sinbo* 4 December 1909.
82. *Hwangsŏng sinmun* 16 February 1906.
83. For simplicity, I have used only the latter title in the text but have kept the separate titles in the notes.
84. *Kongnip sinbo* 18 March 1908.
85. *TaeHan maeil sinbo* 15 September 1909.
86. Government General of Chōsen, *Annual Report on Reforms and Progress in*

Chōsen, 1910–11 (Seoul: Government General of Chōsen, 1911), 87. Consequently, after the 1908 press censorship laws, a major task of the *Kongnip sinbo* was to come up with ways to get the paper into the country. See *Kongnip sinbo* 28 November 1908. Pak Hwan has shown that one Vladivostok paper was confiscated eighty-eight times between 1909 and 1910, sometimes involving more than two thousand copies. See Pak Hwan, "Ku Hanmal Rosia Pŭlladibosŭt'ok aeso kanhaengduin minjokchi: 'Taedong gongbo'" (A Nationalist Newspaper Published in Russia's Vladivostock During the Hanmal Period: "The Great Eastern Forum"), *Han'guk saron* 30 (1993): 107.

87. *Kongnip sinbo* 8 November 1907.
88. *Kongnip sinbo* 21 June 1907, *kisŏ*.
89. *TaeHan minbo* 20 October 1909. Also see 3 June 1908.
90. *Kongnip sinbo* 16 September 1908. Also see *Kongnip sinbo* 8 November 1907.
91. *Kongnip sinbo* 8 July 1908.
92. *Kongnip sinbo* 16 August 1907, *kisŏ*.
93. For another letter claiming that the patriotism of overseas Koreans could urge their compatriots forward, see *Kongnip sinbo* 1 November 1907, *kisŏ*.
94. *TaeHan minbo* 11 August 1909.
95. *Kongnip sinbo* 8 December 1908.
96. *Kongnip sinbo* 28 June 1907.
97. *Kongnip sinbo* 25 March 1908.
98. *TaeHan minbo* 17 February 1909.
99. *Kongnip sinbo* 22 July 1908.
100. *Kongnip sinbo* 22 July 1908.
101. *Kongnip sinbo* 8 November 1907, *kisŏ*.
102. *TaeHan minbo* 14 April 1909.
103. *TaeHan minbo* 9 June 1909.

Epilogue

1. This is the subject of Michael Robinson's *Cultural Nationalism in Colonial Korea, 1920–25* (Seattle: University of Washington Press, 1988).
2. Most famously, the banned *Han'guk minjungsa* (1985). Journals such as *Yŏksa p'ip'yŏng* and *Yŏksa wa hyŏnsil* promoted this approach. For some useful essays on the development of the concept of *minjung*, see Chŏng Ch'angnyŏl et al., eds., *Han'guk minjungnon ŭi hyŏndan'gye* (*The Current State of Debates on the Korean Minjung*) (Seoul: Tolbegae, 1989).
3. The climax of this approach was the twenty-seven volumes edited by Kang Man'gil, *Han'guksa* (*Korean History*) (Seoul: Han'gilsa, 1994). Following the democratic reforms of the 1990s, however, the *minjung* approach has lost much of its political impetus and, thus, support.

4. Pak Ch'ansŭng, "Pundan sidae namHan ŭi Han'guk sahak" (Korean Historiography During the Period of Division in South Korea), in *Han'guk ŭi yŏksaga wa yŏksahak (Korean Historians and Historiography)*, ed. Cho Tonggŏl, Han Yŏngu, and Pak Ch'ansŭng (Seoul: Ch'angjak kwa pip'yŏngsa, 1994), 2: 350–51.

5. For the standard north Korean history, see Sahoe kwahag'wŏn yŏksa yŏn'guso, ed., *Chosŏn chŏnsa (A Comprehensive History of Korea)*, 33 vols. (Pyongyang: Kwahak paekkwasajon ch'ulp'ansa, 1982).

6. Pak Myoung-Kyu has located this dispute over the March First Movement to the liberation period, when different political groups vied to control commemorative ceremonies for the movement. See his "Historical Interpretation in Post-Colonial Korea: Memory, Knowledge, and Power," paper presented at the conference "Between Colonialism and Nationalism: Power and Subjectivity in Korea, 1931–50," University of Michigan, Ann Arbor, 4–6 May 2001.

7. Charles Armstrong, "Centering the Periphery: Manchurian Exile(s) and the North Korean State," *Korean Studies* 19 (1995): 1–19.

8. This competition highlights two streams in the Korean nationalist movements at the expense of ignoring other types of nationalism. See Gi-wook Shin, "Agrarianism: A Critique of Colonial Modernity in Korea," *Comparative Studies in Society and History* 41, no. 4 (October 1999): 784–804.

9. Ross King, "Language, Politics, and Ideology in the Postwar Koreas," in *Korea Briefing: Toward Reunification*, ed. David McCann (Armonk, N.Y.: Sharpe, 1997), 117–19.

10. The precise origin of the neologism *han'gŭl* is somewhat obscure. It appears in journals published in the 1910s and is often credited to Chu Sigyŏng between 1910 and 1913. See King, "Language, Politics, and Ideology in the Postwar Koreas," 111.

11. King, "Language, Politics, and Ideology in the Postwar Koreas," 114.

12. For one example of this type of opposition, see *Chosŏn ilbo* 9 October 1961.

13. These have ranged from as high as eighteen hundred to as low as zero.

14. This is one example offered by Hŏ Ŭng, *Han'gŭl kwa minjok munhwa (Han'gŭl and National Culture)* (Seoul: Sejong Taewang kinyŏm saŏphoe, 1974), 208.

15. Hŏ Ŭng, *Han'gŭl kwa minjok munhwa*, ch. 7. Hŏ's argument includes the need to expel all foreign loan words, especially those from Japanese.

16. Ri Ŭido, "Hangŭlman ssŭginŭn kyŏrye yŏksa ŭi ŭiji" (Writing Only in Korean Is the Historical Will of Our People), *Sŭp'och'ŭ Sŏul* 8 (October 1990): 5.

17. Kim Tonggil, "Han'gŭl munhwagwŏn' ŭn mot irul kkuminga?" (Is a Han'gŭl Cultural Sphere an Unattainable Dream?), *Han'guk Ilbo* 12 October 1984.

18. Hŏ Ŭng, *Han'gŭl kwa minjok munhwa*, 209.

19. This was the *Han'gyŏrye sinmun*.

20. See, for example, Nam Kwangu, *Kugŏ Kukcha nonjip (Essays on National Language and National Script)* (Seoul: Ilchogak, 1982).

21. Han'guk chŏngsin munhwa yŏn'guwŏn p'yŏnch'anbu,, ed., *Han'guk minjok munhwa taebaekkwa sajŏn* (*Encyclopedia of Korean National Culture*) (Seoul: Han'guk chŏngsin munhwa yŏn'guwŏn, 1991), 24: 152.

22. No Taegyu, "Han'gŭl kwa Hanja ŭi sayong piyul ŭi pyŏnhwa" (Changes in the Frequency of Use of *Han'gŭl* and *Hanja*), *Han'gŭl saesosik* 202 (June 1989): 4–6.

23. On Paek Namun, see Pang Kijung, *Han'guk kŭn-hyŏndae sasangsa yŏn'gu: 1930, 40-nyŏndae Paek Nam-un ŭi hangmun kwa chŏngch'i kyŏngje sasang* (*Studies of Korean Modern Thought: The Political Economic Thought of Paek Nam-un in the 1930s and 40s*) (Seoul: Yŏksa p'ip'yŏngsa, 1992).

24. For one example in English, see Chizuko Allen, "Northeast Asia Centered Around Korea: Ch'oe Namson's View of History," *Journal of Asian Studies* 49, no. 4 (1990): 787–806.

25. For a general treatment of the textbook issue, see Chong-Sik Lee, *Japan and Korea: The Political Dimension* (Stanford, Calif.: Hoover Institution Press, 1985), ch. 6.

26. This argument has a long history in English histories of Japan as well. See George Sansom, *A History of Japan* (Stanford, Calif.: Stanford University Press, 1958), 1: 16–17.

27. Takashi Hatada, "An Interpretation of the King Kwanggaet'o Inscription," trans. V. Dixon Morris, *Korean Studies* 3 (1979): 1–18.

28. Suematsu Yasukazu, *Mimana kōbōshi* (*The Rise and Fall of Mimana*) (Tokyo: Ōyashima shuppan, 1949).

29. One exception was Chŏng Inbo, *Chosŏnsa yŏn'gu* (*Research on Korean History*) (Seoul: Soŭl sinmunsa, 1947).

30. Kim Sŏkhyŏng, *Ch'ogi Cho-Il kwan'gye yŏn'gu* (*Studies of Early Korean-Japanese Relations*) (Pyongyang: Sahoe kwahag'won ch'ulp'ansa, 1966).

31. Yi Chinhŭi, *Kwanggaet'o Wang nŭngbi ŭi t'amgu* (*Studies of the King Kwanggaet'o Stele*), trans. Yi Kidong (Seoul: Ilchogak, 1982).

32. For one Japanese repudiation of these myths, see Inoue Hideo, *Kodai Chōsen* (*Ancient Korea*) (Tokyo: Nihon hōsō shuppan kyōkai, 1972). For a recent trilingual symposium on the Kwanggaet'o stele, bringing together historians from Korea, Japan, and China, see Koguryŏ yŏn'guhoe, ed., *Kwanggaet'o hot'ae wangbi yŏn'gu 100 nyŏn* (*100 Years of Research on the Kwanggaet'o Stele*) (Seoul: Hangyŏ munhwasa, 1996).

33. Ch'ŏn Kwanu is known for pursuing this critique through studies of late-Chosŏn reform thinkers, while Kim Yongsŏp did the same in the socioeconomic history of the late Chosŏn dynasty. For an overview of the many other scholars who participated in this critique, see Pak Ch'ansŭng, "Pundan sidae namHan ŭi Han'guk sahak," 2: 331–37.

34. These five points are also reproduced as part of a collection of Yi Kibaek's

essays, "Singminjuŭijŏk Han'guk sagwan pip'yŏng"(A Critique of Colonialist Perspectives in Korean History), in Yi Kibaek, *Minjok kwa yŏksa (The Nation and History)* (Seoul: Ilchogak, 1971), 2–11.

35. See, for example, the roundtable discussion concerning King Kojong and the TaeHan empire, Yŏksa munje yŏn'guso, ed., "Kojong kwa TaeHan Chegugŭl tŭllŏssan ch'oegŭn ŭi nonjaeng" (Recent Debates Concerning Kojong and the TaeHan Empire), *Yŏksa pip'yŏng* 37 (Summer 1997): 224–70.

36. A contemporary article by K. W. Kim went so far as to suggest that under Park, nationalism was not allowed, as it threatened the anticommunist goals of his regime. See K. W. Kim, "Ideology and Political Development in South Korea," *Pacific Affairs* 38, no. 2 (Summer 1965): 164–76.

37. My thanks to Im Chongmyong for pointing out to me the prevalence of the term *kungmin* under the Rhee regime. See his "Ilminjuŭi and the Making of the Republic of Korea as a Modern Nation-State," paper presented at the conference "Between Colonialism and Nationalism: Power and Subjectivity in Korea, 1931–50," University of Michigan, Ann Arbor, 4–6 May 2001.

38. Hong Sŭngi, "Silchŭng sahangnon" (Empiricist Historiography), in No Taedon et al., *Hyŏndae Han'guk sahak kwa sagwan (Contemporary Korean Historiography)* (Seoul: Ilchogak, 1991).

39. Pak Ch'ansŭng, "Pundan sidae namHan ŭi Han'guk sahak," 332–50.

40. This can be seen in recent attempts to refurbish the image of Emperor Kojong, whose generally negative historical appraisal has been blamed by his recent supporters as a legacy of Japanese scholarship. See the comments by Yi T'aejin in Yŏksa munje yŏn'guso, ed., "Kojong kwa TaeHan Chegugŭl tŭllŏssan ch'oegŭn ŭi nonjaeng."

41. The tension between pro-regime historians and those that tried to maintain an independent or oppositional stance divided the field.

42. See the 18 December 1933 editorial in the *Chosŏn ilbo*, as quoted in Chŏng Yŏnghun, "Tan'gun kwa kŭndae Han'guk minjok undong" (Tan'gun and the Modern Korean Nationalist Movement), *Han'guk ŭi chŏngch'i wa kyŏngje* 8 (1995): 50–51.

43. See Paek Namun's critique in his preface to *Chosŏn ponggŏn sahoe kyŏngjesa (A Socioeconomic History of Korean Feudalism)* (reprint, Seoul: Iron kwa silch'ŏn, 1993).

44. John Jorganson, "Tan'gun and the Legitimization of a Threatened Dynasty: North Korea's Rediscovery of Tan'gun," *Korea Observer* 27, no. 2 (Summer 1996): 273–306.

45. This holiday lasted until 1993 when its official status was canceled, according to government officials, because the population had too many work-free holidays.

46. Chŏng Yŏnghun, "Tan'gun kwa kŭndae Han'guk minjok undong," 72–73.

47. Kim, Kyohŏn, *Sindan minsa* (*History of the Divine Tan'gun's People*), trans. Ko Tongnyŏng (Seoul: Han Ppuri, 1986).
48. One example is Yi Kimun, "Han'gugŏ hyŏngsŏngsa," in *Han'guk munhwasa taegye* (*Cultural History of Korea*), ed. Koryŏ Taehakkyo minjok munhwa yŏn'guso (Seoul: Tonga ch'ulp'ansa, 1971), vol. 5.
49. The most prolific territorial historian is Yang T'aejin. See his *Han'guk kungnyŏngsa yŏn'gu* (*Studies of the History of Korean National Boundaries*) (Seoul: Pŏpgyŏng ch'ulp'ansa, 1992).
50. A useful introduction to these various opinions is the roundtable discussion sponsored by the Yŏksa munje yŏn'guso, "Han'guk minjogŭn ŏnje hyŏngsŏngdoeŏnna?" (When did the Korean Nation Form?), *Yŏksa pip'yŏng* 19 (Winter 1992): 16–101.
51. A small minority of scholars exclude themselves from this approach, as can be seen in the preceding note.
52. Charles Armstrong, "Centering the Periphery: Manchurian Exile(s) and the North Korean State," *Korean Studies*, 19 (1995): 1–19.
53. Sahoe kwahag'wŏn yŏksa yŏn'guso, ed., *Chosŏn chŏnsa*.
54. Yi Manyŏl, *Tanjae Sin Ch'aeho ŭi yŏksahak yŏn'gu* (*Studies of the Historiography of Tanjae Sin Ch'aeho*) (Seoul: Munhak kwa pip'yŏngsa, 1990), 12–13.
55. See the volume produced by the Committee for the Commemoration of Sin Ch'aeho, *Tanjae Sin Ch'aeho wa minjok sagwan* (*Sin Ch'aeho and National History*) (Seoul: Hyŏngsŏl ch'ulp'ansa, 1980).
56. Yi Kibaek, "Minjokchuŭi sahak ŭi munje" (Problems in Nationalist History), in Yi Kibaek, *Minjok kwa yŏksa* (*The Nation and History*) (Seoul: Ilchogak, 1978), 12–22; and Michael Robinson, "National Identity in the Thought of Sin Ch'aeho," *Journal of Korean Studies* 5 (1984): 121–42.
57. Yi Manyŏl, *Tanjae Sin Ch'aeho ŭi yŏksahak yŏn'gu*; Committee for the Commemoration of Sin Ch'aeho, *Tanjae Sin Ch'aeho wa minjok sagwan*.
58. Sin Yongha, "Sin Ch'aeho ŭi ch'ogi minjokchuŭi sagwan kwa hugi minjokchuŭi sagwan" (Sin Ch'aeho's Early and Late Nationalist History), in Sin Yongha, *Han'guk kŭndae sahoe sasangsa yŏn'gu* (*Modern Korean Social Thought*) (Seoul: Ilchisa, 1987), 438–81; Han Yŏngu, "Hanmal Sin Ch'aeho ŭi minjokchuŭi saron" (Sin Ch'aeho's Nationalist History During the Hanmal Period), in Han Yŏngu, *Han'guk minjokchuŭi yŏksahak* (*Nationalist Historiography in Korea*)(Seoul: Ilchogak, 1993), 39–84.
59. Henry Em, "Minjok as a Modern and Democratic Construct: With a Focus on Sin Ch'ae-ho's Historiography," in *Colonial Modernity in Korea*, ed. Gi-wook Shin and Michael Robinson (Cambridge, Mass.: Harvard University Press, 1999), 336–61.
60. Two exceptions are Han Yŏngu, "Hanmal Sin Ch'aeho ŭi minjokchuŭi saron"; and Pak Yŏngsŏk, "Tanjae Sin Ch'aeho ŭi Manjugwan" (Sin Ch'aeho's Views

of Manchuria), in Pak Yŏngsŏk, *Hanminjok tongnip undongsa yŏn'gu* (*Studies on the Korean National Independence Movement*) (Seoul: Ilchogak, 1982), 137–54.

61. Kim Tŭkhwang, "Taeryuk sagwan kwa Manju taeryuk" (A Continental Historical Perspective and Manchuria), *Chayu* (May 1979): 79–82.

62. Yu Chŏnggap, *Pukpang yŏngt'oron* (*On the Northern Territories*) (Seoul: Popkyŏng ch'ulp'ansa, 1991).

63. Ibid., 3.

64. Ibid., 227–29.

65. Ibid., 230.

66. For one example attacking materials created by Taejonggyo in the early years of its history, see Pak Kwangyong, "Taejonggyo kwallyŏn munhŏn e wijak mant'a" (The Many Fabrications in Taejonggyo Materials), *Yŏksa pip'yŏng* 16 (Spring 1992): 108–38.

67. Many of these have been published in the journal *Paeksan hakpo*. For a collection of materials relating to jurisdiction issues, see No Yakhyŏn, ed., *Kando Yŏngyu'gwŏn kwan'gye charyojip* (*Materials Relating to the Rights of Possession of Kando*), 2 vols. (Seoul: Paeksan charyowŏn, 1993); Yang T'aejin, *Han'guk kungnyŏngsa yŏn'gu* (*Studies of the History of Korean National Boundaries*) (Seoul: Pŏpgyŏng ch'ulp'ansa, 1992); and Sin Kisŏk, *Kando yŏngyu'gwŏn e kwanhan yŏn'gu* (*Research on the Rights of Possession of Kando*) (Seoul: Tamgudang, 1979).

68. Yang Zhaoquan and Sun Yumei, *Zhong Chao bianjieshi* (*A History of the Sino-Korean Border*) (Changchun: Jilin wenshi chubanshe, 1993).

69. One leading proponent is Ch'oe Changjo, see his *Han'guk ŭi p'ungsu sasang* (*Korean Geomantic Thought*) (Seoul: Minŭmsa, 1986); and his edited volume, *P'ungsu, kŭ salm ŭi chiri saengmyŏng ŭi chiri* (*Essays on Geomancy*) (Seoul: P'urun Namu, 1993). Also see the 1994 volume of the journal *Han'guksa simin kangjwa* for an issue on geomancy edited by Yi Kibaek.

70. Allen, "Northeast Asia Centered Around Korea."

71. Of course, the unifying narrative of the *minjok* adopted by the south opens the government to charges leveled by domestic opponents, especially student groups during the democratic struggle of the 1970s and 1980s, that the very existence of two states violates the historical will of the *minjok*.

Bibliography

Newspapers and Journals

Atlantic Monthly
Cheguk sinmun
Chosŏn Ilbo
Far Eastern Review
Forum
Han'guk Ilbo
Han'gŭl saesosik
Harper's Weekly
Hwangsŏng sinmun
The Independent
Kajŏng chapch'i
Kongnip sinmun
Korean Repository
Korea Review
Maeil sinbo
Manseibo
Missionary Review
New York Times
Outlook
Review of Reviews
Seoul Press
Sŏbuk hakhoe wŏlbo
Sŏu
Sŭp'och'ŭ Sŏul

TaeChosŏn tongnip hyŏphoe hoebo
Taedong hakhoe wŏlbo
Taegŭk hakpo
TaeHan chaganghoe wŏlbo
TaeHan hyŏphoebo
TaeHan maeil sinbo
TaeHan yuhaksaeng hakpo
Taiyō
Tōkyō Asahi shimbun
Tôngnip sinmun
Yorozu chōhō

Books and Periodicals

Akizuki Nozomi. "Chō-Chū kankai kōshō no hottan to kenkai" (The Origin
   and Development of the Sino-Korean Border). *Chōsen gakuho* 132 (July 1989):
   79–108.
Allen, Chizuko. "Northeast Asia Centered Around Korea: Ch'oe Namson's View of
   History." *Journal of Asian Studies* 49, no. 4 (1990): 787–806.
Altman, Albert. "Korea's First Newspaper: The Japanese Chōsen Shimpo." *Journal
   of Asian Studies* 43, no. 4 (August 1984): 685–96.
An Chunggŭn ŭisa chumo charyojip (*A Collection of Materials* by *the Martyr An
   Chunggŭn*). Seoul: Chŏnjugyo chongui kuhyŏn chŏn'guk sajedan, 1990.
Anderson, Benedict. *Imagined Communities: Reflections on the Origins and Spread
   of Nationalism.* Rev. ed. London: Verso, 1991.
Appadurai, Arjun. *Modernity at Large: Cultural Dimensions of Globalization.* Min-
   neapolis: University of Minnesota Press, 1996.
Armstrong, Charles. "Centering the Periphery: Manchurian Exile(s) and the North
   Korean State." *Korean Studies* 19 (1995): 1–19.
Ashcroft, Bill, Gareth Griffiths, and Helen Tiffin, eds. *The Empire Writes Back:
   Theory and Practice in Post-colonial Literature.* London: Routledge, 1989.
Austin, Major Herbert H. "A Scamper Through Korea." In *Korea: Its History, Its
   People and Its Commerce,* edited by Angus Hamilton, Herbert H. Austin, and
   Masatake Terauchi, 151–214. Boston and Tokyo: J. B. Millet, 1910.
Baldwin Jr., Frank P. "The March First Movement: Korean Challenge and Japanese
   Response." Ph.D. diss., Columbia University, 1969.
Balibar, Etienne, and Immanuel Wallerstein. *Race, Nation, Class: Ambiguous Iden-
   tities.* London: Verso, 1991.
Barkin, Elazar. "Post-Anti-Colonial Histories: Representing the Other in Imperial
   Britain." *Journal of British Studies* 33 (April 1994): 180–203.
Bhaba, Homi. *The Location of Culture.* New York: Routledge, 1994.

Bird, Isabella. *Korea Among Her Neighbours.* London: Routledge & Kegan Paul, 1897.

Brinkley, Capt. F., with the collaboration of Baron Kikuchi. *A History of the Japanese People: From the Earliest Times to the End of the Meiji Era.* New York: Encyclopedia Britannica, 1915.

Brook, Timothy, and Andre Schmid, eds. *Nation Work: Asian Elites and National Identities.* Ann Arbor: University of Michigan Press, 2000.

Brownlee, John S. *Japanese Historians and the National Myths, 1600–1945: The Age of Gods and Emperor Jinmu.* Vancouver: University of British Columbia Press, 1997.

——. *Political Thought in Japanese Historical Writing: From Kojiki (712) to Tokushi Yoron (1712).* Waterloo: McMaster University Press, 1991.

Chandra, Vipan. *Imperialism, Resistance, and Reform in Late Nineteenth-Century Korea: Enlightenment and the Independence Club.* Berkeley: Center for Korean Studies, University of California, 1988.

——. "An Outline Study of the Ilchin-hoe (Advancement Society) of Korea." *Occasional Papers on Korea* 2 (March 1974): 43–72.

Chang Yun-Shik, Donald L. Baker, Hur Nam-lin, and Ross King, eds. *Korea Between Tradition and Modernity.* Vancouver: Institute for Asian Research, 2000.

Chatterjee, Partha. *Nationalist Thought and the Colonial World: A Derivative Discourse?* London: Zed, 1986.

Chen, Jerome. *Yuan Shi-k'ai, 1859–1916: Brutus Assumes the Purple.* London: Allen & Unwin, 1961.

Cho Hangnae, ed. *1900 nyŏndae ŭi aeguk kyemong undong yŏn'gu (Studies of the Patriotic Enlightenment Movement of the 1900s).* Seoul: Asea munhwasa, 1992.

Cho Kwang. "Chosŏn hugi ŭi pyŏn'gyŏng ŭisik" (Border Consciousness in the Late Choson). *Paeksan hakpo* 16 (June 1974): 145–82.

Cho Tonggŏl. "Hanmal sasŏ wa kŭŭi kyemongjuŭijŏk hŏsil" (The Strengths and Weaknesses of Enlightenment History Books in the Hanmal Period). In Cho Tonggŏl, *Han'guk minjokchuŭi ŭi sŏngnip kwa tongnip undongsa yŏn'gu (Studies of the Rise of Korean Nationalism and the Independence Movement)*, 141–217. Seoul: Chisik san'ŏpsa, 1989.

Cho Tonggŏl, Han Yŏngu, and Pak Ch'ansŭng, eds. *Han'guk ŭi yŏksaga wa yŏksahak (Korean Historians and Historiography).* 2 vols. Seoul: Ch'angjak kwa pip'yŏngsa, 1994.

Cho Tongil. *Han'guk munhak t'ongsa (A Comprehensive History of Korean Literature).* 2d ed. 5 vols. Seoul: Chisik san'ŏpsa, 1991.

Ch'oe Ch'angjo. "Chosŏn hugi sirhakchadŭl ŭi p'ungsu sasang" (The Geomantic Thought of Sirhak Scholars in the Late Chosŏn Dynasty). *Han'guk munhwa* 11 (1990): 469–504.

340 Bibliography

——. *Han'guk ŭi p'ungsu sasang* (Korean Geomantic Thought). Seoul: Minŭmsa, 1986.

——, ed. *P'ungsu, kŭ salm ŭi chiri saengmyŏng ŭi chiri* (Essays on Geomancy). Seoul: P'urun Namu, 1993.

Ch'oe Chun. *Han'guk sinmunsa* (A History of Korean Newspapers). Rev. ed. Seoul: Ilchogak, 1991.

Ch'oe Kiyŏng. *TaeHan cheguk sigi sinmun yŏn'gu* (Essays on the Newspapers of the TaeHan Empire Period). Seoul: Ilchogak, 1991.

Ch'oe Kyŏnghwan and Chŏng Kyo, eds. *Taedong yŏksa* (History of the Great East). 1905. Reprinted in *Han'guk kaehwagi kyo'gwasŏ ch'ongsŏ*, edited by Han'gukhak munhŏn yŏn'guso. Vol. 17, 1–434. Seoul: Asea munhwasa, 1977.

Ch'oe Munhung, ed. *Myŏngsŏng hwanghu sihae sagŏn* (The Assassination of Queen Min). Seoul: Minŭmsa, 1992.

Ch'oe Sŏgyŏng. *Ilche tonghwa idaeollogi ŭi ch'angch'ul* (The Emergence of Japanese Colonial Assimilation Ideology). Seoul: Sŏgyŏng munhwasa, 1997.

Ch'oe Yongjun. "P'ungsu wa T'aengniji" (Geomancy and the T'aengniji). *Han'guksa simin kangjwa* 14 (1994): 98–122.

Chŏn Kwanu et al. *Wiam Chang Chiyŏn ŭi sasang kwa hwaltong* (The Thought and Activities of Chang Chiyŏn). Seoul: Minŭmsa, 1993.

Chŏng Ch'angnyŏl. "Hanmal ŭi yŏksa insik" (Historical Understanding in the Hanmal Period). In *Han'guk sahak yŏn'gu* (Studies of Korean Historiography), edited by Han'guksa yŏn'guhoe, 187–228. Seoul: Ŭlyu munhwasa, 1991.

Chŏng Ch'angnyŏl, Pak Hyŏnch'ae, Yi Chunmo, Kim Ch'angnak, and Kim Sŏngjae, eds. *Han'guk minjungnon ŭi hyŏndan'gye* (The Current State of Debates on the Korean Minjung). Seoul: Tolbegae, 1989.

Chŏng Chin-sok. *The Korea Problem in Anglo-Japanese Relations: Ernest Thomas Bethell and His Newspapers, the Daehan Maeil Sinbo and the Korean Daily News.* Seoul: Nanam Publications, 1987.

——. "A Study of the Maeil Sinbo (Daily News) — Public Information Policy of the Japanese Imperialists and Korean Journalism Under Japanese Imperialism." *Journal of Social Sciences and Humanities* 52 (December 1980): 59–114.

Chŏng Inbo. *Chosŏnsa yŏn'gu* (Research on Korean History). Seoul: Soŭl sinmunsa, 1947.

Chŏng Inho. *Ch'odŭng TaeHan yŏksa* (An Elementary History of Korea). 1908. Reprinted in *Han'guk kaehwagi kyo'gwasŏ ch'ongsŏ* (A Collection of Textbooks from the Korean Enlightenment Period), edited by Han'gukhak munhŏn yŏn'guso. Vol. 14, 363–539. Seoul: Asea munhwasa, 1977.

Chŏng Kwŏn. "Kyonam kyoyukhoe ŭi hwaltong kwa sŏnggyŏk" (The Activities and Nature of the Kyonam Educational Association). In *1900 nyŏndae ŭi aeguk kyemong undong yŏn'gu* (Studies of the Patriotic Enlightenment Movement of the 1900s), edited by Cho Hangnae, 423–52. Seoul: Asea munhwasa, 1992.

Chŏng Kyo. *TaeHan kyenyŏnsa* (*History of the Waning Years of the TaeHan Empire*). 2 vols. Seoul: Kuksa p'yŏnch'ansa, 1956.

Chŏng Yŏnghun. "Tan'gun kwa kŭndae Han'guk minjok undong" (Tan'gun and the Modern Korean Nationalist Movement). *Han'guk ŭi chŏngch'i wa kyŏngje* 8 (1995): 1–115.

Chu Chino. "Kim T'aegyŏng, Hyŏn Ch'ae." In *Han'guk ŭi yŏksaga wa yŏksahak* (*Korean Historians and Historiography*), edited by Cho Tonggŏl, Han Yŏngu, and Pak Ch'ansŭng. Vol. 2, 35–48. Seoul: Ch'angjak kwa pip'yŏngsa, 1994.

———. "Tongnip hyŏphoe ŭi daeoe insik ŭi kujo wa chŏn'gae" (The Formation and Development of The Independence Club's View of Foreigners). *Hangnim* 8 (1987).

———. "Tongnip hyŏphoe ŭi sahoe sasang kwa sahoe chinhwaron" (The Social Thought and Social Darwinism of the Independence Club). In *Sun Pogi paksa chŏngnyŏn kinyŏm Han'guksa nonch'ong* (*Essays in Commemoration of the Retirement of Sun Pogi*), edited by Sun Pogi paksa chŏngnyŏn kinyŏm wiwŏnhoe. Seoul: Chisik sanŏpsa, 1988.

Cohn, Bernard. *Colonialism and Its Forms of Knowledge: The British in India.* Princeton, N.J.: Princeton University Press, 1996.

Committee for the Commemoration of Sin Ch'aeho. *Tanjae Sin Ch'aeho wa minjok sagwan* (*Sin Ch'aeho and National History*). Seoul: Hyŏngsŏl ch'ulp'ansa, 1980.

Conroy, Hilary. *The Japanese Seizure of Korea: 1868–1910, a Study of Realism and Idealism in International Relations.* Philadelphia: University of Pennsylvania Press, 1960.

Cooper, Frederick, and Ann Laura Stoler, eds. *Tensions of Empire: Colonial Cultures in a Bourgeois World.* Berkeley and Los Angeles: University of California Press, 1997.

Cumings, Bruce. "Archaeology, Descent, Emergence: Japan in British/American Hegemony, 1900–50." In *Japan in the World,* edited by Masao Miyoshi and H. D. Harootunian, 79–111. Durham, N.C.: Duke University Press, 1993.

Deuchler, Martina. *Confucian Gentlemen and Barbarian Envoys: The Opening of Korea, 1875–1885.* Seattle: University of Washington Press, 1977.

———. *The Confucian Transformation of Korea: A Study of Society and Ideology.* Cambridge, Mass.: Harvard University Press, 1992.

Dikötter, Frank. *The Discourse of Race in Modern China.* London: C. Hurst, 1992.

Drake, H. B. *Korea of the Japanese.* London: John Lane, The Bodley Head, 1930.

Duara, Prasenjit. *Rescuing History from the Nation: Questioning Narratives of Modern China.* Chicago: University of Chicago Press, 1995.

Dudden, Alexis. "International Terms: Japan's Engagement in Colonial Control." Ph.D. diss., University of Chicago, 1998.

Duus, Peter. *The Abacus and the Sword: The Japanese Penetration of Korea, 1895–1910.* Berkeley and Los Angeles: University of California Press, 1995.

Eckert, Carter, Ki-baik Lee, Young Ick Lew, Michael Robinson, and Edward W. Wagner. *Korea: Old and New.* Seoul: Ilchogak, 1990.

Edney, Mathew H. *Mapping an Empire: The Geographical Construction of British India.* Chicago: University of Chicago Press, 1997.

Eggert, Marion. "A Borderline Case: Korean Travelers' Views of the Chinese Border (Eighteenth to Nineteenth Century)." In *China and Her Neighbours: Borders, Visions of the Other, Foreign Policy, 10th to 19th Century,* edited by Sabine Dabringhaus and Roderich Ptak, 49–78. Wiesbaden: Harrassowitx Verlag, 1997.

Elias, Norbert. *The Civilizing Process: The History of Manners.* Trans. Edmund Jephcott. New York: Pantheon Books, 1978.

Em, Henry. "Minjok as a Modern and Democratic Construct: With a Focus on Sin Ch'aeho's Historiography." In *Colonial Modernity in Korea,* edited by Gi-wook Shin and Michael Robinson, 336–61. Cambridge, Mass.: Harvard University Press, 1999.

Eto, Shinkichi, and Marius Jansen, trans. *My Thirty Years Dream: The Autobiography of Miyazaki Toten.* Princeton, N.J.: Princeton University Press, 1988.

Farris, William Wayne. *Sacred Texts and Buried Treasures: Issues in the Historical Archaeology of Ancient Japan.* Honolulu: University of Hawai'i Press, 1998.

Gale, James Scarth. *A History of the Korean People.* Reprint, Seoul: Royal Asiatic Society, 1972.

Gellner, Ernest. *Nations and Nationalism.* Ithaca, N.Y.: Cornell University Press, 1983.

Gong, Gerrit W. *The Standard of "Civilization" in International Society.* Oxford: Clarendon Press, 1984.

Government General of Chōsen. *Annual Report on Reforms and Progress in Chōsen (Korea), 1910–11.* Seoul: Government General of Chōsen, 1911.

Government General of Chōsen. *Annual Report on Reforms and Progress in Chōsen (Korea), 1916–17.* Seoul: Government General of Chōsen, 1918.

Government General of Chōsen. *Annual Report on Reforms and Progress in Chōsen (Korea), 1917–18.* Seoul: Government General of Chōsen, 1920.

Government General of Chōsen. *Annual Report on Reforms and Progress in Chōsen (Korea), 1918–21.* Seoul: Government General of Chōsen, 1922.

Ha Ubong. *Chosŏn hugi sirhakcha ŭi Ilbon yŏn'gu (Sirhak Studies of Japan in the Late Chosŏn Dynasty).* Seoul: Ilchisa, 1989.

Haboush, JaHyun Kim. "Constructing the Center: The Ritual Controversy and the Search for a New Identity in Seventeenth Century Korea." In *Culture and the State in Late Chosŏn Korea,* edited by JaHyun Kim Haboush and Martina Deuchler, 46–90. Cambridge, Mass.: Harvard University Press, 1999.

——. *A Heritage of Kings: One Man's Monarchy in the Confucian World.* New York: Columbia University Press, 1988.

Haferkamp, Hans. "From the Intra-Society to the Inter-Society Civilizing Process." *Theory, Culture, and Society* 4 (1987): 545–57.

Hamilton, Angus. *Korea*. London: William Heineman, 1904.

Han Jinchun and Li Yinfun. "Hanwen 'minzu' yici de chuxian ji qichuqi shiyong qingkuang" (The First Appearance of the Chinese Term "Minzu" and Its Early Use). *Minzu yanjiu* 2 (1984): 36–43.

Han U'gun. *Tonghak kwa nongmin ponggi (Tonghak and Peasant Uprisings)*. Seoul: Ilchogak, 1983.

Han Yŏngu. "1910 nyŏndae Yi Sangyong, Kim Kyohŏn ŭi minjokchuŭi yŏksa sosŏl" (The Nationalist Historical Narratives of Yi Sangyong and Kim Kyohŏn in the 1910s). In Han Yŏngu, *Han'guk minjokchuŭi yŏksahak (Nationalist Historiography in Korea)*, 85–122. Seoul: Ilchogak, 1994.

———. *Chosŏn chŏn'gi sahoe sasang yŏn'gu (Essays on the Social Ideology of the Early Chosŏn Dynasty)*. Seoul: Chisik San'ŏpsa, 1983.

———. *Chosŏn hugi sahaksa yŏn'gu (Essays on the Historiography of the Late Chosŏn Dynasty)*. Seoul: Ilchisa, 1989.

———. "Hanmal Sin Ch'aeho ŭi minjokchuŭi saron" (Sin Ch'aeho's Nationalist History During the Hanmal period). In Han Yŏngu, *Han'guk minjokchuŭi yŏksahak (Nationalist Historiography in Korea)*, 39–84. Seoul: Ilchogak, 1993.

Han'guk chŏngsin munhwa yŏn'guwŏn p'yŏnch'anbu, ed. *Han'guk minjok munhwa taebaekkwa sajŏn (Encyclopedia of Korean National Culture)*. 27 vols. Seoul: Han'guk chŏngsin munhwa yŏn'guwŏn, 1991.

Han'guk minjok undongsa yŏn'guhoe, ed. *Ŭibyŏng chŏnjaeng yŏn'gu (Studies of the Ŭibyŏng War)*. Seoul: Chisik san'ŏpsa, 1990.

Han'guk yŏksa yŏn'guhoe, ed. *1894 nyŏn nongmin chŏnjaeng yŏn'gu (Studies of the 1894 Peasant War)*. 4 vols. Seoul: Yŏksa pi'pyŏngsa, 1991–95.

Han'guk yŏsŏng yŏn'guhoe, ed. *Han'guk yŏsŏngsa, kŭndae py'ŏn (Korean Women's History, Modern Volume)*. Seoul: P'ulpit, 1992.

Han'gukhak munhŏn yŏn'guso, ed. *Han'guk kaehwagi kyo'gwasŏ ch'ongsŏ (A Collection of Textbooks from the Korean Enlightenment Period)*. 20 vols. Seoul: Asea munhwasa, 1977.

Harootunian, Harry. *History's Disquiet: Modernity, Cultural Practice, and the Question of Everyday Life*. New York: Columbia University Press, 2000.

Hatada, Takashi. "An Interpretation of the King Kwanggaet'o Inscription." Trans. V. Dixon Morris. *Korean Studies* 3 (1979): 1–18.

———. *Nihonjin no Chōsenkan (Japanese Views of Korea)*. Tokyo: Keiso shobō, 1969.

Hayashi Taisuke. *Chōsen kinseishi (Early Modern Korean History)*. Tokyo: Yoshikawa hanshichi, 1900.

———. *Chōsenshi (Korean History)*. Tokyo: Yoshikawa hanshichi, 1892.

Hŏ Ŭng. *Han'gŭl kwa minjok munhwa (Han'gŭl and National Culture)*. Seoul: Sejong Taewang kinyŏm saŏphoe, 1974.

Hobsbawm, Eric, and Terence Ranger, eds. *The Invention of Tradition*. Cambridge: Cambridge University Press, 1983.

Hong Ponghan, et al. *Chŭngbo munhŏn pigo* (Seoul: Hongmun'gwan, 1907).

Hong Set'ae. "Paektusan'gi" (A Record of Mount Paektu). In *Kando yŏngyu'gwŏn kwan'gye charyojip* (*Materials Relating to the Rights of Possession of Kando*), edited by No Yakhyon. Vol. 2, 314–31. Seoul: Paeksan charyowŏn, 1993.

Hong Sŭngi. "Silchŭng sahangnon" (Empiricist Historiography). In No Taedon, Hong Sŭngi, Yi Hyŏnhŭi, Yi Kibaek, and Yi Kidong, *Hyŏndae Han'guk sahak kwa sagwan* (*Contemporary Korean Historiography*). Seoul: Ilchogak, 1991.

Hong Sungwŏn. *Hanmal Honam chiyŏk ŭibyŏng undongsa yŏn'gu* (*The History of the Ŭibyŏng Movement in the Honam Region During the Hanmal Period*). Seoul: Sŏul taehakkyo ch'ulp'anbu, 1994.

Hoshino, Tokuji. *Economic History of Chosen*. Seoul: Chosŏn unhaeng 1921.

Howland, D. R. *Borders of Chinese Civilization: Geography and History at Empire's End*. Durham, N.C.: Duke University Press, 1996.

Huang, Philip C. *Liang Ch'i-ch'ao and Modern Chinese Liberalism*. Seattle: University of Washington Press, 1972.

Hulbert, Homer. *History of Korea*. Seoul: Methodist Publishing House, 1905.

Hwang Hyŏn. *Maech'ŏn yarok* (*Maech'ŏn's Unofficial History*). Seoul: Kuksa p'yŏnch'an wiwŏnhoe, 1961.

Hwang, Kyung Moon. "Bureaucracy in the Transition to Korean Modernity: Secondary Status Groups and the Transformation of Government and Society, 1880–1930." Ph.D. diss., Harvard University, 1997.

———. "New Conceptualizations of *Kukka* ("State") in Korea, 1896–1910." Paper presented at the annual meeting of the Association of Asian Studies, Boston, 1999.

Hwimun ŭisuk p'yŏnjippu, ed. *Kodŭng sokhak tokpon* (*An Advanced Elementary Reader*). Seoul: Hwimun ŭisuk inswaebu, 1906. Reprinted in *Han'guk kaehwagi kyo'gwasŏ ch'ongsŏ* (*A Collection of Textbooks from the Korean Enlightenment Period*), edited by Han'gukhak munhŏn yŏn'guso. Vol. 5, 1–173. Seoul: Asea munhwasa, 1977.

Hyŏn Ch'ae. *Pot'ong kyogwa Tongguk yŏksa* (*An Ordinary Textbook History of Korea*). Seoul: Ministry of Education, 1898. Reprinted in *Han'guk kaehwagi kyo'gwasŏ ch'ongsŏ* (*A Collection of Textbooks from the Korean Enlightenment Period*), edited by Han'gukhak munhŏn yŏn'guso. Vol. 14, 1–362. Seoul: Asea munhwasa, 1977.

———. *Sinch'an ch'odŭng sohak* (*A New Elementary Primer*). 1909. Reprinted in Han'guk kaehwag; Kyo'gwasŏ ch'ongsŏ (A Collection of Textbooks from the Korean Enlightenment Period), edited by Han'guk munhŏn yŏn'guso. Vol. 7. Seoul: Asea munhwasa, 1977.

——. *Tongguk saryak* (A Brief History of the Eastern Kingdom). 1908. Reprinted in *Han'guk kaehwagi kyo'gwasŏ ch'ongsŏ* (A Collection of Textbooks from the Korean Enlightnment Period), edited by Han'gukhak munhŏn yŏn'guso. Vol. 16, 1–426. Seoul: Asea munhwasa, 1977.

——. *Yunyŏn p'iltok* (An Essential Reader for Youths). 1897. Reprinted in *Han'guk kaehwagi kyo'gwasŏ ch'ongsŏ* (A Collection of Textbooks from the Korean Enlightenment Period), edited by Han'gukhak munhŏn yŏn'guso. Vol. 2, 1–220. Seoul: Asea munhwasa, 1977.

Ihwa Yŏja Taehakkyo Han'guk yŏsŏng yŏn'guso, ed. *Han'guk yŏsŏng kwan'gye charyojip* (A Collection of Materials on Korean Women). 2 vols. Seoul: Ihwa yŏja taehakkyo ch'ulp'anbu, 1980.

Im Chong-myong. "Ilminjuŭi and the Making of the Republic of Korea as a Modern Nation-State." Paper presented at the conference "Between Colonialism and Nationalism: Power and Subjectivity in Korea, 1931–50." University of Michigan, Ann Arbor, 4–6 May 2001.

Inoue Hideo. *Kodai Chōsen* (Ancient Korea). Tokyo: Nihon hōsō shuppan kyōkai, 1972.

Iryon. *Samguk Yusa: Legends and History of the Three Kingdoms of Korea*. Trans. Tae-hung Ha and Grafton Mintz. Seoul: Yonsei University Press, 1972.

Jansen, Marius B. *The Japanese and Sun Yat-sen*. Stanford, Calif.: Stanford University Press, 1954.

Jorganson, John. "'Tan'gun and the Legitimization of a Threatened Dynasty: North Korea's Rediscovery of Tan'gun." *Korea Observer* 27, no. 2 (Summer 1996): 273–306.

Kang Chaeŏn. *Han'guk kŭndaesa yŏn'gu* (Essays on Korean Modern History). Seoul: Hanŭl, 1970.

——. *Han'guk ŭi kaehwa sasang* (Korea's Enlightenment Thought). Trans. Chŏng Ch'angnyŏl. Seoul: Pibong ch'ulp'ansa, 1981.

Kang Man'gil, ed. *Han'guksa* (Korean History). 27 vols. Seoul: Han'gilsa, 1994.

Kang Mansaeng. "Hwangsŏng sinmun ŭi hyŏnsil kaehyŏk kusang yŏn'gu" (A Study of the *Hwangsŏng sinmun*'s Reform Thought). *Hangnim* 9 (1987): 63–120.

Keene, Donald. "The Sino-Japanese War of 1894–95 and Its Cultural Effects." In *Tradition and Modernization in Japanese Culture*, edited by Donald Shively, 121–75. Princeton, N.J.: Princeton University Press, 1971.

Keirstead, Thomas. "Nation and Postnation in Japan: Global Capitalism and the Idea of National History." In *Nation Work: Asian Elites and National Identities*, edited by Timothy Brook and Andre Schmid, 219–39. Ann Arbor: University of Michigan Press, 2000.

Kennedy, Dane. "Imperial History and Post-Colonial Theory." *Journal of Imperial and Commonwealth History* 27, no. 3 (September 1996): 345–63.

——. "The Imperial Kaleidoscope." *Journal of British Studies* 37, no. 4 (October 1998): 460–67.

Kim Ch'unsŏn. "1880–1890 nyŏndae ch'ŏngjo ŭi 'yimin silbyŏn' chŏngch'aek kwa Hanin yijumin silt'ae yŏn'gu" (The Policy of "Populating the Border Regions" in the 1880s and 1890s and the Situation of Korean Migrants). *Han'guk kŭnhyŏndaesa yŏn'gu* 8 (1998): 5–36.

Kim Dong-no. "The Failure of State Reform Movements in Early Modern Korea and Its Relevance to the Mobilization of Resources." In Chang Yun-Shik et al., *Korea Between Tradition and Modernity*, 172–83. Vancouver: Institute for Asian Research, 2000.

Kim, J. Y. "The Kwanggaet'o Stele Inscription." In *Contemporary European Writing on Japan: Scholarly Views from Eastern and Western Europe*, edited by Ian Nish. Kent: Paul Norbury, 1988.

Kim, K. W. "Ideology and Political Development in South Korea." *Pacific Affairs* 38, no. 2 (Summer 1965): 164–76.

Kim, Key-hiuk. *The Last Phase of the East Asian World Order: Korea, Japan and the Chinese Empire, 1860–1882*. Berkeley and Los Angeles: University of California Press, 1980.

Kim Kiju. *Hanmal chaeil Han'guk yuhaksaeng ŭi minjok undong (The Nationalist Movement Among Korean Students in Japan During the Hanmal Period)*. Seoul: Nut'i namu, 1993.

Kim Kyohŏn. *Sindan minsa (History of the Divine Tan'gun's People)*. Reprint, Seoul: Sŏul Kong'insa, 1946.

Kim, Kyohŏn. *Sindan minsa (History of the Divine Tan'gun's People)*. Trans. Ko Tongnyŏng. Seoul: Han Ppuri, 1986.

Kim Sŏkhyŏng. *Ch'ogi Cho-Il kwan'gye yŏn'gu (Studies of Early Korean-Japanese Relations)*. Pyongyang: Sahoe kwahag'wŏn ch'ulp'ansa, 1966.

Kim T'aegyŏng. *Yŏksa kyeryak (A Short History)*. Reprinted in *Han'guk kaehwagi kyo'gwasŏ ch'ongsŏ (A Collection of Textbooks from the Korean Enlightenment Period)*, edited by Han'gukhak munhŏn yŏn'guso. Vol. 15. Seoul: Asea munhwasa, 1977.

Kim Tohyŏng. *TaeHan chegukki ŭi chŏngch'i sasang yŏn'gu (Essays on the Political Ideology of the TaeHan Empire)*. Seoul: Chisiksan'ŏpsa, 1994.

Kim Tukhwang. "Taeryuk sagwan kwa Manju taeryuk" (A Continental Historical Perspective and Manchuria). *Chayu* (May 1979): 79–82.

Kim Yongsŏp. *Chosŏn hugi nongŏpsa yŏn'gu (Research on the Agricultural History of the Late Choson Period)*. 2 vols. Seoul: Ilchogak, 1970–71.

King, Ross. "Language, Politics, and Ideology in the Postwar Koreas." In *Korea Briefing: Toward Reunification*, edited by David McCann, 107–44. Armonk, N.Y.: Sharpe, 1997.

——. "Nationalism and Language Reform in Korea: The *Questione della Lingua* in Precolonial Korea." In *Nationalism and the Construction of Korean Identity*, edited by Hyung Il Pai and Timothy R. Tangherlini, 33–72. Berkeley: Institute of East Asian Studies, University of California, 1998.

Koguryŏ yŏn'guhoe, ed. *Kwanggaet'o hot'ae wangbi yŏn'gu 100 nyŏn (100 Years of Research on the Kwanggaet'o Stele)*. Seoul: Hangyŏn munhwasa, 1996.

Kojiki. Trans. Donald L. Philippi. Tokyo: University of Tokyo Press, 1968.

Koryŏ Taehak Asea Munje Yŏn'guso, ed. *KuHan'guk oegyo munsŏ (Diplomatic Documents of Old Korea)*. 22 vols. Seoul: Koryŏ taehakkyo ch'ulp'ansa, 1965–73.

Koryŏ Taehakkyo Minjok Munhwa Yŏn'guso, ed. *Han'guk munhwasa taegye (Cultural History of Korea)*. 7 vols. Seoul: Koryŏ taehakkyo minjok munhwa yŏn'guso ch'ulp'anbu, 1964–78.

Kuksa p'yŏnch'an wiwŏnhoe, ed. *Kojong sidaesa (History of the Kojong Era)*. 6 vols. Seoul: Kuksa p'yŏnch'an wiwŏnhoe, 1969.

——, ed. *Tongmun hwigo (A Compendium of Diplomatic Documents)*. 4 vols. Seoul: Kuksa p'yŏnch'an wiwŏnhoe, 1978.

——, ed. *Wiam mungo (Writings of Chang Chiyŏn)*. Seoul: Yuchong-sa, 1956.

Kuo T'ing-i and Li Yu-shu, eds. *Qingji Zhong Ri Han guanxi shiliao (Historical Materials on Chinese-Japanese-Korean Relations During the Qing Period)*. 11 vols. Taipei: Chungyang yenchiuyüan chintaishih yenchiuso, 1972.

Ladd, George Trumbell. "The Annexation of Korea: An Essay in 'Benevolent Assimilation.'" *Yale Review* (1911–12): 639–56.

——. *In Korea with Marquis Ito*. London: Longmans, Green, 1908.

Ledyard, Gari."Cartography in Korea." In *The History of Cartography*, edited by J. B. Harley and David Woodward. Vol. 2, no. 2, 235–344. Chicago: University of Chicago Press, 1994.

——. "The Korean Language Reform of 1446: The Origin, Background, and Early History of the Korean Alphabet." Ph.D. diss., University of California at Berkeley, 1966.

Lee, Chae-jin. *China's Korean Minority: The Politics of Ethnic Education*. Boulder, Colo.: Westview Press, 1986.

Lee, Chong-sik. *Japan and Korea: The Political Dimension*. Stanford, Calif.: Hoover Institution Press, 1985.

——. *The Politics of Korean Nationalism*. Berkeley and Los Angeles: University of California Press, 1963.

Lee, Peter, ed. *Anthology of Korean Literature, from Early Times to the Nineteenth Century*. Honolulu: University of Hawai'i Press, 1981.

——, ed. *Sourcebook of Korean Civilization*. Vol. 2: *From the Seventeenth Century to the Modern Period*. Berkeley and Los Angeles: University of California Press, 1994.

Lee, Robert. *The Manchuria Frontier in Ch'ing History.* Cambridge, Mass.: Harvard University Press, 1970.

Legge, James, trans. *The Great Learning.* In *The Chinese Classics,* edited by James Legge. Vol. 1. Hong Kong: Hong Kong University Press, 1970.

Lew Young Ick. "An Analysis of the Reform Documents of the Kabo Reform Movement, 1894." *Journal of Social Sciences and Humanities* 40 (1974): 29–85.

——. "The Conservative Character of the 1894 Tonghak Peasant Uprising: A Reappraisal with Emphasis on Chon Pongjun's Background and Motivation." *Journal of Korean Studies* 7 (1990): 149–80.

——. "Korean-Japanese Politics Behind the Kabo-Ulmi Reform Movement, 1894–1896." *Journal of Korean Studies* 3 (1981): 39–82.

——. "Minister Inoue Kaoru and the Japanese Reform Attempts in Korea During the Sino-Japanese War, 1894–95." *Journal of Asiatic Studies* 27, no. 2 (1984): 145–86.

——. "Reform Efforts and Ideas of Pak Yong-hyo, 1894–95." *Korean Studies* 1 (1977): 21–63.

——. "Yuan Shi-kai's Residency and the Korean Enlightenment Movement, 1885–1894." *Journal of Korean Studies* 5 (1984): 63–108.

Liang Qichao. "Zhengzhixue dajia Bolunzhili zhi xuesho" (The Theories of the Great Politics Scholar, Bluntschli). In Liang Qichao, *Yinbingshi wenji* (*Selected Works of Liang Qichao*). Vol. 10, 31–49. Kunming: Zhonghua shuju, 1941.

Lin Mingde. *Yuan Shikai yu Chaoxian* (*Yuan Shikai and Korea*). Taibei: Zhongyang yanjiuyuan jindaishi yanjiusuo, 1969.

Liu, Lydia. *Translingual Practice: Literature, National Culture, and Translated Modernity in China, 1900–37.* Stanford, Calif.: Stanford University Press, 1995.

Longford, Joseph H. *The Story of Korea.* London: T. Fisher Unwin, 1911.

——. *The Story of Old Japan.* New York: Longmans, Green, 1910.

Luk, Bernard Hung-kay. "State, Nation, Country and Fatherland: An Etymology of Patriotism in Modern Chinese." Paper presented at the Joint Centre for Asia Pacific Studies Conference on Nationalism and Postnationalism, University of Toronto, 7 September 1996.

Malkki, Liisa. *Purity and Exile: Violence, Memory, and National Cosmology Among Hutu Refugees in Tanzania.* Chicago: University of Chicago Press, 1995.

McClintock, Anne. *Imperial Leather: Race, Gender and Sexuality in the Colonial Conquest.* New York: Routledge, 1995.

McKenzie, F. A. *Korea's Fight for Freedom.* New York: Fleming H. Revell, 1920.

——. *The Tragedy of Korea.* London: Hodder & Stoughton, 1908.

Ministry of Education, ed. *Chosŏn yŏksa* (*A History of Chosŏn*). Seoul: Ministry of Education, 1895. Reprinted in *Han'guk kaehwagi kyo'gwasŏ ch'ongsŏ* (*A Collection of Textbooks from the Korean Enlightnment Period*), edited by Han'gukhak munhŏn yŏn'guso. Vol. 11, 1–265. Seoul: Asea munhwasa, 1977.

Ministry of Education, ed. *Chosŏn yŏktae sayak* (*A Brief History of Korea*). Seoul: Ministry of Education, 1895. Reprinted in *Han'guk kaehwagi kyo'gwasŏ ch'ongsŏ* (*A Collection of Textbooks from the Korean Enlightenment Period*), edited by Han'gukhak munhŏn yŏn'guso. Vol. 11, 267–345. Seoul: Asea munhwasa, 1977.

Ministry of Education, ed. *Kugŏ tokpon* (*A Korean Reader*). 1908. Reprinted in *Han'guk kaehwagi kyo'gwasŏ ch'ongsŏ* (*A Collection of Textbooks from the Korean Enlightenment Period*), edited by Han'gukhak munhŏn yŏn'guso. Vol. 6. Seoul: Asea munhwasa, 1977.

Ministry of Education, ed. *Kungmin sohak tokpon* (*An Elementary Reader for Citizens*). Seoul: Ministry of Education, 1895. Reprinted in *Han'guk kaehwagi kyo'gwasŏ ch'ongsŏ* (*A Collection of Textbooks from the Korean Enlightenment Period*), edited by Han'gukhak munhŏn yŏn'guso. Vol. 1, 1–152. Seoul: Asea munhwasa, 1977.

Miyake Hidetoshi. *Ilbon'in ŭi Han'gukkwan* (*Japanese Views of Korea*). Translated by Ha Ubong. Seoul: Pulp'it, 1994.

Murdoch, James. *A History of Japan*. Yokohama: Kelly & Walsh, 1910.

Nam Kwangu. *Kugŏ kukcha nonjip* (*Essays on National Language and National Script*). Seoul: Ilchogak, 1982.

Nihongi: Chronicles of Japan from the Earliest Times to A.D. 697. Trans. W. G. Aston. London: Allen & Unwin, 1956.

No Inhwa. "Hanmal kaehwa chagangp'a ŭi yŏsŏng kyoyukkwan" (Self-Strengthening Reformers' Views on Women's Education in the Hanmal Period). *Han'guk hakpo* 27 (1982): 84–119.

No Taedon, Hong Sŭngi, Yi Hyŏnhŭi, Yi Kibaek, and Yi Kidong. *Hyŏndae Han'guk sahak kwa sagwan* (*Contemporary Korean Historiography*). Seoul: Ilchogak, 1991.

No Taegyu. "Han'gŭl kwa hanja ŭi sayong piyul ŭi pyŏnhwa" (Changes in the Frequency of Use of Han'gŭl and Hanja). *Han'gŭl saesosik* 202 (June 1989): 4–6.

No Yakhyŏn, ed. *Kando Yŏngyu'gwŏn kwan'gye charyojip* (*Materials Relating to the Rights of Possession of Kando*). 2 vols. Seoul: Paeksan charyowŏn, 1993.

O Chuhwan. "Ilcheŭi taeHan ŏron chŏngch'aek" (Japanese Media Policies During the Korean Colonial Period). In *Ilche ŭi munhwa ch'imt'alsa* (*A Hisory of Japanese Cultural Imperialism*), edited by Han Kion, 373–492. Seoul: Minjung sŏgwan, 1970.

Ŏ Yunjung. "Chongjŏng nyŏnp'yo" (A Chronology of Years in Power). In *Ŏ Yunjung chŏnjip* (*The Complete Works of Ŏ Yunjung*), 691–887. Seoul: Asea munhwasa, 1978.

Okakura Kakuzo. *The Ideals of the East*. Rutland, Vt.: Tuttle, 1970.

P'ae Chahyŏk. "Chang Chiyŏn ŭi sasŏ chŏsul kwa yŏksagwan" (Chang Chiyŏn's

Historical Narratives and Perspective). In *Wiam Chang Chiyŏn ŭi sasang kwa hwaltong (The Thought and Activities of Chang Chiyŏn)*, edited by Chŏn Kwanu et al., 308–62. Seoul: Minŭmsa,1993.

Paek Namun. *Chosŏn ponggŏn sahoe kyŏngjesa (A Socioeconomic History of Korean Feudalism)*. Reprint, Seoul: Iron kwa silch'ŏn, 1993.

Pai Hyung Il. *Constructing "Korean" Origins: A Critical Review of Archaeology, Historiography, and Racial Myth in Korean State-Formation Theories*. Cambridge, Mass.: Harvard University Press, 2000.

Pai, Hyung Il, and Timothy R. Tangherlini, eds. *Nationalism and the Construction of Korean Identity*. Berkeley: Institute of East Asian Studies, University of California, 1998.

Pak Ch'angok. "Chosŏnjŏk ŭi Chungguk ijusa yŏn'gu" (A Study of the Migratory History of China's Korean People). *Yŏksa pip'yŏng* 15 (Fall): 179–97.

Pak Ch'ansŭng. *Han'guk kŭndae chŏngch'i sasang yŏn'gu (Studies of Modern Korean Political Ideology)*. Seoul: Yŏksa pip'yŏngsa, 1991.

———. "Pundan sidae namHan ŭi Han'guk sahak" (Korean Historiography During the Period of Division in South Korea). In *Han'guk ŭi yŏksaga wa yŏksahak. Han'guk ŭi yŏksaga wa yŏksahak (Korean Historians and Historiography)*, edited by Cho Tonggŏl, Han Yŏngu, and Pak Ch'ansŭng. Vol. 2, 327–72. Seoul: Ch'angjak kwa pip'yŏngsa, 1994.

Pak Chŏngdong. *Ch'odŭng Taedong yŏksa (An Elementary History of Korea)*. Seoul: Tongmunsa, 1909. Reprinted in *Han'guk kaehwagi kyo'gwasŏ ch'ongsŏ (A Collection of Textbooks from the Korean Enlightenment Period)*, edited by Han'gukhak munhŏn yŏn'guso. Vol. 17, 435–525. Seoul: Asea munhwasa, 1977.

Pak Hwan. "Ku Hanmal Rosia Pŭlladibŏsŭt'ok eso kanhaengduin minjokchi: 'Taedong gongbo'" (A Nationalist Newspaper Published in Russia's Vladivostock During the Hanmal Period: "The Great Eastern Forum"). *Han'guk saron* 30 (1993).

———. *Na Ch'ŏl, Kim Kyohŏn kwa Yun Sebok (Na Ch'ŏl, Kim Kyohŏn, and Yun Sebok)*. Seoul: Tonga Ilbosa, 1992.

———. "Na Ch'ŏl ŭi inmul kwa hwaltong" (Na Ch'ŏl and His Activities). In Pak Hwan, *Manju Hanin minjok undongsa yŏn'gu (Studies of the Nationalist Movement Among Koreans in Manchuria)*, 256–71. Seoul: Ilchogak, 1991.

Pak Kwangyong. "Taejonggyo kwallyŏn munhŏn e wijak mant'a" (The Many Fabrications in Taejonggyo Materials). *Yŏksa pip'yŏng* 16 (Spring 1992): 108–38.

Pak Myoung-Kyu. "Historical Interpretation in Post-Colonial Korea: Memory, Knowledge, and Power." Paper presented at the conference "Between Colonialism and Nationalism: Power and Subjectivity in Korea, 1931–50." University of Michigan, Ann Arbor, 4–6 May 2001.

Pak Ŭnsik. *Han'guk t'ongsa (An Agonizing History of Korea)*. In *Pak Ŭnsik chŏnsŏ*

(*The Complete Works of Pak Ŭnsik*), edited by Tan'guk taehakkyo pusŏl tongyanghak yŏn'guso. Vol. 1. Seoul: Tan'guk taehakkyo ch'ulp'anbu, 1975.

Pak Yŏngsŏk. "Tanjae Sin Ch'aeho ui Manjugwan" (Sin Ch'aeho's Views of Manchuria). In Pak Yŏngsŏk, *Hanminjok tongnip undongsa yŏn'gu* (*Studies on the
Korean National Independence Movement*), 137–548 Seoul: Ilchogak, 1982.

Pang Kijung. *Han'guk kŭn-hyŏndae sasangsa yŏn'gu: 1930, 40-nyŏndae Paek Nam-
un ŭi hangmun kwa chŏngch'i kyŏngje sasang* (*Studies of Korean Modern
Thought: The Political Economic Thought of Paek Nam-un in the 1930s and
40s*). Seoul: Yŏksa p'ip'yŏngsa, 1992.

Patterson, Wayne. *The Korean Frontier in America: Immigration to Hawai'i, 1896–
1910*. Honolulu: University of Hawai'i Press, 1988.

Peng Yingming. "Guanyu woguo minzu gainian lishi de chubu kaocha" (A Preliminary Investigation of the History of Our Country's Concept of Minzu). *Minzu
yanjiu* 2 (1985): 5–11.

Pusey, James. *China and Charles Darwin*. Cambridge, Mass.: Harvard University
Press, 1982.

Robertson, Roland. *Globalisation: Social Theory and Global Culture*. London: Sage,
1992.

Robinson, Michael. *Cultural Nationalism in Colonial Korea, 1920–25*. Seattle: University of Washington Press, 1988.

——. "National Identity in the Thought of Sin Ch'aeho." *Journal of Korean Studies*
5 (1984): 121–42.

Ryang, Sonia. "Japanese Travellers' Accounts of Korea." *East Asian History* 13/14
(June/December 1997) 133–52.

Sahlins, Peter. *Boundaries: The Making of France and Spain in the Pyrenees*. Berkeley
and Los Angeles: University of California Press, 1989.

Sahoe kwahag'wŏn yŏksa yŏn'guso, ed. *Chosŏn chŏnsa* (*A Comprehensive History of
Korea*). 33 vols. Pyongyang: Kwahak paekkwasajŏn ch'ulp'ansa, 1982.

Said, Edward. *Orientalism*. New York: Random House, 1978.

Sansom, George. *A History of Japan*. 3 vols. Stanford, Calif.: Stanford University
Press, 1958.

Schmid, Andre. "Censorship and the *Hwangsŏng sinmun*." In *Korea Between Tradition and Modernity: Selected Papers from the Fourth Pacific and Asian Conference on Korean Studies*, edited by Chang Yun-shik et al., 158–71. Vancouver:
Institute of Asian Research, 2000.

——. "Decentering the 'Middle Kingdom': The Problem of China in Korean Na-
tionalist Thought, 1895–1910." In *Nation Work: Asian Elites and National
Identities*, edited by Timothy Brook and Andre Schmid, 83–107. Ann Arbor:
University of Michigan Press, 2000.

——. "Looking North Toward Manchuria." *South Atlantic Quarterly* 99, no. 1 (Winter 2000): 199–221.

——. "Rediscovering Manchuria: Sin Ch'aeho and the Politics of Territorial History in Korea." *Journal of Asian Studies* 56, no. 1 (February 1997): 26–47.

——. "Tribute, Frontiers and Sinocentricism: A View from South of the Yalu River." Paper presented at the annual meeting of the Association of Asian Studies, Washington D.C., 1998.

Shigeno Yasutsugu, Kume Kunitake, and Hoshino Hisashi. *Kokushikan (A National History)*. 7 vols. Tokyo: Taiseikan, 1890.

Shin, Gi-wook. "Agrarianism: A Critique of Colonial Modernity in Korea." *Comparative Studies in Society and History* 41, no. 4 (October 1999): 784–804.

Shin, Gi-Wook, and Michael Robinson, eds. *Colonial Modernity in Korea*. Cambridge, Mass.: Harvard University Press, 1999.

Shin, Susan. "The Tonghak Movement: From Enlightenment to Revolution." *Korean Studies Forum* 5 (1978/79): 1–79.

Shin Yong-ha. *Formation and Development of Modern Korean Nationalism*. Trans. N. M. Pankaj. Seoul: Daekwang munhwasa, 1989.

Shinoda Jisaku. *Hyakutosan teikaihi (The Boundary Stele of Mount Paektu)*. Tokyo: Rakurō soin, 1938.

Shiratori Kurakichi. *Shiratori Kurakichi zenshū (The Complete Works of Shiratori Kurakichi)*. 4 vols. Tokyo: Iwanami shoten, 1969–71.

——. "Wagaga jōko ni okeru Kanhantō no seiryoku o ronzu" (Concerning Our Power on the Korean Peninsula in Ancient Times). *Chūō kōron* (October 1910): 44–55.

Sin Ch'aeho. "Han'guk kwa Manju" (Korea and Manchuria). In *Tanjae Sin Ch'aeho chŏnjip (The Complete Works of Sin Ch'aeho)*, edited by Tanjae Sin Ch'aeho chŏnjip p'yŏnch'an wiwŏnhoe. Vol. 4, 232–34. Seoul: Hyŏngsŏl ch'ulp'ansa, 1987.

——. "Han'guk minjok chirisang palchŏn" (The Geographical Development of the Korean *minjok*). In *Tanjae Sin Ch'aeho chŏnjip (The Complete Works of Sin Ch'aeho)*, edited by Tanjae Sin Ch'aeho chŏnjip p'yŏnch'an wiwŏnhoe. Vol. 4, 198–99. Seoul: Hyŏngsŏl ch'ulp'ansa, 1987.

——. "Manju munje-e ch'wihayŏ chaeronham" (More Thoughts on the Manchurian Problem). In *Tanjae Sin Ch'aeho chŏnjip (The Complete Works of Sin Ch'aeho)*, edited by Tanjae Sin Ch'aeho chŏnjip p'yŏnch'an wiwŏnhoe. Vol. 4, 238–43. Seoul: Hyŏngsŏl ch'ulp'ansa, 1987.

——. "Toksa sillon" (A New Reading of History). In *Tanjae Sin Ch'aeho chŏnjip (The Complete Works of Sin Ch'aeho)*, edited by Tanjae Sin Ch'aeho chŏnjip p'yŏnch'an wiwŏnhoe. Vol. 1, 467–513. Seoul: Hyŏngsŏl ch'ulp'ansa, 1987.

——. "Yŏksa wa aeguksim ŭi kwan'gae" (The Relation Between History and Patriotism). In *Tanjae Sin Ch'aeho chŏnjip (The Complete Works of Sin Ch'aeho)*, edited by Tanjae Sin Ch'aeho chŏnjip p'yŏnch'an wiwŏnhoe. Vol. 2, 343–59. Seoul: Hyŏngsŏl ch'ulp'ansa, 1987.

Sin Kisŏk. *Kando yŏngyu'gwŏn e kwanhan yŏn'gu* (*Research on the Rights of Possession of Kando*). Seoul: Tamgudang, 1979.

Sin Sŭngha. "Ku Hanmal aeguk kyemong undong sigi Yang Kyecho (Liang Qichao) munjang ŭi chŏnip kwa kŭ yŏnghyang" (The Inception of Liang Qichao's Essays and Their Influence in the Period of the Patriotic Enlightenment Movement During the KuHanmal Period). *Asea yŏn'gu* 41, no. 2 (December 1998): 217–34.

Sin Yongha. *Pak Ŭnsik ŭi sahoe sasang yŏn'gu* (*Essays on the Social Thought of Pak Ŭnsik*). Seoul: Sŏul taehakkyo ch'ulp'anbu, 1982.

——. "Sin Ch'aeho ŭi ch'ogi minjokchuŭi sagwan kwa hugi minjokchuŭi sagwan" (Sin Ch'aeho's Early and Late Nationalist History). In Sin Yongha, *Han'guk kŭndae sahoe sasangsa yŏn'gu* (*Modern Korean Social Thought*), 438–81. Seoul: Ilchisa, 1987.

——. *Tongnip hyŏphoe yŏn'gu* (*Essays on the Independence Club*). Seoul: Ilchogak, 1976.

Suematsu Yasukazu. *Mimana kōbōshi* (*The Rise and Fall of Mimana*). Tokyo: Ōyashima shuppan, 1949.

TaeHan kungmin kyoyukhoe, ed. *Ch'odŭng sohak* (*An Elementary Primer*). Seoul: TaeHan Kungmin kyoyukhoe, 1906. Reprinted in *Han'guk kaehwagi kyo'gwasŏ ch'ongsŏ* (*A Collection of Textbooks from the Korean Enlightenment Period*), edited by Han'gukhak munhŏn yŏn'guso. Vol. 4, 1–431. Seoul: Asea munhwasa, 1977.

Taejonggyo chonggyŏng chŏngsa p'onsu wiwŏnhoe, ed. *Taejonggyo chunggwang yuksimnyŏnsa* (*Sixty Years of Taejonggyo History*). Seoul: Taejonggyo Ch'ongbonsa, 1971.

Takeda, Yukio. "Studies of the King Kwanggaet'o Inscription and Their Basis." *Memoirs of the Research Department of the Tōyō bunko* 47 (1989): 63–78.

Tanaka, Stefan. *Japan's Orient: Rendering Pasts into History*. Berkeley and Los Angeles: University of California Press, 1993.

Tan'guk Taehakkyo Pusŏl Tongyanghak Yŏn'guso, ed. *Chang Chiyŏn chŏnsŏ* (*The Complete Works of Chang Chiyŏn*). 10 vols. Seoul: Tan'guk taehakkyo pusŏl tongyanghak yŏn'guso, 1979–89.

Tanjae Sin Ch'aeho chŏnjip p'yŏnch'an wiwŏnhoe, ed. *Tanjae Sin Ch'aeho chŏnjip* (*The Complete Works of Sin Ch'aeho*). 4 vols. Seoul: Hyŏngsŏl ch'ulp'ansa, 1997.

Terauchi Masatake. "Reforms and Progress in Korea." In *Korea: Its History, Its People and Its Commerce*, edited by Angus Hamilton, Herbert H. Austin, and Masatake Terauchi, 215–309. Boston and Tokyo: J. B. Millet, 1910.

Toby, Ronald. *State and Diplomacy in Early Modern Japan: Asia in the Development of the Tokugawa Bakufu*. Princeton, N.J.: Princeton University Press, 1984.

——. *Tongguk sinsok samgang haengsilto* (A New Illustrated Manual of the Three Relations in Korea). Reprint, Seoul: Taejegak, 1985.

Wagner, Edward. "The Korean *Chokpo* as a Historical Source." In *Studies in Asian Genealogy*, edited by Spencer J. Palmer, 141–52. Provo, Utah: Brigham Young University Press, 1972.

Wakabayashi, Bob Tadashi. *Anti-Foreignism and Western Learning in Early-Modern Japan: The New Theses of 1825*. Cambridge, Mass.: Harvard University Press, 1986.

Weiner, Michael. *The Origins of the Korean Community in Japan, 1910–23*. Manchester: Manchester University Press, 1989.

Wells, Kenneth. *New God, New Nation: Protestants and Self-Reconstruction Nationalism in Korea, 1896–1937*. Honolulu: University of Hawai'i Press, 1990.

Wiam Chang Chiyŏn chŏnsŏ (The Complete Works of Chang Chiyŏn). Seoul: Tan'guk taehakkyo ch'ulp'ansa, 1981.

Wilde, Harry Emerson. *Japan in Crisis*. New York: Macmillan 1934.

Winachakul, Thongchai. *Siam Mapped: A History of the Geobody of a Nation*. Honolulu: University of Hawai'i Press, 1994.

Wright, Mary. "The Adaptability of Ch'ing Diplomacy: The Case of Korea." *Journal of Asian Studies* 17 (May 1958): 363–81.

——. *The Last Stand of Chinese Conservatism: The T'ung-chih Restoration, 1862–74*. Stanford, Calif.: Stanford University Press, 1957.

Wu Han, ed. *Chaoxian lichao shiluzhong de Zhongguo shiliao* (Materials Concerning China in the Chosŏn Veritable Records). 12 vols. Beijing: Zhonghua shuju, 1980.

Yang T'aejin. *Han'guk kungyŏngsa yŏn'gu* (Studies of the History of Korean National Boundaries). Seoul: Pŏpgyŏng ch'ulp'ansa, 1992.

Yang Zhaoquan and Sun Yumei. *Zhong Chao bianjieshi* (A History of the Sino-Korean Border). Changchun: Jilin wenshi chubanshe, 1993.

Yi Chinhŭi. *Kwanggaet'o Wang nŭngbi ŭi t'amgu* (Studies of the King Kwanggaet'o Stele). Trans. Yi Kidong. Seoul: Ilchogak, 1982.

Yi Chunghwan. *T'aengniji* (On Selecting a Village). Trans. Yi Iksŏng. Reprint, Seoul: Ŭlyu munhwasa, 1971.

Yi Haech'ang. *Han'guk sinmunsa yŏn'gu* (Essays on the History of Korean Newspapers). Seoul: Sŏngmun'gak, 1971.

Yi Hunok. "Chang Chiyŏn ŭi yŏksa insik" (Chang Chiyŏn's Historical Understanding). In *Wiam Chang Chiyŏn ŭi sasang kwa hwaltong* (The Thought and Activities of Chang Chiyŏn), edited by Chŏn Kwanu et al., 249–307. Seoul: Minŭmsa, 1993.

Yi Hyŏnhi. "Yi Tongning ŭi *Cheguk sinmun* chŏnnon hwaltong" (The Editorial Activities of Yi Tongning at the *Cheguk sinmun*). Seoul: Minjok munhwasa, 1993.

Yi Hyŏnjong. "Kiho hŭnghakhoe ŭi chojik kwa hwaltong" (The Organization and Activities of the Kiho Society for the Promotion of Education). In 1900 nyŏndae ŭi aeguk kyemong undong yŏn'gu (Studies of the Patriotic Enlightenment Movement of the 1900s), edited by Cho Hangnae, 397–422. Seoul: Asea munhwasa, 1992.

Yi Kibaek. "Minjokchuŭi sahak ŭi munje" (Problems in Nationalist History). In Yi Kibaek, Minjok kwa yŏksa (The Nation and History), 12–22. Seoul: Ilchogak, 1971.

———. A New History of Korea. Trans. Edward Wagner with Edward Schultz. Seoul: Ilchogak, 1984.

———. "Singminjuŭijŏk Han'guk sagwan pip'yŏng"(A Critique of Colonialist Perspectives in Korean History). In Yi Kibaek, Minjok kwa yŏksa (The Nation and History). Seoul: Ilchogak, 1971.

———, ed. Tan'gun sinhwa nonjip (Essays on the Tan'gun Myth). Seoul: Saemunsa, 1988.

Yi Kijun. Hanmal Sŏgu kyŏngjehak toipsa yŏn'gu (The History of the Introduction of Western Economics in the Hanmal Period). Seoul: Ilchogak, 1985.

Yi Kimun. "Han'gugŏ hyŏngsŏngsa" (The Development of the Korean Language). In Han'guk munhwa taegye (Cultural History of Korea), edited by Koryŏ Taehakkyo minjok munhwa yŏn'guso. Vol. 5. Seoul: Tonga ch'ulp'ansa, 1971.

———. "Kaehwagi ŭi kungmun sayong e kwanhan yŏn'gu" (Research on the Use of National Writing in the Kaehwa Period). Han'guk munhwa 5 (1984): 65–84.

———. Kaehwagi ŭi kungmun yŏn'gu (National Language Research During the Enlightenment Period). Seoul: Ilchogak, 1970.

Yi Kuyong. "TaeHan cheguk ŭi sŏngnip kwa yŏlgang ŭi panyŏng" (The Formation of the TaeHan Empire and the Reaction of the Powers). Kangwŏn sahak 1 (December 1985): 75–98.

Yi Kwangnin. "Hwangsŏng sinmun yŏn'gu" (On the Hwangsŏng Sinmun). In Yi Kwangnin, Kaehwap'a wa kaehwa sasang yŏn'gu (Studies of the Enlightenment Party and Enlightenment Thought), 155–95. Seoul: Ilchogak, 1989.

———. "Kaehwagi Han'gugin ŭi asea yŏndaeron" (Korean Theories of Asian Unity in the Enlightenment Period). In Yi Kwangnin, Kaehwap'a wa kaehwa sasang yŏn'gu (Studies of the Enlightenment Party and Enlightenment Thought), 138–54 . Seoul: Ilchogak, 1989.

———. "Yu Kilchun ŭi kaehwa sasang" (The Enlightenment Thought of Yu Kilchun). In Yi Kwangnin, Han'guk kaehwa sasang yŏn'gu (Studies of Korean Enlightenment Thought), 45–92. Seoul: Ilchogak, 1979.

Yi Kwangnin, Yu Chaech'on, and Kim Haktung. TaeHan maeil sinbo yŏn'gu (On the TaeHan maeil sinbo). Seoul: Sogang taehakkyo ch'ulp'ansa, 1986.

Yi Manhyŏng. "KuHanmal aeguk kyemong undong ŭi dae Ŭibyŏnggwan — TaeHan maeil sinborŭl chungsim ŭro" (The Patriotic Enlightenment Movement's View of Ŭibyŏng—Centering on the *TaeHan maeil sinbo*). *Haesa nonmunjip* 18 (1983): 87–117.

Yi Manyŏl. *Han'guk kidokkyo wa minjok undong (Korean Christianity and the Nationalist Movement)*. Seoul : Chongno Sŏjŏk, 1986.

———. *Tanjae Sin Ch'aeho ŭi yŏksahak yŏn'gu (Studies of the Historiography of Tanjae Sin Ch'aeho)*. Seoul: Munhak kwa pip'yŏngsa, 1990.

Yi Minsu, trans. *Abang kangyŏkko (An Investigation of Our Nation's Territory)*. Seoul: Pomunsa, 1995.

———. trans. *Sindan silgi (True Records of Divine Tan'gun)*. Seoul: Hanppuri, 1986.

Yi Pongun. *Kungmun chŏngni (National Language Standardization)*. Seoul: Hakpu p'yŏnjipkuk, 1897.

Yi Sŏnghŭi. "Sŏ-u hakhoe ŭi aeguk kyemong undong kwa sasang" (The Ideology and Patriotic Enlightenment Movement of the Sŏ-u Educational Association). In *1900 nyŏndae ŭi aeguk kyemong undong yŏn'gu (Studies of the Patriotic Enlightenment Movement of the 1900s)*, edited by Cho Hangnae, 291–338. Seoul: Asea munhwasa, 1992.

Yi Sŏngŭn. "Uri kukki chejŏng ŭi yurae wa kŭ ŭi ŭiŭi" (The History and Meaning of the Making of Our Flag), *Kukkasang ŭi chemunje* 2 (July 1959): 177–220.

Yi Wanjae. *Pak Kyusu yŏn'gu (Studies of Pak Kyusu)*. Seoul: Chimmundang, 1999.

Yi Wonjae. *Ch'ugi kaehwa sasang yŏn'gu (Studies of Early Enlightenment Thought)*. Seoul: Minjok munhwa sa, 1989.

Yi Yusŏng. "Yijo hugi kŭn'gi hakpa e issŏsŏ ŭi chŏngt'ongnon ŭi chŏn'gae" (The Development of Theories of Legitimacy During the Late Choson Dynasty by the Kun'gi Group). In *Han'guk ŭi yŏksa insik (Understanding Korean History)*, edited by Yi Yusŏng and Kang Man'gil. Vol. 2, 356–62. Seoul: Changjak kwa Pip'yŏngsa, 1976.

Yŏksa munje yŏn'guso, ed. "Han'guk minjogŭn ŏnje hyŏngsŏngdoeŏnna?" (When Did the Korean Nation Form?) *Yŏksa pip'yŏng* 19 (Winter 1992): 16–101.

———, ed. "Kojong kwa TaeHan Chegugŭl tullŏssan ch'oegŭn ŭi nonjaeng" (Recent Debates Concerning Kojong and the TaeHan Empire). *Yŏksa pip'yŏng* 37 (Summer 1997): 224–70.

Young, Robert. *White Mythologies: Writing History and the West*. New York: Routledge, 1990.

Yu Chŏnggap. *Pukpang yŏngt'oron (On the Northern Territories)*. Seoul: Popkyŏng ch'ulp'ansa, 1991.

Yu Chun'gi. *Han'guk kŭndae yugyo kaehyŏk undongsa (A History of the Confucian Reform Movement in Modern Korea)*. Seoul: Tosŏ ch'ulp'an sammun, 1994.

Yu Kilchun. *Nodong yahak tokpon (A Reader for the Worker's Night School)*. In *Yu Kilchun chŏnsŏ (The Complete Works of Yu Kilchun)*, edited by Yu Kilchun chŏnsŏ p'yŏnch'an wiwŏnhoe. Vol. 2, 261–358. Seoul: Ilchogak, 1996.

——. *Sŏyu kyŏnmun* (*Observations of My Travels to the West*). In *Yu Kilchun chŏnsŏ* (*The Complete Works of Yu Kilchun*), edited by Yu Kilchun chŏnsŏ p'yŏnch'an wiwŏnhoe. Vol. 1. Seoul: Ilchogak, 1996.

——. *TaeHan munjŏn* (*Korean Grammar*). In *Yu Kilchun chŏnsŏ* (*The Complete Works of Yu Kilchun*), edited by Yu Kilchun chŏnsŏ p'yŏnch'an wiwŏnhoe. Vol. 2, 101–247. Seoul: Ilchogak, 1996.

Yu Kilchun chŏnsŏ p'yŏnch'an wiwŏnhoe, ed. *Yu Kilchun chŏnsŏ* (*The Complete Works of Yu Kilchun*). Seoul: Ilchogak, 1996.

Yu Tŭkkong. *Parhaego* (*An Investigation of Parhae*). Reprint, Seoul: Ŭlyusa, 1976.

Yu Yongik. *Kabo kyŏngjaeng yŏn'gu* (*A Study of the Kabo Reforms*). Seoul: Ilchogak, 1990.

Yun Ch'iho. "The Whang-chei of Dai Han, or the Emperor of Korea." *Korean Repository* 4 (1897): 385.

——. *Yun Ch'iho ilgi* (*The Diaries of Yun Ch'iho*). Seoul: Tamgudang, 1971.

Zhang Cunwu. *Qingdai ZhongHan guanxi lunwenji* (*Essays on Sino-Korean Relations During the Qing Dynasty*). Taibei: Shangwu yinshuguan, 1986.

Index

STUDIES OF THE EAST ASIAN INSTITUTE

Selected Titles

Abortion before Birth Control: The Politics of Reproduction in Postwar Japan, by Tiana
   Norgren. Princeton: Princeton University Press, August 2001.
The Reluctant Dragon: Crisis Cycles in Chinese Foreign Economic Policy, by Law-
   rence Christopher Reardon. Seattle: University of Washington Press, 2001.
China's Retreat from Equality: Income Distribution and Economic Transition, Carl
   Riskin, Zhao Renwei, Li Shi, eds. Armonk, N.Y.: M. E. Sharpe, 2001.
Japan's Imperial Diplomacy: Consuls, Treaty Ports, and War with China, 1895–1938,
   by Barbara Brooks. Honolulu: University of Hawai'i Press, 2000.
Japan's Budget Politics: Balancing Domestic and International Interests, by Takaaki
   Suzuki. Boulder: Lynne Rienner Publishers, 2000.
*Cadres and Corruption: The Organizational Involution of the Chinese Communist
   Party*, by Xiaobo Lu. Stanford, Stanford University Press, 2000.
Assembled in Japan: Electrical Goods and the Making of the Japanese Consumer, by
   Simon Partner. Berkeley: University of California Press, 1999.
Nation, Governance, and Modernity: Canton, 1900–1927, by Michael T. W. Tsin.
   Stanford: Stanford University Press, 1999.
Civilization and Monsters: Spirits of Modernity in Meiji Japan, by Gerald Figal,
   Durham: Duke University Press, 1999.
The Logic of Japanese Politics: Leaders, Institutions, and the Limits of Change, by
   Gerald L. Curtis. New York: Columbia University Press, 1999.
Trans-Pacific Racisms and the U.S. Occupation of Japan, by Yukiko Koshiro. New
   York: Columbia University Press, 1999.
Bicycle Citizens: The Political World of the Japanese Housewife, by Robin LeBlanc.
   Berkeley: University of California Press, 1999.
Alignment Despite Antagonism: The United States, Japan, and Korea, by Victor Cha.
   Stanford: Stanford University Press, 1999.
*Contesting Citizenship in Urban China: Peasant Migrants, the State and Logic of
   the Market*, by Dorothy Solinger. Berkeley: University of California Press, 1999.
Japan's Total Empire: Manchuria and the Culture of Wartime Imperialism, by Louise
   Young. Berkeley: University of California Press, 1997.
Honorable Merchants: Commerce and Self-Cultivation in Late Imperial China, by
   Richard Lufrano. Honolulu: University of Hawai'i Press, 1997.
Print and Politics: 'Shibao' and the Culture of Reform in Late Qing China, by Joan
   Judge. Stanford: Stanford University Press, 1996.
Troubled Industries: Confronting Economic Change in Japan, by Robert Uriu. Ithaca:
   Cornell University Press, 1996.
Landownership Under Colonial Rule: Korea's Japanese Experience, 1900–1935, by
   Edwin H. Gragert. Honolulu: University of Hawaii Press, 1994.
Race to the Swift: State and Finance in Korean Industrialization, by Jung-en Woo.
   New York: Columbia University Press, 1991.

Kim Il Sung: The North Korean Leader, by Dae-Sook Suh. New York: Columbia University Press, 1988.

The U.S.–South Korean Alliance: Evolving Patterns of Security Relations, edited by Gerald L. Curtis and Sung-joo Han. Lexington, Mass.: Lexington Books, 1983.

The Foreign Policy of the Republic of Korea, edited by Youngnok Koo and Sungjoo Han. New York: Columbia University Press, 1984.

The Origins of the Korean War: Liberation and the Emergence of Separate Regimes, 1945–1947, by Bruce Cumings. Princeton: Princeton University Press, 1981.